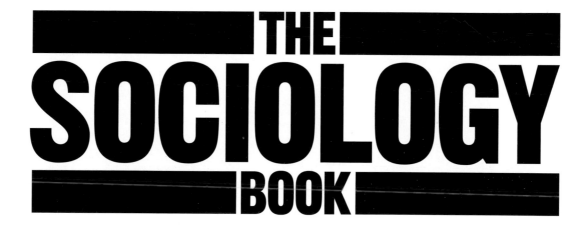

THE SOCIOLOGY BOOK

THE SOCIOLOGY BOOK

DK

DK | Penguin Random House

DK LONDON

SENIOR EDITOR
Sam Atkinson

SENIOR ART EDITOR
Amy Child

EDITORS
Alexandra Beeden
Miezan van Zyl

US EDITORS
Christy Lusiak and Margaret Parrish

MANAGING EDITOR
Esther Ripley

MANAGING ART EDITOR
Karen Self

PUBLISHER
Liz Wheeler

ART DIRECTOR
Phil Ormerod

ASSOCIATE
PUBLISHING DIRECTOR
Liz Wheeler

PUBLISHING DIRECTOR
Jonathan Metcalf

JACKET DESIGNER
Laura Brim

JACKET EDITOR
Claire Gell

JACKET DESIGN
DEVELOPMENT MANAGER
Sophia Tampakopoulos

SENIOR PRODUCER,
PRE-PRODUCTION
Luca Frassinetti

SENIOR PRODUCER
Gemma Sharpe

ILLUSTRATIONS
James Graham

DK DELHI

JACKET DESIGNER
Dhirendra Singh

SENIOR DTP DESIGNER
Harish Aggarwal

MANAGING JACKETS EDITOR
Saloni Singh

original styling by
STUDIO8 DESIGN

produced for DK by
COBALT ID

ART EDITORS
Darren Bland, Paul Reid

EDITORS
Diana Loxley, Marek Walisiewicz,
Christopher Westhorp

First American Edition, 2015
Published in the United States by
DK Publishing
345 Hudson Street
New York, New York 10014

Copyright © 2015
Dorling Kindersley Limited
A Penguin Random House Company
15 16 17 18 19 10 9 8 7 6 5 4 3 2 1
001—282934—July/2015

Published in Great Britain by
Dorling Kindersley Limited.

A catalog record for this book is available
from the Library of Congress.

ISBN: 978-1-4654-3650-4

DK books are available at special discounts
when purchased in bulk for sales promotions,
premiums, fund-raising, or educational use.
For details, contact: DK Publishing Special
Markets, 345 Hudson Street, New York,
New York 10014
SpecialSales@dk.com

Printed and bound in China by
Leo Paper Products Ltd.

A WORLD OF IDEAS:
SEE ALL THERE IS TO KNOW

www.dk.com

CONTRIBUTORS

CHRISTOPHER THORPE, CONSULTANT EDITOR

Our co-consultant and contributor Christopher Thorpe is a sociologist with an interest in social theory, cultural sociology, and British representations of Italy. He has a doctorate in sociology from the University of Aberdeen, Scotland, and is coeditor of the journal *Cultural Sociology*, author of several academic articles, and coauthor of *An Invitation to Social Theory* (2012).

CHRIS YUILL, CONSULTANT EDITOR

Our co-consultant and contributor Chris Yuill is a sociologist and lecturer at Robert Gordon University, Aberdeen, Scotland. His interests include the social dimensions of health, both in the community and the workplace, and what makes for a successful urban space. He is a former committee member of The British Sociological Association and has written several books, including *Understanding the Sociology of Health: An Introduction* (2011)

MITCHELL HOBBS

A lecturer in the department of media and communications at the University of Sydney, Australia, Mitchell Hobbs has a doctorate in media sociology from the University of Newcastle, Australia. He is coauthor of *Communication, New Media and Everyday Life* (2011); author of several national and international studies on global media, cultural flows, and political communication; and has worked in a communications role for former Australian prime minister Julia Gillard.

MEGAN TODD

A senior lecturer in social science at the University of Central Lancashire, England, Megan Todd has a doctorate in sociology from the University of Newcastle, England. Her research interests include gender, sexuality, and violence. She has contributed chapters on intimacies and violence in various publications and is currently writing a textbook on sexualities.

SARAH TOMLEY

A writer, editor, and psychotherapist, Sarah Tomley has contributed to many books on the social sciences, including *The Philosophy Book* (2011) and *The Psychology Book* (2012) in DK's Big Ideas series.

MARCUS WEEKS

A writer and musician, Marcus Weeks studied philosophy and worked as a teacher before embarking on a career as an author. He has contributed to many books on the arts and popular sciences, including various titles in DK's Big Ideas series.

CONTENTS

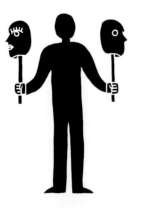

SOCIAL INEQUALITIES

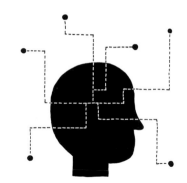

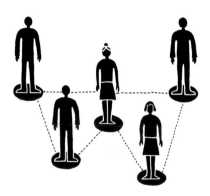

CULTURE AND IDENTITY

WORK AND CONSUMERISM

THE ROLE OF INSTITUTIONS

FAMILIES AND INTIMACIES

INTRODU

Humans are social creatures. Throughout our evolution, from our days of foraging and hunting animals, we have tended to live and work in social groups, which have become progressively larger and more complex. These groups have ranged from simple family units, through clans and tribes, villages and towns, to cities and nation states. Our natural inclination to live and work together has led to the formation of civil societies, which have been shaped by the increasing breadth of our knowledge and sophistication of our technology. In turn, the nature of the society we live in influences our social behavior, affecting virtually every aspect of our lives.

> Sociology was born of the modern ardor to improve society.
> **Albion W. Small**
> **US scholar (1854–1926)**

Sociology is the study of how individuals behave in groups and how their behavior is shaped by these groups. This includes: how groups are formed; the dynamics that animate them; and how these dynamics maintain and alter the group or bring about social change. Today, sociology's scope ranges from the theoretical study of social processes, structures, and systems, to the application of these theories as part of social policy. And, because societies consist of a collection of individual people, there is an inevitable connection between the structures of society as a whole and the behavior of its individual members. Sociologists may therefore focus on the institutions and organization of society, the various social groupings and stratifications within it, or the interactions and experiences of individuals.

Perhaps surprisingly, sociology is a comparatively modern discipline. Although philosophers in ancient China and ancient Greece recognized the existence of civil society and the benefits of social order, their concern was more political than sociological—how society should be organized and governed, rather than a study of society itself. But, just as political

philosophy emerged from these civilizations, sociology appeared as a result of profound changes in Western society during the Age of Enlightenment.

There were several aspects to these changes. Most noticeably, technological advances had provided the machinery that brought about the Industrial Revolution, radically changing methods of production and creating prosperous industrial cities. The traditional certainties based on religious belief were called into question by the philosophy of the Enlightenment. It was not only the authority of the Church that was undermined by this so-called Age of Reason: the old order of monarchies and aristocracies was under threat, with demands for more representative government leading to revolutions in America and France.

Society and modernity
A new, modern society was created from the Age of Enlightenment. Sociology began to emerge at the end of the 18th century as a response to this transformation, as philosophers and thinkers attempted to understand the nature of modernity and its effects on society. Inevitably, some simply

bemoaned the erosion of traditional forms of social cohesion, such as the family ties and community spirit found within small, rural societies, and the shared values and beliefs offered by a common religion. But others recognized that there were new social forces at work, bringing about social change with a potential for both social order and disorder.

In keeping with the spirit of the Enlightenment, these early social thinkers sought to make their study of society objective, and create a scientific discipline that was distinct from philosophy, history, and politics. The natural sciences (physics, chemistry, astronomy, and biology) were well established, and the time was ripe for the study of humans and their behavior.

Because of the nature of the Industrial Revolution and the capitalism that it fostered, the first of the new "social sciences" to emerge was economics, pioneered by Adam Smith's *An Inquiry into the Nature and Causes of the Wealth of Nations*, better known as *The Wealth of Nations*, in 1776. However, at the same time, the foundations of sociology were also being laid, by philosophers and theorists such as Adam Ferguson and Henri de Saint-Simon, and

in the early part of the following century by Auguste Comte, whose scientific approach to the study of society firmly established sociology as a distinct discipline.

Following in Comte's footsteps came three ground-breaking sociologists, whose different approaches to the analysis and interpretation of social behavior set the agenda for the subject of sociology in the 20th century and beyond: Karl Marx, Émile Durkheim, and Max Weber. Each identified a different aspect of modernity as the major factor in creating social order, disorder, and change. Marx, a materialist philosopher and economist, focused on the growth

> ❝
> Human nature is... unbelievably malleable... responding accurately and contrastingly to contrasting cultural traditions.
> **Margaret Mead**
> ❞

of capitalism and the subsequent class struggle; Durkheim on the division of labor brought about by industrialization; and Weber on the secularization and rationalization of modern society. All three have had an enthusiastic following, influencing sociology's major schools of thought to the present day.

A social science
Sociology was a product of the Age of Reason, when science and rational thinking began to reign supreme. Early sociologists were therefore anxious that, for their discipline to be taken seriously, their methods should be seen to be rigorously scientific—no mean feat, given the nature of their subject: human social behavior. Comte laid the ground rules for the new "science" of sociology, based on empirical evidence in the same way as the natural sciences. Marx, too, insisted on approaching the subject scientifically, and Durkheim was perhaps the first to gain acceptance for sociology as a social science in the academic world.

To be scientific, any research method must be quantitative—that is to say, have measurable results. Marx and Durkheim could point to facts, figures, and statistics to back up their theories, but others »

maintained that social research should be more qualitative. Weber especially advocated an interpretive approach, examining what it is like to live in modern society, and the social interactions and relationships that are necessary for social cohesion.

Although this viewpoint was initially dismissed by many as unscientific, sociology has become increasingly interpretive in the latter half of the 20th century, with a methodology that includes a combination of quantitative and qualitative research techniques.

Social reform

For many sociologists, sociology is more than simply the objective study of society, and the quest to analyze and describe social structures and systems. Sociological theories, like theories in the natural sciences, have practical applications, and can be used to improve the society in which we live. In the 19th century, Comte and Marx saw sociology as a way of understanding the workings of society in order to bring about social change. Marx famously said, "The philosophers have only interpreted the world, in various ways. The point, however, is to change it," and his many

followers (sociologists as well as political activists) have taken this to heart.

Durkheim, who was nowhere near as politically radical as Marx, made great efforts to have sociology accepted as an academic discipline. To gain the approval of the authorities, he had to demonstrate not only the subject's scientific credentials, but also its objectivity, especially in light of the political unrest that had existed in Europe for more than a century following the French Revolution. This somewhat "ivory tower" approach, divorced from the real world, dominated sociology for the first part of the 20th century, but as sociologists gradually adopted

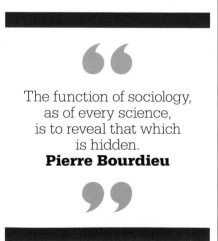

The function of sociology, as of every science, is to reveal that which is hidden.
Pierre Bourdieu

a more interpretive stance, they also advocated sociology as a tool of social reform.

This was particularly noticeable among sociologists with a Marxian perspective and others with a left-wing political agenda. After World War II, sociologists, including Charles Wright Mills and Michel Foucault, examined the nature of power in society and its effects on the individual—the ways in which society shapes our lives, rather than the way we shape society, and how we can resist these forces. Even in more mainstream sociology, the mood was changing, and the scope of the subject broadened from the academic study of society as it is, to include practical applications informing public policy and driving social change. In 1972, Howard Becker, a respected US sociological theorist, wrote: "Good sociology... produces meaningful descriptions of organizations and events, valid explanations of how they come about and persist, and realistic proposals for their improvement or removal."

Institutions and individuals

As a reflection of the increased emphasis on the relevance of sociology, the subject gained greater acceptance, and even

popular interest, in the second half of the 20th century, and as more thinkers turned their attention to social issues, so the scope of sociology broadened. Evolving from the traditional study of the structures and systems of modern society and the forces of social cohesion and causes of social disorder, it began to examine the connections between these areas and the interactions of individuals and social groups.

A century or so ago, sociologists were divided into those who approached the subject on a macro level (looking at society as a whole and the institutions that it is constituted of), and those who approached it on the micro level—focusing on the individual's experience of living within a society. While this distinction still exists to an extent, sociologists now recognize that the two are closely connected and many concentrate their work on groups that fall between these two approaches—social classes; ethnic, religious, or cultural groups; families; or groups that are defined by gender or sexual orientation.

Sociology has also responded to the accelerating pace of change. Since World War II, many social conventions have been challenged, and new social norms have taken their place. In the Western world, the civil rights and women's movements have done much to address racial and gender inequalities, and sociological theories have also helped change attitudes to sexuality and family life. Here, as Zygmunt Bauman advises, "The task for sociology is to come to the help of the individual. We have to be in service of freedom."

The global age

Technological innovations have arguably brought about social changes comparable to—or more far-reaching than—those wrought by the Industrial Revolution. Increased automation and computerization, the rise of the service industries, and the growth of consumer society have all contributed to the shape of society many of us live in today. While some sociologists see this as a continuation of the process of modernity, others believe we are now entering a postmodern, post-industrial age.

Advances in communication and mobility have also made the world a smaller place. Sociologists have recently turned their attention to the importance of cultural and national identity and to the effects of globalization, especially on local communities. With new forms of communication—particularly the Internet and fast international travel—have come entirely new social networks. These do not depend on face-to-face contact, but bring together individuals and groups in ways that were unimaginable even 50 years ago. Modern technology has also provided sociology with a sophisticated means of researching and analyzing the evolution of these new social structures. ∎

> The real political task in a society such as ours is to criticize the workings of institutions that appear to be... both neutral and independent... to criticize and attack them... so that one can fight against them.
> **Michel Foucault**

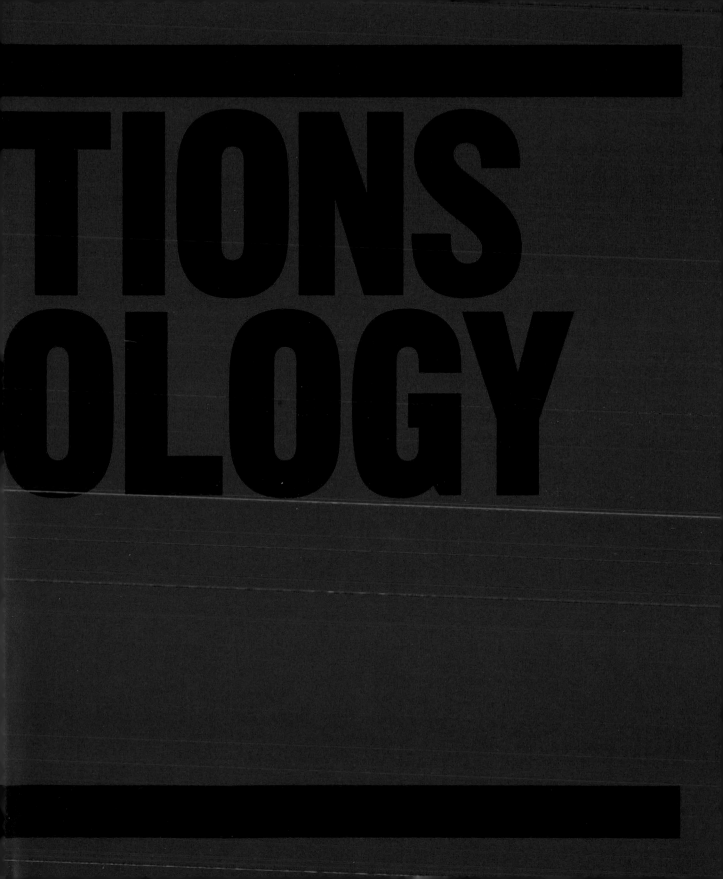

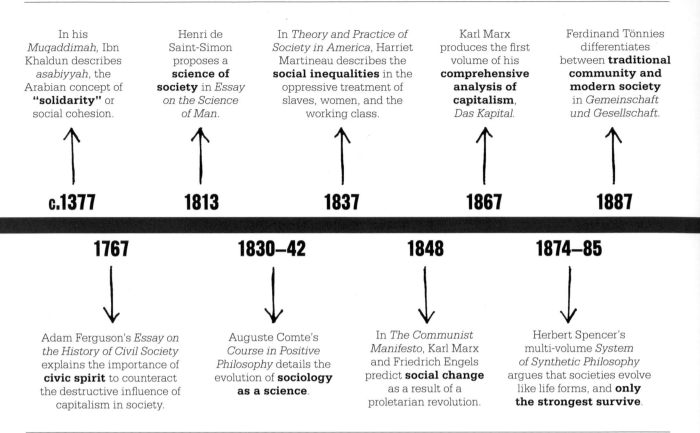

In his *Muqaddimah*, Ibn Khaldun describes *asabiyyah*, the Arabian concept of **"solidarity"** or social cohesion.

Henri de Saint-Simon proposes a **science of society** in *Essay on the Science of Man*.

In *Theory and Practice of Society in America*, Harriet Martineau describes the **social inequalities** in the oppressive treatment of slaves, women, and the working class.

Karl Marx produces the first volume of his **comprehensive analysis of capitalism**, *Das Kapital*.

Ferdinand Tönnies differentiates between **traditional community and modern society** in *Gemeinschaft und Gesellschaft*.

c.1377   **1813**   **1837**   **1867**   **1887**

1767   **1830–42**   **1848**   **1874–85**

Adam Ferguson's *Essay on the History of Civil Society* explains the importance of **civic spirit** to counteract the destructive influence of capitalism in society.

Auguste Comte's *Course in Positive Philosophy* details the evolution of **sociology as a science**.

In *The Communist Manifesto*, Karl Marx and Friedrich Engels predict **social change** as a result of a proletarian revolution.

Herbert Spencer's multi-volume *System of Synthetic Philosophy* argues that societies evolve like life forms, and **only the strongest survive**.

Sociology did not establish its credentials as a discipline until the 20th century, but its many strands of thought, approaches, and fields of study had evolved from centuries of work by historians and philosophers.

Although the first recognizably sociological study was made by Ibn Khaldun in the 14th century, the pioneers of sociology as we know it today only began to emerge from the late 18th century, when society underwent a sea-change in Western Europe: Enlightenment ideas were replacing traditional beliefs, and the Industrial Revolution was transforming the way that people lived and worked. These observers identified social change being driven by forces that became known as "modernity," which included the effects of industrialization and the growth of capitalism, and the less tangible (but no less significant) effects of secularization and rationality.

A social science

Modern society was the product of the Age of Reason: the application of rational thought and scientific discoveries. In keeping with this mood, the pioneers of sociology, such as French philosopher Henri de Saint-Simon and his protégé Auguste Comte, sought to provide verifiable evidence to support theories. Comte believed that not only could the forces of social order be explained by rules similar to the laws of physics and chemistry, but that applied sociology could bring about social reform in the same way that applied sciences had led to technological advances.

Like Comte, Karl Marx believed that the purpose of studying society is not simply to describe or explain it, but also to improve it. He was just as keen to be scientific, but chose as his model the new science of economics, identifying capitalism as the major factor of modernity driving social change.

Almost a century before Marx, the Scottish philosopher Adam Ferguson had warned of the threat to traditional social cohesion posed by the self-interest of capitalism, and both Harriet Martineau and Marx's colleague Friedrich Engels described the social injustices of industrialized capitalist society in the mid-19th century. Another pioneer sociologist, Ferdinand Tönnies, echoed Ferguson's ideas with his description of two very different forms of social cohesion in

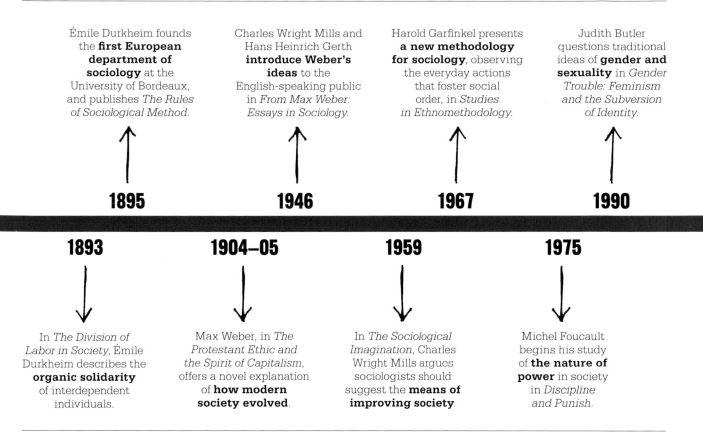

Émile Durkheim founds the **first European department of sociology** at the University of Bordeaux, and publishes *The Rules of Sociological Method*.

Charles Wright Mills and Hans Heinrich Gerth **introduce Weber's ideas** to the English-speaking public in *From Max Weber: Essays in Sociology*.

Harold Garfinkel presents **a new methodology for sociology**, observing the everyday actions that foster social order, in *Studies in Ethnomethodology*.

Judith Butler questions traditional ideas of **gender and sexuality** in *Gender Trouble: Feminism and the Subversion of Identity*.

1895

1946

1967

1990

1893

1904–05

1959

1975

In *The Division of Labor in Society*, Émile Durkheim describes the **organic solidarity** of interdependent individuals.

Max Weber, in *The Protestant Ethic and the Spirit of Capitalism*, offers a novel explanation of **how modern society evolved**.

In *The Sociological Imagination*, Charles Wright Mills argues sociologists should suggest the **means of improving society**.

Michel Foucault begins his study of **the nature of power** in society in *Discipline and Punish*.

traditional and modern societies— a concept variously interpreted by many subsequent sociologists.

Toward the end of the 19th century, sociology proved itself as a field of study distinct from history, philosophy, politics, and economics, largely thanks to Émile Durkheim. Adopting Comte's idea of applying scientific methodology to the study of society, he took biology as his model. Like Herbert Spencer before him, Durkheim saw society as an "organism" with different "organs," each with a particular function.

An interpretive approach

While Durkheim's objective rigor won him academic acceptance, not all sociologists agreed that it was possible to examine social issues with scientific methods, nor that there are "laws" of society to be

discovered. Max Weber advocated a more subjective—"interpretive" approach. Whereas Marx named capitalism, and Durkheim industrialization, as the major force of modernity, Weber's focus was on the effects on individuals of rationalization and secularization.

A strictly scientific discipline was gradually supplanted by a sociology that was a study of qualitative ideas: immeasurable notions such as culture, identity, and power. By the mid-20th century sociologists had shifted from a macro view of society to the micro view of individual experience. Charles Wright Mills urged sociologists to make the connection between the institutions of society (especially what he called the "power elite") and how they affect the lives of ordinary people.

After World War II, others took a similar stance. Harold Garfinkel advocated a complete change of sociological methods, to examine social order through the everyday actions of ordinary people; while Michel Foucault analyzed the way power relations force individuals to conform to social norms, especially sexual norms—an idea taken further in Judith Butler's study of gender and sexuality.

By the end of the century, a balance had been found between the objective study of society as a whole and the interpretive study of individual experience. The agenda had been set by a handful of ground-breaking sociologists, and their various methods are now being applied to the study of society in an increasingly globalized late-modern world. ∎

A PHYSICAL DEFEAT HAS NEVER MARKED THE END OF A NATION
IBN KHALDUN (1332–1406)

IN CONTEXT

FOCUS
Solidarity

KEY DATES
c.622 The first Islamic state is established in Medina.

c.1377 Ibn Khaldun completes *Muqaddimah* (or *Prolegomena*), the introduction to his history of the world.

1835 Volume 1 of Alexis de Tocqueville's *Democracy in America* describes how the association of individuals for mutual purpose benefits political and civil society.

1887 Ferdinand Tönnies writes *Gemeinschaft und Gesellschaft* (*Community and Society*).

1995 Robert Putnam explains the concept of social capital in his article "Bowling Alone," expanded into a book in 2000.

1996 Michel Maffesoli's *Du Nomadisme* continues his study of neotribalism.

The group dynamics of how some societies come to flourish and take over others fascinated Ibn Khaldun, the Arab philosopher and historian. He is best known for his ambitious multivolume history of the world, the *Kitab al-'Ibar*, especially the first part called the *Muqaddimah*. The *Kitab* is seen as a precursor of sociology because of its analyses of Berber and Arabic societies.

Central to Ibn Khaldun's explanation of the success of a society is the Arabic concept of *asabiyyah*, or social solidarity. Originally, *asabiyyah* referred to the family bonds found in clans and nomadic tribes, but as civilizations grew it came to mean a sense of belonging, usually translated today as "solidarity." According to Ibn Khaldun, *asabiyyah* exists in societies as small as clans and as large as empires, but the sense of a shared purpose and destiny wanes as a society grows and ages, and the civilization weakens. Ultimately, such a civilization will be taken over by a smaller or younger one with a stronger sense of solidarity: a nation may experience—but will never be brought down by—a physical defeat but when it "becomes the victim of a psychological defeat... that marks the end of a nation."

This concept of the importance of solidarity and social cohesion in society anticipated many ideas of community and civic spirit in modern sociology, including Robert Putnam's theory that contemporary society is suffering from a collapse of participation in the community. ■

The desert Bedouin tribes were cited by Ibn Khaldun in his theory of group dynamics, in which social and psychological factors contribute to the rise and fall of civilizations.

See also: Ferdinand Tönnies 32–33 ■ Robert D. Putnam 124–25 ■ Arjun Appadurai 166–69 ■ David Held 170–71 ■ Michel Maffesoli 291

MANKIND HAVE ALWAYS WANDERED OR SETTLED, AGREED OR QUARRELED, IN TROOPS AND COMPANIES
ADAM FERGUSON (1723–1816)

IN CONTEXT

FOCUS
Civic spirit

KEY DATES
1748 Montesquieu publishes
The Spirit of the Laws, arguing
that political institutions
should derive from the social
mores of a community.

1767 Adam Ferguson outlines
his views in his book *Essay
on the History of Civil Society*.

1776 With *The Wealth of
Nations*, Adam Smith pioneers
modern economics.

1867 Karl Marx analyzes
capitalism in the first volume
of *Das Kapital*.

1893 Émile Durkheim
examines the importance of
beliefs and values in holding
society together in *The
Division of Labor in Society*.

1993 Amitai Etzioni founds
The Communitarian Network
to strengthen the moral and
social foundations of society.

Progress is both inevitable and desirable, but we must always be aware of the social costs that might be exacted as progress is made. Such was the warning of the philosopher and historian Adam Ferguson, who was one of the "Select Society" of Edinburgh intellectuals of the Scottish Enlightenment, a group that included the philosopher David Hume and economist Adam Smith.

Ferguson believed, as did Smith, that commercial growth is driven by self-interest, but unlike Smith he analyzed the effects of this development and felt it was happening at the expense of traditional values of cooperation and "fellow-feeling." In the past, societies had been based on families or communities, and community spirit was fostered by ideas of honor and loyalty. But the self-interest demanded by capitalism weakens these values, and ultimately leads to social collapse. To prevent commercial capitalism from sowing the seeds of its own destruction, Ferguson

Man is born in civil society...
and there he remains.
Montesquieu
French philosopher (1689–1755)

advocated promoting a sense of civic spirit, encouraging people to act in the interest of society rather than in self-interest.

Ferguson's criticism of capitalism and commercialism meant that his theories were rejected by mainstream thinkers such as Hume and Smith, but they later influenced the political ideas of Hegel and Marx. And because he viewed the subject from a social rather than political or economic angle, his work helped to lay the foundations of modern sociology. ∎

See also: Ferdinand Tönnies 32–33 ▪ Karl Marx 28–31 ▪ Émile Durkheim 34–37 ▪ Amitai Etzioni 112–19 ▪ Norbert Elias 180–81 ▪ Max Weber 220–23

SCIENCE CAN BE USED TO BUILD A BETTER WORLD

AUGUSTE COMTE (1798–1857)

IN CONTEXT

FOCUS
Positivism and the study of society

KEY DATES
1813 French theorist Henri de Saint-Simon suggests the idea of a science of society.

1840s Karl Marx argues that economic issues are at the root of historical change.

1853 Harriet Martineau's abridged translation *The Positive Philosophy of Auguste Comte* introduces Comte's ideas to a wider public.

1865 British philosopher John Stuart Mill refers to Comte's early sociological and later political ideas as "good Comte" and "bad Comte."

1895 In *The Rules of Sociological Method*, Émile Durkheim seeks to establish a systematic sociology.

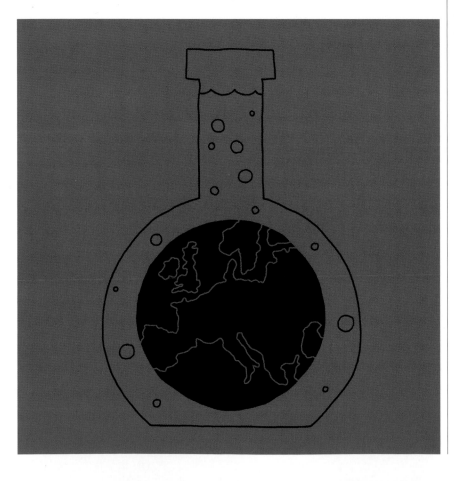

By the end of the 18th century, increased industrialization had brought about radical changes to traditional society in Europe. At the same time, France was struggling to establish a new social order in the aftermath of the French Revolution. Some thinkers, such as Adam Smith, had sought to explain the rapidly changing face of society in economic terms; others, such as Jean-Jacques Rousseau, did so in terms of political philosophy. Adam Ferguson had described the social effects of modernization, but no one had yet offered an explanation of social progress to match the political and economic theories.

See also: Harriet Martineau 26–27 ▪ Karl Marx 28–31; 254–59 ▪
Ferdinand Tönnies 32–33 ▪ Émile Durkheim 34–37 ▪ Max Weber 38–45; 220–23

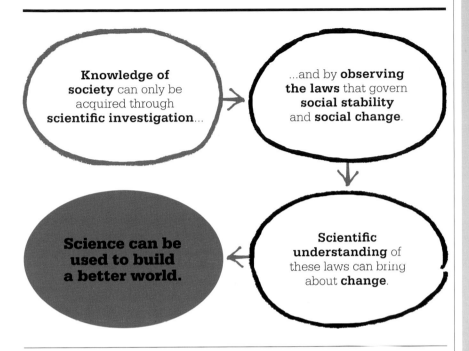

Knowledge of **society** can only be acquired through **scientific investigation**...

...and by **observing the laws** that govern **social stability** and **social change**.

Scientific **understanding** of these laws can bring about **change**.

Science can be used to build a better world.

Auguste Comte

Auguste Comte was born in Montpellier, France. His parents were Catholics and monarchists, but Auguste rejected religion and adopted republicanism. In 1817 he became an assistant to Henri de Saint-Simon, who greatly influenced his ideas of a scientific study of society. After disagreements, Comte left Saint-Simon in 1824, and began his *Course in Positive Philosophy*, supported by John Stuart Mill, among others.

Comte suffered during this time from mental disorders, and his marriage to Caroline Massin ended in divorce. He then fell madly in love with Clotilde de Vaux (who was separated from her husband), but their relationship was unconsummated; she died in 1846. Comte then devoted himself to writing and establishing a positivist "Religion of Humanity." He died in Paris in 1857.

Key works

1830–42 *Course in Positive Philosophy* (six volumes)
1848 *A General View of Positivism*
1851–54 *System of Positive Polity* (four volumes)

Against the background of social uncertainty in France, however, the socialist philosopher Henri de Saint-Simon attempted to analyze the causes of social change, and how social order can be achieved. He suggested that there is a pattern to social progress, and that society goes through a number of different stages. But it was his protégé Auguste Comte who developed this idea into a comprehensive approach to the study of society on scientific principles, which he initially called "social physics" but later described as "sociology."

Understand and transform

Comte was a child of the Enlightenment, and his thinking was rooted in the ideals of the Age of Reason, with its rational, objective focus. The emergence of scientific method during the Enlightenment influenced Comte's approach to philosophy. He made a detailed analysis of the natural sciences and their methodology, then proposed that all branches of knowledge should adopt scientific principles and base theory on observation. The central argument of Comte's "positivism" philosophy is that valid knowledge of anything can only be derived from positive, scientific inquiry. He had seen the power of science to transform: scientific discoveries had provided the technological advances that brought about the Industrial Revolution and created the modern world he lived in.

The time had come, he said, for a social science that would not only give us an understanding of the mechanisms of social order and social change, but also provide us with the means of transforming society, in the same way that the physical sciences had helped to modify our physical environment. »

He considered the study of human society, or sociology, to be the most challenging and complex, therefore it was the "Queen of sciences."

Comte's argument that the scientific study of society was the culmination of progress in our quest for knowledge was influenced by an idea proposed by Henri de Saint-Simon and is set out as the "law of three stages." This states that our understanding of phenomena passes through three phases: a theological stage, in which a god or gods are cited as the cause of things; a metaphysical stage, in which explanation is in terms of abstract entities; and a positive stage, in which knowledge is verified by scientific methods.

Comte's grand theory of social evolution became an analysis of social progress too—an alternative to the merely descriptive accounts of societal stages of hunter-gatherer, nomadic, agricultural, and industrial-commercial. Society in France, Comte suggested, was rooted in the theological stage until the Enlightenment, and social order was based on rules that were ultimately religious. Following the revolution in 1789, French society entered a metaphysical stage, becoming ordered according to

Sociology is, then, not an auxiliary of any other science; it is itself a distinct and autonomous science.
Émile Durkheim

Comte identified three stages of progress in human understanding of the world. The theological stage came to an end with the Enlightenment at the end of the 18th century. Focus then shifted from the divine to the human in a metaphysical stage of rational thought, from which evolved a final stage in which science provides the explanations.

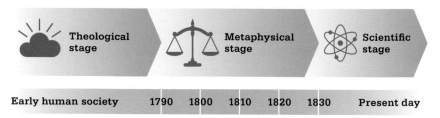

| Theological stage | Metaphysical stage | Scientific stage |

| Early human society | 1790 | 1800 | 1810 | 1820 | 1830 | Present day |

secular principles and ideals, especially the rights to liberty and equality. Comte believed that, recognizing the shortcomings of postrevolutionary society, it now had the possibility of entering the positive stage, in which social order could be determined scientifically.

A science of society

Comte proposed a framework for the new science of sociology, based on the existing "hard" sciences. He organized a hierarchy of sciences, arranged logically so that each science contributes to those following it but not to those preceding it. Beginning with mathematics, the hierarchy ranged through astronomy, physics, and chemistry to biology. The apex of this ascending order of "positivity" was sociology. For this reason, Comte felt it was necessary to have a thorough grasp of the other sciences and their methods before attempting to apply these to the study of society.

Paramount was the principle of verifiability from observation: theories supported by the evidence of facts. But Comte also recognized that it is necessary to have a hypothesis to guide the direction of scientific inquiry, and to determine the scope of observation. He

divided sociology into two broad fields of study: "social statics," the forces that determine social order and hold societies together; and "social dynamics," the forces that determine social change. A scientific understanding of these forces provides the tools to take society into its ultimate, positive stage of social evolution.

Although Comte was not the first to attempt an analysis of human society, he was a pioneer in establishing that it is capable of being studied scientifically. In addition, his positivist philosophy offered both an explanation of secular industrial society and the means of achieving social reform. He believed that just as the

From science comes prediction; from prediction comes action.
Auguste Comte

sciences have solved real-world problems, sociology—as the final science and unifier of the other sciences—can be applied to social problems to create a better society.

From theory to practice

Comte formed his ideas during the chaos that followed the French Revolution, and set them out in his six-volume *Course in Positive Philosophy*, the first volume of which appeared in the same year that France experienced a second revolution in July 1830.

After the overthrow and restoration of monarchy, opinion in France was divided between those who wanted order and those who demanded progress. Comte believed his positivism offered a third way, a rational rather than ideological course of action based on an objective study of society.

His theories gained him as many critics as admirers among his contemporaries in France. Some of his greatest supporters were in Britain, including liberal intellectual John Stuart Mill, who provided him with financial support to enable him to continue with his project, and Harriet Martineau, who translated an edited version of his work into English.

Unfortunately, the reputation Comte had built up was tarnished by his later work, in which he described how positivism could be applied in a political system. An unhappy personal life (a marriage break-up, depression, and a tragic affair) is often cited as causing a change in his thinking: from an objective scientific approach that

The 1830 revolution in France coincided with the publication of Comte's book on positivism and seemed to usher in an age of social progress that he had been hoping for.

examines society to a subjective and quasi-religious exposition of how it should be.

The shift in Comte's work from theory to how it could be put into practice lost him many followers. Mill and other British thinkers saw his prescriptive application of positivism as almost dictatorial, and the system of government he advocated as infringing liberty.

By this time, an alternative approach to the scientific study of society had emerged. Against the same backdrop of social turmoil, Karl Marx offered an analysis of social progress based on the science of economics, and a model for change based on political action rather than rationalism. It is not difficult to see why, in a Europe riven by revolutions, Comte's positivist sociology became eclipsed by the competing claims of socialism and capitalism. Nevertheless, it was Comte, and to a lesser extent his mentor Saint-Simon, who first proposed the idea of sociology as a discipline based on scientific principles rather than

The philosophers have only interpreted the world... the point is to change it.
Karl Marx

mere theorizing. In particular he established a methodology of observation and theory for the social sciences that was taken directly from the physical sciences. While later sociologists, notably Émile Durkheim, disagreed with the detail of his positivism and his application of it, Comte provided them with a solid foundation to work from. Although today Comte's dream of sociology as the "Queen of sciences" may seem naive, the objectivity he advocated remains a guiding principle. ∎

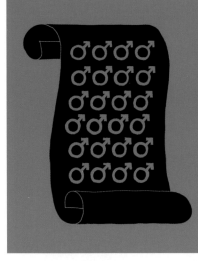

THE DECLARATION OF INDEPENDENCE BEARS NO RELATION TO HALF THE HUMAN RACE
HARRIET MARTINEAU (1802–1876)

IN CONTEXT

FOCUS
Feminism and social injustice

KEY DATES
1791 French playwright and political activist Olympe de Gouges publishes the *Declaration of the Rights of Woman and the Female Citizen* in response to the "Declaration of the Rights of Man and of the Citizen" of 1789.

1807–34 Slavery is abolished in the British Empire.

1869 Harriet Taylor and John Stuart Mill coauthor the essay "The Subjection of Women."

1949 Simone de Beauvoir's *The Second Sex* lays the foundations for "second-wave" feminism of the 1960s–1980s.

1981 The United Nations Convention on the Elimination of All Forms of Discrimination Against Women (CEDAW) is ratified by 188 states.

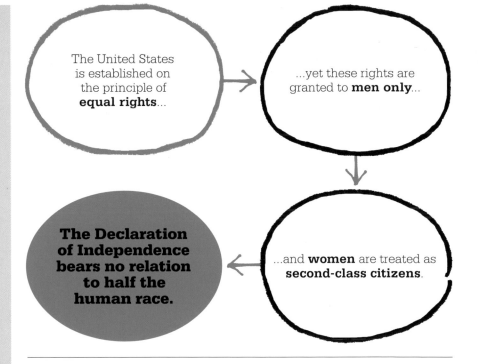

The United States is established on the principle of **equal rights**...

...yet these rights are granted to **men only**...

...and **women** are treated as **second-class citizens**.

The Declaration of Independence bears no relation to half the human race.

I n 1776, the Declaration of Independence proclaimed: "We hold these truths to be self-evident, that all men are created equal, that they are endowed by their Creator with certain unalienable Rights, that among these are Life, Liberty, and the pursuit of Happiness." More than 50 years later, between 1834 and 1836, Harriet Martineau traveled around the US and recorded a very different picture of society. What she saw was a marked discrepancy between the ideals of equality and democracy, and the reality of life in the US.

Before her visit, Martineau had made her name as a journalist writing on political economy and social issues, so on her travels she set down in book form her impressions of US society. Her *Theory and Practice of Society in America* went beyond mere description, however, for it analyzed the forms of social injustice she came across there.

Social emancipator

For Martineau, the degree to which a society can be thought of as civilized is judged by the conditions in which its people live. Theoretical ideals are no measure of how civilized a society is if they do not apply to everybody. The supposed ideals of US society, notably the cherished notion of freedom, were "made a mockery" by the continued practice of slavery, which Martineau identified as the prime example of one section of society having domination over another.

Throughout her life, Martineau campaigned for an end to slavery, but she also applied her principles of what constitutes a civilized

The Continental Congress adopted its highly moral plan for government on July 4, 1776. But Martineau questioned whether social virtues were possible in a society characterized by injustice.

society to identify and oppose other forms of exploitation and social oppression, such as the unjust treatment of the working class in industrial Britain and the subjugation of women in the Western world.

Martineau highlighted the hypocrisy of a society that prided itself on liberty, yet continued to oppress women. This treatment was a particular affront because, as she pointed out, women were half the human race: "If a test of civilization be sought, none can be so sure as the condition of that half of society over which the other half has power." Unlike many of her contemporaries, however, Martineau did not merely campaign for women's rights to education or the vote, but described the ways in which society restricted women's liberty in both domestic and public life.

Martineau was well known in her lifetime, but her contribution to the development of sociology was not recognized until recently. Today, however, she is regarded as not only the first woman to make a methodical study of society, but also the first to formulate a feminist sociological perspective. ∎

Harriet Martineau

Harriet Martineau was born in Norwich, England, the daughter of progressive parents who ensured she had a good education. She showed an early interest in politics and economics, and after the death of her father in 1825, made a living as a journalist. Her success as a writer enabled her to move to London, and in 1834–36 to travel around the US. On her return to England, she published a three-volume sociological critique of the US. Her experiences there confirmed her commitment to campaigning for the abolition of slavery and for the emancipation of women.

Although profoundly deaf since her teenage years, Martineau continued working and campaigning until the 1860s. She had by this time moved to the Lake District, where, housebound by ill health, she died in 1876.

Key works

1832–34 *Illustrations of Political Economy*
1837 *Theory and Practice of Society in America*
1837–38 *How to Observe Morals and Manners*

THE FALL OF THE BOURGEOISIE AND THE VICTORY OF THE PROLETARIAT ARE EQUALLY INEVITABLE

KARL MARX (1818–1883)

IN CONTEXT

FOCUS
Class conflict

KEY DATES
1755 Genevan philosopher Jean-Jacques Rousseau identifies private property as the source of all inequality.

1819 French social theorist Henri de Saint-Simon launches the magazine *L'Organisateur* to promote his socialist ideas.

1807 Georg Hegel interprets historical progress in *The Phenomenology of Spirit*.

1845 In *The Condition of the Working Class in England in 1844*, Friedrich Engels describes the division of capitalist society into two social classes.

1923 The Institute for Social Research is founded and attracts Marxist scholars to the University of Frankfurt.

In the mid-19th century, Europe was characterized by political instability that had begun with the French Revolution. The insurrectionary spirit spread across the continent, and there were attempts to overthrow and replace the old order of monarchies and aristocracy with democratic republics. At the same time, much of Europe was still coming to terms with the changes in society created by industrialization. Some philosophers had explained the problems of the modern industrial world in political terms and offered political solutions, and others such as Adam Smith looked to economics as both the cause of the problems and the answer to them, but there had been little research into the social structure of society.

Between 1830 and 1842, the French philosopher Auguste Comte had suggested that it was possible, and even necessary, to make a scientific study of society. Karl Marx agreed that an objective, methodical approach was overdue and was among the first to tackle the subject. Marx did not set out, however, to make a specifically sociological study, but rather to explain modern society in historical and economic terms, using observation and analysis to identify the causes of social inequality. And where Comte saw science as the means of achieving social change, Marx pointed to the inevitability of political action.

Historical progress

In Marx's time, the conventional explanation of the development of society was of an evolution in stages, from hunting and gathering, through nomadic, pastoral, and agricultural communities to modern commercial society. As a philosopher, Marx was well aware of this idea of social progress and the economic origins of industrial society, but developed his own interpretation of this process.

His primary influence was the German philosopher Georg Hegel, who had proposed a dialectic view of history: that change comes about through a synthesis of opposing forces in which the tension between contradictory ideas is resolved. Marx, however, viewed history as the progression of material circumstances rather than ideas, and took from Hegel the dialectical framework, while

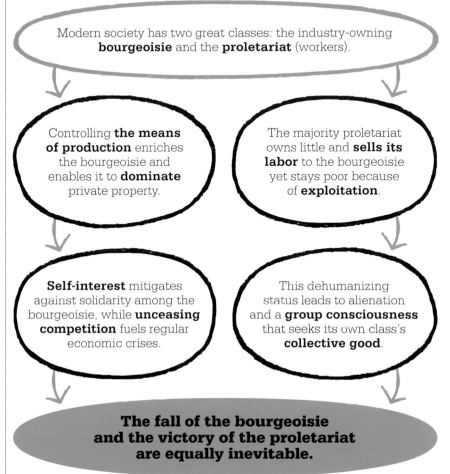

Modern society has two great classes: the industry-owning **bourgeoisie** and the **proletariat** (workers).

Controlling **the means of production** enriches the bourgeoisie and enables it to **dominate** private property.

The majority proletariat owns little and **sells its labor** to the bourgeoisie yet stays poor because of **exploitation**.

Self-interest mitigates against solidarity among the bourgeoisie, while **unceasing competition** fuels regular economic crises.

This dehumanizing status leads to alienation and a **group consciousness** that seeks its own class's **collective good**.

The fall of the bourgeoisie and the victory of the proletariat are equally inevitable.

dismissing much of his philosophy. He was also influenced by French socialist thinkers, such as Jean-Jacques Rousseau, who laid the blame for inequality in civil society on the emergence of the notion of private property.

Marx offered a new approach to the study of historical progress. It is the material conditions in which people live that determine the organization of society, he said, and changes in the means of production (the tools and machinery used to create wealth) bring about socio-economic change. "Historical materialism," as this approach to historical development came to be known, provided an explanation for the transition from feudal to modern capitalist society, brought about by new methods of economic production. Under feudalism, the nobles had controlled the means of agricultural production, as owners of the land that the peasants or serfs worked. With the machine age a new class, the bourgeoisie, emerged as owners of a new means of production. As technology »

Five historical epochs were identified by Marx. Each corresponds to an era in which people were clearly defined by their labor. According to Marx, the determining force of history is the dominant mode of production, which shapes the classes in society. The epochs progress from early human history, when people held things in common, to capitalism in Marx's day, with its two great social classes. In the future lies the classless society of communism.

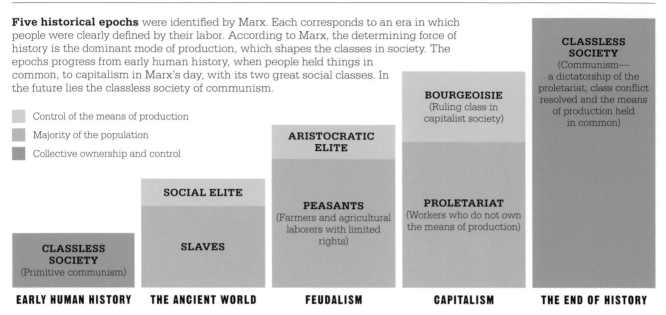

- Control of the means of production
- Majority of the population
- Collective ownership and control

CLASSLESS SOCIETY (Primitive communism)

EARLY HUMAN HISTORY

SOCIAL ELITE

SLAVES

THE ANCIENT WORLD

ARISTOCRATIC ELITE

PEASANTS (Farmers and agricultural laborers with limited rights)

FEUDALISM

BOURGEOISIE (Ruling class in capitalist society)

PROLETARIAT (Workers who do not own the means of production)

CAPITALISM

CLASSLESS SOCIETY (Communism— a dictatorship of the proletariat; class conflict resolved and the means of production held in common)

THE END OF HISTORY

became more prevalent, the bourgeoisie challenged the nobles and brought about a change to the economic structure of society. The opposing elements of feudal society contained the seeds of the capitalist society that replaced it.

Karl Marx's prediction of a communist revolution became a reality in 1917—it did not, however, take place in an advanced industrial nation as he had anticipated, but in Tsarist Russia.

Marx maintained that, as he and Friedrich Engels put it in *The Communist Manifesto*, "the history of all hitherto existing society is the history of class struggles." Whereas feudalism had been characterized by the two classes of nobles or aristocracy and peasants or serfs, modern industrial society had created a bourgeoisie class of capitalists, which owned the means of production, and a proletariat class, which worked in the new industries.

Class conflict

Tension and conflict between the classes in society was inevitable, according to Marx. Therefore, just as feudalism had been replaced, so too would capitalist society and the dominant bourgeoisie. He believed that the proletariat would one day control society, having overthrown the system that had brought it into existence.

It is the method of production of material necessities, Marx argued, that determines the social structure of capitalist society: the classes of capital and labor. Capitalists obtain their wealth from the surplus value of goods produced, in the factories they own, by the labor of the workers. The proletariat, on the other hand, own almost nothing, and in order to survive have to sell their labor to the bourgeoisie.

The relationship between the classes is exploitative, enriching the owners of capital and keeping the working class poor. In addition, the unskilled nature of the work in factories and mills contributes to a feeling of dehumanization and alienation from the process of production, which is aggravated by the threat of unemployment when production exceeds demand.

Over time, however, oppression fosters a class-consciousness in the proletariat—a realization that together the working class can organize a movement for its collective good. The inherent self-interest of capitalism tends to prevent such a development among the bourgeoisie, and constant competition leads to more and

FOUNDATIONS OF SOCIOLOGY **31**

more frequent economic crises. The increasing solidarity of the working class, and weakening of the bourgeoisie, will in time allow the proletariat to take over control of the means of production and bring about a classless society.

A key contribution

Marx's analysis of how capitalism had created socioeconomic classes in the industrial world was based on more than mere theorizing, and as such was one of the first "scientific" studies of society, offering a comprehensive economic, political, and social explanation of modern society. In the process, he introduced several concepts that became central to later sociological thinking, particularly in the area of social class, such as class conflict and consciousness, and the notions of exploitation and alienation.

His ideas inspired numerous revolutionaries, and at one stage in the 20th century, around a third of the world's population lived under a government espousing Marxist principles. But not everyone agreed with the Marxian division of society into classes defined by their economic status, nor the idea that social change is the inevitable result of class conflict. In the generation following Marx, both Émile Durkheim and Max Weber, who along with Marx are often cited as the "founding fathers" of modern sociology, offered alternative views in reaction to his.

Durkheim acknowledged that industry had shaped modern society, but argued that it was industrialization itself, rather than capitalism, that was at the root of social problems.

Weber, on the other hand, accepted Marx's argument that there are economic reasons behind class conflict, but felt that Marx's division of society into bourgeoisie and proletariat on purely economic grounds was too simple. He believed that there were cultural and religious as well as economic causes for the growth of capitalism, and these were reflected in classes based on prestige and power as well as economic status.

Although Marx's influence on sociology in the Western world waned during the first half of the 20th century, the members of the so-called "Frankfurt School" of sociologists and philosophers (including Jürgen Habermas, Erich Fromm, and Herbert Marcuse) remained notable adherents to his principles. After World War II, with the advent of the Cold War, opinion became even more divided. In the US in particular, Marxist theory of any type was largely discredited, while in Europe, especially France, a number of philosophers and sociologists further developed Marx's social ideas.

Today, as new technology is once again transforming our world, and at the same time people are becoming conscious of a growing economic inequality, some of Marx's basic ideas have begun to be revisited by social, economic, and political thinkers. ∎

> 66
> [Marx is] the true father of modern sociology, in so far as anyone can claim the title.
> **Isaiah Berlin**
> **Russo-British philosopher (1909–1997)**
> 99

Karl Marx

Regarded as one of the "founding fathers" of social science, Karl Marx was also an influential economist, political philosopher, and historian. He was born in Trier, Germany, and at his lawyer father's insistence, he studied law, rather than the philosophy and literature he was interested in, at the University of Bonn, and later at Berlin. There he developed his interest in Hegel, and went on to gain a doctorate from the University of Jena in 1841.

After becoming a journalist in Cologne, Marx moved to Paris, where he developed his economic, social, and political theory, collaborating with Friedrich Engels. In 1845 the pair cowrote *The Communist Manifesto*. Following the failure of the revolutions in Europe in 1848, Marx moved to London. After the death of his wife in 1881, his health deteriorated, and he died two years later at 64.

Key works

1848 *The Communist Manifesto*
1859 *A Contribution to the Critique of Political Economy*
1867 *Das Kapital, Volume 1*

GEMEINSCHAFT AND GESELLSCHAFT
FERDINAND TÖNNIES (1855–1936)

IN CONTEXT

FOCUS
Community and society

KEY DATES
1651 English philosopher Thomas Hobbes describes the relationship between man's nature and the structure of society in *Leviathan*.

1848 In *The Communist Manifesto*, Karl Marx and Friedrich Engels lay out the effects of capitalism on society.

1893 Sociologist Émile Durkheim outlines the idea of social order maintained by organic and mechanical solidarity in *The Division of Labor in Society*.

1904–05 Max Weber publishes *The Protestant Ethic and the Spirit of Capitalism*.

2000 Zygmunt Bauman introduces the idea of "liquid modernity" in an increasingly globalized society.

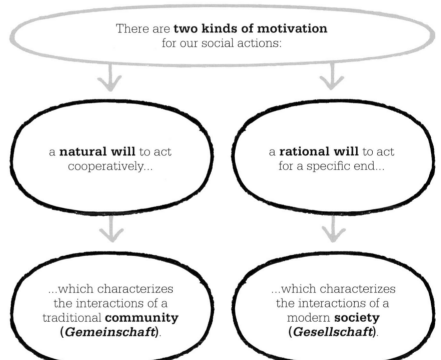

There are **two kinds of motivation** for our social actions:

a **natural will** to act cooperatively...

a **rational will** to act for a specific end...

...which characterizes the interactions of a traditional **community** (*Gemeinschaft*).

...which characterizes the interactions of a modern **society** (*Gesellschaft*).

Toward the end of the 19th century, a number of thinkers turned their attention to the social implications of modernity, and in particular the growth of capitalist industrial society. Among them were Émile Durkheim, Max Weber, and Ferdinand Tönnies, widely regarded as founding fathers of sociology. Tönnies' major contribution to the discipline was his analysis of contrasting types of social groupings in his influential *Gemeinschaft und Gesellschaft*, published in 1887.

In this book, his magnum opus, Tönnies points out what he sees as the distinction between traditional rural communities and modern industrialized society. The former, he argues, are characterized by *Gemeinschaft*, community that is based on the bonds of family and social groups such as the church. Small-scale communities tend to have common goals and beliefs, and interactions within them are based on trust and cooperation.

Triumph of "will"

In large-scale societies such as modern cities, the division of labor and mobility of the workforce have eroded traditional bonds. In place of *Gemeinschaft* there is *Gesellschaft*, association or society. Relationships in such societies are more impersonal and superficial, and based on individual self-interest rather than mutual aid.

The two extremes of *Gemeinschaft* and *Gesellschaft* exist to a greater or lesser extent in every social grouping, but Tönnies argued that the ethos of

Gemeinschaft by its very essence is of an earlier origin than its subject or members.
Ferdinand Tönnies

capitalism and competition had led to a predominance of mere association in the industrial society in which he lived.

At the root of Tönnies' theory was his idea of "will"—what motivates people to action. He distinguished between what he called *Wesenwille*, "natural will," and *Kürwille*, "rational will." *Wesenwille*, he said, is the instinctive will to do something for its own sake, or out of habit or custom, or moral obligation. This is the motivation that underlies the

social order of *Gemeinschaft*, the will to do things for and as a part of the community. On the other hand, *Kürwille* motivates us to act in a purely rational way to achieve a specific goal, and is the type of will behind decisions made in large organizations, and particularly businesses. It is *Kürwille* that characterizes the *Gesellschaft* of capitalist urban society.

Despite his Left-leaning politics, Tönnies was seen as an essentially conservative figure, lamenting modernity's loss of *Gemeinschaft*, rather than advocating social change. Although he had gained the respect of fellow sociologists, his ideas had little influence until many years later. Tönnies' theory, along with his work on methodology, paved the way for 20th-century sociology. Weber further developed Tönnies' notions of will and motivation to social action, and Durkheim's idea of mechanical and organic solidarity echoed the contrast between *Gemeinschaft* and *Gesellschaft*. ∎

Ferdinand Tönnies

Ferdinand Tönnies was born in North Frisia, Schleswig (now Nordfriesland, Schleswig-Holstein, Germany). After studying at the universities of Strassburg, Jena, Bonn, and Leipzig, he was awarded his doctorate at Tübingen in 1877.

In his postdoctoral studies in Berlin and London, Tönnies' interest shifted from philosophy to political and social issues. He became a private tutor at the University of Kiel in 1881, but an inheritance allowed him to focus on his own work. He was also a cofounder of the German

Sociological Society. Because of his outspoken political views, he was not offered a professorship at Kiel until 1913. His Social Democratic sympathies and a public denunciation of Nazism led to his removal from the university in 1931, three years before his death at age 80.

Key works

1887 *Gemeinschaft und Gesellschaft*
1926 *Progress and Social Development*
1931 *Introduction to Sociology*

SOCIETY, LIKE THE HUMAN BODY, HAS INTERRELATED PARTS, NEEDS, AND FUNCTIONS

ÉMILE DURKHEIM (1858–1917)

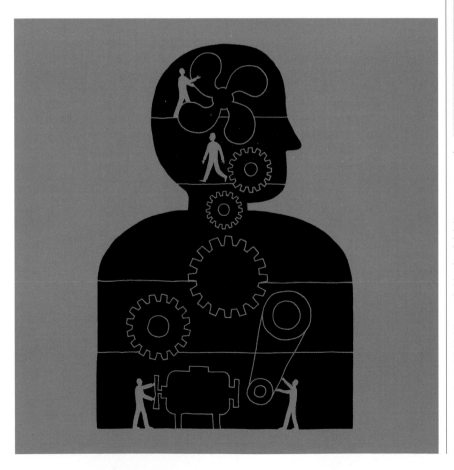

IN CONTEXT

FOCUS
Functionalism

KEY DATES
1830–42 Auguste Comte advocates a scientific approach to the study of society in his *Course in Positive Philosophy*.

1874–77 Herbert Spencer says society is an evolving "social organism" in the first volume of *The Principles of Sociology*.

1937 In *The Structure of Social Action*, Talcott Parsons revives the functionalist approach in his action theory.

1949 Robert K. Merton develops Durkheim's idea of anomie to examine social dysfunction in *Social Theory and Social Structure*.

1976 Anthony Giddens offers an alternative to structural functionalism in *New Rules of Sociological Method*.

S ociology was only gradually accepted as a distinct discipline, a social science separate from philosophy, in the latter half of the 19th century. The intellectual atmosphere of the time meant that for sociology to be recognized as a field of study, it had to establish scientific credentials.

Among those who had studied philosophy but been drawn to the new branch of knowledge was Émile Durkheim, who believed that sociology should be less of a grand theory and more of a method that could be applied in diverse ways to understanding the development of modern society. Now regarded as one of the principal founders of

See also: Auguste Comte 22–25 ▪ Karl Marx 28–31 ▪ Max Weber 38–45 ▪ Jeffrey Alexander 204–09 ▪ Robert K. Merton 262–63 ▪ Herbert Spencer 334

Humankind has evolved from gathering in small, **homogeneous communities** to forming large, **complex societies**.

In traditional society, religion and culture created a **collective consciousness** that provided **solidarity**.

In modern society, the **division of labor** has brought about increased **specialization** and the focus is more on the **individual** than the **collective**...

...and **solidarity** now comes from the **interdependence** of individuals with **specialized functions**.

Society, like the human body, has interrelated parts, needs, and functions.

Émile Durkheim

Born in Épinal in eastern France, Émile Durkheim broke with family tradition and left rabbinical school to follow a secular career. He studied at the École Normale Supérieure in Paris, graduating in philosophy in 1882, but was already interested in social science after reading Auguste Comte and Herbert Spencer.

Durkheim moved to Germany to study sociology. In 1887 he returned to France, teaching the country's first sociology courses at the University of Bordeaux, and later founded the first social science journal in France. He was appointed to the Sorbonne in 1902 and stayed there for the rest of his life, becoming a full professor in 1906. He felt increasingly marginalized by the rise of right-wing nationalist politics during World War I, and after his son André was killed in 1916, his health deteriorated and he died of a stroke in 1917.

Key works

1893 *The Division of Labor in Society*
1895 *The Rules of Sociological Method*
1897 *Suicide*

sociology, with Karl Marx and Max Weber, Durkheim was not the first scholar to attempt to establish the subject as a science; the earlier work of other thinkers inevitably influenced his own ideas.

Forging a scientific model

Auguste Comte had laid the foundations with his theory that the study of human society is the pinnacle of a hierarchy of natural sciences. And, because society is a collection of human animals, the idea grew that of all the natural sciences, biology was the closest model for the social sciences. Not everyone agreed: Marx, for example, based his sociological ideas on the new science of economics rather than biology. But the appearance of Charles Darwin's theory of the origin of species provoked a radical rethink of many conventionally held ideas. This was especially true in Britain, where Darwin's work provided a model of organic evolution that could be applied to many other disciplines.

Among those inspired by Darwin was Herbert Spencer, a philosopher and biologist who likened the development of modern society to an evolving organism, with different parts serving different functions. His writing established the idea of an "organic" model for the social sciences. **»**

Durkheim argued that religions, especially long-established faiths such as Judaism, are fundamentally social institutions that give people a strong sense of collective consciousness.

Durkheim upheld Spencer's functional idea of separate parts serving a purpose and the notion that society was greater than the sum of its individual elements. And Auguste Comte's "positivism" (his belief that only scientific inquiry yields true knowledge) helped to shape the scientific methodology that Durkheim felt would reveal how modern society functions.

Durkheim focused on society as a whole and its institutions, rather than the motivations and actions of individuals within society; above all, he was interested in the things that hold society together and maintain social order. He argued that the basis for sociological study should be what he called "social facts," or "realities external to the individual" that can be verified empirically.

Like the other pioneering sociologists, Durkheim tried to understand and explain the factors

Is it our duty to seek to become a... complete human being, one quite sufficient unto himself; or... to be only a part of a whole, the organ of an organism?
Émile Durkheim

that had shaped modern society, the various forces known as "modernity." But where Marx had associated them with capitalism, and Weber with rationalization, Durkheim connected the development of modern society with industrialization, and in particular the division of labor that came with it.

A functional organism

What differentiates modern society from traditional ones, according to Durkheim, is a fundamental change in the form of social cohesion; the advent of industrialization has evolved a new form of solidarity. Durkheim outlined his theory of the different types of social solidarity in his doctoral thesis, "The Division of Social Labor."

In primitive societies, such as hunter-gatherer groups, individuals do much the same jobs, and although each could be self-sufficient, society is held together by a sense of a common purpose and experience, and commonly held beliefs and values. The similarity of individuals in such

a society fosters what Durkheim called "collective consciousness," which is the basis of its solidarity.

But as societies grew in size and complexity, people began to develop more specialized skills, replacing self-reliance with interdependence. The farmer, for example, relies on the blacksmith to shoe his horses, while the blacksmith relies on the farmer to provide his food. The mechanical solidarity, as Durkheim refers to it, of traditional society becomes replaced by an organic solidarity based not on the similarity of its individual members, but their complementary differences.

This division of labor reaches its peak with industrialization, when society has evolved to become a complex "organism" in which individual elements perform specialized functions, each of which is essential to the well-being of the whole. The idea that society is structured like a biological organism composed of distinct parts with specialized functions became a significant approach to sociology, known as functionalism.

The "social fact"—by which he meant a thing that exists without being subject to any individual will upon it—that Durkheim identifies as driving this evolution from mechanical to organic solidarity is the increase in "dynamic density," or population growth and concentration. The competition for resources becomes more intense, but with the increased population density comes the possibility of greater social interaction within the population itself, triggering a division of labor to more efficiently deal with its demands.

In modern society, the organic interdependence of individuals is the basis for social cohesion. But Durkheim realized that the division of labor that came with rapid industrialization also brought social problems. Precisely because it is built on the complementary differences between people, organic solidarity shifts the focus from the community to the individual, replacing the collective consciousness of a society— the shared beliefs and values that provide cohesiveness. Without that framework of norms of behavior,

A beehive is created by the division of labor of industrious insects. As well as producing a functioning whole, the bees maintain a symbiotic relationship with the flora of their environment.

people become disoriented and society unstable. Organic solidarity can only work if elements of mechanical solidarity are retained, and members of society have a sense of common purpose.

The speed of industrialization, according to Durkheim, had forced a division of labor so quickly on modern society that social interaction had not developed sufficiently to become a substitute for the decreasing collective consciousness. Individuals felt increasingly unconnected with society, and especially the sort of moral guidance that mechanical solidarity had previously given them. Durkheim used the word anomie to describe this loss of collective standards and values, and its consequent sapping of individual morale. In a study of patterns of suicide in different areas, he showed the importance of anomie in the despair that leads someone to take their own life. In communities where collective beliefs were strong, such as among Catholics, the suicide rate was lower than elsewhere, which confirmed for Durkheim the value of solidarity to the health of a society.

An academic discipline

Durkheim based his ideas on thorough research of empirical evidence, such as case studies and statistics. His major legacy was the establishment of sociology as an academic discipline in the tradition of the positivist doctrine of Comte—that social science is subject to the same investigative methods as the natural sciences.

Durkheim's positivist approach was met with skepticism, however. Sociological thinkers from Marx onward rejected the idea that something as complex and unpredictable as human society is

Society is not a mere sum of individuals. Rather, the system formed by their association represents a specific reality which has its own characteristics.
Émile Durkheim

consistent with scientific research. Durkheim also went against the intellectual mood of the time by looking at society as a whole rather than at the experience of the individual, which was the basis of the approach adopted by Max Weber. His concept of "social facts" with a reality of their own, separate from the individual, was dismissed, and his objective approach was also criticized for explaining the basis of social order but not making any suggestions to change it.

But Durkheim's analysis of society as composed of different but interrelated parts, each with its own particular function, helped to establish functionalism as an important approach to sociology, influencing among others Talcott Parsons and Robert K. Merton.

Durkheim's explanations of solidarity were an alternative to the theories of Marx and Weber, but the heyday of functionalism lasted only until the 1960s. Although Durkheim's positivism has since fallen out of favor, concepts introduced by him, such as anomie and collective consciousness (in the guise of "culture"), continue to figure in contemporary sociology. ■

THE IRON CAGE

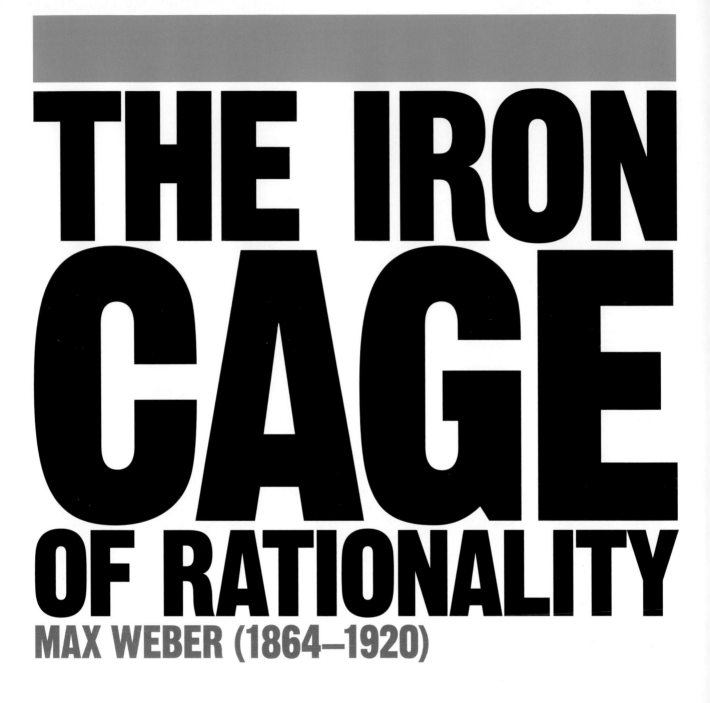

OF RATIONALITY

MAX WEBER (1864–1920)

IN CONTEXT

FOCUS
Rational modernity

KEY DATES
1845 Karl Marx notes down 11 "Theses on Feuerbach" and introduces the idea of historical materialism—that economics, rather than ideas, drive social change.

1903 German sociologist Georg Simmel examines the effects of modern city life on the individual in *The Metropolis and Mental Life.*

1937 In *The Structure of Social Action,* Talcott Parsons puts forward his action theory, which attempts to integrate the contrasting (subjective–objective) approaches of Weber and Durkheim.

1956 In *The Power Elite,* Charles Wright Mills describes the emergence of a military-industrial ruling class as the result of rationalization.

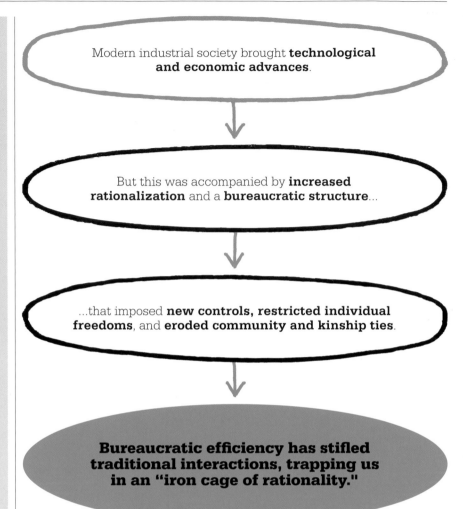

Modern industrial society brought **technological and economic advances**.

But this was accompanied by **increased rationalization** and a **bureaucratic structure**...

...that imposed **new controls, restricted individual freedoms**, and **eroded community and kinship ties**.

Bureaucratic efficiency has stifled traditional interactions, trapping us in an "iron cage of rationality."

Until the latter half of the 19th century, the economic growth of the German states was based on trade rather than production. But when they made the shift to large-scale manufacturing industry, of the sort that had urbanized Britain and France, the change was rapid and dramatic. This was especially noticeable in Prussia, where the combination of natural resources and a tradition of military organization helped to establish an efficient industrial society in a very short time.

Germany's unfamiliarity with the effects of modernity meant it had not yet developed a tradition of sociological thought. Karl Marx was German by birth, but he based his sociological and economic ideas on his experiences of industrialized society elsewhere. However, toward the end of the century, a number of German thinkers turned their attention to the study of Germany's emergent modern society. Among them was Max Weber, who was to become perhaps the most influential of the "founding fathers" of sociology.

Weber was not concerned with establishing sociology as a discipline in the same way as Auguste Comte and Émile Durkheim in France, who sought universal "scientific laws" for society (in the belief, known as "positivism," that science could build a better world).

While Weber accepted that any study of society should be rigorous, he argued that it could not be truly objective, because it is the study not so much of social behavior but of social action, meaning the ways in which individuals in society interact. This action is necessarily subjective, and needs to be interpreted by focusing on the subjective values that individuals associate with their actions.

This interpretive approach, also called *verstehen* ("understanding"), was almost the antithesis of the objective study of society. Whereas Durkheim's approach examined the structure of society as a whole, and the "organic" nature of its many interdependent parts, Weber sought to study the experience of the individual.

Weber was heavily influenced by Marx's theories, especially the idea that modern capitalist society is depersonalizing and alienating. He disagreed, however, with Marx's materialist approach and its emphasis on economics rather than culture and ideas, and with Marx's belief in the inevitability of proletarian revolution. Instead,

Weber synthesized ideas from both Marx and Durkheim to develop his own distinctive sociological analysis, examining the effects of what he saw as the most pervasive aspect of modernity: rationalization.

An "iron cage"
In arguably his best-known work, *The Protestant Ethic and the Spirit of Capitalism* (1904–05), Weber describes the evolution of the West from a society governed by tribal custom or religious obligations to an increasingly secular organization based on the goal of economic gain.

Industrialization had been achieved through advances in science and engineering, and the capitalism that accompanied it called for purely rational decisions based on efficiency and cost-benefit analysis (assessing the benefits and costs of projects). While the rise

> The fate of our times is characterized... above all... by the disenchantment of the world.
> **Max Weber**

of capitalism had brought many material benefits, it also had numerous social drawbacks; traditional cultural and spiritual values had been supplanted by rationalization, which brought with it a sense of what Weber called "disenchantment" as the »

The 1936 film *Modern Times* depicts actor Charlie Chaplin as an assembly line worker subject to the dehumanizing effects of modernity and rationalization.

> ...the world could one day be filled with nothing but those little cogs, little men clinging to little jobs and striving toward bigger ones.
> **Max Weber**

intangible, mystical side of many people's day-to-day lives was replaced by cold calculation.

Weber recognized the positive changes brought about by increased knowledge, and the prosperity that resulted from logical decision-making rather than the dictates of outdated religious authorities. But rationalization was also changing the administration of society by increasing the level of bureaucracy in all kinds of organizations. Having been brought up in Prussia, where well-established military efficiency became the model for the newly industrialized state, this development would have been especially noticeable to Weber.

Bureaucracy, Weber believed, was both inevitable and necessary in modern industrial society. Its machinelike effectiveness and efficiency is what enables society to prosper economically, which meant its growth in scope and

power was apparently unstoppable. However, whereas the eclipse of religion meant that people were liberated from irrational social norms, a bureaucratic structure imposed a new form of control and threatened to stifle the very individualism that had led people to reject dogmatic religious authority. Many members of modern society now felt trapped by the rigid rules of bureaucracy, as if in an "iron cage" of rationalization. Moreover, bureaucracies tend to produce hierarchical organizations that are impersonal, and with standardized procedures that overrule individualism.

Dehumanization

Weber was concerned with these effects on the individual "cogs in the machine." Capitalism, which had promised a technological utopia with the individual at its heart, had instead created a society dominated by work and money,

> The fully developed bureaucratic apparatus compares with other organizations exactly as does the machine with the non-mechanical modes of production.
> **Max Weber**

overseen by an uncompromising bureaucracy. A rigid, rule-based society not only tends to restrict the individual, but also has a dehumanizing effect, making people feel as though they are at the mercy of a logical but godless system. The power and authority of a rational bureaucracy also affects the relationships and interactions of individuals—their social actions. These actions are no longer based on ties of family or community, nor traditional values and beliefs, but are geared toward efficiency and the achievement of specific goals.

Because the primary goal of rationalization is to get things done efficiently, the desires of the individual are subservient to the goals of the organization, leading to a loss of individual autonomy. Although there is a greater degree of interdependence between people as jobs become more and more specialized, individuals feel that

The German Chancellery in Berlin is the headquarters of the German government. The civil servants who work there are a bureaucracy tasked with implementing government policy.

their worth in society is determined by others rather than by their own skills or craftsmanship. The desire for self-improvement is replaced with an obsessive ambition to acquire a better job, more money, or a higher social status, and creativity is valued less than productivity.

In Weber's view, this disenchantment is the price modern society pays for the material gains achieved by bureaucratic rationalization. The social changes it causes are profound, affecting not only our system of morality but also our psychological and cultural makeup. The erosion of spiritual values means our social actions are instead based on calculations of cost and benefit, and become a matter more of administration than moral or social guidance.

Social actions and class

While Weber often despaired of the soulless side of modern society, he was not completely pessimistic. Bureaucracies may be difficult to destroy, but because they are created by society he believed they can also be changed by society. Where Marx had predicted that the

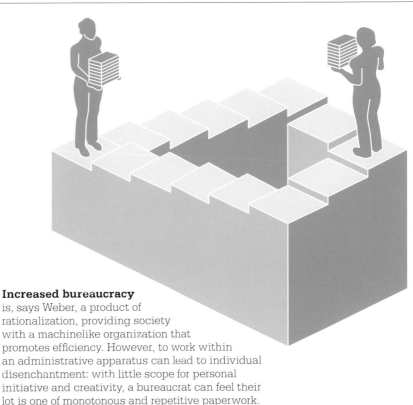

Increased bureaucracy
is, says Weber, a product of rationalization, providing society with a machinelike organization that promotes efficiency. However, to work within an administrative apparatus can lead to individual disenchantment: with little scope for personal initiative and creativity, a bureaucrat can feel their lot is one of monotonous and repetitive paperwork.

...what can we oppose to this machinery... to keep a portion of mankind free from this... supreme mastery of the bureaucratic way of life.
Max Weber

exploitation and alienation of the proletariat by capitalism would inevitably lead to revolution, Weber felt communism led to even greater bureaucratic control than capitalism. Instead, he advocated that within a liberal democracy, bureaucracy should only have as much authority as members of society are prepared to allow it. This is, he said, determined by the social actions of individuals as they try to improve their lives and their "life chances" (or opportunities).

Just as society had progressed from the "charismatic" authority of kinship ties and religion, through the patriarchal authority of feudal society, to the modern authority of rationalization and bureaucracy, so too individual behavior had evolved from emotional, traditional, and value-based social actions to "instrumental action"—action

based on the assessment of costs and consequences, which Weber considered the culmination of rational conduct. In addition, he identified three elements of social stratification in which these social actions could be taken, affecting different aspects of a person's "life chances." As well as the economically determined social class, there is also status class based on less tangible attributes such as honor and prestige, and party class based on political affiliations. Together these help the individual to establish a distinct position in society.

A gradual acceptance

Weber's innovative perspective formed the foundation of one of the major approaches to sociology in the 20th century. By introducing the idea of a subjective, interpretive » examination of individuals' social actions, he offered an alternative to Durkheim's positivism by pointing out that the methodology of the natural sciences is not appropriate to the study of the social sciences, and to Marx's materialist determinism by stressing the importance of ideas and culture over economic considerations.

Although Weber's ideas were highly influential among his contemporaries in Germany, such as Werner Sombart and Georg Simmel, they were not widely accepted. He was regarded in his lifetime as a historian and economist rather than a sociologist, and it was not until much later that his work received the attention it deserved. Many of his works were only published posthumously, and few were translated until well after his death. Sociologists at the beginning of the 20th century felt antipathy toward Weber's approach because they were anxious to establish the

Franz Kafka, a contemporary of Weber, wrote stories depicting a dystopian bureaucracy. His work engages with Weberian themes such as dehumanization and anonymity.

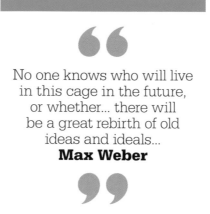

> No one knows who will live in this cage in the future, or whether... there will be a great rebirth of old ideas and ideals...
> **Max Weber**

credentials of sociology as a science; his notion of subjective *verstehen* and his examination of individual experience rather than of society as a whole was seen as lacking the necessary rigor and objectivity. And some critics, especially those steeped in the ideas of Marxian economic determinism, disputed Weber's account of the evolution of Western capitalism.

Nevertheless, Weber's ideas gradually became accepted, as the influence of Durkheim's positivism began to wane. Weber was, for example, an influence on the critical theory of the Frankfurt School, centered around Goethe University in Frankfurt, Germany. These thinkers held that traditional Marxist theory could not fully account for the path taken by Western capitalist societies, and so sought to draw on Weber's anti-positivist sociological approach and analysis of rationalization. Escaping the rise of Nazism, members of the Frankfurt School took these ideas to the US, where Weber's insights were enthusiastically received, and where his influence was strongest in the period following World War II. In particular, American sociologist Talcott Parsons

attempted to reconcile Weber's ideas with the then dominant positivist tradition in sociology established by Durkheim, and to incorporate them into his own theories. Parsons also did much to popularize Weber and his ideas within US sociology, but it was Charles Wright Mills who, with Hans Heinrich Gerth, brought the most important of Weber's writings to the attention of the English-speaking world with their translation and commentary in 1946. Wright Mills was especially influenced by Weber's theory of the "iron cage" of rationality, and developed this theme in his own analysis of social structures, in which he showed that Weber's ideas had more significant implications than had previously been thought.

The rational gone global

By the 1960s, Weber had become mainstream, and his interpretive approach had all but replaced the positivism that had dominated sociology since Durkheim. In the last decades of the 20th century, Weber's emphasis on the social actions of individuals, and their relationship to the power exerted by a rationalized modern society, provided a framework for contemporary sociology.

More recently, sociologists such as British theorist Anthony Giddens have focused on the contrast between Durkheim's approach to society as a whole, and Weber's concentration on the individual as the unit of study. Giddens points out that neither approach is completely right or wrong, but instead exemplifies one of two different perspectives—the macro and micro. Another aspect of Weber's work—that of culture and ideas shaping our social structures

The conditions within semiconductor fabrication plants, where workers wear masks and "bunny suits," are a visible symptom of rationalization and the stifling of human interactions.

more than economic conditions—has been adopted by a British school of thought that has given rise to the field of cultural studies.

Weber and Marx

In many ways, Weber's analysis proved more prescient than Marx's. Despite his dismissal of Marx's interpretation of the inevitability of historical change, Weber predicted the endurance, and global triumph, of the capitalist economy over traditional models as a result of rationalization. He also foresaw that a modern technological society would rely upon an efficient bureaucracy, and that any problems would not be of structure but management and competence: too rigid a bureaucracy would paradoxically decrease rather than increase efficiency.

More significantly, Weber realized that materialism and rationalization created a soulless "iron cage," and if unchecked would lead to tyranny. Where Marx had a vision of workers' emancipation and the establishment of a utopian communist state, Weber argued that in modern industrial society everybody's lives—those of both owners and workers—are shaped by the ongoing conflict between impersonal, organizational efficiency and individual needs and desires. And in recent decades, this has proved to be the case, as economic "rational calculation" has led to the eclipse of high-street sole traders by supermarkets and shopping malls, and the export of manufacturing and clerical jobs from the West to lower-wage economics worldwide. The hopes and desires of individuals have, in many cases, been contained by the iron cage of rationalization. ■

Max Weber

Max Weber is one of the founding fathers of sociology, along with Karl Marx and Émile Durkheim. Born in Erfurt into a German middle-class intellectual family, Weber received his doctorate in 1888 and held professorial posts at the universities of Berlin, Freiburg, and Heidelberg. His knowledge of economics, history, politics, religion, and philosophy serve as the terrain out of which so much sociological thinking in these areas has developed and grown.

Although Weber's professional legacy remains outstanding, his personal life was a troubled one, and in 1897 he had a breakdown following the death of his father. In spite of his untimely death in 1920, at the age of 56, Weber's account of the role of religion in the rise of capitalism remains a sociological classic.

Key works

1904–1905 *The Protestant Ethic and the Spirit of Capitalism*
1919–1920 *General Economic History*
1921–1922 *Economy and Society: An Outline of Interpretive Sociology*

MANY PERSONAL TROUBLES MUST BE UNDERSTOOD IN TERMS OF PUBLIC ISSUES

CHARLES WRIGHT MILLS (1916–1962)

IN CONTEXT

FOCUS
The sociological imagination

KEY DATES
1848 In *The Communist Manifesto*, Karl Marx and Friedrich Engels describe progress in terms of class struggles and depict capitalist society as a conflict between the bourgeoisie and proletariat.

1899 In *The Theory of the Leisure Class*, Thorstein Veblen suggests that the business class pursues profit at the expense of progress or social welfare.

1904–05 Max Weber describes a society stratified by class, status, and power in *The Protestant Ethic and the Spirit of Capitalism*.

1975 Michel Foucault looks at power and resistance in *Discipline and Punish*.

D uring the Cold War that developed after World War II, very few US sociologists openly adopted a socialist standpoint, particularly during the anti-communist witch-hunt that was known as McCarthyism. Yet Charles Wright Mills went against the grain; his most influential books criticized the military and commercial power elites of his time.

Wright Mills risked not only falling foul of the authorities during this "Red Scare" era of the 1940s and 1950s, but also rejection by mainstream sociologists. However, he was no apologist for Marxist ideology and instead presented a

See also: Karl Marx 28–31 ▪ Max Weber 38–45 ▪ Michel Foucault 52–55 ▪ Friedrich Engels 66–67 ▪ Richard Sennett 84–87 ▪ Herbert Marcuse 182–87 ▪ Thorstein Veblen 214–19

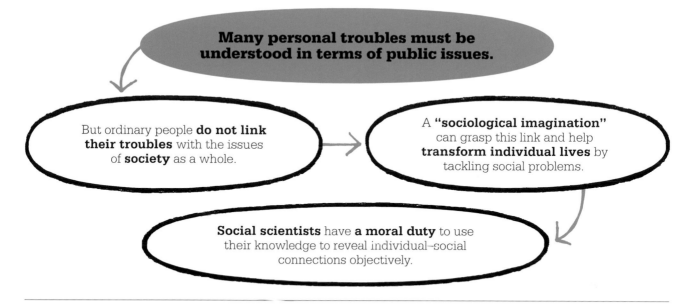

Many personal troubles must be understood in terms of public issues.

But ordinary people **do not link their troubles** with the issues of **society** as a whole.

A **"sociological imagination"** can grasp this link and help **transform individual lives** by tackling social problems.

Social scientists have **a moral duty** to use their knowledge to reveal individual–social connections objectively.

critique of the effects of modernity, pointing out what he saw as the complacency among his fellow intellectuals that had allowed the oppression of "mass society."

Wright Mills' maverick stance belied the firm foundations on which it was based. He had been a brilliant and uncompromising student of sociology, and especially admired the work of Max Weber, whose idea of rationalization inspired the central theme of his own social thinking.

Dehumanized society

For Weber, modern society was replacing traditional customs and values with rational decision-making in a dehumanizing process that affected not only the culture but also the structure of society. He noted that rational social organization is not necessarily based on reason, or for the welfare of all. Weber also provided Wright Mills with a more sophisticated notion of class than the simple

economic model proposed by Marx, introducing the elements of status and power as well as wealth.

With a thorough understanding of Weber's theories, and the belief that they were more radical than had been thought previously, Wright Mills set about applying them to his own analysis of the effects of rationalization in mid-20th century Western society.

He focused his attention first on the working class in the US, criticizing organized labor for collaborating with capitalists and thus allowing them to continue to oppress the workforce. But his was not a Marxist attack on capitalism; he felt Marxism failed to address the social and cultural issues associated with the dominance of commercial industry.

Next, he examined the most obvious product of rationalization: the bureaucratic middle classes. He maintained that by the mid-20th century the US middle classes, alienated from the processes of

production, had become divorced from traditional values, such as pride in craftsmanship, and dehumanized by ever-increasing rationalization. In his view, they were now "cheerful robots"—finding pleasure in material things, but intellectually, politically, and socially apathetic—without any control over their circumstances.

The failure of the working class, and the inability of the middle class, to take control allowed **»**

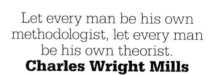

Let every man be his own methodologist, let every man be his own theorist.
Charles Wright Mills

The collapse of the auto industry in Detroit brought ruin to the city, but many workers did not link their poverty to the actions of a power elite, which included union leaders.

society to be shaped by what Wright Mills called a power elite. This, he emphasized, was not necessarily an economic elite, but one that included military, political, and union leaders too. Whereas Weber had argued half a century earlier that rationalization meant that the business elite made the decisions, Wright Mills said that a new military–industrial ruling class had been created. He believed that this was a turning point marking the transition from the modern age to what he called a "Fourth Epoch." Rationalization, which had been assumed to produce freedom and social progress, was increasingly having the opposite effect.

This was not just a problem for liberal democracies, which now faced the prospect of being powerless to control social change, but also for the communist states in which Marxism had proved equally unable to provide a means of taking control. At the heart of the

> "
>
> Neither the life of an individual nor the history of a society can be understood without understanding both.
> **Charles Wright Mills**
>
> "

problem, according to Wright Mills, is the fact that ordinary people in "mass society" are unaware of the way in which their lives are affected by this concentration of political and social power. They go about their lives without realizing how the things that happen to them are connected to the wider social context. Each individual's troubles, such as becoming unemployed, or ending up homeless or in debt, are perceived as personal and not in terms of forces of historical change. As Wright Mills puts it, "They do not possess the quality of mind essential to grasp the interplay of men and society, of biography and history, of self and world"— the quality that he calls "the sociological imagination."

It was the lack of sociological imagination that was to blame for the emergence of the power elite. In *The Sociological Imagination*, published in 1959, Wright Mills turns his sights from society to sociology and the social sciences themselves. Because it is difficult for the ordinary person to think of their personal troubles

in terms of larger public issues, it is up to sociologists to enlighten, inspire, and instruct them—to provide essential knowledge and information.

What ought to be?

Wright Mills was highly critical of academic sociology of the time, which was, in his opinion, remote from everyday experience; more concerned with providing "grand theory" than becoming involved in social change. Wright Mills took the pragmatic view that knowledge should be useful, and felt that it was the moral duty of sociologists to take the lead. It was time, he said, for intellectuals to leave their ivory towers and provide people with the means of changing society for the better, and transforming their individual lives by encouraging public engagement in political and social issues.

His attack on the social science establishment called into question the very notion of what sociology was about. At that time, social scientists were striving to be neutral observers, objectively describing and analyzing social, political, and economic systems. But Wright Mills was calling for them to address the ways in which rationalization and the shift of social control to an elite were affecting people on an individual level too. The adoption of a sociological imagination implied a move from the objective study of "what is" to a more subjective answer to the question of "what ought to be?" He advocated that power should effectively be transferred to an intellectual elite.

A pioneering spirit

Unsurprisingly, Wright Mills' criticism of sociology was met with hostility and he became isolated from the mainstream. His interpretation of the changing nature of the class struggle was also largely dismissed. The conservative establishment also shunned him, rejecting his claims of a concentration of power in the military, business, and political elite, which was seen as a direct attack on the basis of Cold War policy in the West.

Nevertheless, the books and articles of Wright Mills were widely read, and became influential

Unemployment can lead to people blaming themselves for their situation. But a sociological imagination would, says Wright Mills, prompt such people to look to wider causes and effects.

outside the social science establishment. The philosophers and political activists who emerged from the period of McCarthyism were particularly attracted to his description of a power elite. Many of his ideas were adopted by the social movements of the US New Left (a term that Wright Mills popularized in his "Letter to the New Left" in 1960), which in turn paved the way for sociologists such as the German scholar Herbert Marcuse to adopt a New Leftist approach in the 1960s.

Wright Mills' ideas were, in many ways, ahead of their time, and his untimely death in 1962 meant that he did not live to see many of them gain general acceptance. His work foreshadowed the emergence of new socialist thinkers, especially in France, with the counterculture of the 1960s. Michel Foucault's emphasis on the notion of power bears a particularly strong resemblance to ideas that were first raised by Wright Mills.

Today, the so-called War on Terror in the aftermath of the 9/11 attacks and the disastrous financial crises of the early 21st century have led to a growing realization that much of our everyday lives is shaped by wider social and historical issues. US urban policy analyst Professor Peter Dreier claimed in 2012 that Wright Mills would have loved the Occupy Wall Street movement against social and economic inequality. This example of ordinary people objecting to a power elite that they claim is controlling society and affecting their lives is the sociological imagination being exhibited in a campaign for social change. ∎

Charles Wright Mills

Fiercely independent and critical of authority, Charles Wright Mills attributed his unconventional attitudes to an isolated and sometimes lonely childhood because his family moved around frequently. He was born in Waco, Texas, and initially studied at Texas A&M University, but found the atmosphere there stifling and left after his first year. He transferred to the University of Texas in Austin, graduated in sociology and gained a master's degree in philosophy. An obviously talented, but difficult, student, he went on to study at the University of Wisconsin, where he fell out with his professors and refused to make revisions to his doctoral thesis. He was, however, eventually awarded his PhD in 1942. By this time, he had taken up a post at the University of Maryland, and with one of his doctoral supervisors, Hans Gerth, wrote *From Max Weber: Essays in Sociology*.

In 1945 Wright Mills moved, on a Guggenheim fellowship, to Columbia University, where he spent the rest of his career. Although his outspoken criticism of the social science establishment saw him pushed out of the mainstream, he gained much popular attention. His career ended abruptly when he died of heart disease in 1962, at the age of only 45.

Key works

1948 *The New Men of Power: America's Labor Leaders*
1956 *The Power Elite*
1959 *The Sociological Imagination*

PAY TO THE MOST COMMONPLACE ACTIVITIES THE ATTENTION ACCORDED EXTRAORDINARY EVENTS
HAROLD GARFINKEL (1917–2011)

IN CONTEXT

FOCUS
Ethnomethodology

KEY DATES
1895 Émile Durkheim advocates a strict scientific methodology for the social sciences in *The Rules of Sociological Method*.

1921–22 Max Weber's methodological individualism is explained in *Economy and Society*, published posthumously.

1937 Talcott Parsons attempts to form a single, unified social theory in *The Structure of Social Action*.

1967 Harold Garfinkel publishes *Studies in Ethnomethodology*.

1976 Anthony Giddens incorporates ideas of Garfinkel's ethnomethodology into mainstream sociology in his book *New Rules of Sociological Method*.

The structure of society is not determined **"top down"** by a limited set of general rules.

↓

Instead, the rules are built **"bottom up,"** from our small exchanges and interactions.

↓

These rules can be seen in our **spontaneous behavior** in everyday life, rather than in social structures and institutions.

↓

Pay to the most commonplace activities the attention accorded extraordinary events.

In the 1930s, the US sociologist Talcott Parsons embarked upon a project of bringing together the various strands of sociology in a single, unified theory. His 1937 book *The Structure of Social Action* combined ideas from Max Weber, Émile Durkheim, and others, and attempted to present a universal methodology for sociology. In the years after World War II, Parsons' ideas gained him a significant number of supporters.

Among his admirers was Harold Garfinkel, who studied under Parsons at Harvard. While many of the followers were attracted by the idea of a "grand theory" of sociology, Garfinkel picked up on Parsons' idea of examining the roots of social order, rather than social change, and in particular his methods of researching the subject.

The workings of society
Parsons had suggested a "bottom up" rather than "top down" approach to analyzing the foundations of social order. This meant that to understand how social order is achieved in society, we should look at micro interactions and exchanges rather than at social structures and institutions.

See also: Émile Durkheim 34–37 ▪ Max Weber 38–45 ▪ Anthony Giddens 148–49 ▪ Erving Goffman 190–95; 264–69 ▪ Talcott Parsons 300–01

This approach turned traditional sociological methodology on its head: until then, it had been thought that people's behavior could be predicted by finding the underlying "rules" of society.

Garfinkel took the idea further, developing what amounted to an alternative to the conventional sociological approach, which he called ethnomethodology. The underlying rules of social order are built from the ways that people behave in reaction to different situations, and it is by observing everyday interactions that we can gain insight into the mechanisms of social order.

New perspectives

One category of experimental methods Garfinkel advocated became known as "breaching experiments." These were designed to uncover social norms—the expected, but largely unnoticed, ways people construct a shared sense of reality. Breaching these norms—for example by asking his students to address their parents

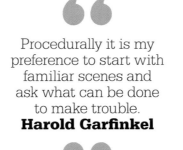

Procedurally it is my preference to start with familiar scenes and ask what can be done to make trouble.
Harold Garfinkel

formally as "Mr. X" or "Mrs. X" or to act as though they were lodgers—often provoked exasperation or anger, as the foundations of the social order were challenged.

Ethnomethodology not only offered an alternative method of social research, but also indicated a flaw in conventional methodology. According to Garfinkel, social researchers support their theories with evidence from specific examples, but at the same time

they use the theories to explain the examples—a circular argument. Instead, they should examine particular social interactions independently, and not set out to find an overall pattern or theory. He referred to jury deliberation and standing in lines as "familiar scenes" that we simply know how to organize intelligibly in recognizable ways. Any social setting, he argued, can "be viewed as self-organizing with respect to the intelligible character of its own appearances as either representations of or as evidences of a social order."

Garfinkel's approach was set out in *Studies in Ethnomethodology* in 1967. In an age when "alternative" ideas were popular, Garfinkel attracted a large following, despite his impenetrable writing style. His ideas were initially dismissed by mainstream sociologists, but by the end of the 20th century had become more generally accepted, perhaps not as an alternative to sociological methodology, but offering an additional perspective to the field of social order. ■

Harold Garfinkel

Born in Newark, New Jersey, Harold Garfinkel studied business and accounting at the University of Newark, then later earned an MA at the University of North Carolina. At the same time, he began his writing career, and one of his short stories, "Color Trouble," was included in the anthology *The Best Short Stories, 1941*.

After noncombatant service in the army during World War II, he studied under Talcott Parsons at Harvard, where he

gained his PhD He then taught at Princeton and Ohio State universities before settling in 1954 at the University of California. Garfinkel retired in 1987, but continued to teach as an emeritus professor until his death in 2011.

Key works

1967 *Studies in Ethnomethodology*
2002 *Ethnomethodology's Program*
2008 *Toward a Sociological Theory of Information*

An orderly line is a collectively negotiated, member-produced form of organization that is based on the unspoken rules of social interaction in a public space.

WHERE THERE IS POWER THERE IS RESISTANCE

MICHEL FOUCAULT (1926–1984)

IN CONTEXT

FOCUS
Power/resistance

KEY DATES
1848 Karl Marx and Friedrich Engels describe the oppression of the proletariat by the bourgeoisie in their book *The Communist Manifesto*.

1883 Friedrich Nietzsche introduces the concept of the "Will to Power" in *Thus Spoke Zarathustra*.

1997 Judith Butler's *Excitable Speech: A Politics of the Performative* develops Foucault's idea of power/knowledge in relation to censorship and hate speech.

2000 In *Empire*, Italian Marxist sociologist Antonio Negri and US scholar Michael Hardt describe the evolution of a "total" imperialist power, against which the only resistance is negation.

The power to maintain social order, or to bring about social change, has conventionally been seen in political or economic terms. Until the 1960s, theories of power usually fell into two types: ideas of the power of government or state over citizens; or the Marxist idea of a power struggle between the bourgeoisie and the proletariat. However, these theories tended to concentrate on power at the macro level, either ignoring the exercise of power at lower levels of social relations, or seeing it as a consequence of the primary exercise of power (or only of secondary importance).

See also: Karl Marx 28–31 ▪ Max Weber 38–45 ▪ Charles Wright Mills 46–49 ▪ Herbert Marcuse 182–87 ▪ Erich Fromm 188 ▪ Jürgen Habermas 286–87

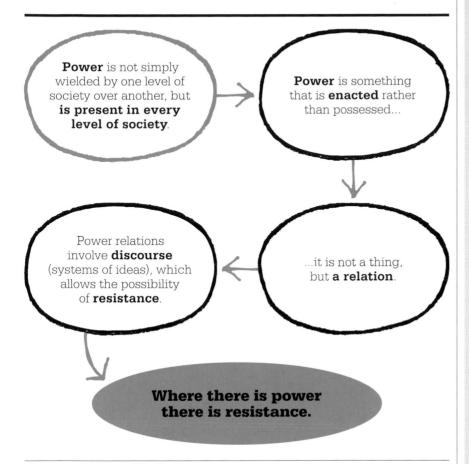

Power is not simply wielded by one level of society over another, but **is present in every level of society**.

Power is something that is **enacted** rather than possessed...

...it is not a thing, but **a relation**.

Power relations involve **discourse** (systems of ideas), which allows the possibility of **resistance**.

Where there is power there is resistance.

Michel Foucault

A brilliant polymath, influential in the fields of philosophy, psychology, politics, and literary criticism as well as sociology, Michel Foucault was often associated with the structuralist and post-structuralist movements in France, but disliked being labeled as such. He was born in Poitiers, France, and studied philosophy and psychology at the École Normale Supérieure in Paris. He taught in Sweden, Poland, and Germany in the 1950s, and received his doctorate in 1959. He lectured in Tunisia from 1966 to 1968 and when he returned to Paris was appointed head of philosophy at the University of Vincennes. Two years later, he was elected to the Collège de France as professor of "the history of systems of thought." He died in 1984, one of the first prominent victims of HIV/AIDS-related illness in France.

Key works

1969 *The Archaeology of Knowledge*
1975 *Discipline and Punish: The Birth of the Prison*
1976–84 *The History of Sexuality* (three volumes)

Michel Foucault, however, thought that in today's Western liberal societies, these approaches are an oversimplification. Power, he said, is not just exercised by the state or capitalists, but can be seen at every level of society, from individuals through groups and organizations to society as a whole. In his words, "power is everywhere, and comes from everywhere." He also disagreed with the traditional view of power as something that can be possessed and wielded, like a weapon. This, he says, is not power, but a capacity to exercise power—it does not become power until some action is taken. Power is therefore not something someone has, but something that is done to others, an action that affects the action of others.

Power relations

Instead of thinking of power as a "thing," Foucault sees it as a "relation," and explains the nature of power through examination of the power relations present at every level of modern society. For example, a power relation exists between a man and the state in which he lives, but at the same time, there are different forms of power relation between him and his employer, his children, the organizations to which he belongs, and so on. »

Foucault acknowledges that power has been, and continues to be, the major force in shaping social order, but describes how the nature of power relations has changed from medieval times to today. What he calls the "sovereign" exercise of power, such as public torture and executions, was the method that authority figures in feudal society used to coerce their subjects into obedience. With the advent of the Enlightenment in Europe, however, violence and force were seen as inhuman and, more importantly, as an ineffective means of exercising power.

Surveillance and control

In place of harsh physical punishment came a more pervasive means of controlling behavior: discipline. The establishment of institutions such as prisons, asylums, hospitals, and schools characterized the move away from the notion of merely punishing to a disciplinary exercise of power: specifically, acting to prevent people from behaving in certain ways. These institutions not only removed the opportunity for transgression, but provided the conditions in which people's

conduct could be corrected and regulated, and above all monitored and controlled.

This element of surveillance is especially important in the evolution of the way power is exercised in modern society. Foucault was particularly struck by the Panopticon, the efficient prison design inspired by British philosopher Jeremy Bentham, with a watchtower that enabled continual observation of inmates. The cells, Foucault points out, are backlit to prevent inmates from hiding in shadowy recesses. Prisoners can never be certain of when they are under surveillance, so they learn to discipline their behavior as if they always are. Power is no longer exercised by coercing people to conform, but by establishing mechanisms that ensure their compliance.

Regulating conduct

The mechanisms by which power is exercised, the "technology of power," have since become an integral part of society. In the modern Western world, social norms are imposed not so much by enforcement, as by exercising "pastoral" power, guiding people's

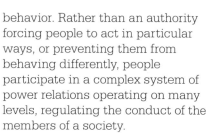

Foucault's *History of Sexuality*... warns us against imagining a complete liberation from power. There can never be a total liberation from power.
Judith Butler

behavior. Rather than an authority forcing people to act in particular ways, or preventing them from behaving differently, people participate in a complex system of power relations operating on many levels, regulating the conduct of the members of a society.

This pervasive sort of power is determined by the control society has over people's attitudes, beliefs, and practices: the systems of ideas Foucault refers to as "discourse." The belief system of any society evolves as people come to accept certain views, to the point that

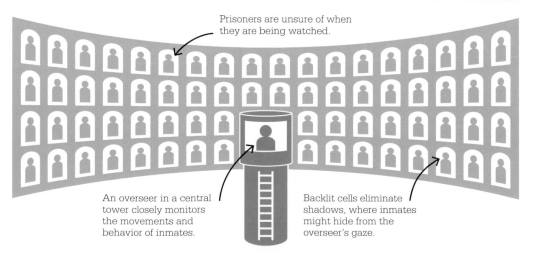

The Panopticon, designed by Bentham, is the supreme eye of power for Foucault. The circular space enables a permanent visibility that guides prison inmates to comply with their own disciplining and control. Foucault argues that not only prisons, but all hierarchical structures (such as hospitals, factories, and schools) have evolved to resemble this model.

Prisoners are unsure of when they are being watched.

An overseer in a central tower closely monitors the movements and behavior of inmates.

Backlit cells eliminate shadows, where inmates might hide from the overseer's gaze.

A shepherd tending his flock is the analogy Foucault uses to describe "pastoral" power, whereby people are guided to act in certain ways and then allow themselves to be governed.

these views become embedded in that society, defining what is good and bad, and what is considered normal or deviant. Individuals within that society regulate their behavior according to these norms, largely unaware that it is the discourse that is guiding their conduct, as it makes opposing thoughts and actions unthinkable.

Discursive regimes

Discourse is constantly reinforced, as it is both an instrument and an effect of power: it controls thoughts and conduct, which in turn shape the belief system. And because it defines what is right and wrong, it is a "regime of truth," creating a body of what is considered undeniable common knowledge.

Foucault challenged the idea that "knowledge is power," saying that the two are related more subtly. He coined the term "power–knowledge" for this relationship, noting that knowledge creates power, but is also created by power. Today, power is exercised by controlling what forms of knowledge are acceptable, presenting them as truths, and excluding other forms of knowledge. At the same time, accepted knowledge, the discourse, is actually produced in the process of exercising power.

Unlike the way power had traditionally been used to compel and coerce people to behave in a particular way, this form of power–knowledge has no immediately recognizable agent or structure. And because of its all-pervasive nature, it would appear to have

nothing specific that can be resisted. Indeed, Foucault points out that political resistance, in the form of revolution, may not lead to social change, as it challenges only the power of the state, not the ubiquitous, everyday way in which power today is exercised.

However, Foucault argues that there is a possibility of resistance: what can be resisted is the discourse itself, which can be challenged by other, opposing discourses. Power that relies on complicity implies at least some degree of freedom of those subject to it. For the discourse to be an instrument of power, those subject to it must be involved in a power relation, and he argues that if there is a power relation, there is also a

possibility of resistance—without resistance, there is no need for the exercise of power.

The deployment of power

Foucault's concepts of power–knowledge and discourse are subtle and at the time were rejected by many scholars as speculative and vague. But his lectures and writings became enormously popular, despite the difficult concepts and his sometimes convoluted prose style. The ideas of power described in *Discipline and Punish* and *The History of Sexuality* gradually gained acceptance by some in the mainstream of sociology (if not among historians and philosophers), and eventually influenced the analysis of how discourse is used in society as an instrument of power in many different arenas.

The development of modern feminism, queer theory, and cultural studies owes much to Foucault's explanation of how norms of behavior are enforced. Today, opinion is still divided as to whether his theories are the somewhat vague conclusions of poor research and scholarship or whether he should be considered one of the 20th century's most original and wide-ranging thinkers in the social sciences. ∎

Discourse transmits and produces power; it reinforces it, but also undermines and exposes it.
Michel Foucault

GENDER IS A KIND OF IMITATION FOR WHICH THERE IS NO ORIGINAL

JUDITH BUTLER (1956–)

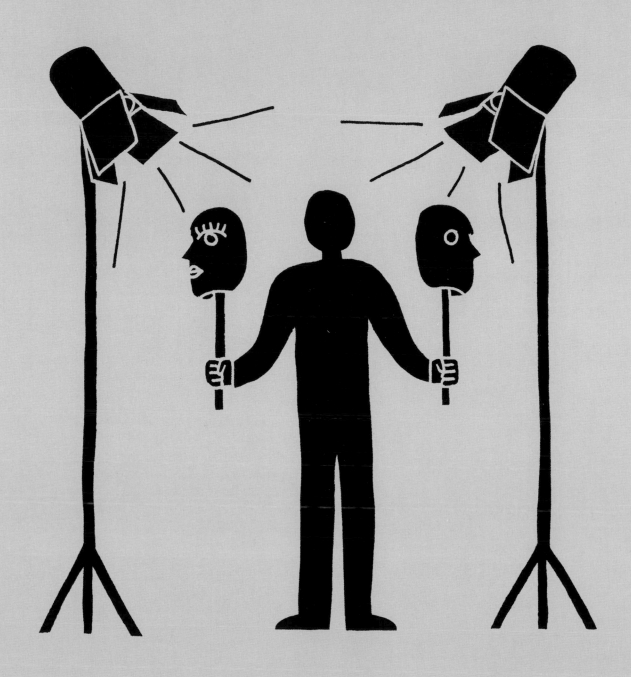

People perform in **ways that are expected** of them by their culture.

Traditional **expectations of gender** are based on how most people behave in their culture.

Gender is a kind of imitation for which there is no original.

Gender is **what you do**, rather than a universal notion of **who you are**.

I t was not until after World War II that gender and sexuality were recognized as issues for sociological study. The so-called "second-wave" feminism of the 1960s to 1980s snowballed from the insight of the French feminist Simone de Beauvoir in *The Second Sex* (1949) that "one is not born a woman: one becomes one." Her idea that there is a difference between sex (what determines whether one is biologically female or male) and gender (the social forces that act upon one to be feminine or masculine) paved the way for a reappraisal of the role of gender in society. It also kick-started the women's liberation movement of the following decades.

Attitudes toward sex in Western society were also being reshaped by the work of anthropologists, such as Margaret Mead. Her studies of tribes in the South Pacific and Southeast Asia showed that many behavioral differences between males and females were culturally, rather than biologically, determined. These findings were shocking when published in the 1930s, but were more openly considered by a post-war generation that was addressing previously taboo subjects—such as promiscuity and extramarital sex—as social phenomena rather than deviant behavior.

Challenging convention
At the forefront of this examination of sexual conventions in Western society was Michel Foucault, who tackled the subject head-on in 1976 in *The History of Sexuality*. Running through this text was his central theory of the way that

See also: Michel Foucault 52–55; 302–03 ▪ Margaret Mead 176–77
Adrienne Rich 304–09 ▪ Jeffrey Weeks 324–25 ▪ Steven Seidman 326–31

> Gender is an impersonation...
> becoming gendered involves
> impersonating an ideal that
> nobody actually inhabits.
> **Judith Butler**

power in society is exerted by the imposition of social norms, and in particular that not only our gender but our sexuality is shaped by the culture in which we live. Just as de Beauvoir had brought the issue of gender into the social sphere, Foucault broadened the debate significantly to include sexual orientation, and indeed the whole of sexual behavior.

The generation after Foucault grew up in an era marked by a relaxation of sexual mores: the "free love" of the 1960s, acceptance (or at least, decriminalization) of homosexuality in many countries, and the sexual liberation brought by the Women's Lib movement.

Gender identities

Among the "baby boomers" of the post-war generation was US scholar Judith Butler, who took these ideas yet further. While accepting de Beauvoir's main point that gender is a social construct, Butler felt that traditional feminism ignores the wider implications of this notion, and merely reinforces male and female stereotypes. Gender is not as simple, she contends, as masculinity and femininity, nor is sexuality as simple as gay and straight. Gender and sexuality are neither as polarized in this way, nor as fixed and unchanging as we have come to believe, but can be fluid, covering a whole spectrum of gender identities. »

Gay Pride events, which were first held in the US in 1971 to protest against persecution of gays, challenged the notion that sexuality was confined to masculinity and femininity.

Judith Butler

One of the most influential figures in feminist and LGBTI issues from the 1990s onward, Judith Butler has also been a prominent activist in anti-war, anti-capitalism, and anti-racism movements. Her parents were of Russian and Hungarian Jewish descent. She studied at Yale University, where she received her doctorate in philosophy in 1984. In 1993, after teaching at various universities, she took up a post at the University of California, Berkeley, and was appointed Maxine Elliot Professor of Rhetoric and Comparative Literature in 1998. Other posts include chair of the board of the International Gay and Lesbian Human Rights Commission. She was awarded the Theodor W. Adorno Prize in 2012. Butler lives with her partner, the political theorist Wendy Brown, in California.

Key works

1990 *Gender Trouble: Feminism and the Subversion of Identity*
1993 *Bodies That Matter: On the Discursive Limits of "Sex"*
2004 *Undoing Gender*

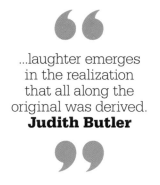

> ...laughter emerges
> in the realization
> that all along the
> original was derived.
> **Judith Butler**

Butler argues that both sex and gender are socially, not biologically determined. At the heart of her argument is the idea that "gender is not something that one is, it is something one does... a 'doing' rather than a 'being'."

Conventionally, our anatomical sex (female or male) is considered to be the cause of our gender (femininity or masculinity), according to the cultural norms associated with them. But Butler challenges the idea of a stable and coherent gender identity. According to her, it is the things that we do, our "gender acts," that determine our gender, and even the way we perceive our biological sex. When we behave in ways that are "appropriate" to our sex, we are imitating the norms of gender identity, which are based on the ways that each sex behaves. We are performing a role that does not in fact exist; in essence, there is no original template for "female" or "male"—the original itself is derived. So, if one is born female, one behaves in what is considered to be a "feminine" way (by, for example, desiring a male partner), and comes to accept the fact that sex with men is associated with that gender.

It is, Butler says, these "gender acts"—which include such things as dress, mannerisms, and all sorts of everyday activities as well as sexual activity and choice of sexual partner—that determine the sex we perceive ourselves to be. Even the language we use reinforces the social norms, ensuring that we perform in a certain way.

Subversive acts

Butler claims that, crucially, it is the constant repetition of this kind of performance that molds gender identity, so that ."..the actors themselves come to believe and to perform in the mode of belief."

To escape the restrictiveness of this kind of sexual typecasting, Butler advocates subversion, deliberately performing in a way that goes against the conventional gender acts. Using what she calls "performativity of gender," such as cross-dressing or drag, the norms are challenged, but also one's perception of gender and even sex can be changed. Butler insists that this should not be merely a trivial lifestyle choice—we cannot wake up and decide what gender we want to be that day—but a genuine act of subversion, and like the gender acts it is subverting, one that is performed on a regular

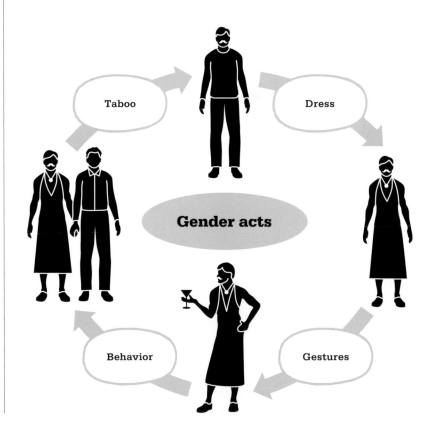

Gender identity, according to Butler, is not a part of a person's essence but the product of actions and behaviors. It is the repeated performing of these actions and behaviors—combined with the taboos imposed by society—that produce what is seen as an essentially masculine or feminine identity.

Priscilla, Queen of the Desert is a 1994 cult movie about two drag queens and a transsexual. Some claim it merely reproduces stereotypes; others that it brings LGBTI issues to the fore.

basis, through constant repetition. In this way, the sexual norms imposed by society are "troubled," shown to be artificial and based on a nonexistent status quo, and the rights of all kinds of different sexual identities (straight, gay, lesbian, transgender, and beyond) can be asserted as having equal validity.

Controversy and change

Butler's widening of the issue of sexuality and gender was a cornerstone of what came to be known as queer theory. As well as moving the discussion away from traditional ideas of masculinity and femininity to include a broad spectrum of sexuality and gender identity, her ideas showed how our perceptions of sexuality are socially molded, rather than an essential part of us. But she is also a political activist, and beneath her theories of gender are the Foucauldian ideas of power and how it is exercised in

Drag is subversive to the extent that it reflects on the imitative structure by which... gender is itself produced and disputes heterosexuality's claim on naturalness.
Judith Butler

society. It is not necessarily just our sexual identity that is shaped by repeated performance of certain behaviors, but our whole social and political outlook. Butler maintains that we can challenge other aspects of the status quo by deliberately performing in new, subversive ways.

Butler has faced considerable criticism, not least from feminist thinkers such as US scholar Martha Nussbaum. Some have argued that she implies a lack of free will in those imitating the sexual norms of society, whereas in fact those norms have frequently been broken by those who felt uncomfortable with them. And, as with many postmodern thinkers, her writing has attracted the criticism that its convoluted form conceals some basically simple ideas. Butler has, however, more

followers than critics, and the field of gender and sexuality in sociology has been much influenced by her broadening of its scope. Whether in part as a result of her work, or simply contemporary with it, there has been increasing liberalization of attitudes to different forms of sexuality in Western society, to the extent that same-sex couples and LGBTI issues are accepted in mainstream and popular culture almost without controversy in some places, changing the nature of the "gender acts" that inform our individual sexual identities. But in those countries where the cultural mores continue to be restrictive, and regimes push ferociously straight agendas, the impact of those not conforming to the rigid sexual norms is that much greater, and more clearly demonstrates the power of subversion. ■

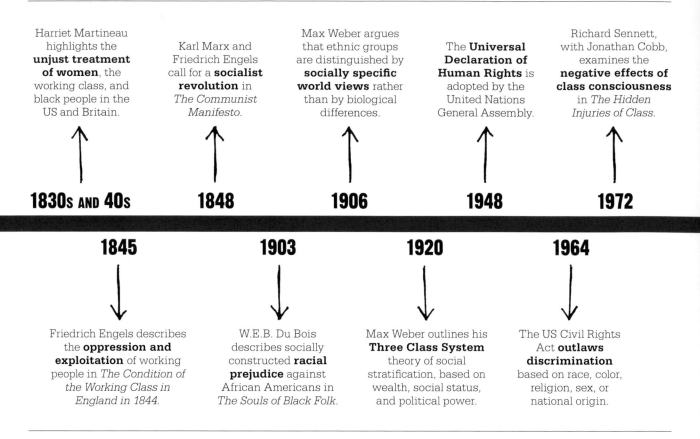

1830s AND 40s
Harriet Martineau highlights the **unjust treatment of women**, the working class, and black people in the US and Britain.

1848
Karl Marx and Friedrich Engels call for a **socialist revolution** in *The Communist Manifesto*.

1906
Max Weber argues that ethnic groups are distinguished by **socially specific world views** rather than by biological differences.

1948
The **Universal Declaration of Human Rights** is adopted by the United Nations General Assembly.

1972
Richard Sennett, with Jonathan Cobb, examines the **negative effects of class consciousness** in *The Hidden Injuries of Class*.

1845
Friedrich Engels describes the **oppression and exploitation** of working people in *The Condition of the Working Class in England in 1844*.

1903
W.E.B. Du Bois describes socially constructed **racial prejudice** against African Americans in *The Souls of Black Folk*.

1920
Max Weber outlines his **Three Class System** theory of social stratification, based on wealth, social status, and political power.

1964
The US Civil Rights Act **outlaws discrimination** based on race, color, religion, sex, or national origin.

T he modernity that emerged from Enlightenment ideas and the technological innovations of the Industrial Revolution offered the promise not only of greater prosperity but also of a more just society. In Europe, at least, the absolute power of monarchs, the aristocracy, and the Church was challenged, and old dogmas were discredited by rational and scientific thought. At the same time, advances in technology brought mechanization to many trades and gave birth to new industries, increasing wealth and bringing hope of improvement to people's working lives.

Class consciousness
As the modern industrialized society became established, however, it became apparent that

it was not the utopian dream that had been expected. By the 19th century, many thinkers had begun to realize that this progress came at a cost, and that some of the promises had yet to be kept. Instead of becoming more just, modern industrial society had created new inequalities.

Among the first to study the new social order was Friedrich Engels, who saw the emergence of a working class exploited by the owners of the mills and factories. With Karl Marx, he identified oppression of this class as the result of capitalism, which in turn fueled and fed off industrialization. Marx and Engels considered the social problems of industrial society in material, economic terms, and saw inequality as a division between the working class (the

proletariat) and the capitalist class (the bourgeoisie). Later sociologists also recognized that social inequality is manifested in a class system, but suggested that the stratification was more complex. Max Weber, for example, proposed that as well as economic situation, status and political standing also play a part. Perceptions of class and the issue of class consciousness became focuses for sustained sociological study of inequality, including the concept of "habitus," as explained by Pierre Bourdieu.

Racial oppression
While Engels and Marx concentrated on the economic disparity between the classes, others realized that it was not only the working classes that suffered social injustice. Harriet Martineau

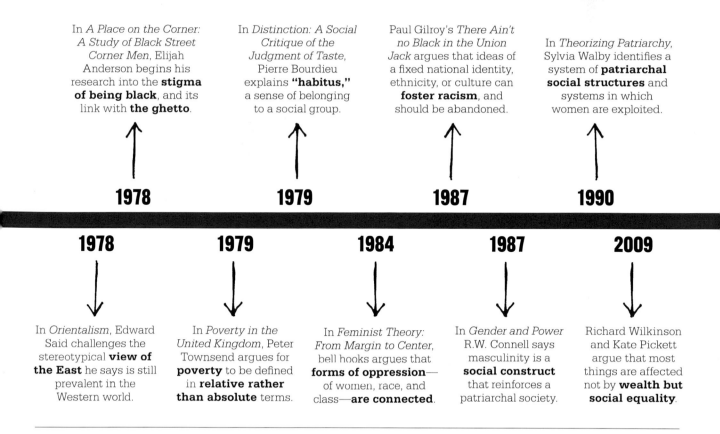

In *A Place on the Corner: A Study of Black Street Corner Men*, Elijah Anderson begins his research into the **stigma of being black**, and its link with **the ghetto**.

In *Distinction: A Social Critique of the Judgment of Taste*, Pierre Bourdieu explains **"habitus,"** a sense of belonging to a social group.

Paul Gilroy's *There Ain't no Black in the Union Jack* argues that ideas of a fixed national identity, ethnicity, or culture can **foster racism**, and should be abandoned.

In *Theorizing Patriarchy*, Sylvia Walby identifies a system of **patriarchal social structures** and systems in which women are exploited.

1978   **1979**   **1987**   **1990**

1978   **1979**   **1984**   **1987**   **2009**

In *Orientalism*, Edward Said challenges the stereotypical **view of the East** he says is still prevalent in the Western world.

In *Poverty in the United Kingdom*, Peter Townsend argues for **poverty** to be defined in **relative rather than absolute** terms.

In *Feminist Theory: From Margin to Center*, bell hooks argues that **forms of oppression**—of women, race, and class—**are connected**.

In *Gender and Power* R.W. Connell says masculinity is a **social construct** that reinforces a patriarchal society.

Richard Wilkinson and Kate Pickett argue that most things are affected not by **wealth but social equality**.

highlighted the gap between the Enlightenment ideal of equal rights and the reality of modern society. Her experiences in the US, where she encountered slavery, showed that even in a democracy founded on ideals of liberty, some groups— women, ethnic minorities, and the working classes—were excluded from participation in shaping society. The connection she made with these various forms of oppression was re-explored by bell hooks some 150 years later.

Even when slavery was finally abolished, true emancipation was incomplete; the political exclusion of black people—by being denied the vote—persisted in the USA well into the 20th century. Black people in the USA and Europe also faced prejudices as a hangover from slavery and European colonialism

that have persisted to the present day. Sociologists such as W.E.B. Du Bois examined the position of ethnic groups in predominantly white European industrial societies, and in the 20th century attention became focused on the connections between race and social inequality. Elijah Anderson began his study of black people and their association with the concept of "the ghetto"; Edward Said analysed negative Western perceptions of "the East"; and British sociologists such as Paul Gilroy sought to find ways of eradicating racism in modern multicultural societies.

Gender equality
Women likewise struggled for political suffrage, but even after this had been achieved they faced

injustice in societies that remained fundamentally patriarchal through the 20th century and up to the present day. It had taken "first wave" feminism over a century to get women the vote, and the task of the second wave, starting soon after World War II, was to examine and overcome persistent social injustice based on gender.

Rather than simply addressing the economic and political factors underlying the continued oppression of women, Sylvia Walby suggested a comprehensive analysis of the social systems that maintain society's patriarchal structure, while R.W. Connell pointed out the prevalence of conventional perceptions—socially constructed forms—of masculinity that reinforce the concept of patriarchal society. ∎

I BROADLY ACCUSE THE BOURGEOISIE OF SOCIAL MURDER

FRIEDRICH ENGELS (1820–1895)

IN CONTEXT

FOCUS
Class exploitation

KEY DATES
1760 The Industrial Revolution begins when the "flying shuttle" weaving machine shifts textile manufacture to England.

1830s–40s The British railway system expands rapidly, allowing easy movement of people, products, and capital.

1844 Graham's Factory Act lowers the minimum age for working in factories in the UK to eight years old.

1848 Marx and Engels publish *The Communist Manifesto*.

1892 James Keir Hardie is the first socialist elected to the British parliament.

1900 The Labour Party is formed in Britain to represent the interests of the workers and trade unionists.

Living in England from 1842 to 1844, the German philosopher Friedrich Engels had seen, first-hand, the devastating effects of industrialization on workers and their children. The bourgeoisie, or capitalist class, he said, knowingly causes the workers' "life of toil and wretchedness... but takes no further trouble in the matter."

He claimed the bourgeoisie was turning a blind eye to their part in the early deaths of their workers, when it was within their power to change things, so he accused them of "social murder."

In the 1840s, England was seen as the workshop of the world; it enjoyed a unique position at the center of the Industrial Revolution. Engels observed that it was

In the 1840s, **mortality in working class streets** in Manchester was 68 percent higher than in those of the "first class."

↓

Bourgeois society condemned the workers to **unhealthy living conditions, insecure wages**, and **physical** and **mental exhaustion**.

↓

If society puts people in such a position that they die an **early and unnatural death**, it is murder.

↓

I broadly accuse the bourgeoisie of social murder.

See also: Karl Marx 28–31 ▪ Peter Townsend 74 ▪ Richard Sennett 84–87 ▪ Max Weber 220–23 ▪ Harry Braverman 226–31 ▪ Robert Blauner 232–33

undergoing a massive but silent transformation that had altered the whole of English civil society.

Industrialization had driven down prices, so handcrafted work, which was more expensive, was less in demand; workers moved to the cities only to endure harsh conditions and financial insecurity. The industrialized, capitalist economy lurched from boom to bust, and workers' jobs could quickly disappear. Meanwhile, the bourgeoisie grew richer by treating the workers as disposable labor.

The legacy of industrialism

In Engels' first book, *The Condition of the Working Class in England in 1844*, he described the appalling way of life of the workers, or proletariat, in Manchester, London, Dublin, and Edinburgh, and found similar situations in all these cities. He reported filthy streets with pools of stagnant urine and excrement, filled with the stench of animal putrefaction from the tanneries. Widespread cholera outbreaks occurred, along with constant

epidemics of consumption and typhus. Workers were packed into one-room huts or the cellars of damp houses that had been built along old ditches to save the house-owner money. They lived in conditions that defied all consideration of cleanliness and health, Engels said—and this in Manchester, "the second city of England, the first manufacturing city of the world."

The proletariat were worked to the point of exhaustion, wearing cheap clothing that gave no protection against accidents or the climate. They could buy only the food spurned by the bourgeoisie, such as decaying meat, wilted vegetables, "sugar" that was the refuse of soap-boiling firms, and cocoa mixed with earth.

When work disappeared and wages failed, even this meager diet proved impossible, and many workers and their families began to starve; this caused illness and a continued inability to work, should work become available. Doctors were unaffordable, and very often

entire families starved to death. The worker, Engels explained, could only obtain what he needed— healthy living conditions, secure employment, and a decent wage— from the bourgeoisie, "which can decree his life or death." He was insistent that this hugely exploitative, capital-owning class should therefore take immediate steps to change workers' conditions and stop its careless murder of an entire social class. ■

Working-class families in England during the 1840s endured social deprivation, crippling financial instability, and terrible sickness due to the effects of industrial capitalism.

Friedrich Engels

Political theorist and philosopher Friedrich Engels was born in Germany in 1820. His father was a German industrialist who struggled with Engels' reluctance to attend school or work in the family business. As a teenager, he wrote articles under the pseudonym Friedrich Oswald, which gained him access to a group of left-wing intellectuals.

After working for a short time in a family factory in Manchester, England, he became interested in communism. In 1844 he traveled to Paris, where he met Karl Marx and became his colleague and

financial sponsor. They jointly wrote *The Communist Manifesto*, and worked together until Marx's death in 1883, after which Engels completed the second and third volumes of *Das Kapital*, along with many books and articles of his own.

Key works

1845 *The Condition of the Working Class in England in 1844*
1848 *The Communist Manifesto*
1884 *The Origin of the Family, Private Property and the State*

THE PROBLEM OF THE 20TH CENTURY IS THE PROBLEM OF THE COLOR LINE

W.E.B. DU BOIS (1868–1963)

IN CONTEXT

FOCUS
Race and ethnicity

KEY DATES
1857 US Chief Justice Roger B. Taney rules against a petition for freedom from enslaved Dred Scott, saying that blacks cannot be granted citizenship and therefore equal protection under the law because they are inferior to whites.

1906 Max Weber says that shared perceptions and common customs, not biological traits, distinguish ethnic groups from each other.

1954 The legal case of "Brown vs Board of Education" rules that establishing "separate but equal" schools for black and white children is unconstitutional.

1964 The Civil Rights Act outlaws public segregation and ends discrimination based on race, color, religion, or sex.

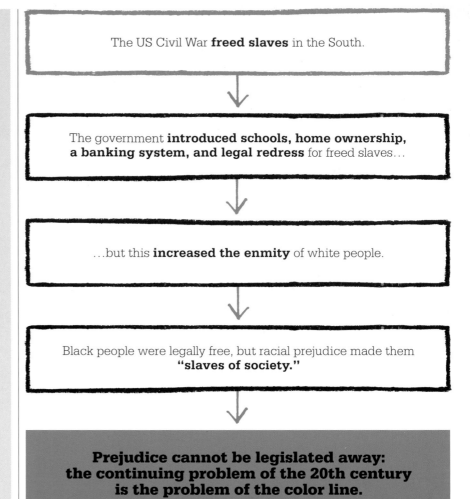

The US Civil War **freed slaves** in the South.

↓

The government **introduced schools, home ownership, a banking system, and legal redress** for freed slaves…

↓

…but this **increased the enmity** of white people.

↓

Black people were legally free, but racial prejudice made them **"slaves of society."**

↓

Prejudice cannot be legislated away: the continuing problem of the 20th century is the problem of the color line.

Toward the end of the 19th century, the US social reformer and freed slave Frederick Douglass drew attention to the continuing prejudice against black people in the US. He claimed that although blacks had ceased to belong to individuals, they had nevertheless become slaves of society. Out of the depths of slavery, he said, "has come this prejudice and this color line," through which white dominion was asserted in the workplace, the ballot box, the legal courts, and everyday life.

In 1903, W.E.B. Du Bois investigated the idea of the color line in *The Souls of Black Folk*. A literary, sociological, and political landmark, it examines the changing position of African-Americans from the US Civil War and its aftermath to the early 1900s, in terms of the physical, economic, and political relations of black and white people in the South. It concludes that "the problem of the 20th century is the problem of the color line"—the continuing division between the opportunities and perspectives of blacks and whites. Du Bois

begins his study by pointing out that no white person is willing to talk about race explicitly, choosing instead to act out prejudice in various ways. But what they really want to know is this: "How does it feel to be a problem?"

Du Bois finds the question unanswerable, because it only makes sense from a white perspective—black people do not see themselves as "a problem." He then examines how this duality of perspective has occurred and gives the example of his first encounter with racism. While

See also: Harriet Martineau 26–27 ▪ Paul Gilroy 75 ▪ Edward Said 80–81 ▪ Elijah Anderson 82–83 ▪ bell hooks 90–95 ▪ Stuart Hall 200–01

at primary school, a new pupil refused to accept a greeting card from Du Bois, at which point "it dawned on me that I was different from the others."

He felt like them in his heart, he says, but realized that he was "shut out from their world by a vast veil." Initially undaunted, he says that he felt no need to tear down the veil until he grew up and saw that all the most dazzling opportunities in the world were for white people, not black people. There was a color line, and he was standing on the side that was denied power, opportunity, dignity, and respect.

Identity crisis

Du Bois suggests that the color line is internal too. Black people, according to him, see themselves in two ways simultaneously:

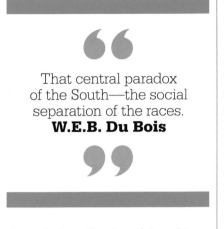

> That central paradox of the South—the social separation of the races.
> **W.E.B. Du Bois**

through the reflection of the white world, which views them with amused contempt and pity, and through their own sense of self, which is more fluid and less well defined. These combine to form what Du Bois calls a double-consciousness: "...two souls, two thoughts, two unreconciled strivings; two warring ideals in one dark body."

The unfolding history of the black person in the US is, Du Bois claims, the history of this inner conflict, which itself is a result of the external, worldly battle between black and white people. He suggests that a black person wants to merge the double-consciousness into one state, and find a true African-American spirit that does not Africanize America, nor "bleach his African soul in a flood of white Americanism."

The Freedmen's Bureau

How had black people become the "problem"? To try to explain this issue, Du Bois looks to the history of slavery in the US and the turning point of the Civil War. **»**

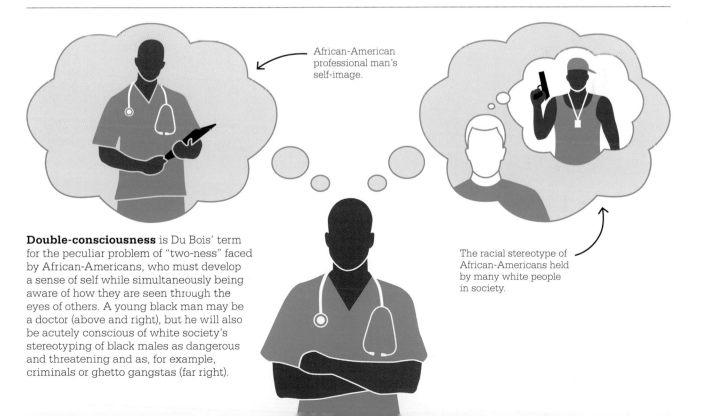

African-American professional man's self-image.

The racial stereotype of African-Americans held by many white people in society.

Double-consciousness is Du Bois' term for the peculiar problem of "two-ness" faced by African-Americans, who must develop a sense of self while simultaneously being aware of how they are seen through the eyes of others. A young black man may be a doctor (above and right), but he will also be acutely conscious of white society's stereotyping of black males as dangerous and threatening and as, for example, criminals or ghetto gangstas (far right).

Ulysses S. Grant and his generals advance on horseback in the Civil War. In 1868 the votes of a new black electorate were vital to Grant's election as Republican president.

According to him, slavery was the real cause of the war, which started in 1861. As the Union army of the northern states marched into the South, slaves fled to join it. At first, slaves were returned to their owners, but the policy changed and they were kept as military labor.

In 1863, slaves were declared free, and the government set up the Bureau of Refugees, Freedmen, and Abandoned Lands (also called the Freedmen's Bureau) to issue food, clothing, and abandoned property to the "flood" of destitute fugitive former slaves (men, women, and children). However, the Bureau was run by military staff ill-equipped to deal with social reorganization. The Bureau was also hampered by the sheer size of the task: the promise of handing over slave-driven plantations to former slaves "melted away" when it became clear that over 800,000 acres were affected.

One of the great successes of the Bureau was the provision of free schools for all children in the South.

Slavery is gone, but its shadow still lingers… and poisons… the moral atmosphere of all sections of the republic.
Frederick Douglass
US social reformer (c.1818–1895)

Du Bois points out that this was seen as a problem, because "the South believed an educated Negro to be a dangerous Negro." The opposition to black education in the South "showed itself in ashes, insult, and blood."

At the same time, the Bureau sowed division in legal matters. According to Du Bois, it used its courts to "put the bottom rail on top"—in other words, it favored black litigants. Meanwhile, the civil courts often aided the former slavemasters. Du Bois describes white people as being "ordered about, seized, imprisoned, and punished over and over again" by the Bureau courts, while black people were intimidated, beaten, raped, and butchered by angry and revengeful (white) men.

The Bureau also opened a Freedman's Bank in 1865 to handle the deposits of former slave men and women. This initiative was hampered by incompetency, and the bank eventually crashed, taking the dollars of the freedmen with it. Du Bois says that this was the least of the loss, because "all the faith in saving went too, and much of the faith in men; and that was a loss that a nation which today sneers at Negro shiftlessness has never yet made good."

The Bureau had set up a system of free (non-slave) labor and ex-slave proprietorship, secured the recognition of black people as free people in courts of law, and founded common schools. The greatest failing of the Bureau was that it did not establish goodwill between the former masters and the ex-slaves; in fact, it increased enmity. The color line remained, but instead of being explicit it now operated in more subtle ways.

Compromise or agitation?

Following the post-war period known as the Reconstruction, some of the newly won black rights started to slip away. A ruling in a US legal case (Plessy vs Ferguson, 1896) made segregation in public places permissible and set a pattern of racial separation in the South that lasted until Brown vs Board of Education, 1954. Anxiety caused by modernity also fueled a rebirth of the Ku Klux Klan and its nativist white supremacism, accompanied by a rise in racist violence, including lynchings.

In 1895 the African-American politican Booker T. Washington had given a speech now known as "the Atlanta Compromise." He suggested that black people should be patient, adopt white middle-class standards, and seek self-advancement by self-improvement and education to show their worth. By foregoing political rights in return for economic rights and legal justice, Washington argued that social change would be more likely in the longer term. This accommodating stance became the dominant ideology of the time.

Du Bois disagreed strongly, and in *The Souls of Black Folk* he said that while black people did not expect full civic rights immediately, they were certain that the way for a people to gain their rights "is not by voluntarily throwing them away." Du Bois had hoped to eliminate racism and segregation through social science, but he came to believe that political agitation was the only effective strategy.

Stretching the color line

In 1949, Du Bois visited the Warsaw Ghetto in Poland, where two-thirds of the population had been killed during the Nazi occupation, and 85 percent of the city lay in ruins. He was shocked by the experience, which he said gave him a "more complete understanding of the Negro problem." Faced with such absolute devastation and destruction, and knowing that it was a direct consequence of racist segregation and violence, Du Bois reassessed his analysis of the color line and declared it a phenomenon that can occur to any cultural or ethnic group. In his 1952 essay for the magazine *Jewish Life*, "The Negro and the Warsaw Ghetto," he writes: "The race problem... cut across lines of color and physique and belief and status and was a matter of... human hate and prejudice." It is therefore not color that matters so much as the "line," which can be drawn to articulate difference and hatred in any group or society.

Activist and scholar

Du Bois became one of the founder members of the civil rights organization, the National Association for the Advancement of Colored People (NAACP). His ideas were concerned with people of African descent everywhere, and during the 1920s he helped found the Pan-African Association in Paris, France, and organized a series of pan-African congresses around the world. However, at the time of writing about the African soul, in the early 1900s, he said that the conditions that were necessary to achieve a true and unified African-American spirit had not yet been reached.

Du Bois applied systematic methods of fieldwork to previously neglected areas of study. The use of empirical data to catalog the details of black people's lives enabled him to dispel widely held stereotypes. For example, he produced a wealth of data on the effects of urban life on African-Americans in *The Philadelphia Negro* (1899), which suggests that rather than being caused by anything innate, crime is a product of the environment. His pioneering sociological research and thinking was a huge influence on later prominent civil rights leaders, including Dr. Martin Luther King, Jr. Du Bois is recognized as one of the most important sociologists of the 20th century. ■

W.E.B. Du Bois

William Edward Burghardt Du Bois was a sociologist, historian, philosopher, and political leader. He was born in Massachusetts three years after the end of the Civil War.

After graduating from high school, Du Bois studied at Fisk University, Nashville, and the university of Berlin, Germany, where he met Max Weber. In 1895 he became the first African American to receive a PhD when he gained a doctorate in history at Harvard University. From 1897 to 1910 he was professor of economics and history at Atlanta University, and from 1934 to 1944 he was chairman of the department of sociology. In 1961 Du Bois moved to Ghana, Africa, to work on the *Encyclopedia Africana*, but died two years later. He wrote numerous books, articles, and essays, and founded and edited four journals.

Key works

1903 *The Souls of Black Folks*
1920 *Darkwater: Voices from Within the Veil*
1939 *Black Folk, Then and Now*

THE POOR ARE EXCLUDED FROM THE ORDINARY LIVING PATTERNS, CUSTOMS, AND ACTIVITIES OF LIFE
PETER TOWNSEND (1928–2009)

IN CONTEXT

FOCUS
Relative poverty

KEY DATES
1776 Scottish economist Adam Smith says the necessities of life include, "whatever the custom of the country renders it indecent for creditable people, even of the lowest order, to be without."

1901 British sociologist Seebohm Rowntree publishes *Poverty: A Study of Town Life*.

1979 Peter Townsend publishes *Poverty in the United Kingdom*.

1999 The UK government carries out the Poverty and Social Exclusion survey of Britain.

2013 French economist Thomas Piketty publishes *Capital in the 21st Century*, documenting extreme income inequality in 20 countries.

Poverty was defined by the social campaigner Seebohm Rowntree at the beginning of the 20th century as a state in which "total earnings are insufficient to obtain the minimum necessaries for the maintenance of merely physical efficiency." This is the "subsistence level" definition of poverty, which has been used by governments to determine the cost of a person's basic needs such as food, rent, fuel, and clothing.

Food banks have faced surging demand in recent years. They meet basic needs, but often include non-essential foodstuffs that are now considered normal for people to have.

However, in 1979 the British sociologist Peter Townsend said that "poverty" should be defined not in absolute terms, but in terms of relative deprivation. He indicated that every society has an average level in terms of living conditions, diet, amenities, and the type of activities people can participate in. Where an individual or family lacks the resources to obtain these, they are socially excluded from normal life, as well as being materially deprived. Other factors, such as poor skills or bad health, must also be taken into account.

Townsend—a leading campaigner who cofounded the Child Poverty Action Group—pointed out that there was an assumption that poverty had been steadily decreasing in affluent societies. But he drew attention to the increasing income gap between those at the top and lower levels of society, and said that when a country becomes wealthier, but income distribution is markedly uneven, the number of people in poverty is bound to increase. ∎

See also: Karl Marx 28–31 ▪ Friedrich Engels 66–67 ▪ Richard Sennett 84–87

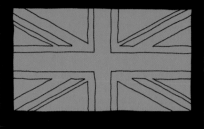

THERE AIN'T NO BLACK IN THE UNION JACK

PAUL GILROY (1956–)

IN CONTEXT

FOCUS
Racism

KEY DATES
18th–19th centuries
Biological-based ideas of race are used to justify slavery and colonialism.

1940s The Nazi party uses "race" to justify political inequality and introduces ideas of "racial purity."

1950 UNESCO declares that "race" is a social myth.

1970s Michel Foucault argues that biological ideas of race, linked with certain essential traits, arose with colonialism.

1981 US sociologist Anne Wortham publishes *The Other Side of Racism*, identifying five black movements that prevent society from reaching a position "beyond racism."

1987 Paul Gilroy publishes *There Ain't No Black in the Union Jack*.

In his book *There Ain't No Black in the Union Jack*, British sociologist Paul Gilroy focuses on racism in Britain in the 20th century. He points out that in the 1970s Britain worried about its "national decline" almost obsessively, and many commentators ascribed this to the "dilution of homogenous and continuous national stock"— specifically, Gilroy says, to the arrival of black people in Britain.

Gilroy indicates that fixed notions of nationality, such as "Britishness," may not be intentionally racist, but they have racist consequences. In seeking to define Britishness, 20th-century writers always seemed to imagine a white Britain—black people were seen as permanent outsiders. They were denied authentic national membership on the basis of their "race," and it was often assumed that their allegiance lay elsewhere.

While accepting that the idea of race has been a historical and political force, Gilroy says that it is no more than a social construct, a concept created in society. Where some sociologists have suggested a discussion of "ethnicity" or "culture" instead, Gilroy proposes that we should abandon all of these ideas. Whatever terms we use, he says, we are creating a false idea of "natural" categories by putting disparate people into different groups, leading to a division between "them" and "us."

Raciology

According to Gilroy, all these types of discussion leave us enmeshed in what he calls "raciology"—a discourse that assumes certain stereotypes, prejudices, images, and identities. Anti-racists find themselves inverting the position of racist thinkers, but are nevertheless unable to displace the idea of racism altogether. The solution, Gilroy suggests, lies in refusing to accept racial divisions as an inescapable, natural force, and instead developing "an ability to imagine political, economic, and social systems in which 'race' makes no sense." ∎

See also: Michel Foucault 52–55; 270–77 ▪ W.E.B. Du Bois 68–73 ▪ Elijah Anderson 82–83 ▪ bell hooks 90–95 ▪ Benedict Anderson 202–03

A SENSE OF ONE'S PLACE

PIERRE BOURDIEU (1930–2002)

IN CONTEXT

FOCUS
Habitus

KEY DATES
1934 The essay "Body Techniques" by French sociologist and anthropologist Marcel Mauss lays the foundations for Pierre Bourdieu's re-elaboration of the concept of "habitus."

1958 Max Weber suggests that "a specific style of life can be expected from those who wish to belong to the circle."

1966 English historian E.P. Thompson says class is "a relationship that must always be embodied in real people and in a real context."

2003 US cultural theorist Nancy Fraser says that capitalist society has two systems of subordination—the class structure and the status order—which interact.

From Marx to Durkheim and Weber to Parsons, sociologists have been keen to determine how the social class system is reproduced, in the belief that it is structurally bound to economics, property ownership, and financial assets.

But in the 1970s Pierre Bourdieu claimed, in *Distinction*, that the issue was more complex: social class is not defined solely by economics, he said, "but by the class habitus which is normally associated with that position." This concept was first discussed by the 13th-century Italian theologian Thomas Aquinas, who claimed that the things people want or like, and

See also: Karl Marx 28–31 ▪ Émile Durkheim 34–37 ▪ Friedrich Engels 66–67 ▪ Richard Sennett 84–87 ▪ Norbert Elias 180–81 ▪ Paul Willis 292–93

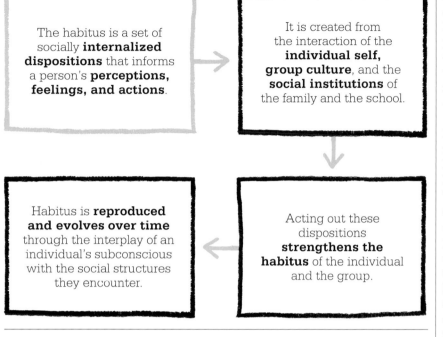

The habitus is a set of socially **internalized dispositions** that informs a person's **perceptions, feelings, and actions**.

It is created from the interaction of the **individual self, group culture**, and the **social institutions** of the family and the school.

Acting out these dispositions **strengthens the habitus** of the individual and the group.

Habitus is **reproduced and evolves over time** through the interplay of an individual's subconscious with the social structures they encounter.

the way they act, is because they think of themselves as a certain kind of person: each of us has a particular inclination, or habitus.

Bourdieu, however, develops the idea significantly. He defines habitus as an embodied set of socially acquired dispositions that lead individuals to live their lives in ways that are similar to other

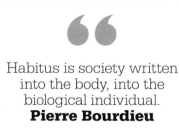

Habitus is society written into the body, into the biological individual.
Pierre Bourdieu

members of their social class group. An individual from one class will "know" that something is "pretentious" or "gaudy," whereas a person from another class will see the same thing as "beautiful" or "stunning." He suggests that a child learns these things from their family, and then from their school and peers, who demonstrate to the growing child how to speak and act, and so on. In this way, he says, "the social order is progressively inscribed in people's minds."

Class dispositions
While researching class divisions in France in the 1960s, Bourdieu noticed that people of the same class exhibited similar cultural values. The things they knew and valued, the way they spoke, their choice of clothes and decoration of the body, and their views on art, leisure, and entertainment

activities were all similar to one another. The French upper classes, he noted, enjoyed reading poetry, philosophy, and politics. They liked going to classic or avant-garde theater, museums, and classical-music concerts; they enjoyed going camping and mountaineering.

Within the working classes, Bourdieu found that people liked reading novels and magazines, betting, visiting music halls and boutiques, and owning luxury cars. The choices were relatively limited and they were determined not by cost, but by taste. He realized that people who were members of a certain class, or "class fraction" (class subset), shared tastes because they shared dispositions, or "habitus." They had somehow come to like and dislike the same things. And this awareness of shared habitus gave them a distinct sense of place; they "fitted" into this or that class.

The construction of habitus is due neither to the individual nor the existing environment—it is created through the interplay of the subjective mind with the structures and institutions around him or **»**

Fox hunting is a leisure pursuit that feels natural to some as a result of their habitus, or disposition. The same tendency makes other types of activity (such as karaoke) feel strange.

her. Individuals are born into a particular social class group. Each is defined by a specific lifestyle, referred to by Bourdieu as the habitus of the group. Every social class group has a group habitus that simultaneously defines, and differentiates it from, all the other group habitus in society.

The habitus of the group is also inscribed in the bodily dispositions and gestures of the individual. The social class of a person can be discerned from how they walk, talk, laugh, cry, and so on—from everything they do, think, and say. For the most part, because they are born and raised within a particular group habitus, individuals are generally unaware of the ways in which habitus both enables and restricts how they think, perceive, act, and interact with the world around them.

Habitus—as the embodiment of the dispositions of the wider group to which the individual belongs—provides people with a clear sense of the type of person they are and what it is that people like themselves should think and feel, as well as the manner in which they should behave.

Habitus gives individuals a unique "sense of one's place," because their internalized self perfectly matches the structure of their external world. But if they were to stray into the "fields" (institutions or structures) of a different class, they would feel like "a fish out of water," wrong-footed at every turn.

Forms of capital

Bourdieu maintains that the habitus of an individual is made up of different types and amounts of capital (economic, cultural, and social), which he redefined as "the set of actually usable resources and powers" that a person has.

Economic capital refers, quite simply, to monetary resources and property. A person's cultural capital is their capacity to play "the culture game"—to recognize references in books, films, and theater; to know how to act in given situations (such as apt manners and conversation at the dinner table); to know what to wear and how; and even who "to look down your nose at." Because habitus defines a person within any situation as being of a certain class or class fraction, it is critical in delineating the social order.

Bourdieu says the habitus is often obvious through "judgments of classification," which are pronounced about a thing, such as a painting, but act to classify the person speaking. Where one person describes a painting as "nice," and another as "passé," we learn little about the artwork, but much more about the person and their habitus. People use these judgments deliberately to distinguish themselves from their neighbors and establish their class.

In addition to economic and cultural capital, people may have social capital—human resources (friends and colleagues) gained through social networks. These relationships give a sense of mutual obligation and trust, and may offer access to power and influence.

This idea of social capital can be seen in the success of social networking websites such as Facebook and LinkedIn, which provide ways for individuals to increase their social capital. Bourdieu also saw scholastic capital (intellectual knowledge), linguistic capital (ease in the command of language, determining who has the authority to speak and be heard), and political capital (status in the political world) as playing a part in class.

The class game

The class struggle, outlined so comprehensively by Marx, can be played out on an individual level using Bourdieu's terms. He says that an individual develops within relationships (the family and school), before entering various social arenas or "fields" (such as institutions and social groups), where people express and constantly reproduce their habitus. Whether or not people are successful in the fields they enter depends on the type of habitus they have and the capital it carries.

Every field has a set of rules that reflects the group habitus, to the extent that the rules seem "common sense" to them. People are recognized for their "symbolic capital" and its worth within the field. Their symbolic capital represents the total of all their other forms of capital, and is reflected as prestige, a reputation for competence, or social position.

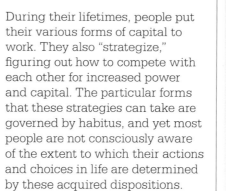

Those who talk of equality of opportunity forget that social games… are not 'fair games.'
Pierre Bourdieu

During their lifetimes, people put their various forms of capital to work. They also "strategize," figuring out how to compete with each other for increased power and capital. The particular forms that these strategies can take are governed by habitus, and yet most people are not consciously aware of the extent to which their actions and choices in life are determined by these acquired dispositions.

The possibility of change

Because Bourdieu's idea of cultural capital rests so heavily on the constantly reproduced habitus, which is embedded in all of us, he seems quite pessimistic about the possibility of social mobility.

However, the habitus *is* open to change through different forces within the field. The interaction of institutions and individuals usually reinforces existing ideas, but it is possible for someone from a lower social class to gain cultural capital by, for instance, being sent to a "good" school. This might raise their economic capital—and their children, in turn, might be privately schooled and benefit from increased economic and cultural capital and a different habitus. So, for Bourdieu, all forms of capital are interrelated: people convert their economic capital into cultural and social capital in order to improve their life chances.

Bourdieu's habitus has had a major impact on sociological debate in the last few decades. More than any other idea, it captures the extent to which impersonal social structures and processes influence what are regarded as seemingly unique personal dispositions. In short, habitus brings together insights of a number of prominent thinkers in one compact and versatile concept. ∎

Pierre Bourdieu

Born in 1930 in a rural village in southwest France, Pierre Bourdieu was the only son of a postman. A teacher recognized his potential and recommended he go to Paris to study. After graduating from the prestigious École Normale Supérieure with a degree in philosophy, he taught at the University of Algiers during the Algerian Liberation War (1956–62).

While in Algeria, he undertook ethnographic studies that resulted in his first book, *The Sociology of Algeria* (1958). On his return to France he became Director of Studies at the École des Hautes Études en Sciences Sociales, Paris, and began an acclaimed career in social studies. He believed research should translate into action, and was involved in many political protests against inequality and domination. Bourdieu died in 2002.

Key works

1979 *Distinction: A Social Critique of the Judgment of Taste*
1980 *The Logic of Practice*
1991 *Language and Symbolic Power*

THE ORIENT IS THE STAGE ON WHICH THE WHOLE EAST IS CONFINED
EDWARD SAID (1935–2003)

The idea of "the Orient" evolved from Western colonial powers and is a politically dangerous and culturally biased idea that continues to infect Western views of the Eastern world. This powerful argument is made by Edward Said in his influential text, *Orientalism* (1978).

The concept of Orientalism, he says, works in two important ways: it presents the East as one homogenous region that is exotic, uncivilized, and backward; and at the same time, it constructs and fixes the West's idea of the East in a simplified, unchanging set of representations.

European "experts" (historians, scientists, and linguists) report on what **"the Orient"** is like, from their own perspective.

↓

Their ideas are reduced still further into **stereotypes and representations that construct and fix Western views of "the East"** and its peoples...

↓

...and fuel and **perpetuate Western fears** about the East, especially Arabs, as **dangerous and "other."**

↓

The Orient is the stage on which the whole East is confined.

See also: Michel Foucault 52–55 ▪ W.E.B. Du Bois 68–73 ▪ Paul Gilroy 75 ▪ Elijah Anderson 82–83 ▪ Stuart Hall 200–01 ▪ Benedict Anderson 202–03 ▪ Stanley Cohen 290

Said explains that the idea of modern Orientalism arose when a French army led by Napoleon Bonaparte conquered Egypt in 1798. This conquest was significant because Napoleon took with him not only soldiers, but also scientists, philologists, and historians. These experts were given the job of recording and categorizing what they saw. In describing their experience of "the Orient" as objective knowledge, their words gained an unquestionable authority and influence in Europe.

Categorizing the East

However, as Said suggests, they were looking at the peoples around them through the lens of imperialist conquest. They saw themselves as the superior power and therefore as superior people. They drew an imaginary line between Us and Them, West and East, and began to define both sides in opposition to one another. Where the peoples of the East were perceived as irrational, uncivilized, lazy, and backward, those of the West were rational, civilized, hardworking, and progressive. The reports sent back to Europe by Napoleon's "experts" meant that the East was presented to Europeans in a highly packaged way; the East was explained by the West, and in the process molded to suit the Europeans. This idea of what "Orientals" were like was appropriated and disseminated widely by literary figures such as Lord Byron, who romanticized the Orient but continued to emphasize its inalienable difference.

Perpetuating fear

The problem continues, Said says, because the idea of the Orient has prevented people in the West from being able to view the East in all its complexity. The same repertory of images keeps arising: the Orient is seen as a place of mythical exoticism—it is the home of the Sphinx, Cleopatra, Eden, Troy, Sodom and Gomorrah, Sheba, Babylon, and Muhammad.

Orientalism is a framework used to understand the unfamiliar, says Said, but at the same time it tells

A memorial to victims of the bombing in Oklahoma in 1995. The attack was first blamed by media on "Muslims" and "Arabs" (the Other), but was the work of a white American.

us that the peoples of the East are different and frightening. In this context, "the Arab" is viewed as a violent fanatic, and Western nations feel the need to protect themselves from "the infiltration of the Other." The challenge, he says, is to find a way of coexisting peacefully. ▪

Edward Said

Cultural theorist and literary critic Edward Said was the founder of postcolonial studies. Born in West Jerusalem during the British Mandate in Palestine, his father was a wealthy Palestinian-American of Christian faith, and Said went to private international schools in Lebanon, Egypt, and the US. He later studied at Princeton and Harvard before becoming a professor of English Literature at Columbia University, where he taught until his death in 2003. Said wrote prolifically on a wide range of topics, including music and Palestinian issues.

Said stated that he was politicized by the Six Day War of 1967 between Israel and its Arab neighbors, after which he became an important voice for the Palestinian cause, especially in the US. In 1999 he founded an Arab-Israeli orchestra with the conductor Daniel Barenboim, in the belief that music transcends politics.

Key works

1978 *Orientalism*
1979 *The Question of Palestine*
1993 *Culture and Imperialism*

THE GHETTO IS WHERE THE BLACK PEOPLE LIVE
ELIJAH ANDERSON (1943–)

IN CONTEXT

FOCUS
The iconic ghetto

KEY DATES
1903 W.E.B. Du Bois says the problem of the 20th century is the problem of the color line.

Early 20th century Blacks migrate from the rural South to cities throughout the US.

1920 Black political leader Marcus Garvey holds an international convention in Harlem, the traditionally black area of New York City.

1960s There is a "white flight" from areas in the US where black people live, leading to "black ghettos."

1972 The Equal Employment Opportunity Act is passed in the US.

1992 Riots take place in Los Angeles after police are filmed beating a black motorist, Rodney King, and then acquitted of his assault.

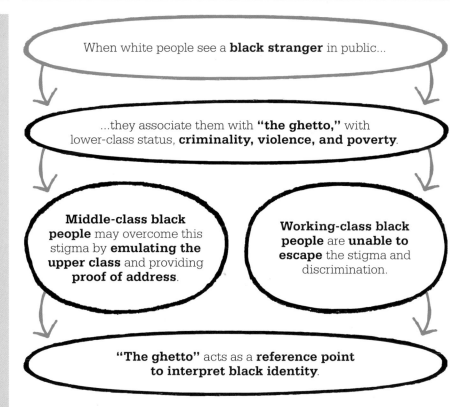

When white people see a **black stranger** in public...

...they associate them with **"the ghetto,"** with lower-class status, **criminality, violence, and poverty**.

Middle-class black people may overcome this stigma by **emulating the upper class** and providing **proof of address**.

Working-class black people are **unable to escape** the stigma and discrimination.

"The ghetto" acts as a **reference point to interpret black identity**.

In 2012, Elijah Anderson wrote "The Iconic Ghetto," which argued that many Americans associate the ghetto with a place where "the black people live." He said that to these same Americans, the ghetto symbolizes a lawless, impoverished, drug-infested, chaotic area of the city, ruled by violence. So when they think of "black people," they imagine them as immoral, drug-addicted, criminal "hoods," deserving of prejudice and discrimination.

See also: Michel Foucault 52–55 ▪ W.E.B. Du Bois 68–73 ▪ Paul Gilroy 75 ▪ Edward Said 80–81

Working-class black people who live in impoverished areas are, says Anderson, routinely stigmatized and "demoralized by racism."

Anderson gives the example of a racist incident while he was on holiday in a "pleasant Cape Cod town full of upper-middle-class white vacationers." As he enjoyed a jog through the town, a middle-aged white man blocked the road with his car, and shouted "Go home!" to Anderson. Bemused, Anderson later questioned what the man meant, and realized that it was an order to "go home" to the ghetto. The institution of the ghetto is persistent, says Anderson, and it leads many to think that the black person's place is most often in the ghetto, not in middle-class society.

Iconic status

Most black people in America do not come from a ghetto, and legally they have access to the same schooling and job opportunities as white people. However, because "the ghetto" has reached iconic status, it operates as a mindset, and black people of all classes find themselves having to prove that they are not from the ghetto before they do anything else. Anderson says that middle-class black people do this by "speaking white" (mimicking the formal speech style of upper-middle-class whites), or demonstrating exceptional intelligence, manners, and poise. They deal with insults by laughing them off with friends, but in fact these small events, like Anderson's jogging incident, can make "the scales fall from one's eyes" and induce a feeling of having been a fool for believing that they fitted seamlessly into society.

Disproving the ghetto

Middle-class black people can work to disabuse others of this "assessment," Anderson says, but the problem for poorer black people is less easily solved. If they actually live in a ghetto, how can they distance themselves from all its associations? How do working-class black people signify that they are not violent drug addicts, or in any way counteract the prejudice already operating against them?

Anderson points to the shooting of Trayvon Martin in 2012: the unarmed, innocent 17-year-old was shot dead by a neighborhood watch coordinator, who said Martin looked "out of place." This exposes the danger of many white people's belief that black people come from, and should remain in, "the ghetto," not white neighborhoods.

According to Anderson, the idea that black people have a specific "place" in society (the "ghetto") persists in the imagination of white people. This is despite a black presence in every social class and neighborhood. The iconic ghetto acts to continually stigmatize people with black skin, and treat them as "dangerous outsiders." ▪

Elijah Anderson

Elijah Anderson is one of the leading urban ethnographers in the US. He was born on a plantation in Mississippi during World War II. His parents were originally sharecroppers who picked cotton, but after his father's experience of fighting as a soldier in Europe during the war, the family found the racism of the South intolerable and moved to Chicago and then Indiana, both in the north of the country.

Anderson studied sociology at Indiana University and then Chicago, where his dissertation on black streetcorner men became his first book, *A Place on the Corner* (1978). He was Vice President of the American Sociological Association (ASA) in 2002, and has won many awards, including the ASA's Cox-Johnson-Frazier Award.

Key works

1990 *Streetwise*
1999 *Code of the Street: Moral Life of the Inner City*
2012 "The Iconic Ghetto"

The black man is treated as a dangerous outsider until he proves he is worthy of trust.
Elijah Anderson

THE TOOLS OF FREEDOM BECOME THE SOURCES OF INDIGNITY

RICHARD SENNETT (1943–)

IN CONTEXT

FOCUS
Class inequality

KEY DATES
1486 Italian philosopher Giovanni Pico della Mirandola says that unlike animals, people search for meaning and dignity in life.

1841 In "Self-Reliance," US philosopher and essayist Ralph Waldo Emerson sees self-reliance as a moral imperative that enables individuals to shape their own destiny.

1960s French philosopher Jean-Paul Sartre says that a class society is a society of resources unfairly distributed because some people have arbitrary power.

1989 British academic Richard Hoggart says, "Every decade we swiftly declare we have buried class, each decade the coffin stays empty."

S ociologists and economists traditionally accepted the idea that social class was linked to money: as workers earned higher incomes and gained more possessions, they would move into the middle class and enjoy not just prosperity, but also an increased sense of dignity. But this concept was challenged when US sociologist Richard Sennett, in collaboration with Jonathan Cobb, investigated a paradox that seemed to afflict working-class people who moved into the middle class.

What Sennett discovered in his interviews with workers, as outlined in *The Hidden Injuries of Class,* published in 1972, was

See also: Friedrich Engels 66–67 ▪ W.E.B. Du Bois 68–73 ▪ Pierre Bourdieu 76–79 ▪ Elijah Anderson 82–83 ▪ Georg Simmel 104–05 ▪ Samuel Bowles and Herbert Gintis 288–89 ▪ Paul Willis 292–93

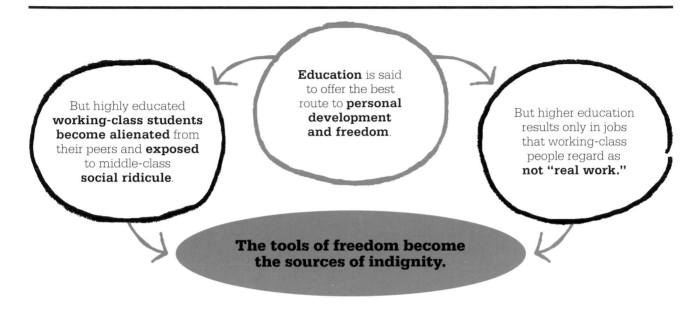

Education is said to offer the best route to **personal development and freedom**.

But highly educated **working-class students become alienated** from their peers and **exposed** to middle-class **social ridicule**.

But higher education results only in jobs that working-class people regard as **not "real work."**

The tools of freedom become the sources of indignity.

---

that an increase in material power and freedom of choice was accompanied by a significant crisis in self respect. In reaching for greater freedom, workers were being asked to use "tools," such as education, that left them feeling alienated and incapable.

Immigration and racism

To explain how this might be happening, Sennett looked first at the history of the working class in the US. During the urbanization of the 19th century, rural workers moved from small farms to towns and then cities, which grew quickly under this sudden influx. In addition, most US cities had large enclaves of newly arrived European immigrants from Ireland, Italy, Poland, and Greece,

Immigrants disembark from a ship in New York in the early 20th century. These "foreigners" were often used for cheap labor, which led to hostility from some US citizens.

for example. Here the old languages were spoken and cultural traditions were kept alive.

This mass immigration meant that industrialists soon realized that unskilled labor was cheaper than machine production. So they hired large numbers of immigrants

and switched the focus of their machinery to replacing the more expensive, skilled labor. Hostility arose toward the newcomers and there was a rise in racist attitudes.

A kind of "moral hierarchy" among nationalities soon gained widespread acceptance. Western »

The pyramid of achievement

Middle- and upper-class people at the top look down on those below.

The working-class laborer climbs the achievement pyramid, striving for a high-status job.

As the laborer moves up the pyramid, he feels a sense of betrayal—both to himself and to those he has left behind.

ACADEMIC AND PROFESSIONAL JOBS

The laborer experiences conflicting emotions as he ascends the pyramid.

TRADES AND MANUAL LABOR JOBS

Europeans (apart from the Irish) were at the top of this hierarchy; they were seen as diligent, hard working, and skilled. However, at the opposite end of the scale, Sennett notes that "Slavs, Bohemians, Jews, and Southern Europeans… were accused of dirtiness, secretiveness, or laziness." The new immigrants found that they could depend only on their countrymen for support, so ethnic communities flourished.

But during the mid-20th century, US cities underwent urban renewal programs that broke up the immigrant communities. Immigrant families were integrated into the larger society, which had different attitudes of social respect from their own. In the wider US society, higher educated, "cultured" people were treated with the most respect. An honest, hard-working man or woman who may have been highly regarded in the "old neighborhood" was now viewed with disdain and suspicion for being ignorant and "foreign."

Education and failure
Sennett says that the working class was being challenged to become "cultured"; education seemed to be the way to acceptance and respect. However, there were several notable problems with this. First, to people who had always valued hard, physical labor, the "pen-pushing" jobs of the middle class

were not considered "real work." These jobs were not worthy, so a worker could not view himself with respect while doing them.

In addition, although intellect and education were held in high esteem by the middle and upper classes, it seemed to the workers that "the educated" did nothing worth respecting; on the contrary, they were often seen to use their privileged position to cheat, lie, and avoid working, while at the same time commanding high salaries. How, therefore, could a worker aim to maintain his dignity and self-respect in this position?

The workers interviewed by Sennett use the word "educated" to stand for a range of experiences and feelings that move beyond pure schooling. Education's elevated status results from the fact that it is thought to increase rationality and develop the finest human capacities. But Rissarro, a shoeshine boy turned bank clerk, explains how this works differently across the social divisions. He believes that people of a higher class have the power to judge him because they are more "internally developed." Despite Rissarro's rise to professional employment, his

The educated… middle-class people… [with] the 'right' values stand out from a mass whose understanding… they believe inferior to their own.
Richard Sennett

middle-class colleagues look down on him and he lacks respect for himself, because he feels that he is not doing "real work." He accepts society's admonitions to "better himself," but he feels like an imposter and is puzzled by his sense of discomfort. He believes that the only explanation is that there is something wrong with him.

Sennett maintains that workers tend to see their failure to fit in and achieve respect as personal failure, not as a condition of societal divisions and inequalities. He quotes James, a highly educated son of an immigrant, who sees himself as a failure, whatever he does. "If I really had what it takes," he says, "I could make this school thing worthwhile." On the other hand, if he "had the balls to go out into the world" and get a real job, that would earn him real respect. James holds himself responsible for not having more self-confidence and for having failed to "develop."

The political is personal

This conjunction of class and self is a uniquely US phenomenon, says Sennett, that is tied up with the prizing of "the individual." Success in IQ tests and schooling is seen as a way of freeing an individual from his or her social conditions at birth—everyone who truly has merit or intelligence will rise. This belief in equality of opportunity is at the heart of the American Dream.

Working-class children do not have the same opportunities as children from more affluent backgrounds, and those who strive to excel are seen as traitors. They are exiled from their peer groups, with a subsequent loss of self-worth. The tools of freedom are a source of indignity for them, both at school and at college, where they are looked down on for not knowing the rules and lacking in wider cultural knowledge. Their educational achievement exposes them not to respect but to disdain from the middle-class people around them and they suffer a sense of failure and alienation.

According to Scottish-American businessman Andrew Carnegie, the justice of industrial capitalism is that society will always reward "a man of talent." If a person is worthy of escaping poverty, he or she can do so. If he or she does not have the ability to "make it," however, what right does that person have to complain? As Sennett notes: in a meritocracy, if you fail, you have no merit. Failure to succeed is due to personal inadequacy. In this way the inequalities of class become hidden by the widespread "personal failures" of working people.

The Hidden Injuries of Class is a subtle and sensitive exploration of working-class lives that exposes how social difference can be made to appear as simply a question of character, competence, and moral resolve, when it is essentially a matter of inherited class. ∎

Arthur Miller was a working-class boy who rose to become one of the leading US dramatists of the mid-20th century—he was, however, largely looked down upon by US critics.

Richard Sennett

Literary author and sociologist Richard Sennett was born in Chicago to parents with communist beliefs. Both his father and uncle fought as internationalists in the civil war in Spain. Sennett was brought up by his mother in one of the first racially mixed public housing projects.

Sennet studied cello at Juilliard in New York City, but a wrist operation in 1964 brought his musical career to an end. He began a career in sociology at Harvard University, and has taught at Yale and the London School of Economics (LSE). In the 1970s he cofounded The New York Institute for the Humanities with writers Susan Sontag and Joseph Brodsky. Sennett made his name with *The Hidden Injuries of Class*, which he wrote after spending four years researching with Jonathan Cobb. He is married to sociologist Saskia Sassen.

Key works

1972 *The Hidden Injuries of Class* (in collaboration with Jonathan Cobb)
1974 *The Call of Public Man*
2005 *The Culture of the New Capitalism*

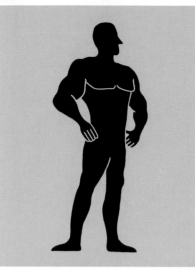

MEN'S INTEREST IN PATRIARCHY IS CONDENSED IN HEGEMONIC MASCULINITY
R.W. CONNELL (1944–)

IN CONTEXT

FOCUS
Hegemonic masculinity

KEY DATES
1930s Italian social theorist Antonio Gramsci uses the term "hegemony" to explain how the views of the dominant class become seen as "common sense."

1957 US sociologist Helen Hacker writes about the social nature of masculinity.

1985 Carrigan, Connell, and Lee publish *Toward a New Sociology of Masculinity*.

1990 US sociologists Messner and Sabo use hegemony to explain homophobia and violence at sporting events.

1993 US sociologist James Messerschmidt publishes *Masculinities and Crime*.

2003 Japanese sociologist Masako Ishii-Kuntz traces the emergence of diverse masculinities in Japan.

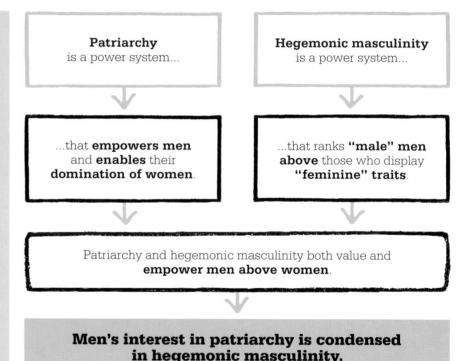

Patriarchy is a power system...

...that **empowers men** and **enables** their **domination of women**.

Hegemonic masculinity is a power system...

...that ranks **"male" men above** those who display **"feminine" traits**.

Patriarchy and hegemonic masculinity both value and **empower men above women**.

Men's interest in patriarchy is condensed in hegemonic masculinity.

It is often assumed that masculinity is a natural, biological state that cannot be altered. R.W. Connell claims, however, that it is not a fixed thing, but an acquired identity: there is no one pattern of masculinity that is found everywhere or over any extended period of time, and, she says, we should speak about masculinities, not masculinity, when exploring what it means to "be a man."

Masculinity also has multiple definitions within multicultural societies. In any one setting, such as a school or workplace, a particular form of masculinity will be seen as the "best" and most effective way to be a man.

This idea lies behind Connell's concept of hegemonic masculinity, which claims that in any time or place, different forms of masculinity are organized into a hierarchy. The dominant form—seen as the ideal masculinity and the one that others will be judged against—is the hegemonic form. It will constitute that society's idea of "manliness" and those few men who can embody this form of masculinity will be "the most honored and desired."

Subordinate masculinity

Subordinated or marginalized forms of masculinity are those that deviate from the norm; men espousing these suffer humiliation, exclusion, and loss of privilege. When the masculine role moves toward a more "female" position (as in homosexuality), there is a corresponding loss of status and power. In this way, the patriarchal

position aligns with the hegemonic ideal in Western societies. As men reap significant benefits from maintaining dominance over women, their general interest and investment in patriarchy is formidable—it is what gives them social, cultural, and economic control. The closer a man's masculinity is to the hegemonic ideal, the more power he has.

Practicing gender

Connell claims that the European/American hegemonic form, which is linked closely to the patriarchal ideal of the powerful, aggressive, unemotional male who will often use violence to get his way, is being extended across the world through processes of globalization. The media glamorizes the hegemonic ideal through its adulation of ruthless billionaire entrepreneurs and fit, contact-sports stars.

Women are complicit in recognizing a hierarchy of masculinities, according to Connell. Their continued loyalty to

> Most men find it difficult to be patriarchs... but they fear letting go of the benefits.
> **bell hooks**

patriarchal religions and romantic narratives, and their perpetuation of gender expectations of children, sustains the power of the patriarchal ideal and the hegemonic masculinity associated with it. By describing masculinity within the terms of hegemony or hierarchy, Connell grants it a fluidity, which means that there is an opportunity for change. A move to establish a version of masculinity that is open to equality with women, she says, would constitute a positive hegemony. ■

Exclusion of homosexual desire from the definition of masculinity is, according to Connell in *The Men and the Boys*, an important feature of modern-day hegemonic masculinity.

R.W. Connell

R.W. Connell was born in Australia in 1944 as Robert William ("Bob") Connell. A transsexual woman, Connell completed her transition late in life and took the first name of Raewyn. Educated in high schools in Manly and North Sydney, Connell went on to gain degrees from the universities of Melbourne and Sydney.

During the 1960s Connell was an activist in the New Left. She became one of the youngest people to attain an academic

chair when she was appointed professor of sociology at Macquarie University, New South Wales, in 1976. Although best known for her work on the social construction of masculinities, Connell has also lectured extensively and written on poverty, education, and the northern hemisphere bias of mainstream social science.

Key works

1987 *Gender and Power*
1995 *Masculinities*
2000 *The Men and the Boys*

WHITE WOMEN HAVE BEEN COMPLICIT IN THIS IMPERIALIST WHITE-SUPREMACIST CAPITALIST PATRIARCHY

BELL HOOKS (1952–)

IN CONTEXT

FOCUS
**Feminism and
intersectionality**

KEY DATES
1979 The Combahee River
Collective, a black feminist
lesbian organization in the
US, claims it is essential to
consider the conjunction of
"interlocking oppressions."

1980s US economist Heidi
Hartmann says that in the
"unhappy marriage" of Marxist
feminism, Marxism (the
husband) dominates feminism
(the wife), because class
trumps gender.

1989 US law professor
Kimberlé Crenshaw uses
"intersectionality" to describe
patterns of racism and sexism.

2002 German sociologist
Helma Lutz claims at least 14
"lines of difference" are used in
power relations, including age,
gender, skin color, and class.

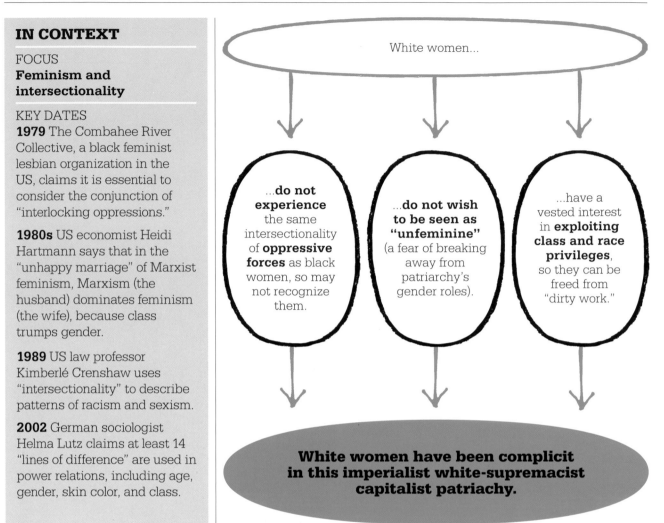

White women...

...**do not
experience**
the same
intersectionality
of **oppressive
forces** as black
women, so may
not recognize
them.

...**do not wish
to be seen as
"unfeminine"**
(a fear of breaking
away from
patriarchy's
gender roles).

...have a
vested interest
in **exploiting
class and race
privileges**,
so they can be
freed from
"dirty work."

**White women have been complicit
in this imperialist white-supremacist
capitalist patriachy.**

The "second-wave" feminists
of the 1960s to 1980s
presented a far more
formidable and thoroughgoing
challenge to male domination than
earlier feminists. Their broadening
agenda included issues such as
legal inequalities, sexuality, rape,
the family, and the workplace.

But the US feminist bell hooks
criticized the feminism of the 1980s
in particular as representing the
view of privileged white women.
In *Feminist Theory: From Margin
to Center*, published in 1984, she
claimed that an emphasis on

women as the "sisterhood" masked
what she saw as the "opportunism
of bourgeois white women."

hooks says that the situation is
more complicated than the second-
wave feminists recognized. Worse
still, these women helped maintain
an intersecting network of
oppressive forces that impacted the
lives of working-class women of
color: white women have been
complicit in perpetuating white
patriarchal domination.

In 1989, US lawyer Kimberlé
Crenshaw described the criss-
crossing forces of oppression as

"intersectionality." She likened this
to a place where traffic flows in four
directions. Discrimination, like
traffic, may flow in one direction or
another. If an accident happens at
an intersection, it could have been
caused by cars traveling from any
number of directions—sometimes
from all directions. If a black
woman is harmed because she
is "at the intersection," this may
have been caused by sex or race
discrimination, or both.

As a lawyer, Crenshaw found
that black women in the workplace
were discriminated against on both

Second-wave feminism of the 1960s to 1980s, with its emphasis on "sisterhood," is criticized by hooks as opportunistic and as representing the interests of middle-class white women.

counts—being black and female—but fell through a legal loophole. They were the last to be hired and the first to be laid off, but their employers denied this had anything to do with discrimination. When a case went to court, the judge ruled that they could not have been laid off because they were women, as other women still worked in the firm. Neither could the reason have

been their color, as black men still worked there. The law could only deal with one or other form of oppression, not the two together.

Hierarchy systems

bell hooks was to take the idea of intersectionality still further. In *The Will to Change* (2004), she says: "I often use the phrase 'imperialist white-supremacist capitalist patriarchy' to describe the interlocking political systems that are the foundation of our nation's politics." The phrase is used to describe a set of systems that combine to situate people within the power hierarchies of society.

White supremacy is the assumed superiority of lighter-skinned or "white" races over others. While hooks acknowledges that "those who allow [racial] prejudice to lead them to hostile

acts are in the minority no matter the class standing of the neighborhood," racial prejudice is still apparent in beliefs that a person is lazy, stupid, or more violent, for instance, because of their racial background. This form of stereotyping means that an Indian doctor or Hispanic teacher might be viewed as less competent than white Europeans.

Capitalism refers to the economic system that is characterized by private or corporate ownership of firms and goods, together with control over the prices, goods, and the labor force. It has an inherent hierarchy: those who own the means of production and control the labor force are privileged over the workers. hooks agrees with the US writer and prominent activist Carmen Vázquez, who she »

> It was clear to black women... that they were never going to have equality within the existing white-supremacist capitalist patriarchy.
> **bell hooks**

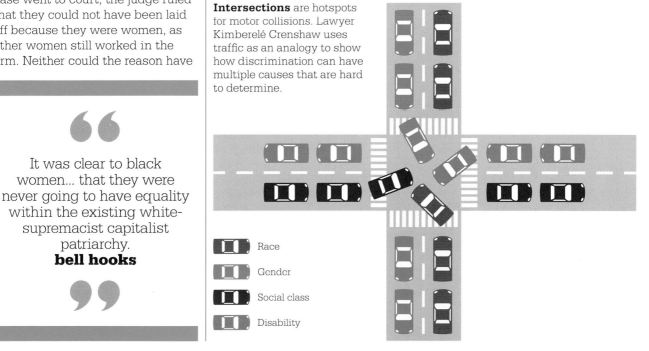

Intersections are hotspots for motor collisions. Lawyer Kimberelé Crenshaw uses traffic as an analogy to show how discrimination can have multiple causes that are hard to determine.

Race

Gender

Social class

Disability

quotes as saying that the "American capitalist obsession for individualism" means that "anything goes so long as it gets you what you want." Capitalism values money more than people, so the wealthy are seen as more important than the poor.

The attitudes encased in white supremacy and capitalism continue to cause problems, according to hooks. Imperialism and colonialism also remain relevant because, historically, non-white peoples and their countries' resources have been plundered and exploited by white supremacist capitalists in their pursuit of wealth.

The rules of patriarchy

hooks defines patriarchy as "a political-social system that insists that males are inherently dominating, superior to everything… and endowed with the right to dominate and rule over the weak and to maintain that dominance through various forms of psychological terrorism and violence." She says that of all the interlocking political systems we encounter, this is the one we learn the most about while growing up. In *The Will to Change*, hooks explains how she and her brother were schooled in the meaning of "patriarchy."

At church they were told God was a man and had created man to rule the world and everything in it. Women were created to obey and serve men. Men must be strong, provide for their family, strategize, and lead—they could also expect to be served. These are the patriarchal gender roles that are apparent in

Only privileged women had the luxury to imagine working outside the home would provide them with an income… to be economically self-sufficient.
bell hooks

every institution of a community, from families, schools, and sports arenas to courtrooms.

If challenged, these ideas may be reinforced through violence; but sometimes the cold stares or mockery of a group of peers is enough to pull someone back into behavior more appropriate to their gender role. A crying boy or an angry girl may quickly become aware of having transgressed the gender roles that have been defined for them.

One of the most insidious things about patriarchy, hooks says, is that it is not spoken about, and we cannot dismantle a system as long as we are in "collective denial about its impact on our lives." Men rarely even know what the word "patriarchy" means—they don't use the term in everyday life, despite rigidly enforcing its rules while also suffering from them. Boys submit to the rule of the father just as girls do, and neither talks about what is happening to them.

The aim of feminism

This interlocking system, hooks says, means there is no sense in making "equality between the sexes" the goal of feminism. Since men are not equals among themselves in white supremacist, capitalist, patriarchal class structure, "which men do women want to be equal to?"

She notes that women in lower-class and poor groups, particularly black women, would not define women's liberation as equality with men, because men in their groups are also exploited and oppressed—

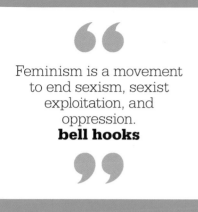

> Feminism is a movement to end sexism, sexist exploitation, and oppression.
> **bell hooks**

they too may lack social, political, and economic power. While these women are aware that patriarchy gives those men privileges, they tend to see exaggerated expressions of male chauvinism in their own group as stemming from a sense of powerlessness compared to other male groups.

The continuing effect of imperialist, white-supremacist, capitalist patriarchy is a complex "intersectionality" that must be examined in its totality of effect on women, if feminists are to improve the lives of all women. hooks claims that black women

have been suspicious of the feminist movement since its inception. They realized that if its stated aim was equality with men, it could easily become a movement that would mostly improve the social standing of middle- and upper-class women. Privileged white women, hooks argues, have not been anxious to call attention to race and class privilege because they benefit from these; they could "count on there being a lower class of exploited, subordinated women to do the dirty work they were refusing to do."

Privilege and politics

Women with multiple social privileges (such as being white, heterosexual, and wealthy), may see a situation as demonstrating just one form of oppression, rather than the intersectionality of many different types of oppression. This may be due in part to ignorance, hooks suggests—in the town in which she grew up, black people frequently traveled to the white district to work, but white people did not visit her neighborhood. They had no knowledge or experience of that world at all.

In addition, according to hooks, some women tend to shun identification with any political movement, especially one that is considered radical; or they do not wish to be associated with a "women's rights" movement of any form. This fear of being seen to join a movement that challenges male rights and behaviors has been inculcated into them from an early age through the influence of patriarchy, whose rules they continue to abide by and enforce.

Once we see that it is the system of patriarchy, and not men, that is the problem, we can then begin to find an answer, suggests hooks. She says that feminists must call attention to the diversity of women's social and political reality, and recognize that race and class oppression are also feminist issues. The feminist movement will then not solely benefit any specific group of women or privilege women over men. The real solution lies, hooks maintains, in changing the philosophical structures that underlie oppression. For this reason, feminism is a political movement, not a "romantic notion of personal freedom." ∎

bell hooks

US social activist and scholar Gloria Jean Watkins took the name of her maternal great-grandmother, Bell Hooks, as a pen name to honor her and to gain strength from her ability to "talk back." She uses lowercase letters to signal to the reader to focus on her ideas, rather than herself.

Born in 1952 in rural Kentucky, her father was a janitor and her mother was a parent to their seven children. She went to a racially segregated school, but then attended an integrated high school, where she became acutely aware of differences in race and

class. In 1973 hooks gained a degree in English from Stanford University, then took an MA and a PhD before becoming a professor of ethnic studies at the University of Southern California. Since writing her first book at the age of 19, she has published more than 30 books on different topics.

Key works

1981 *Ain't I a Woman?*
1984 *Feminist Theory: From Margin to Center*
2000 *Feminism is for Everybody*

THE CONCEPT OF "PATRIARCHY" IS INDISPENSABLE FOR AN ANALYSIS OF GENDER INEQUALITY

SYLVIA WALBY (1953–)

IN CONTEXT

FOCUS
Patriarchy

KEY DATES
1792 Mary Wollstonecraft, English advocate of women's rights, publishes *A Vindication of the Rights of Woman*.

1969 In *Sexual Politics*, US feminist Kate Millett says patriarchy is a universal power relationship that is all-pervasive and enters into all other forms of social divisions.

1971 Italian feminist Mariarosa Dalla Costa argues that women's unwaged labor is an essential part of the functioning of capitalism.

1981 In "The Unhappy Marriage of Feminism and Marxism," US feminist economist Heidi Hartmann suggests that the "dual systems" of capitalism and patriarchy oppress women.

In 1990, the British sociologist Sylvia Walby published *Theorizing Patriarchy*, a groundbreaking book that claims "patriarchy" is a highly complex phenomenon made up of many intersecting forces. Whereas earlier feminists had focused on identifying a single cause of patriarchy, linked to a particular historical era or culture, Walby defines patriarchy as "a system of social structures and practices in which men dominate, oppress, and exploit women." She claims there are six interacting structures: the family household, paid work, the state, male violence, sexuality, and cultural institutions. To examine

See also: Karl Marx 28–31 ▪ Judith Butler 56–61 ▪ bell hooks 90–95 ▪ Teri Caraway 248–49 ▪ Christine Delphy 312–17 ▪ Ann Oakley 318–19

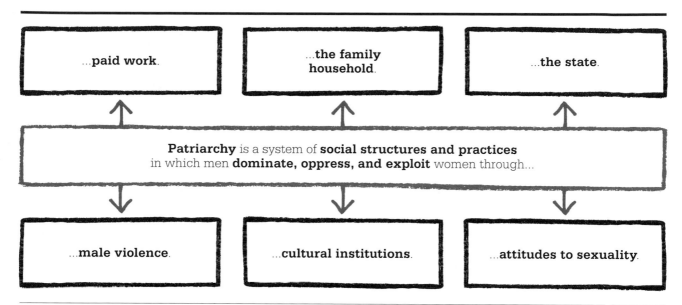

…paid work.	…the family household.	…the state.

Patriarchy is a system of **social structures and practices** in which men **dominate, oppress, and exploit** women through…

…male violence.	…cultural institutions.	…attitudes to sexuality.

these six structures, Walby looks back through the struggles and work of previous feminists.

First-wave feminism

Walby notes that the "first wave" of feminism of the 19th and early 20th centuries in Europe and the US focused on the private, rather than public, nature of patriarchy. At this time, she says, married women were excluded from paid employment, so patriarchal domination occurred mainly within the family, where it was "the man in his position as husband or father who [was] the direct oppressor and beneficiary… of the subordination of women." The idea of "domesticity" intensified during this era. Middle-class women were confined to the private sphere; they were denied the right to vote, own property,

or to gain higher-level education, and violence by husbands was legally sanctioned.

The first-wave feminists addressed these issues on a legal level, but Walby maintains that the significant rights they won for women failed to eliminate all forms of inequality. This was because the family and the household continued to function effectively as

a "patriarchal mode of production." Patriarchy within the household is the first of Walby's six patriarchal structures; it undervalues the work of housewives (as unpaid labor), while apparently valuing them only within this role (this was women's "rightful place")

Walby points out that in Marxist terms, housewives are the producing class, while husbands »

Emmeline Pankhurst (1858–1928) was a militant, first-wave feminist who fought hard to advance women's basic rights and to secure married women the vote in the UK.

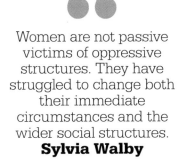

> Women are not passive victims of oppressive structures. They have struggled to change both their immediate circumstances and the wider social structures.
> **Sylvia Walby**

are the class that benefits "individually and directly" from women's unpaid labor.

Women within capitalism

By the 20th century, capitalism had become the dominant global economic model. As capitalism grew, women lost forms of work that had once been open to them (in textiles, for instance) through the growth of industrialization. They moved into a position that was disadvantaged in two ways: vertical segregation (being offered employment only in the lower grades of work) and horizontal segregation (being seen as suitable only for particular areas of work). For this reason, Walby proposes that "patriarchal relations in paid work," which give men the highest opportunities in jobs available and level of employment, constitute the second of the six structures that maintain patriarchy.

However, Walby notes that in the 20th century an interesting conflict began to arise between patriarchy and capitalism, because they had rival interests in the exploitation of women's labor.

As she says: "if women are working for capitalists they have less time to work for their husband."

Conflicts between patriarchy in the home and in the workplace have often been resolved through the intervention of Walby's third patriarchal structure: the state. For example, during World War II, British women were needed to work in munitions factories. The trade unions were unhappy about this and persuaded the UK government to introduce legislation (the Restoration of the Pre-War Practices Act 1942) to ensure that women would be removed from employment in factories at the end of the war. In this way, women were moved to service the public or private arenas according to the needs of men, regardless of their own preferences.

In the West, the state has also intervened to enhance women's rights, such as the 1970 Equal Pay Act in the UK. However, many of the apparent gains have led to little change in practice, with women still earning less than men. Walby says that this is because the state is "a site of patriarchal relations," which is necessary to patriarchy as a whole. She notes that there have been important changes in state policy over the last 150 years but these also include some very significant limitations. "The state is still patriarchal as well as capitalist and racist," she says.

Male violence and sexuality

The fourth of Walby's six structures is male violence against women. Domestic violence includes controlling or threatening behavior, and violence or abuse between intimate partners or family members. These intimate relationships are power-structured (as is the case with all of

patriarchy's six structures) and work through a set of arrangements whereby one person is controlled by another. Men's violence (or threatened violence) against women plays an important part in their continuing control and domination of women.

The fifth of the structures is sexuality. Walby says that societies prize heterosexual relationships above all others, in many cases seeing them as the only permissible option. Sexuality is a major area in which men exercise domination of women: they impose their ideas of femininity onto women and have constructed sexual practices that revolve around male notions of desire.

Walby points out that the second-wave feminists of the 1960s to 1980s looked at a wider range of "unofficial" inequities than the first-wave feminists. They queried sexuality, the family, the workplace, and reproductive rights—although some present-day, third-wave feminists have criticized them for "unfinished business." However, when oppressive laws on sexuality were abolished, some of the hard-won changes became traps for women. Sexual liberty led to the mainstreaming of pornography and

> Male violence against women is sufficiently common and repetitive... to constitute a social structure.
> **Sylvia Walby**

The automobile industry has a long history of using women as sex objects to sell cars (despite the deeply tenuous link to the product), positioning them as a focus of male fantasy and desire.

increased exploitation of women in prostitution, the sex industry, and human trafficking.

The last of Walby's six structures is culture; specifically, a society's cultural institutions. She claims that patriarchy permeates key social institutions and agents of socialization in society, including education, religion, and the media, all of which "create the representation of women within a patriarchal gaze." The world's religions, for example, continue to exclude women from the top positions and seem determined to restrict them to the "caring" rather than executive level—this, they say, is more "natural" for them. Women are thereby defined from a patriarchal viewpoint and kept firmly "in their place."

A shift to public patriarchy
The notions of private and public patriarchy are important for Walby in distinguishing other ways in which power structures intersect to affect women. She points out, for example, that British women of Afro-Caribbean origin are more likely to experience public patriarchy (finding it hard to gain

higher paid employment, for instance), while British Muslim women are more likely to experience higher levels of private patriarchy (affecting their abilities to leave the house or choose their preferred form of dress).

Since writing *Theorizing Patriarchy*, Walby has noted that while conventional "wisdom" sees the family as still central to women's lives, it has become less important. However, this has resulted, she suggests, in women working more, shifting them from the realms of private patriarchy into greater levels of public patriarchy. Women in the West are now exploited less by "individual patriarchs," such as their fathers and husbands, and more by men collectively, via work, the state, and cultural institutions.

Central to Walby's examination of patriarchy is her insistence that we see patriarchy neither as purely structural (which would lock women into subordinate positions within cultural institutions) nor as pure agency (the actions of individual men and women). She says that if we see patriarchy as fundamentally about structure, we are in danger of seeing women as passive victims. On the other hand, if we see women as locked into patriarchy through their own, voluntary actions, we may see them "as colluding with their patriarchal oppressors."

In *Theorizing Patriarchy*, Walby gives an account of patriarchy that explains both changes in structure (such as changes in the capitalist economy) and of agency (the campaigns of the three waves of feminism). She says major shifts must be made both within women themselves and by the society and cultures that surround them if we are to make meaningful progress. ∎

Sylvia Walby

Professor Sylvia Walby is a British sociologist whose work in the fields of domestic violence, patriarchy, gender relations, and globalization has found wide acceptance and acclaim. She graduated in sociology from the University of Essex, UK, in 1984, and went on to gain further degrees from the universities of Essex and Reading.

In 1992, Walby became the founding President of the European Sociological Association, and in 2008 she took up the first UNESCO Chair in Gender Research, to guide its research into gender equality and women's human rights. In the same year she was awarded an OBE for services to equal opportunities and diversity. Walby has taught at many leading institutions, including the London School of Economics (LSE) and Harvard University.

Key works

1986 *Patriarchy at Work*
1990 *Theorizing Patriarchy*
2011 *The Future of Feminism*

> When patriarchy loosens its grip in one area it only tightens it in other arenas.
> **Sylvia Walby**

MODERN

LIVING

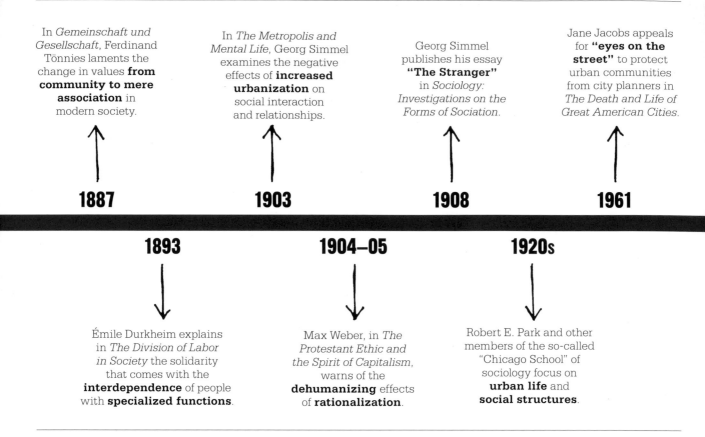

In *Gemeinschaft und Gesellschaft*, Ferdinand Tönnies laments the change in values **from community to mere association** in modern society.

In *The Metropolis and Mental Life*, Georg Simmel examines the negative effects of **increased urbanization** on social interaction and relationships.

Georg Simmel publishes his essay **"The Stranger"** in *Sociology: Investigations on the Forms of Sociation*.

Jane Jacobs appeals for **"eyes on the street"** to protect urban communities from city planners in *The Death and Life of Great American Cities*.

1887

1903

1908

1961

1893

1904–05

1920s

Émile Durkheim explains in *The Division of Labor in Society* the solidarity that comes with the **interdependence** of people with **specialized functions**.

Max Weber, in *The Protestant Ethic and the Spirit of Capitalism*, warns of the **dehumanizing** effects of **rationalization**.

Robert E. Park and other members of the so-called "Chicago School" of sociology focus on **urban life** and **social structures**.

A s prehistory's primitive human groups began to settle down in one place, the foundations of civilization were laid. From these early beginnings, humans increasingly lived together in larger and larger groups, and civilization grew further with the establishment of villages, towns, and cities. But for the greater part of human history, most people lived in rural communities. Large-scale urbanization came about only with the Industrial Revolution, which was accompanied by a huge expansion of towns and cities, and massive numbers of people migrating to work in the factories and mills that were located there.

Living in an urban environment became as much an aspect of "modernity" as industrialization and the growth of capitalism, and

sociologists from Adam Ferguson to Ferdinand Tönnies recognized that there was a major difference between traditional rural communities and modern urban ones. This alteration of social order was ascribed to a variety of factors by an assortment of thinkers: to capitalism by Karl Marx; to the division of labor in industry by Émile Durkheim; to rationalization and secularization by Max Weber. It was Georg Simmel who suggested that urbanization itself had affected the ways in which people interact socially—and one of the fundamental characteristics of modern living is life in the city.

Community in the city
Simmel examined not only the new forms of social order that had arisen in the modern cities, but also the

effects upon the individual of living in large groups, often separated from traditional community ties and family. Building upon his work, the so-called Chicago School of sociology, spearheaded by Robert E. Park, helped to establish a distinct field of urban sociology. Soon, however, sociologists changed the emphasis of their research from what it is like to live in a city, to what kind of city we want to live in.

Having evolved to meet the needs of industrialization, the city—and urban life, with all its benefits and disadvantages—was felt by many sociologists to have been imposed on people. The Marxist sociologist Henri Lefebvre believed that the demands of capitalism had shaped modern urban society, but that ordinary people could take control of their

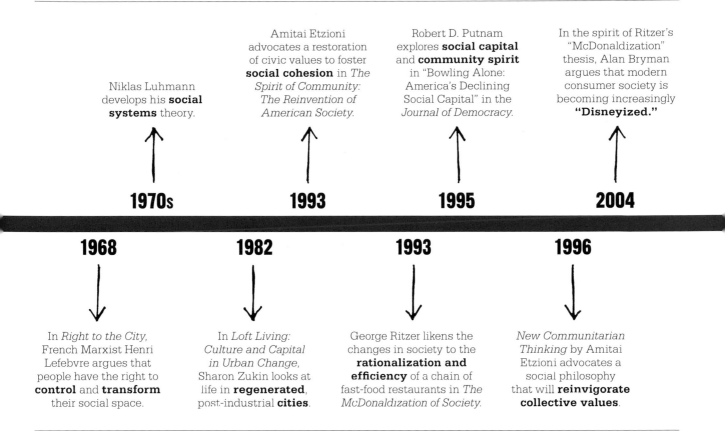

Niklas Luhmann develops his **social systems** theory.

Amitai Etzioni advocates a restoration of civic values to foster **social cohesion** in *The Spirit of Community: The Reinvention of American Society*.

Robert D. Putnam explores **social capital** and **community spirit** in "Bowling Alone: America's Declining Social Capital" in the *Journal of Democracy*.

In the spirit of Ritzer's "McDonaldization" thesis, Alan Bryman argues that modern consumer society is becoming increasingly **"Disneyized."**

1970s   **1993**   **1995**   **2004**

1968   **1982**   **1993**   **1996**

In *Right to the City*, French Marxist Henri Lefebvre argues that people have the right to **control** and **transform** their social space.

In *Loft Living: Culture and Capital in Urban Change*, Sharon Zukin looks at life in **regenerated**, post-industrial **cities**.

George Ritzer likens the changes in society to the **rationalization and efficiency** of a chain of fast-food restaurants in *The McDonaldization of Society*.

New Communitarian Thinking by Amitai Etzioni advocates a social philosophy that will **reinvigorate collective values**.

urban environment, what he called their "social space." Similarly (but from a different political standpoint), Jane Jacobs advocated that people should resist the plans of urban developers and create environments that encouraged the formation of communities within the city.

In the late 20th century, several sociologists took up this idea of the loss of community in our increasingly individualized Western society. A communitarian movement emerged, led by US sociologist Amitai Etzioni, suggesting new ways to restore community spirit in what had become an impersonal society. Robert D. Putnam also gave prominence to the idea of community in his explanation of "social capital," and the value and benefits of social interaction.

Not everyone agreed, however, that the answer to the social problems of urban life was a return to traditional community values. Niklas Luhmann pointed out that the problem today is one of communication between social systems that have become increasingly fragmented and differentiated. In the post-industrial age, with all its new methods of communication, new strategies for social cohesion need to be found.

Post-industrial cities
The nature of cities began to change in the late 20th century, as the manufacturing industries moved out or disappeared. While some cities became ghost towns, others became centers of the service industries. As working-class areas were gentrified, and

industrial buildings became desirable postmodern living spaces, the concept of modern metropolitan life became associated with prosperity rather than gritty industrialization.

This manifested itself not only in the transformation of urban living spaces, as described by Sharon Zukin in the 1980s, but throughout the postmodern social order. George Ritzer likened the efficiency and rationalization of the service industries to the business model pioneered by fast-food chain McDonalds, and Alan Bryman has noted how a US entertainment culture created by Disney has influenced modern consumerism. Modern urban society, having been created by industrialization, is now being shaped by the new demands of post-industrial commerce. ∎

STRANGERS ARE NOT REALLY CONCEIVED AS INDIVIDUALS BUT AS STRANGERS OF A PARTICULAR TYPE
GEORG SIMMEL (1858–1918)

IN CONTEXT

FOCUS
Mental life of the metropolis

KEY DATES
19th century Urbanization begins taking place on a large scale in Europe and the US.

From 1830 Nascent sociology claims to offer the means to understand the changes brought about in society by the Industrial Revolution.

1850–1900 Key social thinkers such as Ferdinand Tönnies, Émile Durkheim, and Karl Marx express concerns about the effect of modernization and industrialization on society.

From the 1920s Simmel's work on the impact of urban life influences the development of urban sociology in the US by a group of sociologists, known collectively as the Chicago School.

The Industrial Revolution was accompanied in Europe and the US by urbanization from the 19th century onward. For many people, this resulted in increased freedom as they experienced liberation from the constraints of traditional social structures. But in tandem with these developments came growing demands from capitalist employers for the functional specialization of people and their work, which meant new restrictions and curtailments of individual liberty.

German sociologist Georg Simmel wanted to understand the struggle faced by the city dweller in preserving autonomy and individuality in the face of these overwhelming social forces. He discovered that the increase in human interaction that was brought about by living and

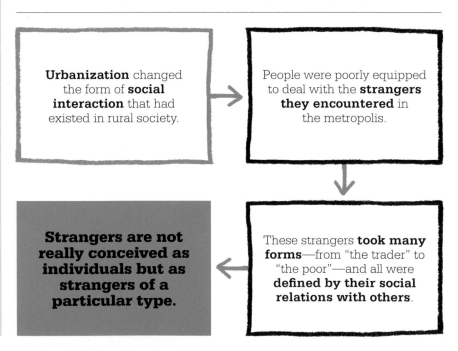

Urbanization changed the form of **social interaction** that had existed in rural society.

People were poorly equipped to deal with the **strangers they encountered** in the metropolis.

These strangers **took many forms**—from "the trader" to "the poor"—and all were **defined by their social relations with others**.

Strangers are not really conceived as individuals but as strangers of a particular type.

See also: Karl Marx 28–31 ▪ Ferdinand Tönnies 32–33 ▪ Émile Durkheim 34–37 ▪ Max Weber 38–45 ▪
Zygmunt Bauman 136–43 ▪ Thorstein Veblen 214–19 ▪ Erving Goffman 264–69 ▪ Michel Foucault 270–77

working in an urban environment profoundly affected relationships between people. He set out his findings in *The Metropolis and Mental Life*. Whereas in pre-modern society people would be intimately familiar with those around them, in the modern urban environment individuals are largely unknown to those who surround them. Simmel believed that the increase in social activity and anonymity brought about a change in consciousness.

The rapid tempo of life in a city was such that people needed a "protective organ" to insulate them from the external and internal stimuli. According to Simmel, the metropolitan "reacts with his head instead of his heart"; he erects a rational barrier of cultivated indifference—a "blasé attitude." The change in consciousness also leads to people becoming reserved and aloof. This estrangement from traditional and accepted norms of behavior is further undermined by the money culture of cities, which reduces everything in the metropolis to a financial exchange.

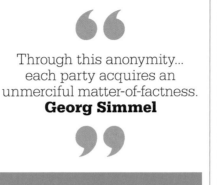

> Through this anonymity...
> each party acquires an
> unmerciful matter-of-factness.
> **Georg Simmel**

Simmel says that the attitude of the metropolitan can be understood as a social-survival technique to cope with the mental disturbance created by immersion in city life— an approach that enables people to focus their energies on those who matter to them. It also results in them becoming more tolerant of difference and more sophisticated.

Space in the metropolis

Degrees of proximity and distance among individuals and groups were central to Simmel's understanding of living in a metropolis, and ideas about social space influenced one of his best-known concepts: the social role of "the stranger," which is set out in an essay in *Sociology*. In the past, he says, strangers were encountered only rarely and fleetingly; but urbanite strangers are not drifters—they are "potential wanderers." Simmel says that the stranger (such as a trader), or the stranger group (his example is "European Jews"), is connected to the community spatially but not socially; he or she is characterized by both "nearness and remoteness"—*in* the community but not *of* it.

The stranger was one of many social types described by Simmel, each becoming what they are through their relations with others; an idea that has influenced many sociologists, including Zygmunt Bauman. Erving Goffman's concept of "civil inattention," whereby people minimize social interaction in public—by avoiding eye contact, for instance—is also informed by one of Simmel's insights: his notion of the "blasé attitude." ▪

Georg Simmel

Born in Berlin in 1858 to a prosperous Jewish family, Georg Simmel is one of the lesser-known founders of sociology. He studied philosophy and history at the University of Berlin and received his doctorate in 1881. Despite the popularity of his work with the German intellectual elite, notably Ferdinand Tönnies and Max Weber, he remained an outsider and only gained his professorship at Strasbourg in 1914.

He developed what is known as formal sociology, which derives from his belief that we can understand distinct human phenomena by concentrating not on the content of interactions but on the forms that underlie behavior. But it is his study of life in a metropolis that remains his most influential work, as it was the precursor to the development of urban sociology by the so-called Chicago School in the 1920s.

Key works

1900 *The Philosophy of Money*
1903 *The Metropolis and Mental Life*
1908 *Sociology*

THE FREEDOM TO REMAKE OUR CITIES AND OURSELVES
HENRI LEFEBVRE (1901–1991)

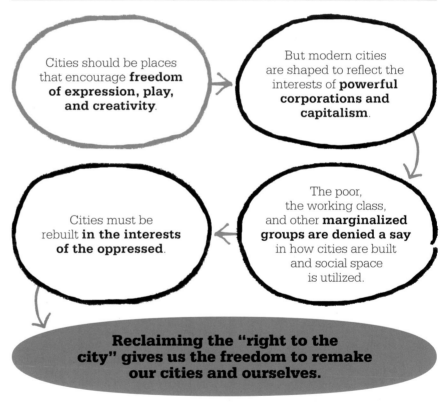

Cities should be places that encourage **freedom of expression, play, and creativity**.

But modern cities are shaped to reflect the interests of **powerful corporations and capitalism**.

The poor, the working class, and other **marginalized groups are denied a say** in how cities are built and social space is utilized.

Cities must be rebuilt **in the interests of the oppressed**.

Reclaiming the "right to the city" gives us the freedom to remake our cities and ourselves.

The city need not be seen as a concrete jungle—grimy, unpleasant, and threatening. For French sociologist and philosopher Henri Lefebvre, who dedicated most of his life to the study of urban society, it is an exciting and complex combination of power relationships, diverse identities, and ways of being.

Writing in the 1960s and 1970s, Lefebvre maintained that one of the most fascinating aspects of the city is not simply the people in it, but

See also: Karl Marx 28–31 ▪ Ferdinand Tönnies 32–33 ▪ Peter Townsend 74 ▪ Elijah Anderson 82–83 ▪
Georg Simmel 104–05 ▪ Jane Jacobs 108–09 ▪ Amitai Etizoni 112–19 ▪ Sharon Zukin 128–31 ▪ Saskia Sassen 164–65

Vast, impersonal malls serve the interests of consumer capitalism. The construction of such spaces often leads to the displacement of the area's original, working-class residents.

the fact that it is an environment that both reflects and creates society. Applying a Marxist perspective to his analysis, Lefebvre also says that urban spaces are shaped by the state and serve the interests of powerful corporations and capitalism. Parts of the city mirror the class relations contained within it: the opulence of some areas reveals the power and wealth of elites, while run-down inner-city areas and ghettos outside the center indicate the displacement and marginalization of the poor, the working class, and other excluded groups.

Public and private

Many modern cities, for example, have become dominated by private spaces, such as shopping malls and office complexes, built in the service of capitalism. The loss of public space has severely restricted the arenas in which people can meet on an equal footing with others, so eroding their personal freedoms and stifling their means to satisfy their social and psychological needs. This can lead to serious social problems, such as crime, depression, homelessness, social exclusion, and poverty.

Considerable power is wielded by those who own and control urban spaces—architects, planners, "the merchant bourgeoisie, the intellectuals, and politicians," according to Lefebvre. But he believes that decisions about the exact nature of the urban environment—what takes place in it, how social space is built and used—should be open to all. Ordinary people should participate in creating a space that reflects their needs and interests—only by claiming this "right to the city" can major social issues be addressed.

Lefebvre's vision is of cities that pulse with life and are vibrant expressions of human freedom and creativity, where people can play, explore their creative and artistic needs, and achieve some form of self-realization. City streets should, he says, be designed to encourage this type of existence—they may be raw, exciting, and untamed but precisely because of this they will remind people that they are alive.

Lefebvre's demand for the right to the city is not simply a call for a series of reforms but for a wholesale transformation of social relations within the city, if not wider society—it is, in essence, a proposal for a radical form of democracy, whereby control is wrested from elites and turned over to the masses. This, he says, is only achievable by groups and class factions "capable of revolutionary initiative." ▪

Henri Lefebvre

Marxist sociologist and philosopher Henri Lefebvre was born in Hagetmau, France, in 1901. He studied philosophy at the Sorbonne, Paris, graduating in 1920. He joined the French Communist Party in 1928 and became one of the most prominent Marxist intellectuals in France. He was, however, later expelled by the Communist Party and became one of its fiercest critics. In 1961 he was appointed professor of sociology at the University of Strasbourg, before moving to Nanterre in 1965. Lefebvre was a prolific writer on a wide range of subjects. His work challenged the dominant capitalist authorities and as such was not always well received, but has gone on to influence several disciplines, including geography, philosophy, sociology, political science, and architecture.

Key works

1968 *Right to the City*
1970 *The Urban Revolution*
1974 *The Production of Space*

THERE MUST BE EYES ON THE STREET
JANE JACOBS (1916–2006)

IN CONTEXT

FOCUS
Urban community

KEY DATES
1887 Ferdinand Tönnies' *Gemeinschaft und Gesellschaft* stirs sociological interest in the bonds of community in urban society.

From the 1950s Inner city neighborhoods in Western cities experience waves of pressure from city planners.

2000 US sociologist Robert D. Putnam argues in *Bowling Alone* that community values have eroded since the 1960s.

2002 In *The Rise of The Creative Class*, US sociologist and economist Richard Florida cites Jacobs as an influence on his theories of creativity.

2013 Increased use of camera surveillance in US cities after 9/11 results in the identification of suspects wanted for the Boston Marathon bombings.

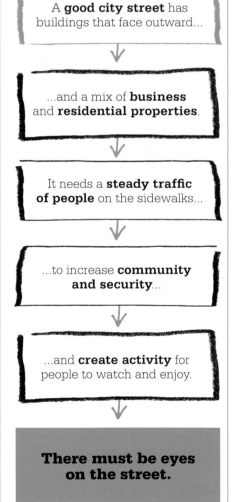

A **good city street** has buildings that face outward...

...and a mix of **business and residential properties**.

It needs a **steady traffic of people** on the sidewalks...

...to increase **community and security**...

...and **create activity** for people to watch and enjoy.

There must be eyes on the street.

Jane Jacobs spent her working life advancing a distinct vision of the city—in particular focusing on what makes a successful urban community. Her ideas were formed from her observations of urban life in the neighborhood of West Greenwich Village, New York, where she lived for more than 30 years.

Jacobs was opposed to the large-scale changes to city life that were occurring in New York during the 1960s, led by city planner and her archrival Howard Moses; these included slum-clearance projects and the building of high-rise developments. At the heart of her vision is the idea that urban life should be a vibrant and rich affair, whereby people are able to interact with one another in dense and exciting urban environments. She prefers chaos to order, walking to driving, and diversity to uniformity.

For Jacobs, urban communities are organic entities—complex, integrated ecosystems—that should be left to grow and to change by themselves and not be subject to the grand plans of so-called experts and technocrats. The best judges of how a city should be—and how it should

Jane Jacobs' vision of what a city street should be like is exemplified by this New York scene of vibrant urban life, with residential apartments, street-level businesses, and sidewalk bustle.

evolve—are the local residents themselves. Jacobs argues that urban communities are best placed to understand how their city functions, because city life is created and sustained through their various interactions.

Ballet of the sidewalk

Jacobs notes that the built form of a city is crucial to the life of an urban community. Of prime importance are the sidewalks. The streets in which people live should be a tight pattern of intersecting sidewalks, which allow people to meet, bump into each other, converse, and get to know one another. She calls this the "ballet of the sidewalk," a complex but ultimately enriching set of encounters that help individuals become acquainted with their neighbors and neighborhood.

Diversity and mixed-use of space are also, for Jacobs, key elements of this urban form. The commercial, business, and residential elements of a city should not be separated out but instead be side by side, to allow for greater integration of people. There should also be a diversity of old and new buildings, and people's interactions should determine how buildings get used and reused.

Finally, urban communities flourish better in places where a critical mass of people live, work, and interact. Such high-density—but not overcrowded—spaces are, she feels, engines of creativity and vibrancy. They are also safe places to be, because the higher density means that there are more "eyes on the street": shopkeepers and locals who know their area and provide a natural form of surveillance ▪

Jane Jacobs

Jane Jacobs was a passionate writer and urbanist. She left Scranton, Pennsylvania for New York in 1935, during the Great Depression. After seeing the Greenwich Village area for the first time, she relocated there from Brooklyn—her interest in urban communities had begun. In 1944 she married, and moved into a house on Hudson Street.

It was when Jacobs was working as a writer for the magazine *Architectural Forum* that she first began to be critical of large top-down urban regeneration schemes. Throughout her life she was an activist and campaigner for her community-based vision of the city.

In 2007 the Rockefeller Foundation created the Jane Jacobs Medal in her honor to celebrate urban visionaries whose actions in New York City affirm her principles.

Key works

1961 *The Death and Life of Great American Cities*
1969 *The Economy of Cities*
1984 *Cities and the Wealth of Nations*

ONLY COMMUNICATION CAN COMMUNICATE
NIKLAS LUHMANN (1927–1998)

IN CONTEXT

FOCUS
Systems of communication

KEY DATES
1937 US sociologist Talcott Parsons discusses systems theory in *The Structure of Social Action*.

1953 Austrian philosopher Ludwig Wittgenstein's concept of language games is published posthumously and influences Luhmann's ideas on communication.

1969 *Laws of Form* by British mathematician George Spencer-Brown underpins Luhmann's ideas about structural differentiation.

1987 German sociologist Jürgen Habermas engages Luhmann in critical debate about systems theory.

2009 Luhmann's ideas are applied by Greek scholar Andreas Mihalopoulos in his analysis of the criminal justice and legal systems.

Modern society has **distinct social systems** (the economy, the law, education, politics, and so on).

These **systems give meaning to the world**, yet they consist not of people but of **communications**.

Each **system** processes activities and problems in its own distinctive way, so **cannot connect to other systems** without assistance.

Structural couplings enable **restricted communications** between the different communication systems.

Modernity's defining feature, according to German sociologist Niklas Luhmann, is advanced capitalist society's differentiation into separate social systems— the economic, educational, scientific, legal, political, religious, and so on. Luhmann argues that the term "society" refers to the system that encompasses all the other systems: society is, he says, the system of systems.

Individuals, Luhmann insists, are socially meaningless. Society's base element is not the human actor but "communication"—a term that he defines as the "synthesis of information, utterance, and understanding" arising out of the

See also: Max Weber 38–45 ▪ Jürgen Habermas 286–87 ▪ Talcott Parsons 300–01 ▪ Herbert Spencer 334 ▪ Alfred Schütz 335

activities and interactions, verbal and nonverbal, within a system. Luhmann argues that just as a plant reproduces its own cells in a circular, biological process of self-production, so a social system is similarly self-sustaining and develops out of an operation that possesses connectivity—emerging when "communication develops from communication." He likens communication to the structural equivalent of a chemical.

Structural couplings

Luhmann uses George Spencer-Brown's ideas on the mathematical laws of form to help define a system, arguing that something arises out of difference: a system is, according to this theory, a "distinction" from its environment. And, says Luhmann, a system's environment is constituted by other systems. For example, the environment of a family system includes other families, the political system, the medical system, and so on. Crucially, each individual system can only make sense of the

events—the activities and ways of communicating—peculiar to itself; it is relatively indifferent to what takes place in the other systems (and the wider society). So, for example, the economic system is functionally dedicated to its own interests and is uninterested in moral issues, except where these might have an impact on the profitability of economic activities and transactions—whereas moral concerns are of great consequence in, say, the religious system.

Luhmann identifies this lack of systems integration as one of the major problems confronting advanced capitalist societies. He identifies what he calls "structural couplings"—certain forms and institutions that help to connect separated systems by translating the communications produced by one system into terms that the other can understand. Examples include a constitution, which couples the legal and political systems, and a university, which couples the educational and, among others, economic systems.

Artists protest at BP's sponsorship of London's Tate Britain art gallery, reflecting the protesters belief that the system of corporate enterprise is not compatible with that of the art world.

"Structural coupling" is a concept that helps to account for the relationship between people (as conscious systems) and social systems (as communications).

Despite its extreme complexity, Luhmann's theory is used worldwide as an analytical tool for social systems. His critics say that the theory passes academic scrutiny, but operationally it fails to show how communication can take place without human activity. ▪

Humans cannot communicate; not even their brains can communicate; not even their conscious minds can communicate.
Niklas Luhmann

Niklas Luhmann

Niklas Luhmann studied law at the University of Freiburg, Germany, from 1946 to 1949, before becoming a civil servant in 1956. He spent 1960 to 1961 on sabbatical at Harvard University, studying sociology and administrative science, where he was taught by Talcott Parsons.

In 1966 Luhmann received his doctorate in sociology from the University of Münster and in 1968 he became professor of sociology at the University of

Bielefeld, where he remained. Luhmann was the recipient of several honorary degrees, and in 1988 he was the winner of the prestigious Hegel Prize, awarded to prominent thinkers by the city of Stuttgart. He was a prolific writer, with some 377 publications to his name.

Key works

1972 *A Sociological Theory of Law*
1984 *Social Systems*
1997 *Theory of Society* (two volumes)

SOCIETY
SHOULD ARTICULATE
WHAT IS GOOD
AMITAI ETZIONI (1929–)

IN CONTEXT

FOCUS
Communitarianism

KEY DATES
1887 *Gemeinschaft und Gesellschaft* (*Community and Society*) by Ferdinand Tönnies extols the value of community.

1947 German thinker Martin Buber's *Paths to Utopia* anticipates the modern communitarianism movement.

1993 The Communitarian Network, a nonpartisan, transnational, and nonprofit coalition is founded.

1999 US scholar and republican communitarian Stephen Goldsmith joins former president George W. Bush's advisory team for social policy.

2005 British sociologist Colin Gray publishes an article entitled "Sandcastles of Theory," arguing that Etzioni's work is overly utopian.

From the end of World War II to the early 1970s, the US experienced rapid economic growth, which resulted in increasing prosperity and upward social mobility for the vast majority of its citizens. The social and political landscape of the country changed too, with the Civil Rights movement, organized opposition to the Vietnam War, the sexual revolution, and feminism becoming prominent.

In 1973, however, the oil crisis and stock market crash sent the US economy into sudden decline and—according to sociologist Amitai Etzioni—the basis of traditional values on which US culture was founded began to crumble.

The response to this cultural and moral crisis, and to the concurrent rise of the ideology of individualism and liberal economic policy—where the free market is allowed to operate with minimal government intervention—was the emergence of the social philosophy of communitarianism. In Etzioni's words, its aims were to: "...restore civic virtues, for people to live up to their responsibilities and not merely focus on their

A responsive community is one whose moral standards reflect the basic human needs of all its members.
Amitai Etzioni

entitlements, to shore up the moral foundations of society." The guiding principle of his form of communitarianism is that society should articulate what is good, through the shared consensus of its members and the principles embodied in its communities and institutions.

Furthermore, for Etzioni, it was not enough for sociologists to *think* about and contemplate social life; rather, they should be actively involved in trying to *change* society for the better. By the early 1990s, a growing number of US social thinkers—including sociologists

---

Amitai Etzioni

Amitai Etzioni was born in Germany in 1929 and by the age of seven was living in Palestine with his family. In 1946 he left education to join the Palmach and fight for the creation of Israel. Some five years later he was a student in an institution where the Jewish existential philosopher Martin Buber had worked. Buber's focus on the "I and Thou" relationship resonates throughout Etzioni's approach toward communitarian living.

In 1951 Etzioni enrolled in the Hebrew University of Jerusalem, where he gained BA and MA

degrees; in 1958 he obtained his PhD in sociology from the University of California, Berkeley. His first post was at New York's Columbia University where he served for 20 years. In 1980 he became a professor at George Washington University, where he serves as the director of the Institute for Communitarian Policy Studies.

Key works

1993 *The Spirit of Community: The Reinvention of American Society*

See also: Karl Marx 28–31 ▪ Ferdinand Tönnies 32–33 ▪ Émile Durkheim 34–37 ▪ Richard Sennett 84–87 ▪ Jane Jacobs 108–09 ▪ Robert D. Putnam 124–25 ▪ Anthony Giddens 148–9 ▪ Daniel Bell 224–25 ▪ Robert N. Bellah 336

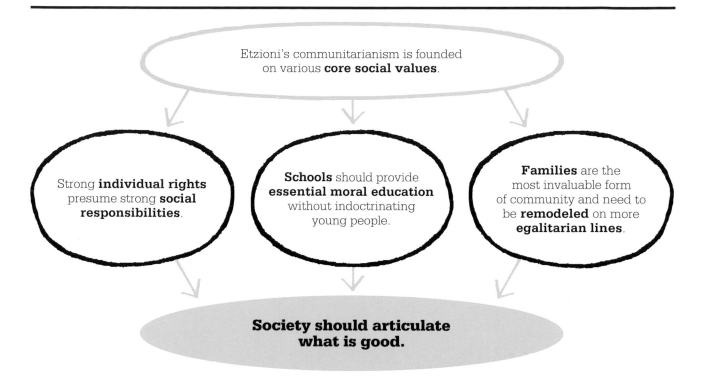

Etzioni's communitarianism is founded on various **core social values**.

Strong **individual rights** presume strong **social responsibilities**.

Schools should provide **essential moral education** without indoctrinating young people.

Families are the most invaluable form of community and need to be **remodeled** on more **egalitarian lines**.

Society should articulate what is good.

Robert D. Putnam, Richard Sennett, and Daniel Bell—self-consciously sought to extend communitarian ideals from the university campus into the wider society.

Responsibilities and rights

The roots of Etzioni's ideas lie in the work of earlier theorists, such as German sociologist Ferdinand Tönnies, who had distinguished between two types of social ties, *Gemeinschaft* (community) and *Gesellschaft* (association). The first referred to personal relationships and face-to-face interactions that created communal society; the

second to ties created by rational self-interest, bureaucracies, and formal beliefs.

Tönnies held that the defining principles of *Gesellschaft* in modern society represented a backward step in the development of human

relations compared to the high levels of solidarity found in traditional forms of communal living—*Gemeinschaft*. Although Etzioni developed the communitarian thinking of Tönnies, he believed that Tönnies overemphasized the »

Life in pre-industrial societies was strongly focused on communal living (as in the European village scene shown here), but Etzioni says this was often at the expense of the individual.

communal at the expense of the individual. Tönnies' contemporary Émile Durkheim, on the other hand, feared that modernity might threaten social solidarity; for him, individuals had to be social beings whose ambitions and needs coincided with the group.

Etzioni says that *Gemeinschaft* communities also have drawbacks: they can often be oppressive, authoritarian, and hinder individual growth and development. His updated form of communitarianism is designed to achieve the optimum degree of equilibrium between the individual and society, between community and autonomy, and between rights and responsibilities.

Etzioni argues that striking a balance between individual rights and community responsibilities is essential, because one cannot exist without the other. Moreover, he claims that present-day Americans have lost sight of the ways in which the fortunes of the individual and those of the community are bound up with one another. Americans have a strong sense of entitlement—expectations that the community

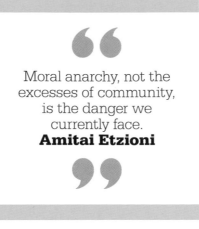

> Moral anarchy, not the excesses of community, is the danger we currently face.
> **Amitai Etzioni**

will provide services, and respect and uphold individual rights—but a weakened sense of moral obligation to the community, both local and national. For example, most young Americans claim that, if charged with a crime, it is their inalienable right to be judged by their peers, yet only a small minority would be willing to do jury service.

According to Etzioni, this major decline in "social capital"—the relations founded on the shared values of reciprocity, trust, and a sense of obligation—across US

society has been brought about by an excess of individualism and is what makes it necessary, more than ever, for the US to adopt the moral principles of communitarianism.

What is a community?

For Etzioni, communities are webs of social relations "that encompass shared meanings and above all else shared values." The views of a community cannot be imposed by an outside group or internal minority, but must be "generated by the members of community in a dialogue that is open to all and fully responsive to the membership." Etzioni's community is inherently democratic, and each community is nested "within a more encompassing one." This definition of community is applicable to a variety of forms of social organization, from micro

Chinatowns, found in Western cities, exemplify Etzioni's community living. Recreating this culture on foreign soil is made possible by the inhabitants upholding shared norms and values.

Communities rather than individuals are, says Etzioni, the elemental building blocks of society, and society comprises multiple, overlapping communities. People are therefore characteristically members of many different intersecting communities.

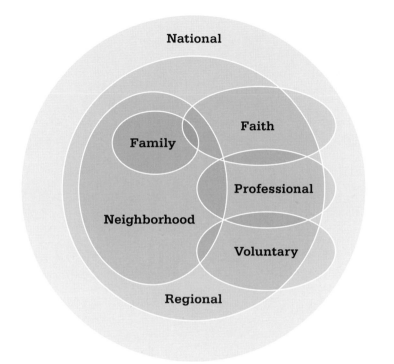

formations, such as families and schools, through macro formations, such as ethnic groups, religions, or nation-states.

Communities need not be geographically concentrated: for example, the Jewish community in New York is dispersed across the city but nevertheless maintains a strong sense of moral solidarity through core institutions such as synagogues and faith-based schools. Etzioni even counts online Internet-based communities as legitimate forms of community, provided that members are committed to, and share, the same values. Conversely, some classically conceived communities, such as villages, do not meet Etzoni's criteria if the aggregate of the people comprising the village are not bound by an obvious commitment to shared norms and values.

Communities are not always virtuous: some may be harsh and confining, or they may be founded on shared values that are far from ethical. Etzioni cites the example of an Afrikaaner village in South Africa whose members supported and colluded in lynching.

The communal society

Rather than just operating at the intellectual level, Etzioni proposes four aspects of how a communitarian society should be implemented and organized. He does this by identifying the core aspects of communitarian society and the functions each one plays in relation to the wider social whole.

The first aspect is what Etzioni calls the "moral voice"—the name given to the shared set of collectively assembled norms and values on which the interpersonal and moral conduct that binds community members is based. No society can thrive without a solid moral order, especially if reliance on state intervention in public matters is to be kept to a minimum. By identifying and establishing a moral voice, it is no longer necessary to rely on either individual conscience or law enforcement agencies to regulate the conduct of community members. When communities value certain behaviors—such as avoiding alcohol abuse and not speeding—antisocial behaviors are prevented, and tend to be curbed effectively.

Second is the "communitarian family." Bringing a child into this world not only obligates the parents to the child but the family to the community too. When children are raised poorly, the consequences must usually be faced not just by the family but by the entire »

Two-parent families, Etzioni claims, are far better equipped to undertake the job of rearing children than one-parent families, because it is a "labor intensive, demanding task."

School leavers should enroll for military service (as at these barracks in Germany in 2011), Etzioni argues, because it instills self-discipline and builds character and community spirit.

community. It is for this reason, according to Etzioni, that the procreation, and bringing up, of children should be considered a communitarian act. Etzioni argues that parents have a moral responsibility to the community to raise their children to the best of their ability; and the communities have an obligation to help them in their efforts. Communities should support and encourage, rather than stigmatize, parents who take a respite from work in order to spend time with their children.

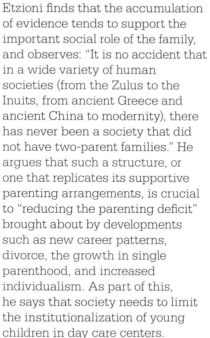

Education, particularly character formation, is the essential family task.
Amitai Etzioni

Etzioni finds that the accumulation of evidence tends to support the important social role of the family, and observes: "It is no accident that in a wide variety of human societies (from the Zulus to the Inuits, from ancient Greece and ancient China to modernity), there has never been a society that did not have two-parent families." He argues that such a structure, or one that replicates its supportive parenting arrangements, is crucial to "reducing the parenting deficit" brought about by developments such as new career patterns, divorce, the growth in single parenthood, and increased individualism. As part of this, he says that society needs to limit the institutionalization of young children in day care centers.

Etzioni's third principle sets out the functions of the "communitarian school." Schools should do far more than transmitting skills and knowledge to pupils. They should build upon the task of character formation initiated by parents to help lay the foundations for a stable

sense of self, of purposefulness, and the ability to control impulses and defer immediate gratification. In particular, the values of discipline, self-discipline, and internalization—the integration of the values of others into one's own sense of self—play a major role in the child's psychological development and wellbeing.

As part of his emphasis on self-discipline, Etzioni argues that all school leavers should undertake a mandatory year of national service. Doing so, he claims, would provide "a strong antidote to the ego-centered mentality as youth serve shared needs."

Fourth, and finally, Etzioni puts forward measures intended to counter the loss of traditional community while also serving as the basis on which to build new communities. These include changing what US sociologist Robert N. Bellah termed "habits of the heart." Etzioni's measures include fostering a "community environment" in which thinking about our individual actions in

The imbalance between rights and responsibilities has existed for a long time.
Amitai Etzioni

terms of their consequences for the wider community becomes second nature; working out conflicts between individual career aspirations and goals and commitments to the community; redesigning the physical, lived environment in order "to render it more community-friendly"; and seeking to reinvest more of our personal and professional resources back into the community.

Criticisms

Etzioni's communitarianism is a response to a range of real concerns about the deterioration of private and public morality and shared values, the decline of the family, high crime rates, and civic and political apathy across US society.

Volunteers play an important part in thousands of organizations across North America and Western Europe, including community tree-planting projects in many neighborhoods.

His vision of a more democratic, just, and egalitarian society is commended by scholars and commentators from a wide range of ideological positions. However, Etzioni's work has also drawn criticism. For example, some supporters of feminism object strongly to communitarianism as an attempt to undo women's economic liberation. They argue that a mother with a full-time job now spends more quality time with her children than the average homemaker did 30 years ago. Beatrix Campbell has accused the communitarians of a "nostalgic crusade," pointing out that the kind of mother they evoke did not exist.

US sociologist and political theorist Richard Sennett claims Etzioni's work fails to address the nature of political and economic power other than in the vaguest of terms, and does not provide a convincing account of what might motivate individuals to commit to

Today there is increasing interest among youngsters... in finding careers... [in which] you can combine 'making it' with something meaningful.
Amitai Etzioni

communitarian principles and values. If, as Etzioni claims, US culture is self-obsessed and overly individualistic, then he fails to provide an answer as to why anyone would choose to take on responsibility to a community that would make demands of them and potentially impinge upon their individual rights.

In spite of criticisms, many of the ideas at the heart of Etzioni's communitarianism have influenced governments. In his book *The Third Way,* British sociologist Anthony Giddens sees Etzioni's work as central to the framework of the political philosophy known as the Third Way, developed by former British prime minister Tony Blair. Etzioni's work appealed to the UK's New Labour government in two distinct ways: first, it provided middle ground between the political Left, with its overemphasis on the role to be played by the State, and the political Right, with its exaggerated support of the free market and championing of the individual; second, it presented the notion of citizenship as something that has to be earned through the fulfillment of shared expectations and obligations. ■

MCDONALDIZATION AFFECTS VIRTUALLY EVERY ASPECT OF SOCIETY

GEORGE RITZER (1940–)

IN CONTEXT

FOCUS
McDonaldization

KEY DATES
1921–1922 Max Weber's *Economy and Society*, which analyzes the relationship between rationality and bureaucracy, is published in Germany.

1961 US entrepreneurs Richard ("Dick") and Maurice ("Mac") McDonald sell their pioneering fast-food burger business to Ray Kroc, who develops it worldwide.

1997 The sushi restaurant chain YO! Sushi opens in Britain, self-consciously using the McDonald's model.

1999 British sociologist Barry Smart edits *Resisting McDonaldization*, a wide-ranging collection of critical responses to Ritzer's McDonaldization thesis.

German sociologist Max Weber argued that a defining feature of the shift from traditional to modern society was the ever-growing number of aspects of life that were organized and enacted along rational, as opposed to emotionally oriented or value-laden, lines.

Developing Weber's ideas, US sociologist George Ritzer claims that the process has reached new levels in both North American and Western European culture, and is now manifested in unprecedented ways. According to Ritzer, author of the 1993 sociological classic *The McDonaldization of Society*, this "wide-ranging process of

See also: Karl Marx 28–31 ▪ Max Weber 38–45 ▪ Roland Robertson 146–47 ▪ Herbert Marcuse 182–87 ▪ Harry Braverman 226–31 ▪ Karl Mannheim 335

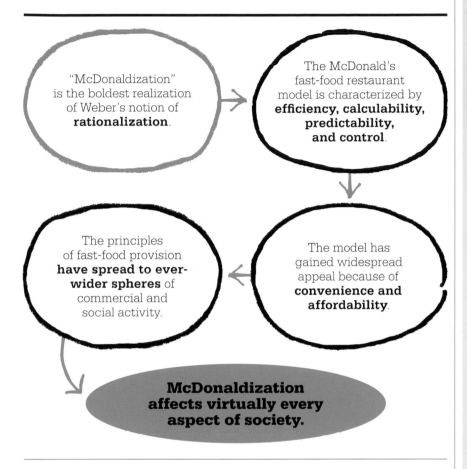

George Ritzer

George Ritzer was born in 1940 in New York City. His father drove a taxi and his mother worked as a secretary. Ritzer claims that his upbringing inspired him to work as hard as he could at his studies in order to distance himself from the often lowly standard of living that characterized his "upper lower-class" childhood.

Since 1974, George Ritzer has been at the University of Maryland, where he is now Distinguished University Professor. While the McDonaldization thesis is his best-known and most influential contribution to sociological theory, he is primarily a critic of so-called consumer society and has published prolifically across a wide range of areas.

Key works

1993 *The McDonaldization of Society: An Investigation into the Changing Character of Social Life*
1999 *Enchanting a Disenchanted World: Revolutionizing the Means of Consumption*
2004 *The Globalization of Nothing*

rationalization" is most clearly exemplified by the McDonald's fast-food restaurant chain.

The McDonald's way

Wherever you are in the world, a McDonald's restaurant never seems to be far away. In fact, there are around 35,000 restaurants in more than 100 countries around the globe. And no matter where that happens to be, there is a virtually flawless level of uniformity and reliability. This familiarity of experience is a definitive feature of McDonald's restaurants all over the world and it is directly attributable to the strong emphasis the McDonald's corporation places on rationalization. Ritzer terms this development "McDonaldization," and claims that the tendencies and processes it refers to have infiltrated, and now dominate, "more and more sectors of American society as well as the rest of the world." He argues that McDonaldization has five main components: efficiency, calculability, predictability, control, and "the ultimate irrationality of formal rationality."

Efficiency refers to the bureaucratic principles employed by the corporation as it strives, from the level of organizational structure down to the interactions between employees and customers, to find »

A McDonald's next to Xi'an's historic Drum Tower. McDonald's opened its first outlet in China in 1990. By 2014, with 2,000 premises, it was China's second-biggest restaurant chain.

the optimum means to an end. For example, food preparation: burgers are assembled, cooked, and distributed in an assembly-line fashion because this is the most efficient way. Not only is this true in terms of the time taken to prepare food, but also the space necessary for doing so. Moreover, the physical layout of a McDonald's restaurant is designed in such a way that employees and customers alike behave in an efficient manner. A culture of efficiency is cultivated and maintained by staff adhering to a strict series of standardized norms, regulations, rules, and operational procedures.

Calculability refers to things that are counted and quantified; in particular, there is a tendency to emphasize quantity (the "Big Mac") over quality. Ritzer notes that many aspects of the work of employees at McDonald's are timed, because the fast-paced nature of the restaurant environment is intended to ensure maximum productivity.

Predictability affects the food products, restaurant design, and employee and customer interactions. Irrespective of the geographic setting, or the time of day or night, when customers enter a restaurant they want to know what to expect—and knowing what it is they want, where to find the menu, and how to order, they will be able to pay, eat, and leave.

Control is closely linked to technology. The machinery used to cook the food served in McDonald's restaurants dominates both employees and customers. The machines dictate cooking times, and so the pace of work for the employees; and the machines produce a uniform product so customers cannot specify how they would like their food to be cooked. Ritzer argues that—in time—

> 66
> McDonald's has become more important than the United States itself.
> **George Ritzer**
> 99

technologies that are more predictable and easier to control than people may come to replace employees entirely.

Finally, Ritzer assesses the costs of this otherwise beneficial rationalization. He acknowledges his debt to Weber in observing that, paradoxically, rational systems seem to spawn irrationalities and unintended consequences. The ultimate irrationality, Ritzer emphasizes, is the dehumanizing effects that the McDonald's model has on both employees and customers.

He notes that McDonald's employees work in mindless, production-line style jobs, often in cramped circumstances for little pay. There is virtually no scope for innovation and initiative on behalf of employees, either individually or collectively, resulting in worker dissatisfaction and alienation, and high staff-turnover rates.

The customers line up to buy and eat unhealthy food in what Ritzer describes as "dehumanizing settings and circumstances." Moreover, the speed of production and consumption in McDonald's restaurants means that, by definition, customers cannot be served high-quality food, which requires more time to prepare.

Principles of modernity

Ritzer argues that the sociological significance of these five principles of McDonaldization is their extension to an ever-greater number of spheres of social activity. In essence, the dominant cultural template for organizing all manner

> Within sociology, theory is one of the least likely elements to be McDonaldized, yet it too has undergone that process, at least to some extent.
> **George Ritzer**

of collective and individual actions and interactions is now shaped by efficiency, calculability, predictability, control, and rationalization costs.

This is an extension of Weber's argument that, once set in motion, the process of rationalization is self-perpetuating and proliferates until it covers virtually every aspect of social life. To remain competitive in the market, firms must adhere to the principles of rationality and efficiency being used by others. Ritzer cites a host of examples to substantiate his claims, including fast-food chains, such as Subway, and children's toy stores, such as Toys "R" Us. All of these corporations have self-consciously adopted McDonald's principles as a way of organizing their activities.

While Ritzer admires the efficiency and capacity to adapt to change demonstrated by the McDonald's fast-food chain since its inception in 1940, he is simultaneously wary of the

YO! Sushi restaurants in the UK enhance McDonald's rationalization approach by making the creation and distribution of the food into an urban, Tokyo-style eating experience.

dehumanizing effects that the pursuit of rationalization can lead to. Echoing Weber's notion of the "iron cage," Ritzer argues that although McDonald's has assumed iconic status as a highly efficient and profitable Western corporation, the spread of its principles across an increasing number of spheres of human activity leads to alienation.

As a transnational corporation, McDonald's plays a significant role as a carrier of Western rationality. To this end, according to Ritzer, McDonaldization is one of the key elements of global cultural homogenization. However, critics of this position, such as British sociologist John Tomlinson, rebut this charge by using the concept of glocalization. Tomlinson acknowledges that McDonald's is a global brand, but points out that it does make allowances for local contingencies and contexts. An example of this is the adaptation of products to conform to local dietary conventions, such as including vegetarian burgers on menus in India.

Two decades after it first appeared, Ritzer's McDonaldization thesis remains as pertinent as ever, if not more so. Ritzer and others have continued to work to apply, recalibrate, and update it across a range of topics, including the sociology of higher education. A collection of essays edited by British social thinkers Dennis Hayes and Robin Wynyard, *The McDonaldization of Higher Education*, contains a range of arguments that draw upon Ritzer. For example, Hayes claims that the traditional value-base on which higher education was founded— from college to postgraduate university-level education— is rapidly being replaced by standardization, calculability, and so on. Furthermore, argues Hayes, the McDonaldization of higher education holds true for students as much as it does for academic institutions and staff because, increasingly, the former approach education with a rational mindset as a means to an end, rather than as an end in itself. ∎

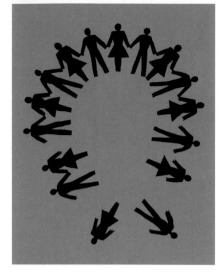

THE BONDS OF OUR COMMUNITIES HAVE WITHERED
ROBERT D. PUTNAM (1941–)

IN CONTEXT

FOCUS
Social capital

KEY DATES
1916 The term "social capital" is coined by US social reformer L.J. Hanifan, and refers to intangible things that count in daily life, such as "good will, fellowship, sympathy, and social intercourse."

2000 Finnish sociologist Martti Siisiäinen critically compares Pierre Bourdieu and Robert D. Putnam's respective concepts of social capital.

2000 The Saguaro Seminar at Harvard University produces "Better Together," a report led by Putnam and a team of scholars aimed at addressing the "critically low levels" of social capital in the US.

2013 Dutch social thinker Marlene Vock and others use the concept of social capital in "Understanding Willingness to Pay for Social Network Sites."

A recurrent theme animating early social thinkers was the fear that modern society was eroding traditional forms of community life, social cohesion, and a shared sense of solidarity. As valid as those concerns about change were, the 19th century was also a great era of voluntarism, during which people cooperated and established many of the institutions—such as schools, missions for the poor, and charities—that we know today.

Social capital grows from **a sense of common identity** and shared values such as **trust, reciprocity, good will, and fellowship**...

...which help to create the **voluntary associations and civic institutions** that bind communities together.

But our lifestyles are increasingly individualized and we have **disengaged from public affairs**, and even friends and neighbors.

The bonds of our communities have withered.

See also: Karl Marx 28–31 ▪ Pierre Bourdieu 76–79 ▪ Richard Sennett 84–87 ▪ Jane Jacobs 108–09 ▪ Amitai Etizoni 112–19 ▪ Sharon Zukin 128–31

Putnam's Saguaro Seminar, founded in 1995, is named after the cactus that he regards as a social metaphor—"it takes a long time to develop, and then it serves lots of unexpected purposes."

However, by the late 20th century, the state had taken on many of these responsibilities and the civic connections that once unified people had gone into decline.

The social glue that binds together individuals and wider collectives is referred to as "social capital" by the US sociologist Robert Putnam, and is reproduced through voluntary associations and social and civic networks. Americans today are wealthier than in the 1960s, says Putnam, but at the cost of a shared sense of moral obligation and community.

Three different types of links make up this social capital: bonds, bridges, and linkages. Bonds are forged from a sense of common identity, including family, friends, and community members. Bridges extend beyond shared identity to include colleagues, associates, and acquaintances. Linkages connect individuals or groups further up or lower down the social hierarchy. Differences in the type of social capital binding people are important. For example, bonds with

friends and family can help to secure a job, or provide a source of comfort at times of emotional need. But bonds can be restricting, too: in immigrant communities, bonds with fellow immigrants can hinder the formation of social bridges and linkages, which makes integration into wider society more difficult.

Civic engagement

Putnam's study *Bowling Alone* applies the concept of social capital to US society. He shows that the demise of traditional suburban neighborhoods and the increasing solitude that commuters and workers face daily—listening to iPods, or sitting in front of computer screens—means that people are not just far less likely to engage with voluntary and community-based initiatives, but also to spend less time socializing with friends, neighbors, and family.

Putnam uses ten-pin bowling to illustrate his point: the number of Americans taking up the sport has increased, but the proportion who join a team is in decline. People are literally "bowling alone" because the traditional community values of trust and reciprocity have been eroded, which impacts negatively upon voluntary associations and civically oriented organizations, from parent/teacher associations (PTAs) to local council committees. Since Putnam set up the Saguaro Seminar initiative in 1995 to look into aspects of civic engagement, his concept of social capital has become vastly influential, and has been applied to a wide range of phenomena spanning neighborhood quality of life and crime rates to voting behavior and church attendance. ▪

Robert D. Putnam

Robert David Putnam was born in 1941 in New York, and raised in the small town of Clinton, Ohio. With a degree from the University of Oxford, UK, and a doctorate from Yale, he directs the Saguaro Seminar and is the Malkin professor of Public Policy at Harvard University.

In 1995 his article "Bowling Alone: America's Declining Social Capital" began a debate about civic engagement and Putnam was invited to meet with then President Bill Clinton. Since then, with the article having become a book in 2000, his reputation has grown. In 2013 President Barack Obama awarded him the National Humanities Medal for his contributions to understanding and trying to ameliorate community life in the US.

Key works

2000 *Bowling Alone: The Collapse and Revival of American Community*
2002 *Democracies in Flux*
2003 *Better Together* (with Lewis M. Feldstein)

> The core idea of social capital theory is that social networks have value.
> **Robert Putnam**

DISNEYIZATION REPLACES MUNDANE BLANDNESS WITH SPECTACULAR EXPERIENCES

ALAN BRYMAN

IN CONTEXT

FOCUS
Disneyization

KEY DATES
1955 Walt Disney opens the first Disneyland to the general public in California, attracting 50,000 visitors on its first day.

From the 1980s The term "globalization" is used increasingly to refer to the growing interconnectedness of the world.

1981 In *Simulacra and Simulation*, Jean Baudrillard says, "Disneyland is presented as imaginary in order to make us believe that the rest is real, whereas all of Los Angeles and the America that surrounds it are no longer real, but belong to... the order of simulation."

1983–2005 Disney parks are opened in Tokyo, Paris, and Hong Kong.

1993 US scholar George Ritzer publishes *The McDonaldization of Society*.

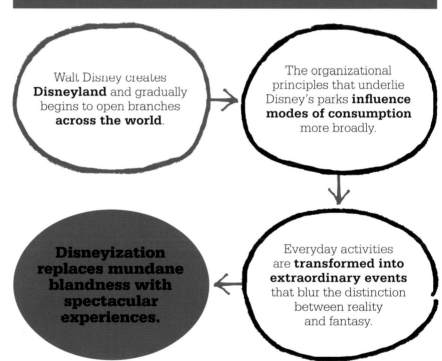

Walt Disney creates **Disneyland** and gradually begins to open branches **across the world**.

The organizational principles that underlie Disney's parks **influence modes of consumption** more broadly.

Everyday activities are **transformed into extraordinary events** that blur the distinction between reality and fantasy.

Disneyization replaces mundane blandness with spectacular experiences.

Modern consumer culture creates issues that have far-reaching implications. British professor Alan Bryman is interested in the impact that Disney theme parks have upon wider society and in how their model is influencing the ways in which services and products are made available for consumption.

Bryman argues that "Disneyization" lies at the heart of contemporary consumer society. The phenomenon is profoundly shaping our shopping experiences because, he says, the principles underlying the organization of such parks are increasingly dominating other areas: "Thus, the fake worlds of the Disney parks, which represent

See also: George Ritzer 120–23 ▪ Sharon Zukin 128–31 ▪ Jean Baudrillard 196–99 ▪ Arlie Hochschild 236–43

a nonexistent reality, become models for American society." Furthermore, Disneyization is also occurring in the rest of the world.

Blurring fantasy and reality

Bryman identifies four aspects to Disneyization: theming, hybrid consumption, merchandizing, and emotional labor.

Theming involves drawing on widely recognized cultural sources to create a popular environment—for example, using rock music as the theme of Hard Rock Café.

Hybrid consumption refers to areas where different kinds of consumption become interlinked: airports and sports arenas, for example, become shopping malls.

Merchandizing involves the promotion and sale of goods with copyrighted images and logos. For example, literature and films such as the *Harry Potter* series or *Shrek* generate a plethora of products from t-shirts to video games.

The term "emotional labor" was coined by Arlie Hochschild in *The Managed Heart* to describe

The Buddha Bar has franchises throughout the world and is an example of Bryman's "theming" theory, whereby a cultural source (in this case, religion), is used to create a product or venue.

a person altering their outward behavior to conform to an ideal. In Disneyization, this occurs where a job appears to become more of a performance, with a scripted interaction, dressing up, and the impression of having endless fun.

The effect of these processes is that they can transform everyday occurrences, such as shopping and eating, into spectacular and sensational events. At the same time, however, the tendency to repackage things in a sanitized format undermines the authenticity of other experiences and places.

Ultimately this blurs the distinction between fantasy and reality. Bryman cites the fashion for trying to bestow character on somewhere by associating it with a well-known cultural totem, leading to England's Nottinghamshire becoming "Robin Hood Country" and Finland's Lapland "Santa Claus Land."

Bryman proposes Disneyization as a parallel notion to George Ritzer's McDonaldization, a process by which the principles of the fast-food restaurant (McDonald's itself is merely a symbol) come to dominate more and more sectors of society. McDonaldization is grounded in the idea of rationalization and produces sameness. Theme parks echo this in several ways, but Disneyization is essentially about increasing the inclination to consume (goods and services), often through variety and difference. The popularity of theming and merchandizing suggests that Disneyization has become an integral part of modern life and identity. ∎

Alan Bryman

British sociologist Alan Bryman is a professor of organizational and social research in the school of management at the University of Leicester, England. Prior to this he worked at the University of Loughborough for 31 years. Bryman is interested in methodological issues and different aspects of consumer culture. His specializations include combining qualitative and quantitative research methods; Disneyization and McDonaldization; and effective leadership in higher education. He is widely published in all three areas.

Bryman is unable to understand the disdain of fellow intellectuals for all things Disney; his love of the cartoons and parks has greatly inspired his academic work, which has become influential in both cultural and sociological studies.

Key works

1995 *Disney and his World*
2004 *The Disneyization of Society*

LIVING IN A LOFT IS LIKE LIVING IN A SHOWCASE

SHARON ZUKIN

IN CONTEXT

FOCUS
Gentrification and urban life

KEY DATES
1920s US sociologist Robert E. Park coins the term "human ecology" and is a leading figure in establishing the "Chicago School" and its systematic study of urban life.

1961 Jane Jacobs' *The Death and Life of Great American Cities* is published, becoming one of the most influential post-war studies of urban environments.

1964 British sociologist Ruth Glass invents the word "gentrification" to describe the displacement of working-class occupiers by middle-class incomers.

1970s Artists begin to move into former factory buildings in Lower Manhattan.

C ities are dynamic places of change and renewal for people, communities, ideas, and the built environment. Social thinkers have always been drawn to the study of urban life, especially during times of rapid change. The period of metropolitan growth from the 19th century onward, the transformation of cities and the movement into suburbia that followed World War II, and changes in the structure of the urban village in the 1960s have all been the subjects of intense study.

Another such period occurred in the 1980s, when many cities in the Western world had been radically altered by the loss of manufacturing

See also: Georg Simmel 104–05 ▪ Henri Lefebvre 106–07 ▪ Jane Jacobs 108–09 ▪ Alan Bryman 126–27 ▪
Saskia Sassen 164–65

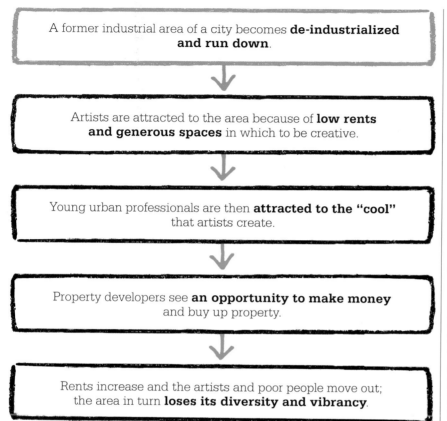

A former industrial area of a city becomes **de-industrialized and run down**.

⬇

Artists are attracted to the area because of **low rents and generous spaces** in which to be creative.

⬇

Young urban professionals are then **attracted to the "cool"** that artists create.

⬇

Property developers see **an opportunity to make money** and buy up property.

⬇

Rents increase and the artists and poor people move out; the area in turn **loses its diversity and vibrancy**.

to replace the mass production of modernism and the uniformity of suburban living with the individualization of a space once used for mass production (since many loft spaces had once been workshops or factories). In a loft, the privacy of the detached suburban house was replaced by a non-hierarchical layout that opens up "every area... to all comers." This space and openness creates an impression of informality and equality, transforming the loft into a "tourist attraction" or a showcase—a place that demands to be seen.

Urban regeneration

Zukin also closely examined the costs of urban regeneration and loft living. On the surface, the movement of people back into virtually abandoned districts appears to be a positive process, breathing new life into old buildings and places. However, Zukin questions this assumption, arguing that regeneration »

industries and the growing impacts of globalization. A new generation of scholars began to investigate inner city decline, the processes of urban regeneration, and what gives somewhere its distinctive sense of place. Prominent among them has been Sharon Zukin, author of the influential 1982 work, *Loft Living*.

The meanings of space

Zukin moved into a loft—a former garment factory and artist's studio—in Greenwich Village, New York, in 1975. She became interested in what these new residential spaces meant to their occupiers, and was particularly concerned by the impact that

their use as dwellings was having on long-established communities in New York.

Zukin reiterated the ideas of thinkers such as French philosopher Gaston Bachelard, who argued, in *The Poetics of Space* (1958), that a home was more than a space for living; it represented the "psychic state" of the inhabitants. For example, in Victorian times, houses were divided into rooms with specific functions (drawing room, dressing room, and so on), providing a series of intimate spatial encounters.

The psychic state of a loft-dweller, argued Zukin, was that of a search for authenticity—an attempt

Bare walls, exposed beams, and unexpected architectural details provide the authenticity sought by buyers of urban loft apartments.

Chelsea Market is a New York food hall created in the 1990s in a derelict factory in the Meatpacking District. Zukin says the area is a far cry from the one-time "no-go zone" of butchery.

benefits specific groups at the expense of others. She claims that regeneration leads to a process whereby poor or marginalized groups are effectively pushed out of the areas in which they have been living, sometimes for generations, to make way for more elite groups. The result can be a uniform urban experience, which Zukin has identified in parts of New York and other cities around the world.

The steps of gentrification

Zukin argues that gentrification is more than, as she puts it, a "change of scene." It is a "radical break with suburbia... toward the social diversity and aesthetic promiscuity of city life." Gentrifiers, according to her, have a distinctive culture and milieu (they are interested, for example, in restoring historical architectural detail), which leads to "a process of social and spatial differentiation." In her study of Lower Manhattan, Zukin argues that gentrification is a process within which a number of steps can be clearly identified.

The first step was a decline in traditional manufacturing industry. Just a couple of generations ago, New York had a working waterfront that employed tens of thousands and a hinterland in Manhattan that was packed, in the areas around Greenwich Village, with small-scale workshops and factories making textiles and clothes. The buildings housing the workshops typically had high ceilings and lots of light, and were known as "lofts."

The textile firms began to go out of business from the 1950s onward, as more and more of the US's textiles production was "off-shored" by large corporations to countries in Asia where labor costs were lower. US workers were left unemployed, and the affected districts of New York became deindustrialized and run-down. By the 1970s, much of Lower Manhattan had become derelict.

Creative space

The second step took place in the 1970s, after the abandoned workplaces had become home to the poor and marginalized. Because the buildings were intended to be factories, the floors were not subdivided into multiple rooms, as you would find in an apartment block, but were instead open plan with tall windows. A space that accommodated lots of people needing good natural light, while they worked on sewing machines, also proved to be the ideal studio environment for artists. In the early 1970s, when New York was hit by an economic crisis, private rents citywide went down because demand for properties decreased. Stereotypically, artists struggle to make ends meet and often seek out cheap places in which to live and work. Lower Manhattan's old factory lofts therefore had appeal and the area became home to many artists.

This was an organic regeneration of these old neighborhoods: there was no official city government plan to convert the lofts into live-in studios. As more

Much of what made [New York City's] neighborhoods unique lives on only in the buildings, not the people.
Sharon Zukin

artists moved to the area, it developed a cultural vibrancy; the presence of the artists meant that secondary businesses—such as coffee shops, restaurants, and art galleries—opened to support their activities. The area became increasingly funky and edgy, and proved attractive to the new class of young urban professionals who wanted to live somewhere new, exciting, and different from the staid, post-war homes in which they had grown up.

The third and decisive step in gentrification was reached when young professionals began to move into the area—in this case, to become part of the urban bohemian environment and lifestyle. There were now people with money interested in living in what had previously been an undesirable area. The fact that this new and more affluent group suddenly wanted to live in the area attracted the attention of profit-driven developers, who began to buy up comparatively cheap property— often, criticizes Zukin, with subsidies from the city authorities— and convert it into apartments that resembled the lofts in which the artists lived. As a result, rents began to steadily increase. Artists and poor people found it hard to afford to live there anymore, and they begin to move out.

The final step in gentrification was reached when the area was colonized by the more affluent middle and upper classes. The galleries and coffee shops remained, but the mix of people, the vibrancy, and the cultural activity that had made the area popular was lost. In effect, the artists became unwitting accomplices of gentrification, and then its victims: their success in breathing new life into Lower

> 66
>
> It's just inexorable, this authenticity in the visual language of sameness.
> **Sharon Zukin**
>
> 99

Manhattan resulted ultimately in their exclusion from what they had helped to regenerate.

The search for urban soul

Zukin's work has been influential in clarifying what drives change in modern cities: the cultural and consumerist needs of some social groups wishing to pursue a certain lifestyle, rather than the development of new forms of industry. However, for Zukin this way of life is just another form of consumerism that is ultimately empty, offering a "Disneyfied" experience in which diversity and authenticity are marginalized

by the prevalent cultural forms and lifestyles promoted by multinational media companies. The result is that poor and marginalized groups are effectively excluded from urban life.

A naked city

Zukin's more recent work, such as *Naked City*, has focused on how gentrification and consumerism have created bland, homogenous, middle-class areas and robbed cities of the authenticity that most people long for. She also notices that the pace of gentrification has sped up. What used to take decades to unfold now only seems to require a few years: an area is deemed to be "cool" and very rapidly the developers move in and begin a process that fundamentally alters its character, invariably destroying what was special. In fact, the distinctiveness of a neighborhood has actually become a tool of capitalist developers—one that results in the exclusion of the characters who first gave an area its real "soul." The challenge for planners is to find ways of preserving people as well as buildings and streetscapes. ∎

Sharon Zukin

Sharon Zukin is currently a professor of sociology at Brooklyn College in New York, and at the CUNY Graduate Center. She has received several awards, including the Wright Mills Award and the Robert and Helen Lynd Award for career achievement in urban sociology from the American Sociological Association.

She is the author of books on cities, culture, and consumer culture, and a researcher on urban, cultural, and economic change. Her work has mainly focused on how cities are affected by processes such as gentrification, and investigating the dominant driving processes in urban living. She is also an active critic of the many changes that are occurring within New York and other cities.

Key works

1982 *Loft Living: Culture and Capital in Urban Change*
1995 *The Cultures of Cities*
2010 *Naked City: The Death and Life of Authentic Urban Places*

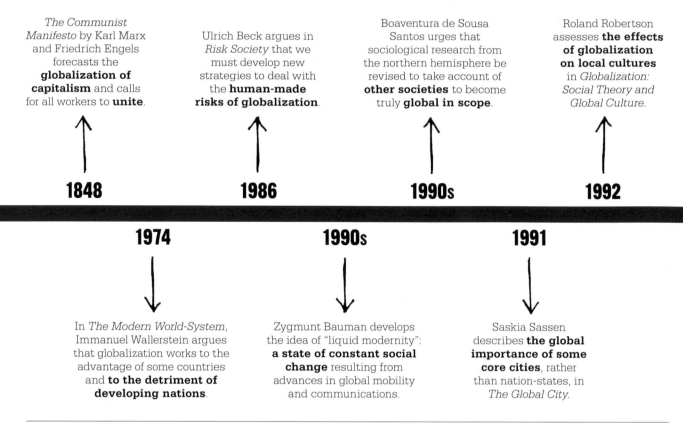

1848

The *Communist Manifesto* by Karl Marx and Friedrich Engels forecasts the **globalization of capitalism** and calls for all workers to **unite**.

1986

Ulrich Beck argues in *Risk Society* that we must develop new strategies to deal with the **human-made risks of globalization**.

1990s

Boaventura de Sousa Santos urges that sociological research from the northern hemisphere be revised to take account of **other societies** to become truly **global in scope**.

1992

Roland Robertson assesses **the effects of globalization on local cultures** in *Globalization: Social Theory and Global Culture*.

1974

In *The Modern World-System*, Immanuel Wallerstein argues that globalization works to the advantage of some countries and **to the detriment of developing nations**.

1990s

Zygmunt Bauman develops the idea of "liquid modernity": **a state of constant social change** resulting from advances in global mobility and communications.

1991

Saskia Sassen describes **the global importance of some core cities**, rather than nation-states, in *The Global City*.

Sociology grew out of a desire to understand, and suggest ways of improving, the modern society that had emerged during the Enlightenment, and especially the effects of industrialization, rationalization, and capitalism. But as the discipline of sociology became more firmly established in the latter part of the 20th century, it became apparent that there was another force driving social change: globalization.

International trade had been in force for centuries, with multinational corporations rooted in the trading empires of the 16th and 17th centuries, so the idea of globalization was nothing new. However, since the Industrial Revolution, the pace of progress in transport and communication had accelerated. In the 20th century, the telegraph and aviation revolutionized international connections, and post-World War II information technology has sustained this pattern.

Network society

While many people feel that the world has entered a new, post-industrial, postmodern age, others see globalization as simply a continuation of the process of modernity. Zygmunt Bauman, for example, argues that what began with industrialization has now entered a mature, "late modern" stage as technology has become ever more sophisticated. The nature of technological progress means this stage is characterized by a "liquid modernity"—a state of constant change.

Perhaps the most noticeable social effect of these technological advances has been from the improvement of communications. From telephones to the Internet, the world has become increasingly interconnected, and social networks now transcend national boundaries. Information technology has not only made commercial transactions quicker and easier than ever, but has also connected individuals and communities that had previously been isolated.

Manuel Castells was among the first to identify the social effects of this network society, while Roland Robertson argued that rather than having a homogenizing effect (by creating a universal model of society), globalization was in fact merging with local cultures to produce new social systems.

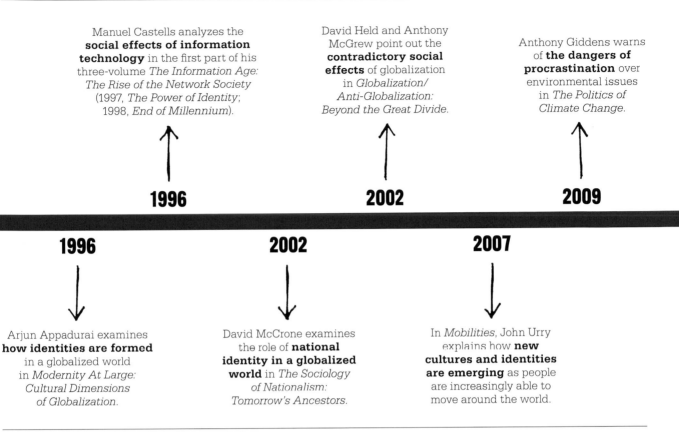

Manuel Castells analyzes the **social effects of information technology** in the first part of his three-volume *The Information Age: The Rise of the Network Society* (1997, *The Power of Identity*; 1998, *End of Millennium*).

David Held and Anthony McGrew point out the **contradictory social effects** of globalization in *Globalization/ Anti-Globalization: Beyond the Great Divide.*

Anthony Giddens warns of **the dangers of procrastination** over environmental issues in *The Politics of Climate Change.*

1996   **2002**   **2009**

1996   **2002**   **2007**

Arjun Appadurai examines **how identities are formed** in a globalized world in *Modernity At Large: Cultural Dimensions of Globalization.*

David McCrone examines the role of **national identity in a globalized world** in *The Sociology of Nationalism: Tomorrow's Ancestors.*

In *Mobilities*, John Urry explains how **new cultures and identities are emerging** as people are increasingly able to move around the world.

Another aspect of late modernity is the ease with which people now travel worldwide. Just as the migration from the countryside to the cities after industrialization created new social structures, increased mobility in the late 20th century has changed social patterns. Economic migration has become increasingly common as people move not just into the new global cities, but internationally in search of work and prosperity. As Arjun Appadurai and others have pointed out, this has led to cultural changes, including a questioning of how identities are formed.

Culture and environment

Many sociologists have tried to assess globalization's impact on local cultures, and the changing nature of national identities. In Western countries, an influx of migrants from different cultures has changed attitudes to race, religion, and culture, especially as second- and third-generation immigrants identify themselves with their host country.

Much of this movement has been driven by economic inequality between nations, which has not been alleviated by globalization. According to Immanuel Wallerstein, it is the spread of capitalism that perpetuates the differences between rich and poor countries. Capitalism reaps an economic advantage by maintaining this difference, and exploiting the resources of developing countries. And because of the increasing contrast between the northern and southern hemispheres, Boaventura de Sousa Santos has urged a change in sociological thinking to include marginalized points of view.

Others, such as Ulrich Beck, have warned of the risks associated with globalization, as traditional ways of life are eroded by advances in new technology and communication. Unlike in the past, we no longer face only natural risks on a local scale, but also human-made crises that have international consequences. Environmental issues are perhaps the greatest threat, but as a society we have tended, as Anthony Giddens has pointed out, to bury our heads in the sand. While enjoying the benefits of modern global society, we continue to put off dealing with the underlying problems, maybe to the point where it is too late to prevent disaster. ■

ABANDON ALL HOPE OF TOTALITY YOU WHO ENTER THE WORLD OF FLUID MODERNITY

ZYGMUNT BAUMAN (1925–)

IN CONTEXT

FOCUS
Liquid modernity

KEY DATES
1848 Karl Marx and Friedrich Engels publish *The Communist Manifesto*, which forecasts the globalization of capitalism.

1929–35 Antonio Gramsci's concept of hegemony shapes Zygmunt Bauman's view that the culture of capitalism is highly resilient.

1957 The ratification of the Treaty of Rome allows for the free flow of workers within the European Economic Community.

1976 Bauman is influenced by Michel Foucault's *Discipline and Punish*, and in particular by his ideas on surveillance.

2008 British sociologist Will Atkinson questions whether Bauman's notion of liquid modernity has been subject to sufficient critical scrutiny.

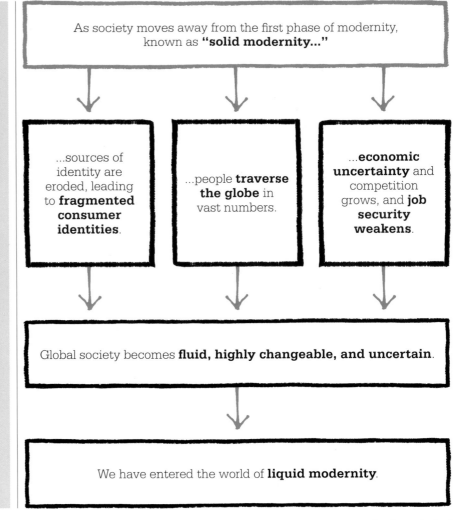

As society moves away from the first phase of modernity, known as **"solid modernity..."**

...sources of identity are eroded, leading to **fragmented consumer identities**.

...people **traverse the globe** in vast numbers.

...**economic uncertainty** and competition grows, and **job security weakens**.

Global society becomes **fluid, highly changeable, and uncertain.**

We have entered the world of **liquid modernity**.

In the late 19th century, societies began to coalesce around urban centers, and Western Europe entered a phase known as modernity, characterized by industrialization and capitalism. According to Polish sociologist Zygmunt Bauman, societies have moved away from that first phase of modernity—which he termed "solid modernity"—and now occupy a period in human history called "liquid modernity." This new period is, according to Bauman, one marked by unrelenting uncertainty and change that affects society at the global, systemic level, and also at the level of individual experience. Bauman's use of the term "liquid" is a powerful metaphor for present-day life: it is mobile, fast-flowing, changeable, amorphous, without a center of gravity, and difficult to contain and predict. In essence, liquid modernity is a way of life that exists in the continuous, unceasing reshaping of the modern world in ways that are unpredictable, uncertain, and plagued by increasing levels of risk. Liquid modernity, for Bauman, is the current stage in the broader evolution of Western—and now also global—society. Like Karl Marx, Bauman believes that human society progresses in a way that means each "new" stage develops out of the stage before it. Thus it is necessary to define solid modernity before it is possible to understand liquid modernity.

Defining solid modernity
Bauman sees solid modernity as ordered, rational, predictable, and relatively stable. Its defining feature is the organization of human

See also: Karl Marx 28–31 ▪ Michel Foucault 52–55 ▪ Max Weber 38–45 ▪ Anthony Giddens 148–49 ▪ Ulrich Beck 156–61 ▪ Antonio Gramsci 178–79

activity and institutions along bureaucratic lines, where practical reasoning can be employed to solve problems and create technical solutions. Bureaucracy persists because it is the most efficient way of organizing and ordering the actions and interactions of large numbers of people. While bureaucracy has its distinctly negative aspects (for example, that human life can become dehumanized and devoid of spontaneity and creativity), it is highly effective at accomplishing goal-oriented tasks.

Another key characteristic of solid modernity, according to Bauman, is a very high degree of equilibrium in social structures—meaning that people live with a relatively stable set of norms, traditions, and institutions. By this, Bauman is not suggesting

Auschwitz concentration camp in Poland was built and run by the Nazis. Bauman cites the Holocaust as a product of the highly rational, planned nature of solid modernity.

that social, political, and economic changes do not occur in solid modernity, just that changes occur in ways that are relatively ordered and predictable. The economy provides a good example: in solid modernity, the majority of people—from members of the working class through to middle-class professionals—enjoyed relatively high levels of job security. As a consequence, they tended to remain in the same geographical area, grow up in the same neighborhood, and attend the same school as their parents and other family members.

Bauman regards solid modernity as one-directional and progressive—a realization of the Enlightenment view that reason leads to the emancipation of humankind. As scientific knowledge advances, so does society's understanding of, and control over, the natural and social worlds. In solid modernism, according to Bauman, this supreme faith in scientific reasoning was embodied in the social and political institutions that »

Zygmunt Bauman

Born in 1925, Zygmunt Bauman is a Polish sociologist from a nonpracticing Polish-Jewish family who were forced to relocate to the Soviet Union in 1939 following the Nazi invasion. After serving in the Polish division of the Red Army, he moved to Israel. In 1971 he settled in England, where he is now professor emeritus of sociology at the University of Leeds.

Bauman is the author of more than 40 books, of which 20 or so have been written since his retirement in 1990. In recognition of his contribution to sociology, he was awarded the Theodor W. Adorno Award in 1998 and the Prince of Asturias Award in 2010. The University of Leeds created the acclaimed Bauman Institute in 2010 in his honor, and in 2013 the Polish director Bartek Dziadosz produced a film of his life and views entitled *The Trouble With Being Human These Days.*

Key works

1989 *Modernity and the Holocaust*
2000 *Liquid Modernity*
2011 *Culture in a Liquid Modern World*

addressed primarily national issues and problems. Enlightenment values were institutionally entrenched in the figurehead of the State—the primary point of reference from which emerged the development of social, political, and economic ideals.

At the level of the individual, claims Bauman, solid modernity gave rise to a stable repertoire of personal identities and possible versions of selfhood. Solid modern individuals have a unified, rational, and stable sense of personal identity, because it is informed by a number of stable categories, such as occupation, religious affiliation, nationality, gender, ethnicity, leisure pursuits, lifestyle, and so on. Social life under the conditions of solid modernity—like the individuals it created—was self-

Bauman's idea of solid modernity was embodied by Enlightenment thinkers such as Isaac Newton (depicted here by William Blake), who used reason to transform society.

assured, rational, bureaucratically organized, and relatively predictable and stable.

From solid to liquid
The transition from solid to liquid modernity, according to Bauman, has occurred as a result of a confluence of profound and connected economic, political, and social changes. The result is a global order propelled by what Bauman describes as a "compulsive, obsessive, and addictive reinventing of the world."

Bauman identifies five distinct, but interrelated, developments that have brought about the transition from solid to liquid modernity. First, nation-states are no longer the "key load-bearing structures" of society; national governments today have considerably less power to determine events both at home and abroad. Second, global capitalism has risen and multi- and transnational corporations have proliferated, resulting in a decentering of state authority.

The population of every country is nowadays a collection of diasporas.
Zygmunt Bauman

Third, electronic technologies and the Internet now allow for near-instant, supranational flows of communication. Fourth, societies have become ever more preoccupied by risk—dwelling on insecurities and potential hazards. And fifth, there has been huge growth in human migration across the globe.

Defining liquid modernity
As Bauman himself observes, attempting to define liquid modernity is something of a paradox, because the term refers to a global condition that is characterized by unrelenting change, flux, and uncertainty. However, having identified the traits of solid modernity, he claims it is possible to define the most prominent aspects of liquid modernity.

At an ideological level, liquid modernity undermines the Enlightenment ideal that scientific knowledge can ameliorate natural and social problems. In liquid modernity, science, experts, university-based academics, and government officials—once the supreme figures of authority in solid modernity—occupy a highly ambiguous status as guardians of the truth. Scientists are increasingly perceived as being as much the cause of environmental and sociopolitical problems as they are the solution. This inevitably leads to increased skepticism and general apathy on the part of the general public.

Liquid modernity has undermined the certainties of individuals regarding employment, education, and welfare. Today, many workers must either retrain or change occupation altogether, sometimes several times—the notion of a "job for life," which was typical in the age of solid modernity, has been rendered unrealistic and unachievable.

The practice of "re-engineering," or the downsizing of firms—a term that Bauman borrows from the US sociologist, Richard Sennett—has become increasingly common, as it enables corporations to remain financially competitive in the global market by reducing labor costs significantly. As part of this process, stable, permanent work—which typified solid modernism—is being replaced by temporary employment contracts that are issued to a largely mobile workforce. Closely related to this occupational instability is the shifting role and nature of

We live in a globalizing world. That means all of us, consciously or not, depend on each other.
Zygmunt Bauman

The key differences between solid and liquid modernity were identified by Bauman as two sets of four characteristics.

Stasis · Design · Movement · Chance · Indeterminacy · Determinacy · Predictability · Unpredictability

Solid modernity   **Liquid modernity**

education. Individuals are now required to continue their education—often at their own expense—throughout their careers in order to remain up to date with developments in their respective professions, or as a means of ensuring they remain "marketable" in case of redundancy.

Concurrent with these changes to employment patterns is the retreat of the welfare state. What was once regarded historically as a reliable "safety net" guarding against personal misfortune such as ill-health and unemployment, state provision of welfare is rapidly being withdrawn, especially in the areas of social housing, state-funded higher education, and national health care.

Fluid identities
Where solid modernity was based on the industrial production of consumer goods in factories and

industrial plants, liquid modernity is instead based on the rapid and relentless consumption of consumer goods and services.

This transition from production to consumption, says Bauman, is a result of the dissolution of the social structures, such as occupation and nationality, to which identity was anchored in solid modernity. »

Welfare states, as Bauman says, have been under pressure recently. In the UK, for example, the National Health Service is being eroded, despite widespread support for the system.

The self-creation of personal identity is undertaken through consumption as traditional sources of identity, such as employment status and family ties, have withered under liquid modernity.

But in liquid modernity selfhood is not so fixed: it is fragmented, unstable, often internally incoherent, and frequently no more than the sum of consumer choices out of which it is simultaneously constituted and represented. In liquid modernity, the boundary between the authentic self and the representation of the self through consumer choice breaks down: we are—according to Bauman— what we buy and no more. Depth and surface meaning have fused together, and it is impossible to separate them out.

Consumption and identity

The central importance of consumption in the construction of individual self-identity goes beyond the acquisition of consumer goods. Without the unchanging sources of identity provided by solid modernity, individuals in the modern world seek guidance, stability, and personal direction from an ever-broadening range of alternative sources, such as lifestyle coaches, psychoanalysts, sex therapists, holistic life-experts, health gurus, and so on.

Self-identity has become problematic for the individual in ways that are historically unprecedented, and the consequence is a cycle of endless self-questioning and introspection that serves only to confound the individual even more. Ultimately, the result is that our experience of ourselves and everyday life is increasingly played out against a backdrop of ongoing anxiety, restlessness, and unease about who we are, our place in the world, and the rapidity of the changes taking place around us.

Liquid modernity thus principally refers to a global society that is plagued by uncertainty and instability. However, these destabilizing forces are not evenly distributed across global society. Bauman identifies and explains the importance of the variables of mobility, time, and space for understanding why. For Bauman, the capacity to remain mobile is an extremely valuable attribute in liquid modernity, because it facilitates the successful pursuit of wealth and personal fulfillment.

Tourists and vagabonds

Bauman distinguishes between the winners and losers in liquid modernity. The people who benefit most from the fluidity of liquid modernity are the socially privileged individuals who are able to float freely around the world. These people, who Bauman refers to as "tourists," exist in time rather than space. By this he means that through their easy access to Internet-based technologies and transnational flights, tourists are able—virtually and in reality—to span the entire globe and operate in locations where the economic conditions are the most favorable and standards of living the highest. By stark contrast, the "vagabonds,"

> In a liquid modern life, there are no permanent bonds, and any that we take up... must be tied loosely so that they can be untied... when circumstances change.
> **Zygmunt Bauman**

> If you define your value by the things you acquire... being excluded is humiliating.
> **Zygmunt Bauman**

as Bauman calls them, are people who are immobile, or subject to forced mobility, and excluded from consumer culture. Life for them involves either being mired in places where unemployment is high and the standard of living is very poor, or being forced to leave their country of origin as economic or political refugees in search of employment, or in response to the threat of war or persecution. Anywhere they stay for too long soon becomes inhospitable.

For Bauman, mass migration and transnational flows of people around the globe are among the hallmarks of liquid modernity and are factors contributing to the unpredictable and constantly changing nature of everyday life: Bauman's social categories of tourists and vagabonds occupy two extremes of this phenomenon.

Applying Bauman's theory

Zygmunt Bauman is considered one of the most influential and eminent sociologists of the modern age. He prefers not to align himself with any particular intellectual tradition—his writings are relevant to a vast range of disciplines, from ethics, media, and cultural studies to political theory and philosophy. Within sociology, his work on liquid

modernity is regarded by the vast majority of thinkers as a unique contribution to the field.

The Irish sociologist Donncha Marron has applied Bauman's concept of liquid modernity to a critical rethinking of consumer credit within the US. Following Bauman's suggestion that consumption of goods and brands is a key feature of how individuals construct personal identity, Marron notes that the credit card is an important tool in this process because it is ideally suited for enabling people to adapt to the kind of fluid ways of living Bauman depicts. The credit card can, for example, be used to fund shopping trips to satisfy consumer desire. It makes paying for things easier, quicker, and considerably more manageable. The credit card of course also serves the function, says Marron, of meeting day-to-day bills and expenses, as people move between jobs or make significant career moves. And the physical card itself

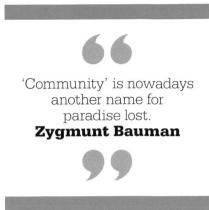

> 'Community' is nowadays another name for paradise lost.
> **Zygmunt Bauman**

can often be co-branded with things the owner is interested in, such as football teams, charities, or stores. These co-branded cards represent a small but revealing means whereby a person is able to select and present a sense of who they are to the outside world. ∎

Bauman's global "tourists" are mobile members of the social elite who possess the wealth and occupational status necessary to enjoy the most positive aspects of liquid modernity.

THE MODERN WORLD-SYSTEM
IMMANUEL WALLERSTEIN (1930–)

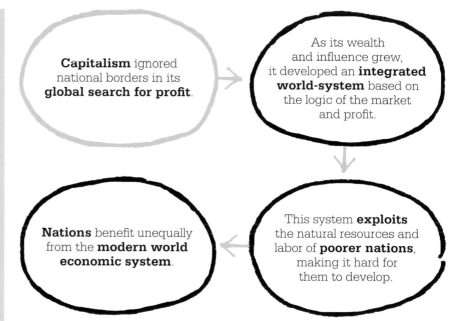

Capitalism ignored national borders in its **global search for profit**.

As its wealth and influence grew, it developed an **integrated world-system** based on the logic of the market and profit.

This system **exploits** the natural resources and labor of **poorer nations**, making it hard for them to develop.

Nations benefit unequally from the **modern world economic system**.

arious nations of the world are interconnected by a global system of economic relationships that sees more-developed nations exploiting the natural resources and labor of developing nations, according to US sociologist Immanuel Wallerstein in *The Modern World-System* (1974). This "world-system" makes it difficult for poor nations to develop, and ensures that rich nations continue to be the primary beneficiaries of global commodity chains and the products and wealth that are created by industrial capitalism.

The world economic system, says Wallerstein, began to emerge in the 16th century, as European nations such as Britain, Spain, and France exploited the resources of conquered and colonized lands. These unequal trade relationships

See also: Karl Marx 28–31 ▪ Roland Robertson 146–47 ▪ Saskia Sassen 164–65 ▪ Arjun Appadurai 166–69 ▪ David Held 170–71

produced an accumulation of capital that was reinvested in expanding the economic system. By the late 19th century, most of the world had been incorporated into this system of commodity production and exchange.

The global stage

Wallerstein's ideas on the origin of modern capitalism extend the theories of Karl Marx to the global stage. Marx focused on how capitalism produces a struggle over "surplus value," which refers to the fact that a worker produces more value in a day than he or she is paid for, and this extra value translates as profit for the employer. Under capitalism, the working class is exploited by wealthy social elites for the surplus value of their labor.

Wallerstein develops this idea to focus on those who benefit from global commodity chains, arguing that there are classlike groupings of nations in the world-system, which he labels "core," "semi-periphery," and "periphery." Core nations are developed societies,

The modern world-system is based on a classlike grouping of nations, and results in unequal economic and trade relationships between those nations.

- **Periphery nations** are powerless and dispossessed; they have narrow economic bases in agriculture and minerals, and provide the semi-periphery and core nations with commodities, raw materials, and cheap labor.

- **Semi-periphery** nations have intermediate levels of affluence and some autonomy and economic diversity.

- **Core nations** are developed, industrialized, and affluent; they dominate at the heart of the modern world-system.

which produce complex products using technologically advanced methods of production. The core nations rely on periphery nations for raw materials, agricultural products, and cheap labor. Semi-periphery nations have a mix of the social and economic characteristics of the other categories.

The unequal nature of this economic exchange between the core and the periphery means that

core nations sell their developed commodities at higher prices than those from the periphery. Those nations in the semi-periphery also benefit from unequal trade relationships with the periphery, but are often at a disadvantage with regards to their economic exchanges with the core.

This world-system, Wallerstein suggests, is relatively stable and unlikely to change. While nations can move "up" or "down" within the system, the military and economic power of states in the core, along with the aspirations of those in the semi-periphery, make it unlikely that global relationships will be restructured to be more equitable.

Wallerstein's ideas on the modern world-system, originating in the 1970s, predate the literature on globalization, which only emerged as a central concern of sociology from the late 1980s and early 1990s. His work is therefore recognized as an early and important contribution to economic globalization and its sociopolitical consequences. ■

Global patterns of wealth and inequality

Social scientists originally discussed global inequalities using the terms "First World" (developed Western nations), "Second World" (industrialized communist nations), and "Third World" (colonized nations). Nations were ranked according to their levels of capitalist enterprise, industrialization, and urbanization, and the argument was that poorer nations simply needed more of the economic features of developed societies to escape poverty.

Wallerstein rejected the idea that the Third World was merely underdeveloped. He focused on the economic process and links underpinning the global economy to show that, although a nation's position in the world-system was initially a product of history and geography, the market forces of global capitalism serve to accentuate the differences between the core and the periphery nations, thereby effectively institutionalizing inequality.

GLOBAL ISSUES, LOCAL PERSPECTIVES
ROLAND ROBERTSON (1938–)

IN CONTEXT

FOCUS
Glocalization

KEY DATES
1582–1922 Beginning with the Catholic countries of Europe and finally the states of East Asia and the Soviet Union, the Gregorian calendar is adopted as the most widely used calendar internationally.

1884 Greenwich Mean Time (GMT) is recognized as the world's time standard, becoming the basis for a global 24-hour time-zone system.

1945 The United Nations (UN) is founded to promote international cooperation.

1980s Japanese businesses develop strategies to adapt global products to local markets, a process they call "glocalization."

1990s Roland Robertson expands the Japanese concept of "glocalization" in his work on globalization.

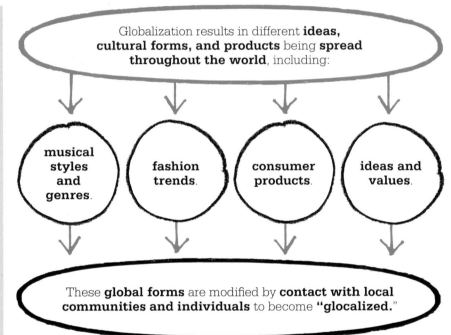

Globalization results in different **ideas, cultural forms, and products** being **spread throughout the world**, including:

musical styles and genres.

fashion trends.

consumer products.

ideas and values.

These **global forms** are modified by **contact with local communities and individuals** to become **"glocalized."**

Globalization is giving rise to new cultural forms, as global products, values, and tastes fuse with their local equivalents. This intermixing of the global and the local, says British sociologist Roland Robertson, is a key feature of modern societies and is producing new creative possibilities.

In *Globalization: Social Theory and Global Culture* (1992), Robertson argues that the cultural dynamics at the heart of globalization can be understood by focusing on the relationships between four areas: "individual selves," "nation-state," a "world system of societies," and "a notion of a common humanity." This focus allows him to examine

See also: George Ritzer 120–23 ▪ Immanuel Wallerstein 144–45 ▪ Saskia Sassen 164–65 ▪ Arjun Appadurai 166–69 ▪ David Held 170–71

Soccer is the "glocal game." Many communities identify with their team and develop distinctive traditions and soccer cultures, which they then bring to international competitions.

the interacting aspects of a person's self-identity and their relationship with national and global cultural influences.

One's self-identity, for example, is defined in relation to a nation, to interactions between societies, and to humankind (ideas regarding sexual orientation, ethnicity, and so on). In this context, Robertson explores the tension between global and local influences on a person's experiences and actions.

Robertson emphasizes "global unicity": the ways in which globalization and cultural exchange seem to be giving rise to a global culture. This is a movement toward a world dominated by Western cultural products and beliefs—such as Hollywood movies and US pop music—and is made possible by the increasing connectivity of societies and by people's awareness of the world as a single sociocultural entity.

But Robertson stresses that the emergence of "global unicity" does not mean the world is moving toward a single global culture in which everything is the same, or "homogenized." On the contrary, he argues that the differences between cultural groups and their products can be sharpened as they encounter cultural flows from other communities. This can lead to a dynamic interaction between local and global cultures, as people modify cultural forms to suit their particular sociocultural context.

Mixing "global" and "local"

To reflect how the global and local relate and intermix, Robertson popularized the term "glocalization." The concept was developed from the practices of transnational companies and their strategy of taking a global product and adapting it for a local market. For example, the fast-food corporation McDonald's has created many "glocalized" burger products in an attempt to appeal to customers outside the US (such as the Chicken Maharaja Mac in India, where Hindus do not eat beef). In sociology, glocalization also refers more broadly to the localization of global cultural products or forms.

Globalization is, then, a twofold process of "universalizing and particularizing tendencies." Some cultural forms, products, and values are transported around the world, where they may be adopted or modified by different societies and individuals. A creative tension then emerges between the local and the global, which can result in cultural innovation and social change; for example, when people tell "local stories" through their adaptation of globally recognized music genres such as Hip Hop, K-Pop, and Indie. ▪

Cultural mélange

The recent rise of global communications has produced what Roland Robertson describes as a "cultural interconnectedness." As global influences mutate and hybridize locally, the result is "glocalized" diversity, or a cultural "mélange," according to Dutch sociologist Jan Nederveen Pieterse. A good example of this global-to-local process is film-making.

Hollywood movies inspired the Indian film industry in the early 20th century. But Indian film-makers focused on modifying Hollywood's output: they wanted to make the art form their own, to appeal to local culture and reflect its distinct forms of expression. In so doing, they initiated a creative engagement between the global and local. Indian cinema draws on a rich body of themes—ranging from the country's ancient epics and myths to traditional drama—and retells them in colorful, distinctive ways. The Hindi films known as "Bollywood" attract audiences well beyond the Indian diaspora.

Local cultures adopt and redefine any global cultural product to suit their particular needs, beliefs, and customs.
Roland Robertson

CLIMATE CHANGE IS A BACK-OF-THE-MIND ISSUE
ANTHONY GIDDENS (1938–)

IN CONTEXT

FOCUS
Giddens' paradox

KEY DATES
1900 Modernity continues
to spread as nations develop
industrial economies and
generate economic growth.

1952 The Great Smog, a toxic,
smokelike air-pollution event
over London, kills an estimated
4,000 people and leads to the
Clean Air Act (1956).

1987 The Montreal Protocol
is agreed, protecting the
ozone layer by phasing out
the production of substances
responsible for ozone depletion.

1997 Agreement of The Kyoto
Protocol, a United Nations
convention intended to reduce
greenhouse gas emissions
from industrialized countries
and prevent climate change.

2009 A renewed commitment
to the reduction of greenhouse
gas emissions is made in the
Copenhagen Accord.

The world is in danger
and globalization is at
least partially to blame,
according to British sociologist
Anthony Giddens. He believes
that modernity has produced
a "runaway world" in which
governments and individuals
face global risks such as climate
change. One of his contributions
to this important area of research
is to provide a sociological
explanation for why governments
and individuals are reluctant to
take immediate action to address
the causes of global warming.

Globalization of modernity

Giddens has been highlighting the
effects of globalization and how it
has been transforming society's
institutions, social roles, and
relationships since the publication
of his book *The Consequences of
Modernity* in 1990. He notes that
the world's developed and newly
industrialized societies are now
characterized by experiences
and relationships that are
dramatically different from those
in pre-industrial societies.

This globalization of modernity
and its consequences marks a new
stage in human civilization, which
Giddens calls "late modernity." He
uses the analogy of "riding onboard
a juggernaut" to illustrate how
the modern world seems to be
"out of control" and difficult to
direct. While life in late modernity
is at times "rewarding" and
"exhilarating," individuals must
also confront new uncertainties,
place trust in abstract systems, and
manage new challenges and risks.

Giddens sees anthropogenic
(human-induced) climate change
as one of the most important risks,
and indeed challenges, confronting
humanity. Industrialized societies
burn significant amounts of
fossil fuels to generate power.

> People find it hard to
> give the same level of
> reality to the future as
> they do to the present.
> **Anthony Giddens**

See also: Zygmunt Bauman 136–43 ▪ Manuel Castells 152–55 ▪ Ulrich Beck 156–61 ▪ David Held 170–71 ▪ Thorstein Veblen 214–19 ▪ Daniel Bell 224–25

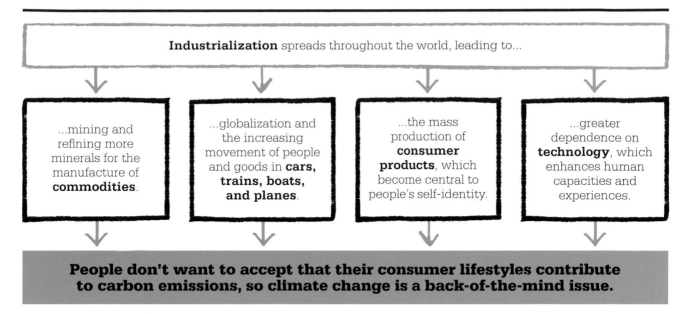

Industrialization spreads throughout the world, leading to...

...mining and refining more minerals for the manufacture of **commodities**.

...globalization and the increasing movement of people and goods in **cars, trains, boats, and planes**.

...the mass production of **consumer products**, which become central to people's self-identity.

...greater dependence on **technology**, which enhances human capacities and experiences.

People don't want to accept that their consumer lifestyles contribute to carbon emissions, so climate change is a back-of-the-mind issue.

A by-product of this energy production is carbon dioxide, which builds up in the upper atmosphere and traps energy from the sun, leading to "global warming" and extreme weather events, such as droughts, floods, and cyclones.

Innovative solutions

In *The Politics of Climate Change* (2009) Giddens argues that because the dangers posed by environmental degradation and climate change are not obvious or immediately visible in everyday life, many people "...do nothing of a concrete nature about them. Yet waiting until such dangers become visible and acute—in the shape of catastrophes that are irrefutably the result of climate change—before being stirred to serious action will be too late."

"Giddens' paradox" is the label that he gives to this disconnect between the rewards of the present and the threat of future dangers and catastrophes.

However, Giddens is optimistic about the future. He believes that the same human ingenuity that gave rise to industrial and high-tech societies can be used to find innovative solutions to reducing carbon emissions. For instance, international cooperation is seeing countries introducing carbon trading schemes and carbon taxes,

which use market forces to reward companies that reduce their greenhouse gas emissions. New technologies are also being researched, developed, and shared, which could potentially end the world's reliance on fossil fuels, and provide cheap and clean sources of energy for both developed and developing societies. ■

Future discounting

According to Giddens, the concept of "future discounting" explains why people take steps to solve present problems but ignore the threats that face them in the future. He notes that people often choose a small reward now, rather than take a course of action that might lead to a greater reward in the future. The same psychological principle applies to risks.

To illustrate his point, Giddens uses the example of a smoker. Why does a young

person take up smoking, when the health risks are widely known? For the teenage smoker it is almost impossible to imagine being 40, the age at which the dangers start to take hold and have potentially fatal consequences. This analogy applies to climate change. People are addicted to advanced technology and the mobility afforded by fossils fuels. Rather than tackle an uncomfortable reality, it is easier to ignore the warnings of climate scientists.

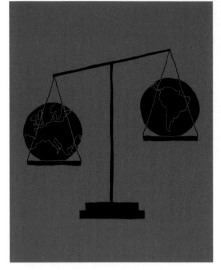

NO SOCIAL JUSTICE WITHOUT GLOBAL COGNITIVE JUSTICE
BOAVENTURA DE SOUSA SANTOS (1940–)

IN CONTEXT

FOCUS
**Epistemologies
of the South**

KEY DATES
1976 G-7 is formed by the world's seven wealthiest and most influential nation-states to discuss global affairs.

1997 Indian scholar Shiv Visvanathan coins the term "cognitive justice," in his book *A Carnival for Science: Essays on Science, Technology, and Development.*

2001 The World Social Forum is founded in Brazil by anti-globalization activists to discuss alternative pathways to sustainable development and economic justice.

2014 British sociologist David Inglis uses de Sousa Santos's ideas about the plurality of knowledge to critically consider the development of cosmopolitan society.

A **Western capitalist world order** has taken root, stratifying nations not only along economic and political lines but also by **forms of knowledge**.

This has resulted in a **cultural battle** in which the global North, with its **culture rooted in science**, regards the global South as **culturally inferior**.

Global equality can only be achieved when cultures enter into a **dialogue based on mutual respect** and acknowledgment of **different forms of knowledge**.

There can be no social justice without global cognitive justice.

The notion that knowledge and culture are inseparable was proposed by French sociologist Émile Durkheim. He claimed that the culture of a group—its collectively produced ideas and ways of thinking about situations and events—shapes the ways in which its members accumulate socially specific knowledge about the world.

Portuguese sociologist Boaventura de Sousa Santos accepts that this link exists and, building upon Immanuel Wallerstein's concept of the world

See also: Zygmunt Bauman 136–43 ▪ Immanuel Wallerstein 144–45 ▪ Roland Robertson 146–47 ▪ Arjun Appadurai 166–69 ▪ Antonio Gramsci 178–79

system, he has extended the idea to what he says is the cultural battle created by globalization. He claims the world is divided into an uneven conflict between dominant ("hegemonic") groups, states, and ideologies on one side, and dominated ("counter-hegemonic") groups, collectives, and ideas on the other. The battle takes place at a number of levels, including the economy, technology, and politics.

Culture and power

De Sousa Santos says that the cultures of the world—and the knowledge embedded within them—are hierarchically arranged and unevenly accessible, in line with wider capitalist power relations. Referring to the philosophical term "epistemology" (from *episteme*, "knowledge"), he argues that the marginalization of some nations by others on the world stage is intimately related to epistemological exclusion. Because the dominant models of social research are those imposed by the

Indigenous tribes, such as Brazil's Kayapó, understand the properties of healing plants. Western pharmaceutical companies exploit this knowledge, but fail to reward the tribes adequately.

global North, he refers to different agendas from the peripheral states as "epistemologies of the South."

In his work, de Sousa Santos acknowledges that his goal is to end these hierarchies of exclusion, because "there is no social justice without global cognitive justice." He maintains that the cultural diversity of the world is matched by its epistemological diversity; recognition of this has to be at the core of any global effort to eradicate current inequalities. The biggest obstacle to this, argues de Sousa Santos, is that the scientific knowledge of the global North is "hegemonic" within the social hierarchy of knowledge.

Technological dominance

The capitalist and imperial order imposed on the global South by the global North has an epistemological foundation. Western powers have developed the capacity to dominate many parts of the world, not least by elevating modern science to the status of a form of universal knowledge, superior to all other types of knowledge. Other non-scientific forms of knowledge, and the cultural and social practices of different social groups informed by these knowledges, are suppressed in the name of modern science. Modern science has colonized our thinking to such an extent that diverging from it is classified as irrational thought. An example of this is the Western media's portrayal of Middle Eastern culture as irrational and excessively emotionally charged, which has "destructive consequences."

Instead, de Sousa Santos is keen to develop a transnational cultural dialogue that will result in

Boaventura de Sousa Santos

Boaventura de Sousa Santos is a professor at the University of Coimbra, Portugal. He earned his doctorate in the US, at Yale, and is a visiting professor at the University of Wisconsin-Madison. He is a defender of strong social and civic movements, which he regards as essential for the realization of participative democracy.

In 2001 de Sousa Santos founded The World Social Forum as a meeting place for organizations opposed to forms of globalization led by neoliberal economic policy and transnational corporate capitalism. He has published widely on globalization, sociology of law and the state, democracy, and human rights.

Key works

2006 *The Rise of the Global Left: The World Social Forum and Beyond*
2007 *Cognitive Justice in a Global World: Prudent Knowledges for a Decent Life*
2014 *Epistemologies of the South*

plurality: an "emancipatory, non-relativistic cosmopolitan ecology of knowledges," which will have at their heart the recognition of difference, and of the right to difference and coexistence. Only by these means, says de Sousa Santos, can we achieve a truly global understanding of how societies work. This vision informs the efforts of groups such as The World Social Forum, which seeks to bring about social and economic justice using alternatives to capitalism. ▪

THE UNLEASHING OF PRODUCTIVE CAPACITY BY THE POWER OF THE MIND

MANUEL CASTELLS (1942–)

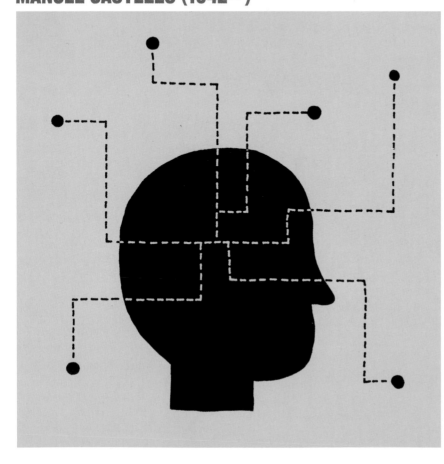

IN CONTEXT

FOCUS
Network society

KEY DATES
1848 Karl Marx and Friedrich Engels' *The Communist Manifesto* forecasts the globalization of capitalism.

1968 Manuel Castells studies under French sociologist Alain Touraine on the subject of social movements and resistance to capitalism.

From 1990 The corporate use of Internet-based technology increases, spreading out to the wider public and domestic life.

1992 US sociologist Harrison White writes "Markets, Networks, and Control," a discussion of network theory.

1999 Dutch sociologist Jan Van Dijk writes *The Network Society*, focusing on social media such as Facebook.

The last 50 years have seen giant leaps in science and developments in Internet-based and digital technologies. According to Spanish sociologist Manuel Castells (whose work straddles communication and information studies and is strongly influenced by Karl Marx), these advances have been shaped by—and played a key role in contributing to—economic, social, and political developments on the world stage. This has led Castells to focus on globalization and its economic and social effects.

For Marx, industrial capitalism was based on the production of consumer goods and commodities.

The "network society" is an **interconnected global community** of interests...

...where access to the network, or the **"space of flows,"** is no longer the preserve of a dominant social group.

This means almost **anyone, anywhere**, can use telecommunications-based technology for any **creative purpose**.

During the 1970s, US sociologist Daniel Bell invoked the term "post-industrialism" to designate the shift toward a service-led economy. Castells argues that the rise to prominence of Internet-based technologies means capitalism now centers on information and knowledge. Human societies, he claims, have left behind the Industrial Age and entered the Information Age, the social–structural expression of which is the "network society."

A networked world

The Information Age is defined by the creation and dissemination of various specialist knowledges such as fluctuations in world oil prices, the financial markets, and so on. In advanced capitalist societies, networks of financial capital and information are now at the heart of productivity and competitiveness.

The shift from the production of goods and services to information and knowledge has profoundly altered the nature of society and social relations. Castells claims that the dominant mode of organizing interpersonal relations, institutions,

and whole societies is networks. Moreover, the malleable and open-ended nature of these networks means that they span the globe.

When classical sociologists such as Karl Marx, Émile Durkheim, and Max Weber use the term "society," it refers primarily to that of a given nation-state. So, for example, it is possible to talk of US society as something different from, as well as sharing similarities with, say, British society. However, in Castells' work, the nation-state has become the globe and everything in it. The world of relatively autonomous nation-states, with their own internally structured societies, is no longer—it has been reimagined as multitudes of overlapping and intersecting networks.

The idea of a fully connected world, wired through the Internet, conjures up images of people in all corners of the planet engaging productively in different types of relations with one another in constantly shifting networks—constrained not by geography or nationality, but only by the capacity of human imagination. It is now possible to access information 24 hours a day through search engines such as Google, and to join chat rooms with people thousands of miles away and engage in instantaneous communication.

Castells elaborates on the concept of networks in a variety of ways. Microelectronics-based networks define the network society and have replaced bureaucracy as the main way of »

BM&FBOVESPA in São Paulo, Brazil, is the largest stock exchange in Latin America. The exclusively electronic trading environment exemplifies the global economy in the Information Age.

The network society is a result of affordable, globally unifying telecommunications technology that has changed how we live, think, and do things. People who may never meet one another can now communicate instantly to trade goods or to exchange information and ideas.

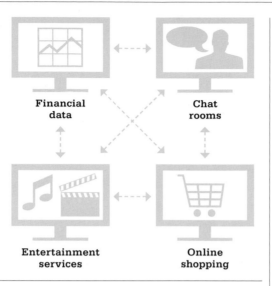

Financial data

Chat rooms

Entertainment services

Online shopping

organizing social relations, because they are far better at managing complexity. As well as the economic networks of financial trade and capital investment, microelectronic networks include political and interpersonal networks. The "network state" includes transnational political bodies such as the European Union, while examples of interpersonal networks are enacted through the Internet, email, and social networking websites such as Facebook and Twitter.

Castells says a network can be defined as follows: it has no "center"; it is made up of a series of "nodes" of varying importance but nevertheless all are necessary in order for the network to operate; the degree of social power peculiar to a network is relative depending on how much information it is able to process; a network only deals with a certain type of information—namely, the type of information relevant to it; and a network is an open structure, able to expand and compress without limits.

Castells emphasizes the high levels of adaptability characteristic of network society. Key here is that

a social order organized into and around networks can lay claim to being highly dynamic, innovative, and geared to ongoing, fast-moving social changes. Castells describes networked social relations as a "dynamic, self-expanding form of human activity" that tends to transform all spheres of social and economic life.

Social dynamics

The matter of whether individuals and institutions participate in, or are excluded from, certain social networks provides Castells with a window on the power dynamics at work in the network society. He concludes that networked relations have changed the structure of society over time.

Castells' initial argument was that individuals working within large multinational finance houses and institutions, and whose professional work is structured within and through networks of global financial flows, comprised the dominant social group—what he calls the "technocratic-financial-managerial elite." Occupying the key posts of command and control within the worldwide system,

this elite's preferred spatiality is the global city—from here it is able to reproduce its cosmopolitan practices and interests.

Meanwhile, in contrast, the lives of the masses tend to be local rather than global—organized around and clustered in places where people live in close physical proximity and social relations are characterized by shared ways of life. Therefore, said Castells, most people build meaningful identities and lives in actual geographically specific locales, the "space of places," rather than in the ethereal and placeless world of electronic networks, the "space of flows."

With the spread of the Internet and social media, however, this view of a unified, cosmopolitan, global elite using the space of flows to exert power came to be seen as overly simplistic. Economically impoverished social groups may find it harder to incorporate into, and center their lifestyles on, Internet-based technologies to the same degree as socially dominant groups, but this is less and less the case. Castells now claims that "people of all kinds, wishing to do all kinds of things, can occupy this space of flows and use it for their own purposes."

> Networks have become the predominant organizational form of every domain of human activity.
> **Manuel Castells**

Anti-capitalist organizations, such as the Anticapitalist Initiative (which expressly refers to itself as a network on its website), have made use of the Internet in creative ways to connect people through a burgeoning network that occupies the space of flows. Castells uses the example of the Zapatistas in Mexico to acknowledge that social power can be accrued through the space of flows by marginalized groups in order to challenge the state and elite institutions. The Zapatistas have been successful in attracting media attention in cyberspace and have used the Internet to perform virtual sit-ins, with software clogging government servers and websites, as well as to plan and coordinate offline events.

Dystopia or utopia?

Castells' twin concepts of Information Age and network society provide a powerful set of analytical tools for understanding the transformative effects that information technology and globalization are having on human life and social relations.

Marx's concept of alienation resonates throughout Castells' work, which represents an attempt to make sense of the furiously paced changes and processes unfolding in the world around us with a view to reclaiming control over them. However, the idea that humans have created a global society they have lost control of and are alienated by is in part indebted to other theorists of globalization such as Anthony Giddens, Ulrich Beck, and Zygmunt Bauman.

Castells' work has many critics. Sociologists such as Bauman say it is utopian considering the "reality" of the social, economic, political, and environmental problems confronting humanity today. Others deny that the present social and economic order is historically unprecedented; British sociologist Nicholas Garnham argues that the network society is more accurately a development of industrialism than a novel stage in human society. British sociologist Frank Webster charges Castells with technological determinism— the view that social relations are intimately shaped by technological developments but are not determined by them; rather, the two influence one another.

Whether or not the network society is novel or beneficial, there is no doubt that the world is increasingly interconnected and reliant on digital technologies, which are reshaping social relations. For Castells, the rise of a global society bound by myriad networks is, ultimately, a positive thing. Enabling people from far-flung places to interact offers the potential for humanity to draw upon its collective productive resources to create a new and enlightened world order. He argues that if we "are informed, active, and communicate throughout the world" then we "can depart for exploration of the inner self, having made peace among ourselves." ∎

> While organizations are located in places... the organizational logic is placeless.
> **Manuel Castells**

Manuel Castells

Manuel Castells Oliván was born in 1942 in Spain. After being active in the student anti-Franco movement, he left Spain for France to study for a PhD in sociology at the University of Paris during the politically turbulent late 1960s.

In the 1980s Castells moved to California—the home of Silicon Valley. A decade or so later he wrote an influential three-volume study about the network society entitled *The Information Age: Economy, Society, and Culture.*

Castells is an influential social scientific thinker. He is a sociologist at the University of Southern California (USC), Los Angeles, contributed to the establishment of the USC Center on Public Diplomacy, and is also a member of the Annenberg Research Network on International Communication (ARNIC).

Key works

1996 *The Information Age: Volume I: The Rise of the Network Society*
1997 *The Information Age: Volume II: The Power of Identity*
1998 *The Information Age: Volume III: End of Millennium*

WE ARE LIVING IN A WORLD THAT IS BEYOND CONTROLLABILITY

ULRICH BECK (1944–2015)

IN CONTEXT

FOCUS
Risk society

KEY DATES
1968 The Club of Rome think tank is founded and in 1972 publishes a report "The Limits to Growth," which identifies the risk posed by excessive population growth.

1984 US sociologist Charles Perrow publishes *Normal Accidents: Living with High-Risk Technologies*.

1999 US sociologist Barry Glassner draws on Ulrich Beck's concept of risk in *The Culture of Fear: Why Americans Are Afraid of the Wrong Things*.

2001 The 9/11 attacks on the US lead to worldwide changes in the perception of the risks posed by international terrorist organizations.

We are entering a new period of **"reflexive" modernity**, which is characterized by **uncertainty and insecurity**.

The **scientific and technological revolution** that delivered progress is now viewed as having **introduced problems of development and global risks**.

Nothing appears fixed anymore and **contradictions emerge between scientists and policymakers** about the **appropriate risk response**.

Loss of respect for institutions and experts creates uncertainty and doubt as we begin to fear we are living in a world that is beyond controllability.

Human societies have always faced dangers, and historically these have usually been "natural" in origin. In recent years, science, technology, and industry have created prosperity, but have also brought about new dangers (for example, those posed by the production of nuclear power), which have focused the thoughts of individuals and societies on a quest for safety and the idea of calculable risk. In the mid-1980s the German sociologist Ulrich Beck claimed that our relationship to society and its

institutions had changed profoundly over the past decades, and that this required a new way of thinking about risk. Beck argues that social life is progressing from a first stage of modernity to an emergent second, or "reflexive," stage. This is shaped by an awareness that control of—and mastery over—nature and society may be impossible. This awareness may itself lead to disenchantment with existing social structures as providers of safety and reassurance.

A key characteristic of this new stage is the emergence of a global "risk society," by which Beck

means that individuals, groups, governments, and corporations are increasingly concerned about the production, dissemination, and experience of risk. We now have to confront problems that previous generations could not imagine, and this requires new societal responses.

In his earlier work, Beck points in particular to the risks posed by nuclear energy, the chemical industry, and biotechnology. He says that the application of science and technology to meet human needs has reached a critical

See also: August Comte 22–25 ▪ Karl Marx 28–31 ▪ Max Weber 38–45 ▪ Anthony Giddens 148–49

threshold; that our advances have opened up the possibility of disasters on an unprecedented scale. Should such a catastrophe occur, it would be so grave that it would be almost impossible to contain its impact or to return to the way things were before.

Qualities of risk

Beck identifies three significant qualities of risk. First, global, irreparable damage: accidents cannot be compensated for, so insurance no longer works. Second, exclusion of precautionary aftercare: we cannot return conditions to the way they were before the accident. Third, no limit on space and time: accidents are unpredictable, can be felt across national borders, and impose their effects over long periods of time.

In terms of dealing with the possibility or likelihood of such calamities happening in the future, traditional methods of risk calculation have become obsolete in relation to many of the new kinds of risks that concern us in the 21st century, such as health pandemics, nuclear meltdowns, or genetically modified foodstuffs. As a result, how do scientists, corporations, and governments try to manage such potentially catastrophic risks?

Real and virtual risk

Beck identifies a strange ambiguity in how society understands risks. On the one hand, they are real—they exist as objective, latent threats at the heart of scientific and technological progress. They cannot be ignored, even if authorities try to pretend they do not exist. At the same time, however, risks are also virtual; that is, they represent current anxieties about events that have yet to—or may never—happen. Nonetheless, it is the apparent threat posed by these risks, the anticipation of disaster, that ushers in new challenges to the power of scientists, corporations, and governments.

Beck observes that no one is an expert on questions of risk, not even the experts themselves. The intrinsic complexity of many risks

> Neither science, nor the politics in power... are in a position to define or control risks rationally.
> **Ulrich Beck**

means that scientists often cannot agree on questions of likelihood, possible severity, or how to set up proper safety procedures. In fact in the public mind, it is these same experts—in their manipulation of genes or splitting of atomic nuclei—who may have created the risks.

However, while there is public skepticism about scientists, Beck notes that they are nevertheless essential in the risk society. Precisely because we cannot feel, hear, smell, or see the risks that »

Ulrich Beck

Ulrich Beck was born in 1944 in the town of Stolp, Germany, which is now part of Poland. From 1966 onward he studied sociology, philosophy, psychology, and political science at Munich University. In 1972 he received his doctorate at Munich University and in 1979 he became a full university lecturer. He was subsequently appointed professor at the universities of Münster and Bamberg.

From 1992 Beck was professor of sociology and director of the Institute for Sociology at Munich's Ludwig Maximilian University; he was also Visiting Professor at the London School of Economics. Beck was one of Europe's most high-profile sociologists; in addition to his academic writing and research he commented on contemporary issues in the media and played an active role in German and European political affairs. He died in 2015.

Key works

1986 *Risk Society*
1997 *What is Globalization?*
1999 *World Risk Society*
2004 *The Cosmopolitan Vision*

we face, we need these experts to help measure, calculate, and make sense of them for us.

Making risks meaningful

Beck notes the important role played by so-called "new social movements" in raising public awareness of risk. For instance, Greenpeace, an independent organization committed to environmental protection, runs many high-profile publicity campaigns to draw attention to the environmental risks both caused and downplayed by corporations and governments.

The media feeds on public anxieties about risk, claims Beck. To increase sales, news providers latch on to stories of corporate or institutional failures to adequately manage risk, or sensationalize stories of the hidden threats posed by technological developments.

While ultimately self-serving, Beck sees this as a positive thing because it helps develop public consciousness about risks and promote open debate. The media makes risks visible and meaningful for people by giving abstract risks

> 66
> Reduced to a formula, wealth is hierarchic, smog is democratic.
> **Ulrich Beck**
> 99

a powerful symbolic form. For example, the consequences of rising global temperatures over many decades into the future can feel slightly unreal and abstract. However, "then-and-now" imagery of retreating glaciers, or footage of polar bears perched perilously on top of dissolving chunks of ice, delivers a powerful message about the immediacy of the risks the world faces.

Among the wider social consequences of living in a risk society is a change in the nature of inequality. In the past, wealthier individuals could protect

themselves from risks, perhaps by paying more to live in a safer community or by having private insurance to provide better medical care. However, people can no longer buy their way out of many modern-day risks. Up to a point, someone could spend their way out of one risk by eating more expensive organic food to avoid the perceived hazards of industrial pesticides. Similarly, wealthier nations might avoid the polluting effects of heavy industry by outsourcing production to rapidly developing nations such as China. Sooner or later, however, these risks "boomerang" back. Here, Beck emphasizes the third quality of risk—that it does not respect boundaries of space and time. Wealth itself provides no certain way to avoid risk—the affluent West cannot ultimately escape the consequences of global warming that will be exacerbated by China's industrialization.

Globalized fears and hopes

In his more recent work on the concepts of "world risk society" and "cosmopolitanism," Beck argues that the process of globalization—

Today's technological societies create risks that may be unknown or almost impossible to quantify. According to Beck, when faced with such unknowable risks, we have three main responses—denial, apathy, or transformation.

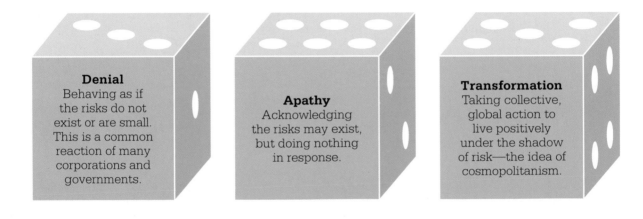

Denial
Behaving as if the risks do not exist or are small. This is a common reaction of many corporations and governments.

Apathy
Acknowledging the risks may exist, but doing nothing in response.

Transformation
Taking collective, global action to live positively under the shadow of risk—the idea of cosmopolitanism.

Surveillance, of both public spaces and private communications, has grown in the Western world in response to the real and perceived dangers posed by terrorist violence.

the growth of interdependency that undermines the influence and power of nation-states—produces its own negative consequences.

These include financial risks and terrorism risks. With the global growth of hedge funds, futures markets, derivatives trading, debt securitization, and credit default swaps, no country can hide behind its borders from the consequences of something going wrong. Acts of terrorist violence, planned and carried out by ideological groups, permeate the boundaries between states by striking at the heart of global cities such as New York and London. Interestingly, Beck observes that global terrorism is one of the few risks that governments are happy to draw attention to for political purposes.

While Beck's overriding focus on risk seems bleak, he also highlights what he sees as the positive possibilities inherent in the growth of risk. He points to the development of what he terms "cosmopolitanism," a concept comprising several components.

First, the existence of global risks calls for a global response: catastrophic risks affect humanity as a whole and must be responded to collectively, beyond the confines of national borders. Second, the level of media attention devoted to risks and catastrophes has the effect of giving more attention to how disasters impact most heavily upon the poor; the media coverage of Hurricane Katrina in the US in 2005, for example, demonstrated to a global audience how poverty worsens the experience of catastrophe. Third, public experience and awareness of risk today draws groups into dialogue with one another; for example, Beck notes how environmental groups and businesses have joined forces to protest at the US government's lack of responsiveness to the problem of climate change.

Risk and reward

Beck's work has been read widely beyond the world of sociology, because it deals in an all-encompassing way with many of the key changes and concerns of recent decades. First published in German in 1986, at a time of new environmental concerns about acid rain and ozone layer depletion, his original concept of the risk society encapsulated and anticipated a number of high-profile environmental issues and accidents, such as the 1984 Bhopal disaster in India—where a gas leak from a chemical plant caused widespread poisoning—and the 1986 Chernobyl nuclear plant explosion in Ukraine. More recently, Beck's analysis has been applied to issues of global terrorism and the near-collapse of the financial system in 2008; it has been taken on board by others as a way of making sense of a diverse array of issues, including international relations, crime control, human health, food safety, social policy, and social work.

Ultimately, a positive strain runs through Beck's work. He argues that the experience of responding to global risk can lead to innovative solutions and constructive social changes. It is only in new encounters with the possibility of catastrophe that collective welfare and common interests can prevail over narrow, selfish concerns and our modern institutions can be reconfigured accordingly. ■

Fears about acid rain and global warming led to the Intergovernmental Panel on Climate Change. Formed in 1988, it reviewed the state of knowledge of the science of climate change.

IT SOMETIMES SEEMS AS IF THE WHOLE WORLD IS ON THE MOVE
JOHN URRY (1946–)

IN CONTEXT

FOCUS
Mobilities

KEY DATES
1830 The world's first inter-city railway opens in England between Liverpool and Manchester.

1840 In Britain the first prepaid adhesive postage stamp, the "Penny Black," revolutionizes the circulation of information and goods.

1903 US brothers Wilbur and Orville Wright make the first powered flight in North Carolina.

From the 1960s
Telecommunications satellites go into orbit, heralding the instantaneous global transmission of information.

1989–91 British scientist Tim Berners-Lee develops the World Wide Web.

2007 British sociologist John Urry publishes *Mobilities*.

Since the 17th century, new technologies have been emerging that have enabled people, objects, and ideas to move around the world more easily than before. British sociologist John Urry advises that the consequences of this increase in global mobility demand that the social sciences develop a "new paradigm" for the study of how goods, people, and ideas circulate. For Urry this movement creates new identities, cultures, and networks, giving rise to cultural diversity, economic opportunities and, at times, new forms of social inequality.

Systems and mobilities
Urry's primary contribution to the study of globalization is his focus on the social systems that facilitate movement. The 20th century, in particular, saw the emergence of cars, telephones, air power, high-speed trains, communications satellites, networked computers, and so on. These interconnecting "mobility systems" are the dynamic heart of globalization, says Urry.

> Being physically mobile has become… a 'way of life' across the globe.
> **John Urry**

He argues that the study of "mobilities" makes apparent the impacts and consequences of globalization. Likewise, the study of the forces preventing mobility—"immobilities"—is essential for comprehending contemporary social exclusion and inequality.

By understanding this global flow, sociology can better explore globalization's social and environmental advantages and costs (such as economic growth or industrial pollutants), as well as the forces driving social change. ∎

See also: Zygmunt Bauman 136–43 ▪ Manuel Castells 152–55 ▪ Saskia Sassen 164–65 ▪ David Held 170–71

NATIONS CAN BE IMAGINED AND CONSTRUCTED WITH RELATIVELY LITTLE HISTORICAL STRAW
DAVID McCRONE

IN CONTEXT

FOCUS
Neo-nationalism

KEY DATES
1707 The Act of Union is ratified and the United Kingdom is officially formed.

1971 British ethnographer Anthony D. Smith publishes his highly influential study, *Theories of Nationalism*.

1983 British sociologist Benedict Anderson publishes *Imagined Communities*, which examines the formation of nationhood.

1998 British sociologist David McCrone argues in *The Sociology of Nationalism* that nationalism operates as a vehicle for a variety of social and economic interests.

2004 Japanese sociologist Atsuko Ichijo explores the apparent contradiction of an "independence in Europe" policy in *Scottish Nationalism and the Idea of Europe*.

The economic, political, and cultural forces that globalization brings to bear have, according to British sociologist David McCrone, coincided with a rise in neo-nationalism, which occurs when a social group within a nation tries to redefine its identity. He argues that all neo-national identities concern smaller entities within larger nation-states: for example, Scotland in the United Kingdom, Catalonia in Spain, the Basque Country that straddles southwestern France and northern Spain, and French-speaking Quebec in Canada.

Both national and neo-national identities are forged from the "raw historical materials" of a common language, cultural myths and narratives, and social ideals. McCrone says that solidarity comes into being whenever enough people invoke these raw materials, or "historical straw," in pursuit of a common cause. Moreover, relatively little historical straw is required to galvanize neo-nationalist sentiment; often only a few symbols are needed to evoke strong feelings in people, such as the Senyera flag of Catalonia, or the fleur-de-lis symbol in Quebec. Although a sense of being distinctively different from the larger state may be the main factor that prompts calls for more autonomy or outright independence, the motivations for neo-nationalist identities or separatism can differ widely. They may, for example, be motivated by perceived unfairness in taxation or resource allocation. ∎

The Basque separatist organization ETA engaged in political and armed conflict with the Spanish and French states from 1959 to 2011, in a quest for political independence.

See also: Émile Durkheim 34–37 ▪ Paul Gilroy 75 ▪ John Urry 162 ▪ David Held 170–71 ▪ Benedict Anderson 202–03 ▪ Michel Maffesoli 291

GLOBAL CITIES ARE STRATEGIC SITES FOR NEW TYPES OF OPERATIONS
SASKIA SASSEN (1949–)

IN CONTEXT

FOCUS
Global cities

KEY DATES
1887 Ferdinand Tönnies says urbanization affects social solidarity by giving rise to a more individualistic society.

1903 Georg Simmel suggests that cities can cause people to adopt an "urban reserve" and blasé attitude.

1920s–40s "Chicago School" sociologists claim that cities have an "urban ecology," in which people compete for employment and services.

From the 1980s British sociologist David Harvey and Spanish sociologist Manuel Castells separately argue that cities are shaped by capitalism, which influences not only their character but also the various interactions of their inhabitants.

Globalization does not take place by itself. According to Saskia Sassen, professor of sociology at Columbia University, New York, certain cities play a key role in generating the economic and cultural flows that connect the world together. These "global cities" exert power and influence well beyond the territory in which they are located.

Sociologists study cities to understand what impact they have on the behavior, values, and opportunities of occupants. In the 20th century, they noted that the large industrial cities of the developed world were forming

Wall Street is the economic engine of the global city of New York. Such cities, Sassen says, are the "terrain where a multiplicity of globalization processes assume concrete, localized forms."

new connections and becoming economically interdependent. These changes were resulting, in part, from trade liberalization and the global expansion of industrial capitalism. Within this new "global economy," central clusters of economic and cultural activity, or "global cities," were forming.

The modern metropolis
Global cities, Sassen advises, produce goods in the form of technological innovations, financial products, and consulting services (legal, accounting, advertising, and so on). These service industries are highly intensive users of telecommunications technologies and are therefore integrated into business networks that stretch across national borders. They are also part of the post-industrial or "service" economies of the developed world, in that their main products are knowledge, innovation, technical expertise, and cultural goods.

Sassen argues in *The Global City* (1991, revised 2001) that the emergence of a global market for financial and specialized services gives global cities a "command and control function" over economic

See also: Ferdinand Tönnies 32–33 ▪ Georg Simmel 104–05 ▪ Henri Lefebvre 106–07 ▪ Zygmunt Bauman 136–43 ▪ Immanuel Wallerstein 144–45 ▪ David Held 170–71

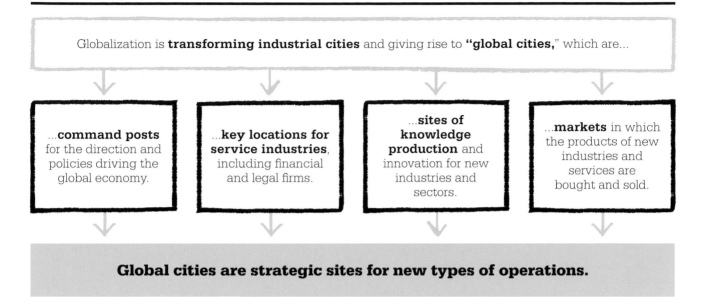

Globalization is **transforming industrial cities** and giving rise to **"global cities,"** which are...

...**command posts** for the direction and policies driving the global economy.

...**key locations for service industries**, including financial and legal firms.

...**sites of knowledge production** and innovation for new industries and sectors.

...**markets** in which the products of new industries and services are bought and sold.

Global cities are strategic sites for new types of operations.

globalization. This is because the headquarters of many major transnational companies are located in global cities. Consultant firms are also "over-represented" in these urban hubs. These companies make the decisions that direct global flows of money and knowledge, and that can cause economic activity to expand or contract in other regions.

The global marketplace

Global cities are also marketplaces where financial goods are bought and sold. New York, London, Tokyo, Amsterdam, Hong Kong, Shanghai, Frankfurt, and Sydney (among others) are major financial centers, home to large banks, businesses, and stock exchanges. In the global city, national and global markets interconnect, which leads to a concentration of financial activity.

Global cities are supported by multifunctional infrastructure. Central business districts provide employment clusters where the employees of local, national, and multinational firms interact. Influential universities and research facilities also contribute to the production of knowledge and innovation, which are central to information-based economies.

Sassen's research shows that global cities are sites where the human activities behind the processes of globalization are performed and their consequences dispersed through the socio-economic networks of the global economy. While global cities are not free from poverty and other forms of social inequality, they are nevertheless cosmopolitan sites of diverse economic and social opportunities. ▪

Multinational urban culture

Sassen's work highlights that global cities are increasingly cosmopolitan. As migrants add new foods, cultural expressions, fashions, and entertainments to the host national culture, this diversity enriches a city.

In a nation-state that encourages multiculturalism and social inclusion, global cities can become even more vibrant sites of cultural innovation as ideas and values are freely shared. This multicultural texturing of a pre-existing national culture also increases economic activity. This is because global cities are more appealing for transitory visitors and migrants, who can maintain aspects of their ethnic and national identities, while embracing the new experiences and values of a cosmopolitan city. The cultural diversity of global cities also means that they are orientated toward supporting the activities of a global economy and a cosmopolitan global culture.

DIFFERENT SOCIETIES APPROPRIATE THE MATERIALS OF MODERNITY DIFFERENTLY

ARJUN APPADURAI (1949–)

IN CONTEXT

FOCUS
Globalization and modernity

KEY DATES
1963 Jacques Derrida introduces the concept of "différance" (difference), which later informs ideas about cultural heterogeneity.

1983 British social thinker Benedict Anderson says that groupings based on the perceptions of their members rather than direct interaction are "imagined communities."

1991 Economic liberalization opens India to globalizing forces as the country tries to integrate into the global order.

2008 Postcolonial studies thinker Richard Brock applies Appadurai's notion of "scapes" to critically consider the cultural construction of the HIV/AIDS pandemic.

The term "globalization" has become associated with the spread of free-market capitalism and the development of borderless economies—the idea of a global trading village. In a sociological context, however, globalization is not just an economic, but a cultural, social, and ideological phenomenon.

Much debate among cultural theorists has addressed the issue of whether globalization necessarily means that the world will become more homogenous—moving toward a "one-world" culture—or whether reactions to the forces of globalization will reinforce diversity in language, culture, and ethnicity.

See also: Zygmunt Bauman 136–43 ▪ Immanuel Wallerstein 144–45 ▪
Roland Robertson 146–47 ▪ Manuel Castells 152–55 ▪ Jeffrey Alexander 204–09

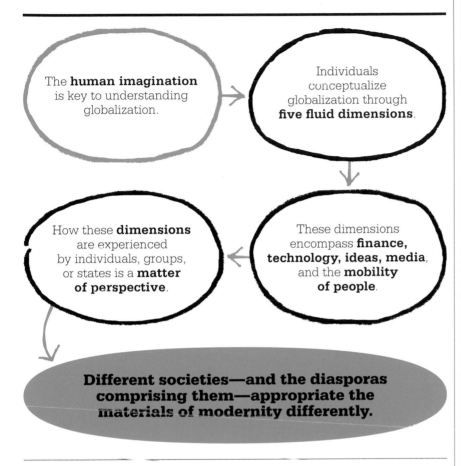

The **human imagination** is key to understanding globalization.

Individuals conceptualize globalization through **five fluid dimensions**.

How these **dimensions** are experienced by individuals, groups, or states is a **matter of perspective**.

These dimensions encompass **finance, technology, ideas, media**, and the **mobility of people**.

Different societies—and the diasporas comprising them—appropriate the materials of modernity differently.

Arjun Appadurai

Born in Mumbai, India, Arjun Appadurai went to the US to study at Brandeis University, near Boston. He attained his master's degree in 1973 and his doctorate from the University of Chicago in 1976.

Appadurai is currently the Goddard Professor in Media, Culture, and Communication at New York University, where he is also Senior Fellow at the Institute for Public Knowledge. He has served as an advisor to the Smithsonian Institution, the National Endowment for the Humanities, the National Science Foundation, the United Nations, and the World Bank. Appadurai founded and is president of the nonprofit group Partners for Urban Knowledge Action and Research, based in Mumbai, and he is one of the founders of *Public Culture*, an interdisciplinary journal focused on transnationalism.

Key works

1990 "Disjuncture and Difference in the Global Cultural Economy"
1996 *Modernity at Large: Cultural Dimensions of Globalization*
2001 *Globalization*

Indian social anthropologist and sociologist Arjun Appadurai has taken this debate in a different direction. He argues that the conventional view of globalization as a form of cultural imperialism fails to reflect the reality of the changes globalization has set in motion. Instead, Appadurai suggests that different societies appropriate the materials of modernity differently.

What this means is that one society, such as China, may take up one aspect of global change (such as economic change) very rapidly, and another aspect (such as ideological change) very slowly, while another society will be different altogether. The result is that globalization does not necessarily denote a uniform and all-encompassing process; rather, nations are more positively disposed toward certain facets of globalization than others, depending on a range of factors, such as the state of the economy, political stability, and strength of cultural identity. For example, China has embraced industrial and information technologies and global economic expansion, while retaining a strong sense of political autonomy.

For Appadurai, the process of globalization is one that leads to "disjunctures" where areas such »

> One man's imagined community is another man's political prison.
> **Arjun Appadurai**

as the economy, culture, and politics do not move in the same direction, thereby causing tensions in society. An example of this is the distance between a promise of consumer goods made by global companies and the ability of local people to afford them.

Appadurai's work addresses how globalization diminishes the role of the nation-state in shaping cultural identity and argues that identity is increasingly becoming deterritorialized by mobility, migration, and rapid communications. People no longer hold coherent sets of ideas, views, beliefs, and practices based on their nationality or membership of a state; instead, new cultural identities are emerging in the interstices between different states and localities—what Appadurai calls translocalities.

Globally imagined worlds

The key to understanding globalization, says Appadurai, is the human imagination. He argues that rather than living in face-to-face communities, we live within imagined ones that are global in extent. The building blocks are five interrelated dimensions that shape the global flow of ideas and information. He calls these dimensions "scapes"—ethnoscapes, mediascapes, technoscapes, finanscapes, and ideoscapes. Unlike landscapes, which are characteristically fixed, Appadurai's "scapes" are constantly changing, and the manner in which they are experienced depends largely on the perspective of the social actors involved.

In this context, social actors may be any one of a number of groupings, such as nation-states, multinational corporations, diasporic communities, families, or individuals. The different ways in which these five scapes can combine means that the imagined world that one person or grouping perceives can be radically different, and no more real, than that seen by another observer.

Shifting scapes

Appadurai first used the term "ethnoscape" in a 1990 essay, "Disjuncture and Difference in the Global Cultural Economy," to describe the flow of people—immigrant communities, political exiles, tourists, guest workers, economic migrants, and other groups—around the globe, as well as the "fantasies of wanting to move" in pursuit of a better life. The increasing mobility of people between nations constitutes an essential feature of the global world, in particular by affecting the politics of nation-states.

Mediascapes refer to the production and distribution of information and images through newspapers, magazines, TV, and film, as well as digital technologies. The multiplying ways in which information is made accessible to private and public interests throughout the world is a major driver of globalization. Mediascapes provide large and complex repertoires of images and narratives to viewers, and these shape how people make sense of events taking place across the world.

Technoscapes represent the rapid dissemination of technology and knowledge about it—either mechanical or informational—across borders. For example, many service industries in Western Europe base their customer-care call centers in India, and Indian software engineers are often recruited by US companies.

Finanscapes reflect the almost instantaneous transfer of financial and investment capital around the globe in the fast-moving world of currency markets, stock exchanges, and commodity speculations.

Ideoscapes are made up of images that are "often directly political," either state-produced and intended to bolster the dominant ideology, or created by counter-ideological movements "oriented to

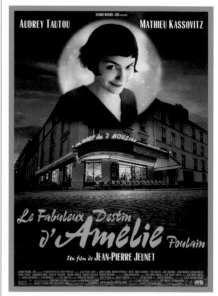

France has embraced many economic dimensions of globalization yet seeks to limit the influence of foreign cultures by, for example, charging a ticket levy to help fund the French film industry.

The perspective of social actors—who may be individuals or groups—is shaped by the position they occupy in relation to the wider culture, society and particular moment in historical time. From within this milieu, they construct a world view.

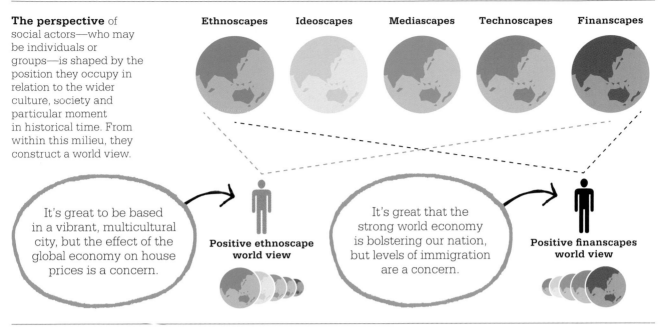

Ethnoscapes Ideoscapes Mediascapes Technoscapes Finanscapes

It's great to be based in a vibrant, multicultural city, but the effect of the global economy on house prices is a concern.

Positive ethnoscape world view

It's great that the strong world economy is bolstering our nation, but levels of immigration are a concern.

Positive finanscapes world view

capturing state power or a piece of it." Examples include ideas about a state built through concepts such as "national heritage," countered by social and political movements that promote the rights of minority groups and freedom of speech.

Sameness and difference

The different "scapes" identified by Appadurai may be, and often are, incongruous and disjointed. For example, social actors in one place may be positively disposed toward economic developments brought about by globalization (that is, they see a positive finanscape), while simultaneously regarding immigration as a threat to national identity and culture (a negative ethnoscape).

By conceptualizing globalization in terms of the five scapes, Appadurai is able to undermine the view of globalization as a uniform and internally coherent process; instead, globalization is understood as a multilayered, fluid, and irregular process—and one that is characterized by ongoing change.

The different scapes are capable of moving together or of following different trajectories, in turn serving either to reinforce or destabilize one another.

Appadurai states that the scapes are constructs of perspective because they are determined by the relation of the viewer to the viewed. If this relation changes, so in turn does the view. In sum, the world view constructed by any social actor is exactly that: it is a view dependent upon the social, cultural, and historical positioning of the actor; and for this reason, who and where we are determines what scapes we see and how we interpret them. There are multiple ways of imagining the world.

The impact of Appadurai's contribution to globalization theory is a significant one, primarily because it does not try to provide an integrated theory of globalization in the orthodox manner of social thinkers such as Immanuel Wallerstein from the US and Spain's Manuel Castells. Quite the opposite; it is Appadurai's

intention to critically deconstruct what he considers the naive view that something as complex and multifaceted as globalization can be explained through one master theory. That said, Appadurai's work has been criticized by the likes of Dutch social thinker Gijsbert Oonk, who questions whether or not his concept of global landscapes can be meaningfully applied when conducting empirical research. ∎

> The new global order cultural economy has to be understood as a complex, overlapping, disjunctive order.
> **Arjun Appadurai**

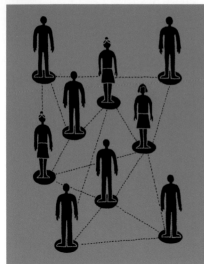

PROCESSES OF CHANGE HAVE ALTERED THE RELATIONS BETWEEN PEOPLES AND COMMUNITIES
DAVID HELD (1951–)

IN CONTEXT

FOCUS
Globalization

KEY DATES
1960s Canadian media theorist Marshall McLuhan claims that the world is contracting into a "global village" through technology.

1974 US sociologist Immanuel Wallerstein publishes *The Modern World-System*, highlighting the social effects of a global economy.

1993 US sociologist George Ritzer claims that systematic methods of production are influencing the operations of institutions and corporations around the world.

2006 German sociologist Ulrich Beck argues that states must embrace multilateral cooperation, transnational institutions, and cosmopolitan identities if they are to prosper in the global age.

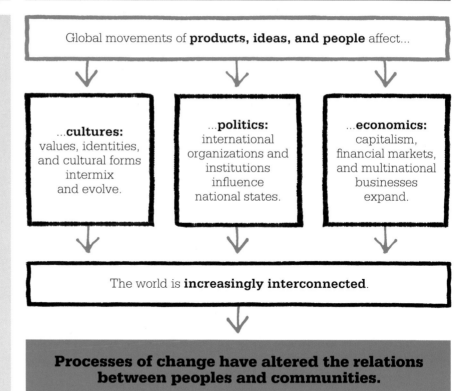

Global movements of **products, ideas, and people** affect...

...**cultures:** values, identities, and cultural forms intermix and evolve.

...**politics:** international organizations and institutions influence national states.

...**economics:** capitalism, financial markets, and multinational businesses expand.

The world is **increasingly interconnected**.

Processes of change have altered the relations between peoples and communities.

The world is becoming smaller due to the mass movement of people and the exchange and flow of products, ideas, and cultural artifacts. These changes, suggests British sociologist David Held, are altering the way communities and individuals are interacting and communicating with one another.

Migration, for example, creates an intermixing of cultures and the development of multicultural societies. People also connect

See also: George Ritzer 120–23 ▪ Immanuel Wallerstein 144–45 ▪
Roland Robertson 146–47 ▪ Ulrich Beck 156–61 ▪ Arjun Appadurai 166–69

Bollywood films in India represent the assymetrical flow of culture around the world. Despite selling more tickets than Hollywood, they make far less revenue from international distribution.

with global cultures, such as music genres or cuisines, blending the global with the local to produce new cultural products.

Held suggests globalization is best understood as a set of processes and changes. Cultural dimensions include the distribution of media products and movement of ideas and people across societies. Political dimensions include the rise of international organizations, institutions, and multinational companies. The economic dimensions include the expansion of capitalism and consumerism.

Change for better or worse?

In *Globalization/Anti-Globalization*, Held examines the views of different sociologists on globalization, organizing them into "hyper-globalists," "skeptics," and "transformationalists."

The hyper-globalists see the forces of globalization as powerful, unprecedented, and as facilitating the development of a global civilization. Some hyper-globalists praise globalization for driving economic development and spreading democracy; others are critical of the spread of capitalism and its social consequences.

The skeptics, by contrast, downplay the extent to which globalization is a new phenomenon and reject the idea that global integration and institutions are undermining the power of the nation-state. They see globalization as marginalizing the developing world, while at the same time benefiting corporations based in developed nations.

The transformationalists, according to Held, best explain the contradictory processes of globalization. They argue that boundaries between the global and local are breaking down, and that the human world is becoming interconnected. They also argue that there is no single cause of globalization, and that the outcomes of these processes are not determined.

Globalization, Held suggests, is giving rise to a new global "architecture" comprised of

multinational companies and institutions, and characterized by asymmetrical cultural and economic flows.

The precise nature of the emerging patterns of inequality and prosperity brought by globalization is not yet clear. Importantly, however, Held sees globalization as a dynamic process that can be influenced: nation-states can embrace policies and relationships that address global problems or risks, be they poverty, pandemics, or environmental damage and change. ▪

David Held

David Held was born in Britain in 1951 and was educated in Britain, France, Germany, and the US. He holds an MSc and a PhD in political science from Massachusetts Institute of Technology (MIT).

In 1984, Held cofounded Polity Press, the highly influential international publisher of social-science and humanities books, where he continues as Director. He has written and edited more than 60 books on democracy, globalization, global governance, and public policy. In 2011 Held resigned his professorial position in political science at the London School of Economics to become Director of the Institute of Global Policy at Durham University in the UK.

Key works

1995 *Democracy and the Global Order*
2002 *Globalization/Anti-Globalization* (coauthor)
2004 *Global Covenant*

CULTURE
IDENTITY

AND

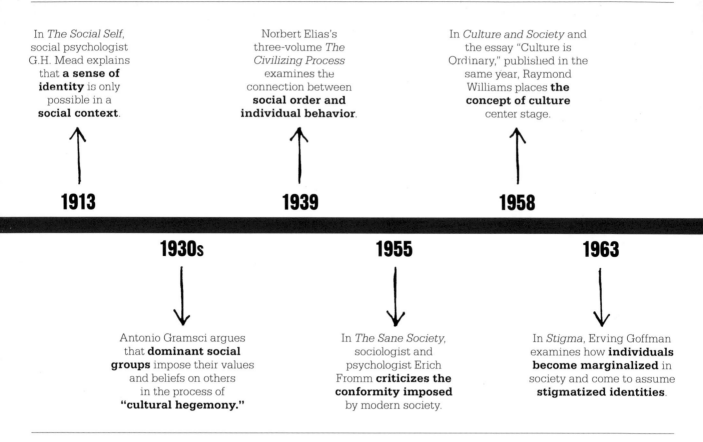

In *The Social Self*, social psychologist G.H. Mead explains that **a sense of identity** is only possible in a **social context**.

1913

Norbert Elias's three-volume *The Civilizing Process* examines the connection between **social order and individual behavior**.

1939

In *Culture and Society* and the essay "Culture is Ordinary," published in the same year, Raymond Williams places **the concept of culture** center stage.

1958

1930s

Antonio Gramsci argues that **dominant social groups** impose their values and beliefs on others in the process of **"cultural hegemony."**

1955

In *The Sane Society*, sociologist and psychologist Erich Fromm **criticizes the conformity imposed** by modern society.

1963

In *Stigma*, Erving Goffman examines how **individuals become marginalized** in society and come to assume **stigmatized identities**.

From its beginnings in the early 19th century, sociology sought to examine not only the institutions and systems that created social order, but also the factors that maintained social cohesion.

Traditionally, this had come from the shared values, beliefs, and experiences of communities, but with the advent of "modernity" in the form of industrialization and secularization, the structure of society was radically transformed. Although it was recognized that modernity had changed the way people associated with one another, it was not until the 20th century that culture—the ways that people think and behave as a group, and how they identify themselves as members of a society—became an object of study in its own right.

The emergence of sociology—the systematic study of how society shapes human interaction and identity—had coincided with the establishment of anthropology and psychology, and there was a degree of overlap between the three disciplines. It is unsurprising, then, that one of the first cultural sociologists was also a pioneering social psychologist, G.H. Mead. He set the scene for a sociological study of culture by highlighting the connection between the individual and society, and especially the notion of a social identity. An individual, he argued, can only develop a true sense of identity in the context of a social group, through interaction with others.

The connections with social psychology continued throughout the 20th century, notably in the

work of Erich Fromm in the 1950s, who argued that many psychological problems have social origins. In the process of connecting with wider society and identifying with a particular culture, individuals are expected to conform with society, and this stifles our individualism so that we lose a true sense of self. Around the same time, Erving Goffman began discussing the problems of establishing a sense of identity, and in the 1960s, he focused on the stigma attached to those who do not conform or are "different."

Culture and social order
Norbert Elias, in the 1930s, had described the imposition of social norms and conventions as a "civilizing process," directly regulating individual behavior.

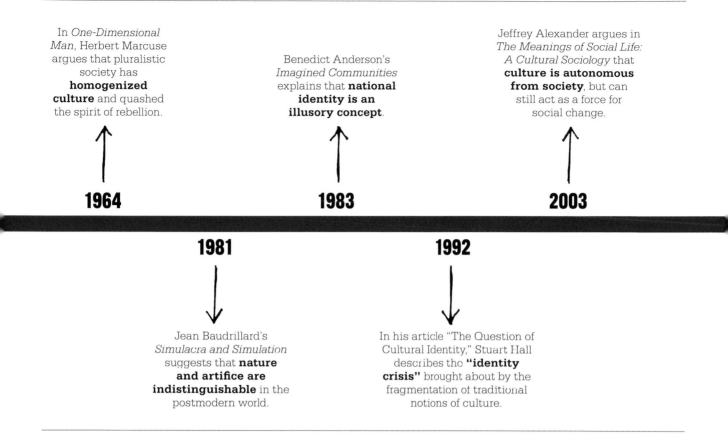

In *One-Dimensional Man*, Herbert Marcuse argues that pluralistic society has **homogenized culture** and quashed the spirit of rebellion.

Benedict Anderson's *Imagined Communities* explains that **national identity is an illusory concept**.

Jeffrey Alexander argues in *The Meanings of Social Life: A Cultural Sociology* that **culture is autonomous from society**, but can still act as a force for social change.

1964

1983

2003

1981

1992

Jean Baudrillard's *Simulacra and Simulation* suggests that **nature and artifice are indistinguishable** in the postmodern world.

In his article "The Question of Cultural Identity," Stuart Hall describes the **"identity crisis"** brought about by the fragmentation of traditional notions of culture.

There is clearly a connection between the regulating power of culture and the maintenance of social order, and some saw it as more than merely a process of socialization. Antonio Gramsci recognized the potential for culture to be used as a means of social control. Through subtle coercion, a dominant culture imposes a "cultural hegemony" in which social norms become so ingrained that anything else is unthinkable.

Michel Foucault developed this idea further in his study of power relations, and others, including Herbert Marcuse, examined the ways in which culture could be used to quell social unrest. Later, another French sociologist, Jean Baudrillard, argued that in the postmodern world, with its explosion of availability of information, culture had become so far removed from the society in which it exists that it bears little relation to reality.

Cultural identity

A distinct branch of culturally oriented sociology emerged in the UK from the latter part of the 20th century: cultural studies. The starting point was Raymond Williams' extensive research into the idea of culture. His work transformed the concept, opening up entirely new areas of study to sociological investigation.

Williams explained that culture is expressed by material production and consumption, and by the creations and leisure pursuits of social groups of a specific time and place—their food, sports, fashion, languages, beliefs, ideas, and customs, as well as their literature, art, and music. Also at the forefront of this British school of cultural studies was Stuart Hall, who suggested that notions of cultural identity are no longer fixed. With significantly improved communications and increased mobility, traditional national, ethnic, class, and even gender identities have all but disappeared—and another British sociologist, Benedict Anderson, goes so far as to suggest that the concept of belonging to any community is illusory.

However, the US sociologist Jeffrey Alexander considered culture to be an independent variable in the structure of society. His cultural sociology examines how culture shapes society through the creation of shared meaning. ∎

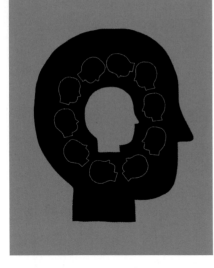

THE "I" AND THE "ME"
G.H. MEAD (1863–1931)

IN CONTEXT

FOCUS
The development of self

KEY DATES
1902 US sociologist Charles Cooley says our views of self reflect the standpoint of significant others in our lives.

1921 In *The Language of Gestures*, German philosopher Wilhelm Wundt says that the mind is inherently social.

1975 US anthropologist Clifford Geertz claims the self is a "distinctive whole and set contrastively against other such wholes."

1980s British-born US social psychologist Hazel Rose Markus suggests we each form a schema based on past social experiences that operates as a self-system.

1999 US psychologist Daniel Siegel suggests that the development of the social self happens in concert with developing brain function.

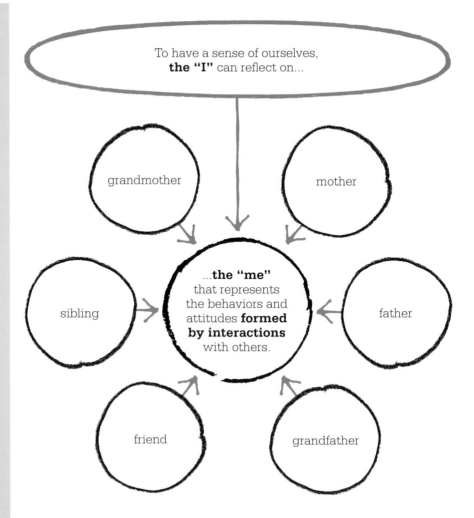

To have a sense of ourselves, **the "I"** can reflect on...

grandmother

mother

sibling

...**the "me"** that represents the behaviors and attitudes **formed by interactions** with others.

father

friend

grandfather

George Herbert Mead was a social psychologist and a philosopher, and he looked to both disciplines in trying to work out what exactly we mean when we talk about the "self." Traditional philosophers and sociologists saw societies as growing from the coming together of individual, autonomous selves, but Mead said the opposite was true—selves emerge from social interactions; they are formed within society.

This concept is prevalent now in psychology and psychotherapy, but when Mead first presented his ideas in 1913 in *The Social Self*, it was a revolutionary point of view. Mead disagreed with the idea that individual, experiencing selves exist in any recognizable way before they are part of the social process. The social process of experience or behavior is "logically prior to the individuals and their individual experiencing which are involved in it."

By this, Mead is suggesting that an individual's consciousness, with all its intentions, desires, and so on, is formed within the context of social relationships, one or more particular languages, and a set of cultural norms. From birth, babies begin to sense communication through gestures, which function as symbols and build "a universe of discourse." Over time, they learn to mimic and "import" the practices, gestures, and eventually words of those around them, so that they can make their own response and receive further gestures and words from others.

Who we are

The pattern of attitudes that the baby experiences and internalizes (learns) creates the sense of "me." In this way, the "me" represents the behaviors, expectations, and attitudes learned through interactions with others.

But Mead says that we also have another sense of ourselves, which he calls the "I." Both the "I" and the "me" are different functions of the self. The "I," like the "me," keeps evolving, but its function is to reflect on the "me," while also

Our view of ourselves, of who we are, is developed from birth through interaction with those closest to us. Individual selves are not the products of biology but rather of this interaction.

seeing the bigger picture: the "me" acts in habitual ways, while the "I" can reflect on these and make self-conscious choices. It allows us to be different, both from other people and our former selves, through reflection on our actions.

Mead's theory of the development of self was pivotal in turning psychology and sociology away from the idea of "self" as being merely internal introspection, and aligning it firmly within a societal context. ∎

Mind can never find expression, and could never have come into existence at all, except in terms of a social environment.
G.H. Mead

G.H. Mead

George Herbert Mead was born in Massachusetts. His father was a minister in the Congregational Church, and he moved the family to Oberlin, Ohio, to teach at the seminary there when Mead was six years old. After graduating from Oberlin College in 1883, Mead worked for a few years as a teacher and then as a railroad surveyor before returning to academia. He began his studies in philosophy and sociology at Harvard University in 1887 and seven years later moved to the University of Chicago, where he worked until his death in 1931. He claimed to have an "activist spirit" and marched in support of women's suffrage and other causes. The philosopher John Dewey acknowledged Mead as having "a seminal mind of the very first order."

Key works

1913 *The Social Self*
1932 *The Philosophy of the Present*
1934 *Mind, Self, and Society*

THE CHALLENGE OF MODERNITY IS TO LIVE WITHOUT ILLUSIONS AND WITHOUT BECOMING DISILLUSIONED

ANTONIO GRAMSCI (1891–1937)

IN CONTEXT

FOCUS
Cultural hegemony

KEY DATES
1846 Karl Marx and Friedrich Engels finish *The German Ideology*; not published until 1932, it later strongly influences Gramsci's thinking about ideology.

1921 The Italian Communist Party is founded.

1922 Benito Mussolini becomes dictator of Italy and a leading figure in the development of Fascism.

1964 The Centre for Contemporary Cultural Studies is established at the University of Birmingham, England, and draws heavily on Gramsci's notion of hegemony.

1985 Inspired by Gramsci's concept of hegemony, Ernesto Laclau and Chantal Mouffe develop a post-Marxist manifesto in *Hegemony and Socialist Strategy*.

According to Marx, **the ruling class controls the economic base** and creates the superstructure of institutions and social relations that **dominate the working class**.

Gramsci claims **class domination also occurs culturally**: the working class are subject to the **ideological illusions** perpetrated by the ruling class.

These illusions must be seen through, and **resisted at all costs**.

The challenge of modernity is to live without illusions and without becoming disillusioned.

The Marxist view of society is that life is an ongoing struggle of competing groups; these groups are determined economically, and under modernity the struggle has intensified into a contest for control between a minority ruling elite and the majority, made up of workers. Italian socialist and social thinker Antonio Gramsci tries to explain why revolution is not precipitated

See also: Karl Marx 28–31 ▪ Friedrich Engels 66–67 ▪ Pierre Bourdieu 76–79 ▪ Zygmunt Bauman 136–43 ▪ Herbert Marcuse 182–87 ▪ Jean Baudrillard 196–99

in a crisis, as it should be according to classical Marxist theory. He argues that repression by the ruling class is insufficient to secure a stable social order; there must also be ideological subjugation. This happens in a complex process whereby the ruling elite propagates its views of the world so that they are accepted as common sense and largely beyond contention. Gramsci calls this "hegemony," a concealed mode of class domination that explains why workers can become Fascists rather than revolutionaries.

The hegemonic struggle

Gramsci claims that hegemony is cultural and that it is involved in a struggle between competing class-based world views, by which is meant sets of values, ideas, beliefs, and understandings of what human beings are like, what society is, and—crucially—what it could be.

Hegemony, he says, involves an invisible mechanism whereby positions of influence in society are always filled by members of an already ruling class—largely with the consent of the subordinated. The ruling class's ideas, which are the dominant ones permeating the whole of society, are propounded by intellectual groups working in its service (often only partially knowingly) such as journalists who disseminate these ideas to the wider population. Constant exposure to them means that the lower classes experience them as natural and inevitable, and come to believe them. Hegemonic ideas shape the thinking of all social classes. It is for this reason, says Gramsci, that the challenge of modernity is not to become disillusioned with the ongoing struggle but to see through the "illusions"—the views propounded by elite groups—and resist them.

Because individuals have the capacity to think critically about the view imposed upon them, which Gramsci calls "counter-hegemonic" thinking, the ruling class's ideological dominance is often in the balance. In Western liberal democracies, the challenge to hegemony is an everyday reality.

The nature and extent of these struggles between competing world views is contingent upon social, political, and economic circumstances. A series of prolonged economic crises leading to high unemployment, for example, is liable to result in a situation in which various counter-hegemonic forces arise in the form of trade unions or protest movements. Gramsci notes that in most capitalist societies the ruling classes face constant opposition and dissent "from below" and have to devote a vast amount of time and energy to managing this situation, with complete control highly unlikely, even for short periods.

Gramsci's ideas emphasize the role of individuals and ideologies in the struggle for social change, and thereby challenge the economic determinism of traditional Marxism. His concept of "cultural hegemony," which recognizes human autonomy and the importance of culture, has had a lasting impact on a number of academic disciplines. ▪

Antonio Gramsci

Antonio Gramsci was born in Sardinia, Italy, in 1891. He was a cofounder of the Italian Communist Party. While serving as the party's leader, he was sentenced to 20 years imprisonment in 1928 by Benito Mussolini, Italy's prime minister and dictator at the time.

Gramsci wrote prolifically while in prison. Although he had a prodigious memory, without the help of his sister-in-law, Tania, who was a frequent visitor, his ideas would not have come to light. This intellectual work did not emerge until several years after World War II, when it was published posthumously in what are known as the *Prison Notebooks*. By the 1950s, his prison writings had attracted interest not only in Western Europe, but also in the Soviet bloc. Due to the poor diet, illness, and bad health he suffered in prison, Gramsci died of a stroke at the age of only 46.

Key works

1975 *Prison Notebooks* (three volumes)
1994 *Pre-Prison Writings*

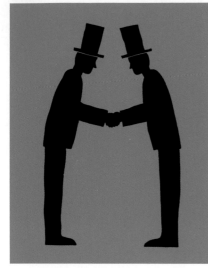

THE CIVILIZING PROCESS IS CONSTANTLY MOVING "FORWARD"
NORBERT ELIAS (1897–1990)

IN CONTEXT

FOCUS
The civilizing process

KEY DATES
c.1500 Feudalism in Western Europe comes to an end and court society emerges.

1690 English philosopher John Locke describes "civil society" as a united body of individuals under the power of an executive.

1850s Auguste Comte asks how the individual can be both a cause and consequence of society.

1958 Max Weber says values and beliefs can cause dramatic change in the social structure.

1962 US anthropologist Robert Redfield says that civilization is a totality of great and little traditions.

1970s Antonio Gramsci says the ruling classes maintain their dominance through the institutions of civil society.

As nations stabilized in the West after the 1500s, **power was centralized** and became the preserve of a small number of people.

These people were no longer revered for their physical strength, but for their **social standing**, reflected in their courtly manners.

To be identified with power, people are encouraged to display the same **"civilized behavior"** as a nation's governing elite.

People (and nations) lacking the right behavior are seen as **inferior and need "civilizing"** into following the rules of the powerful.

To shed light on the West's centralization of national power and increasing global domination over the last 500 years, Norbert Elias turned his attention to the "psychical process of civilization"—the changes in behavior, feeling, and intentions of people in the West since the Middle Ages. He describes these changes, and the effect they have had on individuals, in his famous book *The Civilizing Process*.

Elias draws on history, sociology, and psychoanalysis to conclude that the way in which Western society believes itself to be superior to others is summed up by the concept of "civilization." This is both historical and

See also: W.E.B. Du Bois 68–73 ▪ Paul Gilroy 75 ▪ Pierre Bourdieu 76–79 ▪ Edward Said 80–81 ▪ Elijah Anderson 82–83 ▪ Stuart Hall 200–01

"Good" table manners and "correct" etiquette and deportment were, according to Elias, key components of the cultural template in the spread of the European "civilizing" process.

contemporary, and can refer to all sorts of facts about nations: from general ones such as lifestyles, values, customs, and religions, to personal ones such as levels of bodily hygiene, ways of preparing food, and so on. In every case, Western society stresses that "its" version is the standard against which all others should be judged.

The rise of manners

Elias studied etiquette books and found that a transformation in attitudes toward bodily behaviors was key to this sense of civilization. Westerners had gradually changed their ideas of what was acceptable in terms of facial expressions, control of bodily functions, general deportment, and so on.

Behaviors considered normal in the Middle Ages were thought "barbarous" by the 19th century.

These minor changes resulted in the formation of a courtly class, identifiable by its highly codified manners and disciplined way of living. Warrior knights became quiet courtiers, expressing restraint and maintaining strict control of impulses and emotions. "Civilized" behaviors soon became essential to everyone wishing to trade and socialize with others, from tradesmen to noblemen and women.

Elias says that the process spread ever more widely from the 1500s onward, because "good manners" help people get along more peaceably, and growing towns and cities require such cooperation. The process, he said, at some point became a question of internalizing the social rules of one's parents, rather than one's "betters." However, the rules about what constitutes "good manners" have always been dictated by the upper classes, so "civilization" continues to work toward furthering the interests of the powerful elite.

Elias saw the transformation of manners as an important part of the centralization of power within Western nations, and a sign of the growing interdependency of people during urbanization. But it was also important in colonization during Elias's lifetime. He was writing during the 1930s, when colonial powers such as Britain and France, secure in their sense of national self-consciousness, justified the morality of colonization by claiming it brought civilization, which would be "good" for colonized peoples. ▪

Norbert Elias

Norbert Elias was born in Breslau (now the Polish city of Wrocław) in 1897, to a wealthy Jewish family. After leaving school he served in the German army during World War I. Elias studied philosophy and medicine at Breslau University, gaining a PhD in philosophy in 1924. He then studied sociology with Max Weber's younger brother, Alfred, at Heidelberg, Germany, before moving to Frankfurt University to work with Karl Mannheim.

In 1933 Elias went into exile in Paris and then London, where he finished *The Civilizing Process*. In 1939 the book was published in Switzerland, but sank into oblivion until its republication in West Germany in 1969. A sought-after lecturer, Elias spent his final years traveling in Europe and Africa.

Key works

1939 *The Civilizing Process* (3 volumes)
1939 *The Society of Individuals*
1970 *What is Sociology?*

MASS CULTURE REINFORCES POLITICAL REPRESSION

HERBERT MARCUSE (1898–1979)

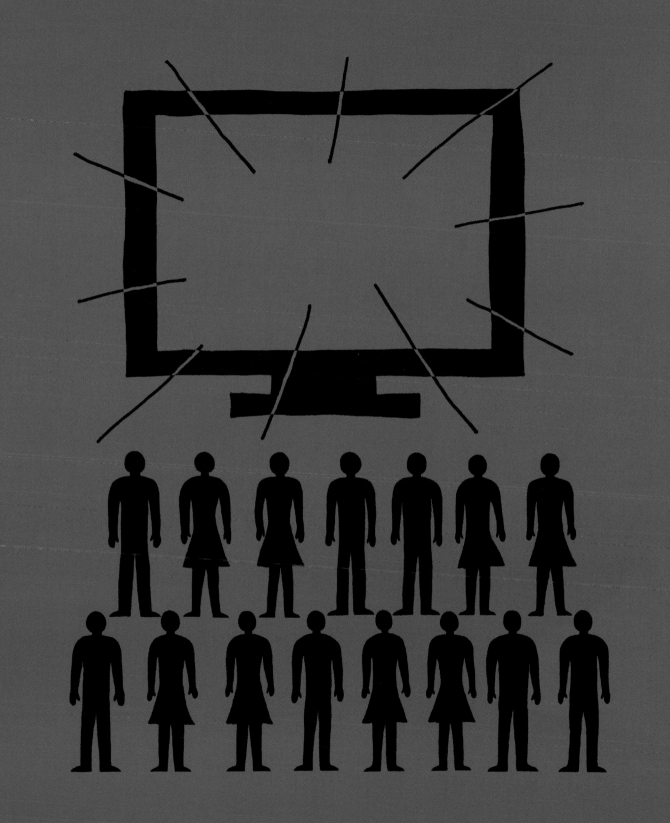

IN CONTEXT

FOCUS
The culture industry

KEY DATES
1840s Karl Marx says there are always at least two classes in capitalist societies: those who own the means of production and those who sell their labor to that group.

1923 The Institute for Social Research is founded in Frankfurt, and gives rise to the new "critical theory" of culture.

1944 German-Jewish émigrés Max Horkheimer and Theodor W. Adorno coin the term "culture industry" in *Dialectic of Enlightenment*.

1963 Canadian sociologist Erving Goffman publishes *Stigma*, in which he claims identity is constructed by other people and society.

1970s–80s Michel Foucault examines the normalizing techniques of modern society.

uring the 20th century, it became apparent that the transformation of society theorized by Karl Marx had failed to materialize. The sociologist and philosopher Herbert Marcuse tried to determine what had happened by urging Marxists to move beyond theory and take into account the real, lived experience of individuals.

Marcuse said that capitalism had somehow integrated the working class: workers who were supposed to be the agents of change had accepted the ideas and ideals of the establishment. They had lost sight of themselves as a class or group and become "individuals" within a system that prized individuality. This seemed to be the route to success, but in abandoning their group, the workers lost all bargaining power.

Freedom to choose

How had the workers been so easily silenced? There was no obvious moment at which this had taken place, so Marcuse examined how rebellion against the status quo seemed to have been so effectively quashed during the 20th century. He started by looking much further

The Statue of Liberty symbolizes the American Dream of a "classless" society with equal opportunity – through hard work, anyone can improve their lives and fulfill their potential.

back, to the end of feudal society in Europe in the late Middle Ages. In this time of transition, people moved from being bound to work for a landowner to being free to find work anywhere, for their own benefit alone. But this "freedom of enterprise was, from the beginning, not altogether a blessing," says Marcuse. Although free to work wherever they wanted, the majority of people had to labor extremely

---

Culture has always played a key role in pointing to possible ways of living that are **outside the social "norm."**

→

But from the 1960s, even **art forms once thought subversive** were subsumed into daily life and appropriated by the media.

↓

The possibility of rebellion has effectively been quashed: mass culture reinforces political repression.

←

By absorbing the media's messages **people accepted society's rules and values** as their own; they realized that to step beyond them would seem neurotic.

See also: Karl Marx 28–31 ▪ Michel Foucault 52–55 ▪ Antonio Gramsci 178–79 ▪ Erving Goffman 190–95 ▪ Jean Baudrillard 196–99 ▪ Thorstein Veblen 214–19 ▪ Daniel Miller 246–47

hard, with no guarantee of work from day to day, and they were frightened about the future.

Centuries later, the machines of the Industrial Revolution promised to lift national economies to such an extent that it was thought a person would no longer need to worry about survival, but might "be free to exert autonomy over a life that would be his own." This was the American Dream, and the hope of most Westerners during the 20th century. If the longed-for freedom was synonymous with choice, individuals were free as never before, because choices in work, housing, food, fashion, and leisure activities continued to widen over the decades.

"False needs"

However, when Marcuse looked closer, he discovered that "a comfortable, smooth, reasonable, democratic un-freedom prevails in advanced industrial civilization"— far from being free, people were being manipulated by "totalitarian" regimes that called themselves democracies, he said. Worse still, people were unaware of the manipulation, because they had internalized the regimes' rules, values, and ideals.

Marcuse goes on to describe government as a state apparatus that imposes its economic and political requirements on its people by influencing their working and leisure time. It does so by creating in people a set of "false needs" and

Desire for "must-have" clothing, gadgets, and inessential goods stems, says Marcuse, from a false sense of "need" that is implanted in us by advertising and the media.

then manipulating people through those needs. Essentially, by convincing people that they have certain needs, and then making it look as though there is a route to satisfying these needs (even though there is not), "vested interests" effectively control the rest of the population.

False needs are not based on real ones such as the necessity for food, drink, clothes, and somewhere to live, but are instead artificially generated and impossible to satisfy in any real sense. Marcuse cites the need "to relax, to have fun... and consume in accordance with the advertisements, to love and hate what others love and hate"—the actual content of these needs (such as the latest "must-have" gadget) is proposed by external forces; it does not naturally arise in someone like the need for water does. Yet these needs feel internally driven because we are bombarded by media messages that promise happiness if you do that or go there. In this way we begin to believe that false needs are real ones.

> The cultural center is becoming a fitting part of the shopping center.
> **Herbert Marcuse**

Marcuse suggests that: "People recognize themselves in their commodities; they find their soul in their automobile, hi-fi set, split-level home, kitchen equipment."

Everything is personal; the individual is paramount, and his or her needs are what matter. This apparent empowerment of the individual is in fact its opposite, according to Marcuse. Social needs—for job security, a decent living standard, and so on—are translated into individual needs, such as your own need for a job to buy »

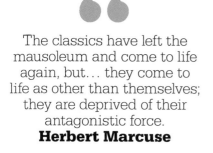

> The classics have left the mausoleum and come to life again... they come to life as other than themselves; they are deprived of their antagonistic force.
> **Herbert Marcuse**

consumer products. If you think you are badly paid, your employer might invite you in to talk "about you." There is no longer any sense of being part of a group that is treated unfairly—all hopes of Marxist rebellion are lost.

A dimensionless world

According to Marcuse, we are caught in a bubble from which there is no escape, because it has become almost impossible to stand outside the system. There used to be "a gap" between culture and

reality that pointed to other possible ways of living and being, but that gap has disappeared. Traditionally, the forms of art considered to represent "culture"— such as the opera, theater, literature, and classical music— aimed to reflect the difficulties encountered by the transcendent human soul forced to live in social reality. It pointed to a possible world beyond gritty reality.

Tragedy, says Marcuse, used to be about defeated possibilities; about hopes unfulfilled and promises betrayed. He cites Madame Bovary, in Gustave Flaubert's novel of that name (1856), as a perfect example of a soul unable to survive in the rigid society in which she lived.

However, by the 1960s, society had become so pluralistic that it could apparently contain everyone and all their chosen lifestyles. Tragedy is no longer even possible as a cultural motif; its discontent is seen as a problem to be solved.

Art has lost its ability to inspire rebellion because it is now part of a mass media, claims Marcuse. Books and stories about individuals who will not conform are no longer

Flaubert's Madame Bovary chose to die rather than "fit in." But modern society has absorbed all forms of lifestyle; so today, Marcuse suggests, she would be offered therapy.

incendiary calls to revolution but must-read "modern classics" that someone might consume on a self-improvement program. The "avant garde and the beatniks" now entertain without troubling people's consciences. Culture is not in a position of dangerous "other," but has been stripped of all its power. Even great works of alienation, he

---

Herbert Marcuse

Born in Berlin in 1898, Herbert Marcuse served with the German army in World War I before completing a PhD in literature in 1922 at the University of Freiburg. After a short spell as a bookseller in Berlin, he studied philosophy under Martin Heidegger.

In 1932, he joined the Institute for Social Research, but he never worked in Frankfurt. In 1934 he fled to the US, where he was to remain. While he was in New York with Max Horkheimer, the latter received an offer from Columbia University to relocate the Institute there and Marcuse joined him.

In 1958 Marcuse became a professor at Brandeis University, Massachusetts, but in 1965 he was forced to resign because of his outspoken Marxist views. He moved to the University of California, and during the 1960s gained world renown as a social theorist, philosopher, and political activist. He died of a stroke, aged 81.

Key works

1941 *Reason and Revolution*
1964 *One-Dimensional Man*
1969 *An Essay on Liberation*

says, have become commercials that sell, comfort, or excite—culture has become an industry.

This flattening of the two dimensions of high culture and social reality has led to a one-dimensional culture that easily determines and controls our individual and social perspectives. There is no other world, or way to live. Marcuse claims that in saying this he is not overstating the power of the media, because the social messages we receive as adults are merely reinforcing the same ones that we have been hearing since our birth—we were conditioned as children to receive them.

The disappearance of class

The compressing of culture and reality is reflected in an apparent leveling of class structure. If all art forms and mass media are part of a homogenous whole, where nothing stands outside of societal approval, people from all social classes will inevitably start doing some of the same things. Marcuse points to the examples of a typist who is made up as attractively as her boss's daughter, or the worker and his boss enjoying the same

Intellectual freedom would mean the restoration of individual thought now absorbed by mass communication and indoctrination.
Herbert Marcuse

The power of the media

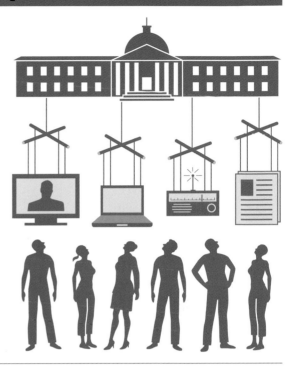

The state and its consumerist forces control the media in the modern world.

The media reflects and disseminates the state's dominant values and ideologies, and manipulates society into buying goods, services, and lifestyles.

Society and individuals are lulled into believing and conforming to the media messages.

TV program. However, according to Marcuse, this kind of assimilation does not indicate the disappearance of classes—it actually reveals the extent to which the needs that serve the establishment have become shared by the underlying population.

The result of this is that classes are no longer in conflict. The social controls have been internalized, and Marcuse says that we are hypnotized into a state of extreme conformity where no one will rebel. There is no longer a sublimated realm of the soul or spirit of inner man, because everything has been or can be translated into operational terms, problems, and solutions. We have lost a sense of inner truth and real need, and can no longer critique society because we cannot find a way to stand outside of it without appearing to have lost our sanity.

Marcuse's ideas about a society that includes everything—in which pluralism defeats the oppositional power of any idea—is particularly relevant in a global age that is dominated by a proliferation of new media. Marcuse was always aware of the importance of scientific knowledge in shaping and organizing not just society but myriad aspects of everyday life. Crucially, and often from a radical and politicized perspective, he could see the potential for both emancipation and domination, which makes his emphasis on the cultural conversation and the role of new technologies in its service especially pertinent. Do these things really bring about social change and liberation, or are they simply tools for increasing manipulation and social oppression by a powerful ruling class? ∎

THE DANGER OF THE FUTURE IS THAT MEN MAY BECOME ROBOTS
ERICH FROMM (1900–1980)

IN CONTEXT

FOCUS
Alienation of self

KEY DATES
1844 Karl Marx says humans become alienated from their own essence as a systemic result of capitalism.

1903 In *The Metropolis and Mental Life*, Georg Simmel suggests urban life breeds alienation and indifference.

1955 Erich Fromm publishes *The Sane Society*.

1956 US sociologist Leo Srole develops an alienation scale.

1959 US sociologist Melvin Seeman says alienation results from powerlessness, normlessness, social isolation, cultural estrangement, and self-estrangement.

1968 Israeli-American sociologist Amitai Etzioni says alienation results from social systems that do not cater to basic human needs.

The German sociologist and psychoanalyst Erich Fromm claimed that during industrialization in the 19th century, God was declared dead, "inhumanity" meant cruelty, and the inherent danger was that people would become slaves.

However, in the 20th century, the problem changed: alienated from a sense of self, people had lost the ability to love and reason for themselves. "Man" effectively died. "Inhumanity" came to mean lacking humanity. People, Fromm advised, were in danger of becoming like robots.

He attributed this sense of alienation to the emergence of Western capitalist societies and believed that a state's social, economic, and political factors intersect to produce a "social character" common to all its citizens. In the industrial age, as capitalism increased its global dominance, states encouraged people to become competitive, exploitative, authoritarian, aggressive, and individualist.

In the 20th century, by contrast, individuals were repositioned by capitalist states to become cooperative consumers, with standardized tastes, who could be manipulated by the anonymous authority of public opinion and the market. Technology ensured that work became more routine and boring. Fromm advised that unless people "get out of the rut" they are in and reclaim their humanity, they will go mad trying to live a meaningless, robotic life. ∎

> Synthetic smiles have replaced genuine laughter... dull despair has taken the place of genuine pain.
> **Erich Fromm**

See also: G.H. Mead 176–77 ▪ Robert Blauner 232–33 ▪ Arlie Hochschild 236–43 ▪ Robert K. Merton 262–63 ▪ Erving Goffman 264–69 ▪ Ann Oakley 318–19

CULTURE IS ORDINARY

RAYMOND WILLIAMS (1921–1988)

IN CONTEXT

FOCUS
Structure of feeling

KEY DATES
1840s Karl Marx argues that the economy determines society's ideas and culture.

1920s Italian Marxist Antonio Gramsci critiques Marx's economic determinism.

1958 Welsh academic Raymond Williams discusses the concept of "structure of feeling" in *Culture and Society*, placing culture firmly at the center of an understanding of social networks.

1964 British sociologist and cultural theorist Richard Hoggart founds the Centre for Contemporary Cultural Studies in Birmingham, England, and is succeeded as director in 1968 by Stuart Hall.

1975 Jean Baudrillard indicates that Marx's focus on economics as the driving force of change is limiting.

While Karl Marx had a keen interest in culture, especially in literature, he regarded the economy as the driver of history: culture and ideas were secondary. Later Marxist thinkers such as Antonio Gramsci and Hungarian theorist Georg Lukács paid more attention to cultural matters; but culture only came to the center of radical theory in the mid-20th century with Raymond Williams' extensive body of work, which included his hugely influential text *Culture and Society*.

Williams detaches the idea of culture from a politically conservative understanding of "tradition," enabling an analysis of what he calls "the long revolution": that difficult but persistent effort to democratize our whole way of life.

The shape of culture

In his essay "Culture is Ordinary" (1958), Williams offers a personal reflection of a journey from the farming valleys of South Wales to the colleges of Cambridge, England. For Williams, the shape of his culture includes mountains, farms, cathedrals, and furnaces; family relationships, political debates, trade skills, languages, and ideas; as well as literature, art, and music, both popular and serious. He describes the shape as a characteristic "structure of feeling," which might be defined as the lived experience (ordinary life) of a community beyond society's institutions and formal ideologies.

Structure of feeling operates, Williams explains, "in the most delicate and least tangible part of our activities." The concept suggests a combination of something that is visible and organized enough to be the subject of study (structure), yet elusive enough to convey the complexities of lived experience (feeling). Williams' emphasis on lived experience served to open up to sociological study whole swathes of popular culture such as television, film, and advertising, which had earlier been seen as culturally insignificant. ∎

See also: Karl Marx 28–31 ▪ Antonio Gramsci 178–79 ▪ Herbert Marcuse 182–87 ▪ Jean Baudrillard 196–99 ▪ Stuart Hall 200–01

STIGMA
REFERS TO AN ATTRIBUTE THAT IS DEEPLY DISCREDITING

ERVING GOFFMAN (1922–1982)

IN CONTEXT

FOCUS
Stigma

KEY DATES
1895 Émile Durkheim explores the concept of stigma and its relation to social order.

1920s The concept of symbolic interactionism emerges at the University of Chicago as the leading US social theoretical model.

1934 *Mind, Self, and Society* by US social psychologist G.H. Mead is published and later influences Goffman's ideas about identity.

2006 In *Body/Embodiment*, Dennis Waskul and Phillip Vannini (eds.) see Goffman's work as a "sophisticated framework" for understanding the sociology of the body.

2014 US sociologist Mary Jo Deegan applies Goffman's theories to the analysis of sex, gender issues, and feminism.

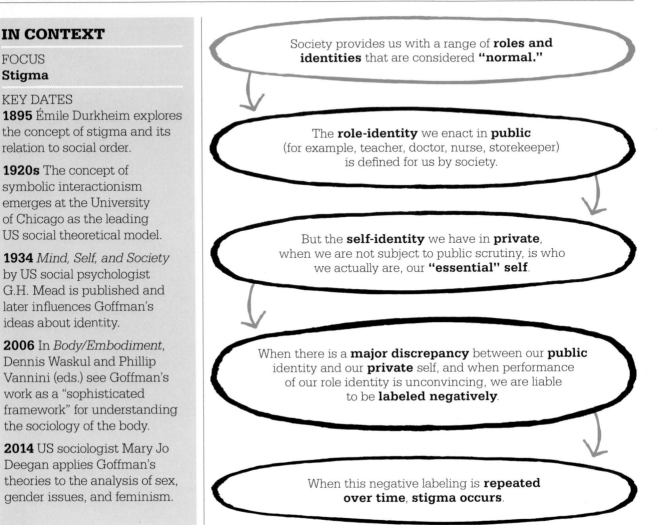

Society provides us with a range of **roles and identities** that are considered **"normal."**

The **role-identity** we enact in **public** (for example, teacher, doctor, nurse, storekeeper) is defined for us by society.

But the **self-identity** we have in **private**, when we are not subject to public scrutiny, is who we actually are, our **"essential" self**.

When there is a **major discrepancy** between our **public** identity and our **private** self, and when performance of our role identity is unconvincing, we are liable to be **labeled negatively**.

When this negative labeling is **repeated over time**, **stigma occurs**.

E rving Goffman was a Canadian sociologist whose work draws heavily on the US social theoretical tradition known as symbolic interactionism. This tradition focuses on micro-level interactions and exchanges between individuals and small groups of people, rather than on the far more impersonal, macro-level relationships between social structures or institutions and individuals. Interactionist thinkers examine issues such as personal identity, selfhood, group dynamics, and social interaction.

The basic idea underpinning symbolic-interactionist thought is that the individual self is first and foremost a social entity: even the most seemingly idiosyncratic aspects of our individual selves, according to symbolic interactionists, are not so much the product of our own unique psychology, but are socially determined and culturally and historically contingent. Who we think we are, who we imagine ourselves to be, and perhaps most importantly, who it is we are able to be, is inextricably bound up

with and mediated by the types of people we interact with and the institutional contexts we inhabit.

Of specific interest to Goffman was the subject of deviance and the socially enacted processes whereby individuals and groups come to be stigmatized (from the Greek word *stigma*, meaning "mark," "brand," or "puncture"), or marked with disgrace. Deviance is implicit in the notion of stigma because, as Goffman points out, stigma occurs whenever an individual or group is perceived to have deviated from the socially

See also: Pierre Bourdieu 76–79 ▪ Georg Simmel 104–05 ▪ G.H. Mead 176–77 ▪ Howard S. Becker 280–85 ▪ Alfred Schütz 335

School teachers perform one of the most "legitimate," highly respected roles in society—Goffman refers to the public roles people enact as their "virtual social identity."

prescribed norms that govern interpersonal conduct. When an individual deviates from these social norms they are stigmatized and marginalized from the wider group or social community to which they belong.

Virtual and actual identity

In his landmark study *Stigma*, Goffman analyzes the behavior of individuals whose identity is believed to be "soiled" or "defective" in some way. He distinguishes between what he refers to as "virtual" and "actual" social identity.

Virtual social identity is the socially legitimate version of selfhood that individuals are expected to present in public—for example, the socially defined traits and behaviors associated with being a medical doctor. Actual social identity is the self-identity

individuals imagine themselves to possess in private—the traits and behaviors the doctor enacts in his or her private life, for example. For Goffman, stigma arises whenever the disparity between virtual and actual social identity becomes untenable—when, for instance, the respected medic is known to drink and smoke excessively outside of work; feelings of embarrassment or shame then ensue, and social interaction breaks down. Stigma results from the fact that members of society share common expectations and attitudes about what to expect from people in certain social situations, and how those people should behave or look.

The concept of stigma

Goffman identifies three important features of the concept of stigma. First, stigma is not inherent to a given individual, attribute, or way of behaving, although some behaviors, such as pedophilia, are universally condemned. The context in which an attribute or behavior is displayed strongly determines how others respond. »

Erving Goffman

Erving Goffman was born in Canada in 1922 to a family of immigrant Ukrainian Jews. After graduating from the University of Toronto in 1945 with a BA in anthropology and sociology, he moved to the University of Chicago, where he attained his MA and PhD For his doctoral dissertation, he undertook fieldwork on a remote island in Scotland. The data he collected there formed the basis for his most celebrated work, *The Presentation of Self in Everyday Life*. He was appointed to the University of Pennsylvania in 1968 and in 1981 was the 73rd President of the American Sociological Association. Goffman died in 1982 of stomach cancer.

Key works

1959 *The Presentation of Self in Everyday Life*
1961 *Asylums: Essays on the Social Situation of Mental Patients and Other Inmates*
1963 *Stigma: Notes on the Management of Spoiled Identity*

Stigma constitutes a special discrepancy between virtual and actual social identity.
Erving Goffman

Second, stigma is a negative classification that emerges out of the interactions and exchanges between individuals or groups, whereby one has the power to classify the other as the possessor of what are considered to be socially undesirable attributes or behaviors. (Goffman refers to non-stigmatized people as "normals.") To this extent, it is a relational concept, because things classified as stigmatized are liable to change, depending on the individuals or groups interacting. Goffman suggests that potentially any attribute or act is stigmatizing, and for this reason some degree of stigmatization is present in virtually all social relationships: we are all capable of being stigmatized at certain times.

The third characteristic of stigma, says Goffman, is that it is "processual": this means that being stigmatized or, more precisely, coming to assume a stigmatized identity, is a socially mediated process that takes place over time. For example, if an individual is made to feel uncomfortable by others because they become excessively inebriated at an office party, then the feelings of embarrassment and shame, while not particularly pleasant and comfortable, are not likely to have any long-term effect on the person's

> **"**
> An attribute that stigmatizes one type of possessor can confirm the usualness of another.
> **Erving Goffman**
> **"**

actual social identity. However, if the excessive behavior continues over a period of time, and through interaction with group members the individual is allocated a deviant status, then their self-conception will be altered as they assume a stigmatized identity.

Types of stigma

In addition to explaining the concept of stigma, Goffman identified three types of stigma. The first type of stigma relates to what he refers to as "deformities" of the body, such as physical disability, obesity, uneven skin tone, baldness, and scarring. The second type of stigma refers to blemishes of character, including, says Goffman, "mental disorder, imprisonment, addiction,

alcoholism, homosexuality, unemployment, suicide attempts, and radical political behavior." He identifies the third type of stigma as tribal stigma, which includes social marginalization on the grounds of ethnicity, nationality, religion, and ideological beliefs. The attributes identified in these three categories of stigma are liable, Goffman claims, to impinge negatively on the ordinary and predicted patterning of social interactions involving the possessor of the attribute, and in turn result in exclusion or marginalization.

Impression management

Goffman also focuses on how individuals try to respond to and cope with negative classification. He suggests that people who are stigmatized actively seek to manage or, where possible, resist the negative social identities attributed to them.

His concept of "impression management" is important in this context because it highlights the various ways people try to present a version of selfhood to others that is as favorable as possible: they adopt different strategies to avoid being stigmatized. These include "concealment" through use of "covers," such as prosthetic limbs in the case of people who feel ashamed of having lost a limb. This is in direct contrast to "disclosure," which involves a person openly acknowledging the discrediting feature(s) of their identity. Where these strategies fail or are simply not feasible, the possessor of a stigma is liable to

Wigs are among the "props" or "covers" that are used by some bald people to attempt to "conceal" their baldness and thereby deflect potential sources of stigma.

seek out social types who they believe will act sympathetically toward them.

Goffman identifies three categories of people in particular who are liable to fulfill this role. The first are "the own": people who have a similarly stigmatized attribute—for example, members of a drug-addiction recovery group. The second category is "the wise": people who work in an institution or agency that supports individuals who possess a stigmatizing trait (care workers, disability officers, nurses, mental health therapists, and social workers, for example). The third category identified by Goffman includes individuals that the stigmatized person knows very well and who are likely to be empathetic toward them, such as the partner of someone with a disability or an addiction.

Crossing boundaries

It is generally accepted within sociology that Goffman's detailed observations of human interactions and of the interpersonal dynamics of small-scale groups remain unparalleled. Anthony Giddens, for example, draws heavily on Goffman's ideas about human behavior and identity formation in his much acclaimed "structuration" theory, which discusses the link between structures and human interaction. Pierre Bourdieu also refers to Goffman's work in his exploration of the extent to which people are able to change who they are and how they feel within certain contexts.

British social thinker Anthony Wootton has argued, however, that Goffman's work universalizes and identifies certain attributes as once and for all liable to be the cause of stigmatizing behavior. But normative expectations and moral

The causes of stigmatization are numerous, but can include idle gossip and negative attitudes that arise from ignorance and/or class- or race-based tensions. This then leads to negative stereotyping of an individual by the wider group. Over time, the individual internalizes these labels to the extent that they inform the person's self-evaluation and identity. By this point, the individual has acquired a stigmatized identity.

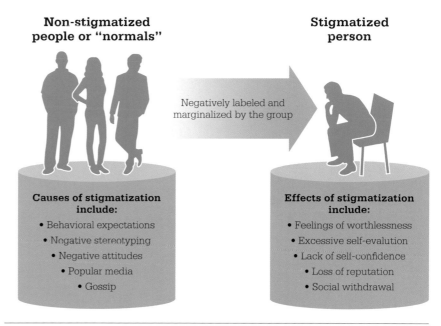

evaluations of certain attributes and behaviors change as society progresses. So, he says, whether or not mental illness and physical disability could still be said to be the cause of stigma is highly questionable in certain social and national contexts.

Goffman's work straddles the disciplinary boundaries between sociology and social psychology—his theories have therefore been taken up by thinkers from a wide range of academic backgrounds. Within sociology, his ideas about stigma have been applied very effectively by British social thinker Gill Green to consider the experiences of people with long-term illness, including those who have contracted the HIV virus. And social worker John Offer has used Goffman's concepts to consider the reintegration of

stigmatized individuals back into the community. Goffman's work also remains relevant politically—in particular, by offering a means of understanding how to address the problem of the stigmatization of minority groups in modern multicultural societies. ∎

> The stigmatized individual may find that he feels unsure how normals will identify and receive him.
> **Erving Goffman**

WE LIVE IN A WORLD WHERE THERE IS MORE AND MORE INFORMATION, AND LESS AND LESS MEANING

JEAN BAUDRILLARD (1929–2007)

IN CONTEXT

FOCUS
Simulacra

KEY DATES
c.360 BCE Greek philosopher Plato says he would banish "the imitator" from his perfect republic.

Early 1800s The Industrial Revolution begins in Europe.

1884 Friedrich Nietzsche says that we can no longer look to God to find meaning in our life, because "God is dead."

1970s Roland Barthes says signs and symbols have ideological functions that they impart to the reader with a "natural" simplicity.

1989 British computer scientist Tim Berners-Lee invents the World Wide Web (www.), an Internet-based hypermedia initiative for global information sharing.

A t the end of the 20th century, the French sociologist Jean Baudrillard announced that "the year 2000, in a certain way, will not take place." He claimed that the apocalypse—the end of the world as we know it—had already occurred, and in the 21st century, we "have already passed beyond the end." He believed this because, he said, there had been a perfect crime—"the murder of the real."

The only way in which we would "know" the year 2000, Baudrillard said, would be the way we now know everything: via the stream of images that are reproduced endlessly for our

See also: Henri Lefebvre 106–07 ▪ Alan Bryman 126–27 ▪ David Held 170–71 ▪
Antonio Gramsci 178–79 ▪ Herbert Marcuse 182–87

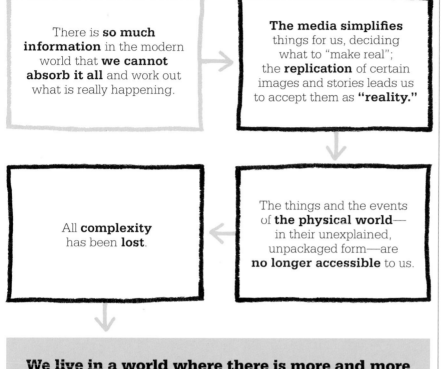

There is **so much
information** in the modern
world that **we cannot
absorb it all** and work out
what is really happening.

The media simplifies
things for us, deciding
what to "make real";
the **replication** of certain
images and stories leads us
to accept them as **"reality."**

All **complexity**
has been **lost**.

The things and the events
of **the physical world**—
in their unexplained,
unpackaged form—are
no longer accessible to us.

**We live in a world where there is more and more
information, and less and less meaning.**

Jean Baudrillard

Born in Reims, France, in
1929, Jean Baudrillard was
the first member of his family
to attend university. His
parents were civil servants,
but his grandparents were
peasant farmers, and he
claimed to have upset the
status quo when he went to
Paris to study, beyond school
level, at the Sorbonne.

During the 1950s
Baudrillard taught German
in secondary schools while
writing a PhD thesis under
the tuition of the Marxist
philosopher Henri Lefebvre.
In 1966, Baudrillard took up a
post at the University of Paris
IX teaching sociology, and
later became a professor in the
subject. His left-wing, radical
attitude made him famous
(and controversial) worldwide.
He broke with Marxism in the
1970s, but remained politically
active all his life. When asked
"Who are you?," he replied,
"What I am, I don't know. I am
the simulacrum of myself."

Key works

1981 *Simulacra and Simulation*
1983 *Fatal Strategies*
1986 *America*
1987 *The Ecstasy of
Communication*

consumption by magazines, TV,
newspapers, film, advertising,
and websites. Reality, according
to Baudrillard, is not whatever
happens in the physical world (that
"reality" is dead), but that which
is capable of being simulated, or
reproduced. In fact, he says, the
real is that "which is already
reproduced." During the 20th
century, representation started
to precede reality, rather than
the other way around.

The map comes first
Baudrillard explains his position
with reference to a short story
by the Argentinian writer and
poet Jorge Luis Borges, in which
cartographers draw up a huge map
of an empire. The map's scale is
1:1, and so the map is as large as
the ground it represents, and covers
the physical landscape of empire
completely. As the empire declines,
the map gradually becomes frayed
and finally ruined, leaving only a
few shreds remaining.

In this allegory, the real and
its copy can be easily identified;
the difference between them is
clear. Baudrillard maintains that
this is how it used to be in the
Renaissance world, when the link
between a thing and its image
was obvious. The image was a
reflection of a profound reality,
and we recognized both its »

Second Life is a virtual world where users re-create themselves digitally. Online marketing advises: "Everyone… is a real person and every place you visit is built by people just like you."

similarity to that reality and its difference. With the start of the industrial age, however, the link between the object and its representation became far less clear, as the original object, or a model of one, could be reproduced hundreds or thousands of times.

Remaking reality
Baudrillard was aware of other Marxist thinkers of the 1960s, such as French theorist Guy Debord, who had drawn attention to the shift in cultural thinking that occurred with the onset of mass production. Debord notes that at this point in history, "the whole life of those societies… presents itself as an… accumulation of spectacles." Thus life becomes condensed into a set of recorded pictures: a family wedding, a holiday in France, and so on. People are more interested in capturing the image—becoming spectators—than in *doing* things: the image, not the event, is central (the modern obsession with taking "selfies" emphasizes how pervasive this has become).

Baudrillard points out that through capitalism, commodities also became detached from themselves. Wheat was no longer simply wheat, for instance, but a

good investment, or a breakfast cereal. Presentation, not substance, dictated value. This was the start of the age of advertising, where the message of the brand overtook the reality of the substance in question. Image became everything.

Simplifying the world
Baudrillard followed the trajectory of this bizarre world of images and spectacles still further. As technology progressed, he says, it became obvious that there was no need to refer to a real object or model at all. The image—which was originally abstracted from something real—could now be created from nothing. It did not need to connect to or reflect anything in the physical world at all. This kind of image he calls a "simulacrum."

As long as an image or set of images is reproducible, Baudrillard maintains, it can create reality. The real is "that which can be reproduced." Once images are replicated and widely disseminated (in magazines or websites, for example), they create a shared reality that people can discuss, in a way that they cannot do with the messy, unstructured physical reality that we used to try to

engage with. They simplify the world and make it manageable. In addition, the reality they create is more exciting and perfect in every way than the one around us.

Dangerous utopias
"Simulacra"—images that have no original in reality—can be produced to create a much more satisfying effect than images that reflect reality. An actress can be "digitally enhanced" to look closer to a culture's ideal image of womanhood, but even this refers back to some kind of reality. For this reason, Baudrillard says that "the territory" of the real has not yet disappeared entirely—fragments remain. But people who find pleasure in looking at these enhanced images may find even more pleasure in images that are completely digitally created—that do not refer back to a "real person" at all. For example, we can look at "perfect" digitally created people

> The real is produced from miniaturized units, from matrices, memory banks, and command models—and with these it can be reproduced an indefinite number of times.
> **Jean Baudrillard**

and worlds, and even re-create ourselves in any shape or form online, in virtual worlds where we are invited to interact with other real/virtual people.

And herein lies the danger, says Baudrillard. Constructed realities can be built to maximize pleasure, so they are far more appealing than reality. We are constructing utopias, because if you have the freedom to construct a world, why not aim at a utopia? But the utopia we are creating in our virtual worlds is tantamount to death: we no longer want the real experience of something, but the experience of being told about the experience of something—in such a way that it is hyperreal, or more real than real. For instance, we prefer to sit in a cinema and enjoy the hyperreal experience of a family reunion than go to one of our own. On screen it is more colorful, noisy, and complete—it seems "so true." Our own lives pale by comparison, except perhaps our virtual lives, on Facebook or elsewhere. Meanwhile, we sit, not moving, looking at a screen.

Too much information

According to Baudrillard, our reality is now dictated by the incredible amount of information that streams into our lives from so many forms of media. He says that, strangely, although the real is disappearing, "it is not because of a lack of it, but an excess of it." An excess of information pouring into our awareness puts an end to information, he says, because we drown in complexity, and reach for the simple solution that is handed

In Disney World, US, countries such as "China" are re-created. These virtual models, says Baudrillard, are far more appealing to Disney's customers than the world "outside."

> " The age of simulation thus begins with a liquidation of all referentials—worse: by their artificial resurrection in systems of signs.
> **Jean Baudrillard** "

to us. Simulacra make sense of the world, even if this is at the cost of complex meaning. The world is becoming ever more superficial.

The simulacra that make up our reality today have been constructed to immediately gratify our desires. Baudrillard says that as virtual reality increases, our ideals and imaginations will recede. We accept what is given, just as we find it far easier to travel from "Germany" to "France" in Disney

World than in Europe. There is no longer a requirement for systems or things to be rational, just to work well, or be "operational." We have created a hyper-reality that is, he says, "the product of an irradiating synthesis of combinatory models in a hyperspace without atmosphere." We seem not to have noticed the fact that only robots can "live" without an atmosphere.

Some critical theorists, such as US philosopher Douglass Kellner, have criticized Baudrillard for moving away from a Marxist interpretation of culture. Marxist geographer David Harvey takes a similar stance, saying that Baudrillard is wrong to insist that there is no reality behind the image. Many theorists, however, including Canadians Arthur and Marilouise Kroker, praise his celebration of postmodern culture and see his work as a vital guide to the cultural dangers of the 21st century. As media ecologist Kenneth Rufo notes, Baudrillard is "full of interesting things, and even his misses... still pack a wallop." ∎

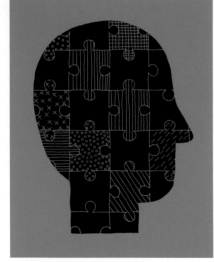

MODERN IDENTITIES ARE BEING DECENTERED
STUART HALL (1932–2014)

IN CONTEXT

FOCUS
Cultural identity

KEY DATES
17th century "The self"
becomes a noun for the first
time, gaining currency as an
idea worthy of investigation.

1900s Max Weber says that
individuals act according to
their subjective interpretations
of the world.

1920s G.H. Mead's idea of
symbolic interactionism
examines the symbols that
allow people to communicate
to each other despite their
subjective interpretations.

1983 Anglo-American
professor Benedict Anderson
says that national identity is
an "imagined community."

2010 British sociologist
Mike Featherstone examines
self-driven identity change
through bodily transformations
such as cosmetic surgery.

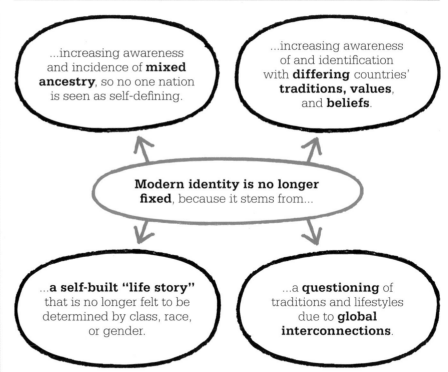

...increasing awareness
and incidence of **mixed
ancestry**, so no one nation
is seen as self-defining.

...increasing awareness
of and identification
with **differing** countries'
**traditions, values,
and beliefs**.

**Modern identity is no longer
fixed**, because it stems from...

...**a self-built "life story"**
that is no longer felt to be
determined by class, race,
or gender.

...a **questioning** of
traditions and lifestyles
due to **global
interconnections**.

In the late 20th century,
sociologists began to speak
about a new "crisis of identity,"
because identity—once seen as
a simple idea—was becoming
increasingly hard to pin down.
Professor Stuart Hall claims that
this is due to the way in which
structural change has been

transforming modern societies,
fragmenting the cultural
landscapes of class, gender,
sexuality, ethnicity, race, and
nationality. These are the
frameworks that we have
traditionally relied upon to
tell us who we are, both within
society and as individuals.

See also: W.E.B. Du Bois 68–73 ▪ Roland Robertson 146–47 ▪ David Held 170–71 ▪ G.H. Mead 176–77 ▪ Norbert Elias 180–81 ▪ Erving Goffman 190–95 ▪ Benedict Anderson 202–03 ▪ Howard S. Becker 280–85

In modern cities different cultures are thrown together. The more our lives are influenced by these diverse cultural traditions, the less sense we have of a fixed national identity.

Hall names three modern ideas of identity: the Enlightenment "self," the sociological "self," and the postmodern "self." The Enlightenment sense of self prevailed from the 17th to the early 20th centuries, and was held to be a complete, autonomous being: a person was born with a firm inner "core" that unfolded with age, but remained unchanged.

In the 1920s, sociologists such as G.H. Mead suggested that identity is formed in relationship with the environment and "significant others," who explain and transmit the values, meanings, and symbols of the child's world. The self in this definition was still seen as an inner core, but it could be modified by society, through internalizing cultural values and meanings. This "interactionist" view of the self, which bridges the gap between the personal and public worlds, became the classic sociological view of the self.

The postmodern self, on the other hand, says Hall, has no stable inner core. It is not fixed in any way, but instead is formed and transformed continuously according to the ways that it is addressed or represented in society. This is a self in process, defined historically rather than biologically. It contains contradictory identities that pull in different directions, and only seems continuous or stable because of the narrative that each of us constructs about ourselves (our "life story").

Detached identities

Hall says that the rapid, continuous, and extensive change that began to take place at the end of the 20th century has added to a sense of instability. Traditions and social practices are constantly examined, challenged, and often transformed by new information stemming from increased global interconnection. The global marketing of styles, places, and images means they pop up in every country, disrupting a traditional sense of fixed nationality and cultural identity.

This "mash up" of global culture means that identities have become detached from specific times, places, histories, and traditions, and we are now faced with a range of identities from which we can choose, when they appeal to us. Within the "discourse" (meanings system) of global consumerism, the differences and cultural distinctions that are used to define identity have become a kind of global currency. For example, jeans and sneakers—once associated with "being American"—are now just as much a part of being a young person in India or Kenya.

Where to the Afro-French philosopher Franz Fanon, black people were always defined as "other" to whites, Hall says that in the global arena, cultures are thrown together "with each 'Other'," where that other is "no longer simply 'out there' but also within." People increasingly come from a mixture of living spaces, ancestry, and birthplaces, and are aware of internally holding a range of identities that may come to the fore at different times. This inner and outer diversity, Hall says, is the force that is shaping our times. ∎

Stuart Hall

Known as the "godfather of multiculturalism," Stuart Hall was born into a Jamaican family that he says played out the conflict between the local and imperial (colonizing) context. His parents were from different social classes and from mixed ancestry; Hall rebelled against their suggestions to play only with "higher color" friends.

In 1952, Hall went to Oxford University, England, and became a key figure in the emerging New Left political movement. He was a cofounder of the *Left Review* in 1957, director of the Centre for Contemporary Cultural Studies, Birmingham, UK, and in 1979, a professor of sociology with the Open University. He also worked with film-makers and artists on black subjectivity.

Key works

1979 *The Great Moving Right Show*
1980 *Encoding/Decoding*
1992 "The Question of Cultural Identity"

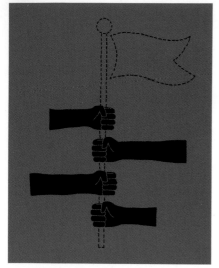

ALL COMMUNITIES ARE IMAGINED
BENEDICT ANDERSON (1936–)

IN CONTEXT

FOCUS
Nationalism

KEY DATES
1800 German philosopher Johann Fichte argues for a centralized state that could isolate itself from the world to develop a *volksgeist*—a nation's distinct sense of self.

1861 Soon after Italian unification, politician Massimo d'Azeglio announces: "We have made Italy. Now we have to make Italians."

1965 British-Czech anthropologist Ernest Gellner suggests that "nationalism is not the awakening of nations to self-consciousness: it invents nations where they do not exist."

1991 French philosopher Étienne Balibar says that "every 'people'… is the project of a national process of ethnicization."

Before the 16th century, the idea of nationalism did not exist. It is a modern concept that we have imagined into being and then convinced ourselves that it has an immemorial past. These are the views of social and political theorist Benedict Anderson, who says that we take the idea of nationalism as a given: if you are born in a certain place, you have a certain nationality, just as you are born a particular gender.

Anderson's book *Imagined Communities* (1983) questions the entire basis of nationalism. He defines "the nation" as "an imagined political community

With the **development of printing**, publishers appealed to the masses with books written in **the most widespread vernacular** languages as well as in Latin.

⬇

This gave the **languages more stability**, and helped to **define groups of people** according to the language they spoke.

⬇

This **unification via a common language** allowed the growth of shared ideas and values, and the idea of **belonging to a nation** grew.

⬇

In a time when belief in **religious rule was in decline**, the concept of **"nationhood"** gave the populace **something to believe in**, and a **cause to die for**.

See also: Paul Gilroy 75 ▪ Edward Said 80–81 ▪ Elijah Anderson 82–83 ▪ Saskia Sassen 164–65 ▪ David Held 170–71 ▪ Stuart Hall 200–01

that is imagined as both limited and sovereign." He explains that it is "imagined" because members of even the smallest nation in the world will never know or even meet most of their fellow-members, but "in the minds of each lives the image of their communion."

National consciousness

The idea of the nation is "limited," Anderson argues, because even the largest of nations has finite boundaries, although these are "elastic" (due, for example, to movement from immigration, emigration, and contested territories). No nation has ever entertained the possibility of making everyone in the world part of "their nation," he says, in the way that a religion, such as Christianity, would like to see everyone joined in one, unified belief system.

Anderson claims that one of the ways in which nationalities revealed their "elastic borders" was via the printing industry. In the 16th century, booksellers catered to the educated, Latin-speaking minorities, but realized they needed to reach larger markets for bigger profits. Unable to cater for

the many regional dialects, they chose the larger ones, and as these dialects gained stability in print, so they created unified fields of communication and helped define what the nation should "look like."

Giving life purpose

Sovereignty is also part of this idea of the nation, Anderson says, because the concept arose during the Enlightenment and an era of revolution. Religions lost their unquestioned grip on people's minds, and it was no longer accepted that monarchs had been divinely chosen by God to rule. The sovereign state allowed the structure of a nation to exist without calling on its people to believe in religious dogma. But with the death of religious rule, questions about the meaning of life went unanswered, according to Anderson. The rationality of the Enlightenment did not suggest any reason for living, or dying—but with the idea of the nation, a new purpose arose. Here was something worth dying for, and it also provided a sense of continuity of purpose that people had previously gained from an idea of the afterlife (such as heaven).

Some have questioned Anderson's theory, in particular with respect to the Arabic world, which continues to use a classical form of language and is still defined by religious belief. However, at a time in which political unrest is rife within "sub-nations" (such as Scotland or Catalonia) around the world, Anderson's idea of imagined nationhood has proved both controversial and hugely influential. *Imagined Communities* has been published in 29 languages. ▪

Benedict Anderson

Benedict Richard Anderson is professor emeritus of international studies, government, and Asian studies at Cornell University, US. Born in Kunming, China, in 1936, he was the son of an Irish father and English mother who had been active in Irish nationalist movements. The family emigrated to California in 1941, and thereafter to Ireland. Anderson was educated at Eton College in Berkshire, England. He took a degree in classics at the University of Cambridge in 1957.

A fascination with Asian politics led Anderson to undertake a PhD at Cornell University, which included a period of research in Jakarta, Indonesia. His public response to the 1965 communist coup there resulted in him being deported from the country, after which he traveled in Thailand for several years before returning to Cornell to teach.

Key works

1983 *Imagined Communities*
1998 *The Spectre of Comparisons*
2007 *Under Three Flags*

> " Nationality, or… nation-ness, as well as nationalism, are cultural artifacts.
> **Benedict Anderson** "

THROUGHOUT THE WORLD CULTURE HAS BEEN DOGGEDLY PUSHING ITSELF CENTER STAGE

JEFFREY ALEXANDER (1947–)

IN CONTEXT

FOCUS
Cultural sociology

KEY DATES
1912 In *The Elementary Forms of the Religious Life*, Émile Durkheim discusses how culture and meaning are interrelated.

1937 US sociologist Talcott Parsons emphasizes the autonomy of culture in *The Structure of Social Action*.

1973 US anthropologist Clifford Geertz stresses the importance of meaning for human social life in *The Interpretation of Cultures*.

1995 In *Fin de Siècle Social Theory*, Alexander criticizes Pierre Bourdieu, the world's leading sociologist of culture.

2014 British sociologist Christopher Thorpe applies Alexander's ideas in his examination of how the British experience Italy.

Sociologists have tended to regard culture as of **secondary importance**.

Material factors—**such as economic wealth and social class**—have been seen as **more influential**.

Alexander **emphasizes the role of culture** for determining social life.

Without culture, **no communication, event, or human interaction** is intelligible.

Within sociology, culture has been doggedly pushing itself center stage.

Many of us live our lives without examining why we habitually do what we do and think what we think. Why do we spend so much of each day working? Why do we save up our money? Why are we interested in gossip about people we don't know? If pressed to answer such questions, we may respond by saying "because that's what people like us do." But there is nothing natural, necessary, or inevitable about any of these things; instead, we behave like this because the culture we belong to compels us to.

The culture that we inhabit shapes how we think, feel, and act in the most existentially pervasive ways. It is not in spite of our culture that we are who we are, but precisely because of it.

US sociologist Jeffrey Alexander argues that culture—the collectively produced ideas, beliefs, and values of a group—is integral to an understanding of human life. Only through culture can humans pry themselves apart from a primordial state to reflect upon, and intervene in, the world around them. In spite of its central role, Alexander maintains that sociologists have historically seen culture as being of secondary importance. As one of the most influential social theorists in the world, Alexander has sought to ensure that the subject of culture takes center stage in the analysis of late-modern society.

Sociology and culture
While early sociological theorists recognized the central importance of culture, they failed—according to Alexander—to take seriously the idea that culture is essential to understanding why people think

See also: Karl Marx 28–31 ▪ Émile Durkheim 34–37 ▪ Max Weber 38–45 ▪ Erving Goffman 190–95 ▪ Talcott Parsons 300–01 ▪ Herbert Blumer 335

> We are not anywhere as reasonable or rational or sensible as we would like to think.
> **Jeffrey Alexander**

and act in the ways they do. Karl Marx, for example, saw mainstream culture as a function of the ideas and values of the ruling class; accordingly, culture served as little more than a veil to blind the majority of people to the profoundly unjust society in which they lived. Max Weber took a different view and argued that Western culture was rational and involved viewing the natural and social worlds in a dispassionate and scientific way; it was devoid of any wider meaning or worth.

For Alexander, both of these views are lacking: Marx's account is overly reductive because it holds that culture is determined by the way society is organized; Weber's account is overly rational because it fails to acknowledge the highly irrational aspects of Western culture—in particular the role of emotions and values in directing the responses of individuals, and even entire nations, to the events taking place around them.

Alexander's theoretical approach was very different, and built upon ideas about religion proposed by French sociologist Émile Durkheim. For Durkheim, religion involved the separation of the sacred—meaning the ideas, icons, and representations of the divine—from the profane, or the functions of everyday life. Alexander saw culture as akin to the sacred—autonomous from, rather than dependent upon, society; enabling rather than solely constraining; and containing both irrational and rational elements. His cultural sociology focuses on understanding how individuals and groups are involved in the creation of meaning by drawing upon collectively produced values, symbols, and discourses—ways of talking about things—and how this in turn shapes their actions.

Three aspects of culture

Alexander defines cultural sociology in terms of three main points, relating to origination, interpretation, and structure. First, culture can be completely autonomous from the material dimensions of social life. Marx's theories about culture became the orthodox way of conceptualizing the relationship between the "social" and the "cultural." In Marx's view, the material base of society (the economy, technologies, and the division of labor) determined the ideal superstructure (the norms, values, and beliefs of culture).

In contrast, Alexander believes that culture cannot be understood as a mere by-product of the "harder," more "real" material dimensions of social life. The notion that material factors determine ideal ones—that economy determines culture—is fundamentally misguided. »

Jeffrey Alexander

Jeffrey Alexander, born in 1947, is the Lillian Chavenson Saden Professor of Sociology at Yale University, and Co-Director for the Center for Cultural Sociology. As part of this role, Alexander established *Cultural Sociology* as a new academic journal to promote cultural sociological ideas and methods.

In the US, and arguably on the world scene generally, notably through his work on *Remembering the Holocaust: A Debate* (2009), he is one of the most distinguished social thinkers of his time. Originally taught by the influential US sociologists Talcott Parsons and Robert Bellah, Alexander carried forward structural-functionalism to its logical conclusion before abandoning it and founding his cultural sociological paradigm.

Key works

2003 *The Meanings of Social Life: A Cultural Sociology*
2012 *Trauma: A Social Theory*
2013 *The Dark Side of Modernity*

> ...the heart of current debates lies between... 'cultural sociology' and the 'sociology of culture.'
> **Jeffrey Alexander**

Instead, culture is, and should be, according to Alexander, considered "an independent variable," detached from the life conditions from which it emerged but able to exert power over the individuals and collectives within that culture.

People's understanding of events is neither natural or inevitable but is determined by the culturally specific language and symbols they use to interpret, code, and make sense of the world. As Alexander says, whether a society is defined as capitalist, socialist, or authoritarian does not bring us any closer to understanding the collective meaning attributed to an event. Instead, this is something that needs to be explored from "inside," in terms of the collectively produced structures, meanings, and symbols that people use to make sense of it.

Second, in order to understand culture, sociologists must adopt an interpretative approach. Alexander compares culture to a text—something that people read and interpret in ways that are socially

> ❝
> The failure of Bourdieu… is that he doesn't recognize that culture has relative autonomy from social structure.
> **Jeffrey Alexander**
> ❞

structured, but partially unique to them, and for this reason cannot be understood in terms of simple cause and effect. How people interpret an event cannot ever be fully predicted but instead requires to be understood retrospectively and from the perspective of the people concerned.

Third, Alexander claims that in the same way that there exist social structures—patterned ways of behaving that exist above and beyond individuals—there are also cultural structures. These are symbolic resources, constellations of signs and symbols that members of a culture draw upon to invest the world with meaning and relevance. People are often only partially aware of these structures—they do not consciously reflect upon the extent to which their conscious and unconscious minds are shaped by them. Nevertheless, those structures are socially produced and patterned. The goal of cultural sociology is to make these structures visible. The ultimate aim is to understand better—and, where desirable, intervene in—the collective actions and reactions to events that take place in the world.

Meaning and the Holocaust
To demonstrate the way social groups are compelled by value-laden meanings and symbols, Alexander draws upon the example of the Nazi Holocaust of World War II. He uses this example because the Holocaust is recognized as one of the most powerful symbols of

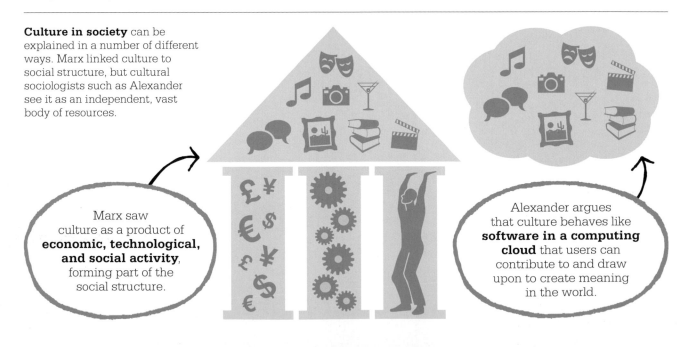

Culture in society can be explained in a number of different ways. Marx linked culture to social structure, but cultural sociologists such as Alexander see it as an independent, vast body of resources.

Marx saw culture as a product of **economic, technological, and social activity**, forming part of the social structure.

Alexander argues that culture behaves like **software in a computing cloud** that users can contribute to and draw upon to create meaning in the world.

human suffering and evil; it is (almost) beyond question that this event could be understood in any other way. Unbelievable as it may seem now, he argues, it is neither natural or inevitable that those events came to be understood as an act of unprecedented evil; rather: "...the category of 'evil' must be seen not as something that naturally exists but as an arbitrary construction, the product of cultural and sociological work."

In his 2001 essay "On the Social Construction of Moral Universalism: The 'Holocaust' from War Crime to Trauma Drama," Alexander demonstrates in rich detail that in the years immediately after World War II the Holocaust was not viewed with anything like the same horror and condemnation as it is now. As a socially distinct ethnic group, European Jews were typically negatively regarded in many societies, which in turn led to a less than empathetic response to their plight. Only as they became more integrated into wider society, and their distinctness as a social

group lessened, did it become possible for individuals and institutions to identify with them psychologically. By the early 1970s, the necessary cultural structures were in place for the Holocaust to be re-evaluated, re-narrated, and symbolically recoded as an act of evil. Only then was it elevated to the level of a traumatic event for all humankind and not just the Jews. On a state visit in 1970, the West German chancellor's "kneefall" at the Warsaw Ghetto memorial has been described by Valentin Rauer, in Alexander's *Social Performance* (2006), as a "symbol in action."

Alexander's cultural sociology is rapidly establishing itself as one of the most innovative and insightful sociological theoretical frameworks. As part of the wider "cultural turn" within the social sciences, his work has helped retrain the analytical focus of social thinkers onto the topic of "meaning." In particular his adaptation and application of Durkheim's work to understanding

An earthquake in 1997 destroyed Giotto's frescoes of St. Francis in the basilica at Assisi, Italy. Mira Debbs reflected on how this loss resulted in socially constructed cultural trauma.

the creation of meaning and its maintenance across a range of areas— including the Holocaust, democracy and civil society, and the 9/11 attacks—have led to more scholars developing and extending his ideas. For example, US sociologist Mira Debbs has analyzed the response in Italy to the destruction in 1997 of the artist Giotto's iconic frescoes in the basilica at Assisi. Such was the sacred status allocated to them in the national imagination that their loss has often been given more prominence than that of human life. Debbs draws upon Alexander's ideas to demonstrate how the narration and coding of the artworks in a particular way—as sacred national treasures—led to such a strong, seemingly irrational, collective emotional response by the majority of Italian people. ∎

Willy Brandt's kneefall at the memorial to the Warsaw Ghetto Uprising in 1970 was an act that symbolized German repentance, triggering a shift in collective identity.

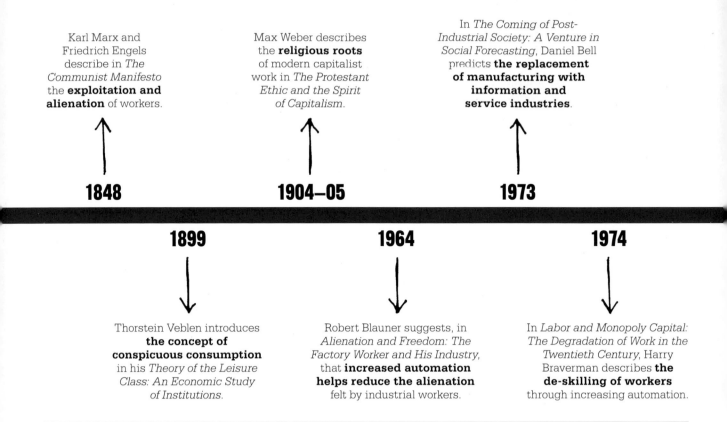

Karl Marx and Friedrich Engels describe in *The Communist Manifesto* the **exploitation and alienation** of workers.

1848

Thorstein Veblen introduces **the concept of conspicuous consumption** in his *Theory of the Leisure Class: An Economic Study of Institutions*.

1899

Max Weber describes the **religious roots** of modern capitalist work in *The Protestant Ethic and the Spirit of Capitalism*.

1904–05

Robert Blauner suggests, in *Alienation and Freedom: The Factory Worker and His Industry*, that **increased automation helps reduce the alienation** felt by industrial workers.

1964

In *The Coming of Post-Industrial Society: A Venture in Social Forecasting*, Daniel Bell predicts **the replacement of manufacturing with information and service industries**.

1973

In *Labor and Monopoly Capital: The Degradation of Work in the Twentieth Century*, Harry Braverman describes **the de-skilling of workers** through increasing automation.

1974

Sociology initially focused its attention on the changes to society that had been brought about by industrialization. A major aspect of modernity was the changing nature of people's working lives: the dramatic shift from agriculture and crafts in rural communities to employment in the new manufacturing industries. Along with this came the growth of capitalism, bringing prosperity to at least some members of society.

Among the first to study the implications of work in modern industrial society were Karl Marx and Friedrich Engels, who saw the emergence of two social classes: an affluent bourgeoisie, or middle class, and an oppressed proletariat, or working class. But as well as the exploitation of the working class, the pair recognized that the repetitive and soulless nature of the work itself alienated the workers, while the division of labor removed any feeling of connection with the finished product or pride in their work. Later, Max Weber pointed out how rationalization and the work ethic combined to force people to work for a specific economic end rather than for the good of the community as a whole. Traditional communal values had been eroded, and replaced with an emphasis on material worth.

Consumer society

For the working class, this translated into a struggle to earn the means to support a family, and resignation to a life of work that was unrewarding in every sense. For the growing capitalist middle class, it meant increased prosperity and leisure. The value that was ascribed to material wealth meant that a person's social status was judged by economic worth.

Toward the end of the 19th century, sociologist Thorstein Veblen pointed out that the bourgeoisie could assert its social status, whether real or not, by conspicuous consumption— spending not on goods and services that were necessary, but luxuries and leisure pursuits that would be noticed. Colin Campbell was later to liken the rise of a "consumer society" in the 20th century to the Romanticism that flourished in reaction to 18th-century rationalism and industrialization. Daniel Miller saw the growth of material consumerism as a potential source of social cohesion—a means of identifying with a social group.

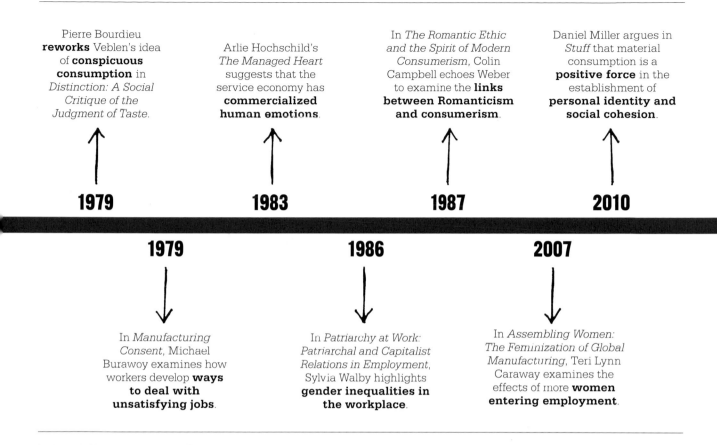

Pierre Bourdieu **reworks** Veblen's idea of **conspicuous consumption** in *Distinction: A Social Critique of the Judgment of Taste.*

Arlie Hochschild's *The Managed Heart* suggests that the service economy has **commercialized human emotions.**

In *The Romantic Ethic and the Spirit of Modern Consumerism*, Colin Campbell echoes Weber to examine the **links between Romanticism and consumerism.**

Daniel Miller argues in *Stuff* that material consumption is a **positive force** in the establishment of **personal identity and social cohesion.**

1979   **1983**   **1987**   **2010**

1979   **1986**   **2007**

In *Manufacturing Consent*, Michael Burawoy examines how workers develop **ways to deal with unsatisfying jobs.**

In *Patriarchy at Work: Patriarchal and Capitalist Relations in Employment*, Sylvia Walby highlights **gender inequalities in the workplace.**

In *Assembling Women: The Feminization of Global Manufacturing*, Teri Lynn Caraway examines the effects of more **women entering employment.**

Industrialization continued to spread across the world in the 20th century, and technological advances led to an increase in automation—in agricultural and traditional crafts as well as in manufacturing industries. Societies, in the industrialized West at least, became more materially prosperous, and fostered the rapid growth of mass consumerism, but sociologists disagreed about the effects of automation on the workforce.

Robert Blauner forecast that automation would free people from mindless tasks and reduce their feelings of alienation. On the other hand, Harry Braverman argued that automation meant workers were no longer required to develop professional skills, had less control over their working lives, and felt yet more alienated. Somewhere between these two views, however, Michael Burawoy suggested that workers reconcile themselves to ultimately dull and oppressive work by recognizing its positive aspects.

Post-industrial work
In the 1970s, around 200 years after the beginning of the Industrial Revolution, the nature of work looked set to change yet again. Daniel Bell predicted that mechanization would take people out of manufacturing industries, and they would be employed predominantly in the information and service industries. To a large extent, in the affluent world at least, this has proved correct. Another change that became apparent in the latter part of the 20th century is that work was no longer seen as a male preserve; more women than ever before are in paid employment.

One effect of the shift into what is now known as the post-industrial world has been identified by Arlie Hochschild. Service industries are more emotionally demanding than manufacturing; in effect, they commercialize emotion, to the extent, she argues, that people can associate their feelings with their work rather than their home lives and leisure. The social effects of these recent changes to the nature of employment have yet to be fully studied; it is too early to tell whether work in the service economy will prove to be any more rewarding, or conducive to social solidarity, than manufacturing work—or if gender inequality will be reduced because more women are in the workforce. ∎

CONSPICUOUS CONSUMPTION OF VALUABLE GOODS IS A MEANS OF REPUTABILITY TO THE GENTLEMAN OF LEISURE

THORSTEIN VEBLEN (1857–1929)

IN CONTEXT

FOCUS
Conspicuous consumption

KEY DATES
1844 Karl Marx discusses class structure in capitalist society in *Economic and Philosophical Manuscripts of 1844*.

1859 Charles Darwin explains his theory of evolution in *On the Origin of Species by Means of Natural Selection*.

1979 Pierre Bourdieu reworks Veblen's theory of conspicuous consumption in *Distinction*.

1992–2005 Studies by US sociologist Richard A. Peterson suggest that snobbery is no longer a determining factor in the consumption practices of the middle class.

From 2011 Veblen's concept of conspicuous consumption influences economic ideas about irrationality and consumer behavior.

The work of US economist and sociologist Thorstein Veblen focuses on the relationship between economy and society, and on how different class groups consume specific goods and services. He draws on the ideas of a number of key theorists, including Karl Marx, British sociologist Herbert Spencer, and British naturalist Charles Darwin. Veblen's insights into capitalist society and the types of consumer behavior it gives rise to are outlined in his most celebrated work, *The Theory of the Leisure Class: An Economic Study of Institutions* (1899).

Capitalism and class

Veblen sees the transition from traditional to modern society as propelled by the development of technical knowledge and industrial production methods. Like Marx, Veblen argues that capitalist society is split into two competing social-class groups: the industrious class made up of workers; and the leisure class, also referred to as the pecuniary or business class (which also includes politicians, managers, lawyers, and so on), which owns the factories and workshops.

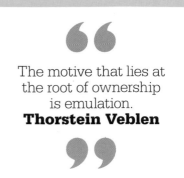

The motive that lies at the root of ownership is emulation.
Thorstein Veblen

The industrious class forms the vast majority of the population and engages in productive labor, such as manual craft and machine work. By contrast, the leisure class is a numerically far smaller, but nevertheless socially and economically privileged, group that is parasitic on the labor of the industrious class. For Veblen, members of this predatory leisure class do not produce anything of any real benefit to the wider good of society. The wealth and privilege they possess derive from driving competition and manipulating workers, with the sole aim of increasing their personal wealth.

Capitalist society is divided into **two classes**.

The **industrious class** produces consumer goods, and the **leisure class** thrives on the profits created by the industrious class.

Members of the leisure class buy **nonessential luxury goods** to display their **wealth, power, and status**.

Conspicuous consumption of valuable goods is a means of reputability to the gentleman of leisure.

See also: Karl Marx 28–31 ▪ Charles Wright Mills 46–49 ▪ Pierre Bourdieu 76–79 ▪ Anthony Giddens 148–49 ▪ Herbert Marcuse 182–87 ▪ Colin Campbell 234–35 ▪ Herbert Spencer 334

Worse still, the privileged class consistently impedes positive social advancement through its deliberate mismanagement of industry and society generally.

Social recognition

Veblen's concept of "conspicuous consumption" is his most renowned contribution to economic and sociological theory. Framed by the Darwinian notion that all life represents an ongoing struggle for resources in the pursuit of advancement of the species (or in the case of human societies, the groups to which individuals belong), Veblen argues that under capitalism the majority of human behavior is determined by struggles for social recognition, status, and power. This is most evident in relation to patterns of consumption and leisure.

Conspicuous consumption refers to spending money on, and consumption of, nonessential luxury goods in order to display to other members of society one's own economic and material wealth. An example of this is the modern business tycoon who buys an expensive yacht so that he can entertain friends and clients. It is not the utility value of the yacht (whether or not it is an effective means of transport) that matters to the tycoon; rather, its value is as a highly conspicuous signifier of the wealth at the tycoon's disposal, for which he will receive both admiration and respect.

Leisure and waste

Closely bound to Veblen's concept of conspicuous consumption is the notion of conspicuous leisure: the vast amount of time that

The concept of "Veblen goods," or luxury goods that signal high status, appeared in economic theory in the 1970s. In a reversal of usual trends, the higher the price of these items, the more they are desired.

Desire for goods increases as price increases.

PRICE OF LUXURY ITEM

DESIRE FOR LUXURY ITEM

members of the leisure class spend in pursuit of activities that are neither economically nor socially productive. Very simply, leisure implies an absence of work. For members of this privileged class who have sufficient distance from economic necessity (the need to work), the nonproductive use of time can be used to further their social prestige and class position. Going on exotic foreign vacations and learning about other countries are classic examples of conspicuous leisure, according to Veblen.

The inevitable consequence of conspicuous leisure and consumption is the production of unnecessary waste. Conspicuous waste, argues Veblen, derives from the amalgamation of conspicuous consumption and conspicuous leisure. The net result of these two activities is that socially valuable resources (the raw materials and human labor essential for the

production of consumer goods and services) and time are wasted. A glaring example of this culture of waste is the depletion of natural resources such as oil and minerals in the manufacture of luxury »

Travel to foreign lands, learning languages, and acquiring knowledge about other cultures were powerful status symbols for wealthy Europeans in the 18th and 19th centuries.

goods and commodities, which in turn gives rise to increased carbon emissions and climate change.

Veblen's concepts of conspicuous consumption and conspicuous leisure are "political" ones because they contain within them a strong moral stance toward the actions and lifestyle of what he sees as the predatory and parasitic leisure class.

Pecuniary emulation

Aside from the wastefulness that the lifestyle of the leisure class necessitates, a further negative consequence of their activities is captured in Veblen's notion of pecuniary emulation. This concept refers to the idea that individuals from lower social-class groups try

> 66
> Wealth is now itself intrinsically honorable and confers honor on its possessor.
> **Thorstein Veblen**
> 99

to emulate, both consciously and unconsciously, the consumption practices of their social "superiors"—members of the leisure class. This is an attempt to signify to others their affiliation to the most socially powerful and dominant groups in society.

Pecuniary emulation is firmly rooted in the idea of ownership: once the immediate material needs of individuals are met, consumer goods are purchased for their utility as signifiers of social-class status and affiliation to the identity and lifestyle of a given social group. In capitalist society, social-class groups are stratified hierarchically. Attached to each class group is a specific amount of social status. Ownership, power, status, and dominance become inextricably bound together, such that the struggle for status is founded primarily in displays of economic wealth and pecuniary respect. Veblen claims that people are constantly comparing themselves— and what they have—to those around them. There are, he says, a number of very real and negative unintended consequences arising from this phenomenon.

Individuals and entire groups are subjected to the pressures of "invidious," or unjust, comparison with one another,

The carbon-copy lifestyle of some middle-class neighborhoods arises from pressure to emulate the consumption practices of residents in an attempt to gain status and prestige.

according to Veblen. As capitalism becomes increasingly competitive, so the process of invidious comparison proliferates. The dominant mode of evaluating other people is "with a view to rating and grading them in respect to relative worth or value." But in addition to generating even more waste across the population, the process of pecuniary emulation does not guarantee the accumulation of social respect or prestige. Here Veblen uses the term "nouveau riche," or recently acquired wealth, to describe people who engage in conspicuous acts of consumption, such as buying flashy cars or designer-brand clothes. This may result in disapproval from people whose wealth or status— and what may be considered as more understated or subtle taste dispositions—is inherited from previous generations. This could serve to alienate the nouveau riche even further from the dominant social groups they aspire to emulate. Purchasing conspicuous consumer goods can lead to the attainment of social prestige, but not in those cases in which the consumers are perceived to be, and often are, exceeding the financial means available to them.

Veblen's legacy

Veblen's ideas on the conspicuous nature of consumption have been influential in the development of sociological analysis and continue to attract controversy and debate in equal measure.

For example, the work of the French theorist Pierre Bourdieu is indebted to Veblen's notions of pecuniary emulation and conspicuous consumption, even though he modified them to fit his theoretical model. Bourdieu maps out how individuals and social-class groups constantly compete with, and differentiate themselves from, one another through the consumption of certain types of socially distinguishing goods and services.

British-born sociologist Colin Campbell, however, sees Veblen's work as overly reductive. He claims that Veblen fails to acknowledge that the acquisition of consumer goods plays an essential and positive part in the way people

> Individuals... seek to excel in pecuniary standing and... gain the esteem and envy of fellow-men.
> **Thorstein Veblen**

are able to construct a sense of self-identity and worth through the products they buy and the activities they pursue.

More recently, sociologists have questioned whether a socially distinct leisure class can really be said to exist at all. British sociologist Mike Savage, for example, has argued that the shifting dynamics of modern class relations means there is no aristocratic leisure class in the modern world. This also means, according to Savage, that there is no longer a clearly identifiable social group whose taste

dispositions and consumption practices are emulated by all other social groups.

Developing this idea further, US sociologist Richard Peterson devised the concept of "cultural omnivore" to refer to an emergent social group—the educated fraction of the middle class working in the new media industries and advertising—that accrues prestige from consuming an eclectic mix of high- and low-brow consumer goods. Social prestige, according to Peterson, is now no longer derived from conspicuous consumption of luxury goods alone, but from the "knowing" and "ironic" consumption of purposively non-luxury items such as retrograde clothing, baseball caps, Dr. Martens boots, and so on.

Despite criticisms and modification of his ideas, Veblen's *The Theory of the Leisure Class*, with its detailed examination of the intended and unintended social consequences of consumer spending and wider consumption patterns in capitalist societies, nevertheless remains an essential reference for economists and sociologists alike. ∎

Thorstein Veblen

Thorsten Veblen was born in Wisconsin to Norwegian immigrant parents. He obtained his undergraduate degree in economics from Johns Hopkins University in 1880; four years later he received his doctorate from Yale University.

Veblen's relationship with the world of institutional academia was a fractious one. In the late 19th century, many universities were strongly affiliated with churches, and Veblen's skepticism about

religion, combined with his odd manner and allegedly monotonous teaching style, meant that he struggled to gain employment. As a result, from 1884 to 1891 he depended on the largesse of his family.

In 1892, his former mentor, J. Laurence Laughlin, joined the University of Chicago, taking Veblen with him as a teaching assistant. It was here Veblen wrote and published *The Theory of the Leisure Class*. Shortly after, he was fired from the University of Chicago and, later, also from the University of Stanford for

his notoriously promiscuous behavior. This culminated in divorce from his wife in 1911. He moved to California, where he passed his remaining years in depressed solitude.

Key works

1899 *The Theory of the Leisure Class: An Economic Study of Institutions*
1904 *The Theory of Business Enterprise*
1914 *The Instincts of Workmanship and the State of the Industrial Arts*

THE PURITAN WANTED TO WORK IN A CALLING; WE ARE FORCED TO DO SO

MAX WEBER (1864–1920)

Max Weber, a founding father of sociology, provides a very different account of the rise of capitalism to that outlined in the work of the two other traditional founders of the discipline, Karl Marx and Émile Durkheim. In *The Protestant Ethic and the Spirit of Capitalism* (1904–05), Weber's most acclaimed work, he offers an analysis of the role played by religious ideas, beliefs, and values—particularly Protestantism—in the rise of modern capitalism.

For Weber, the definitive feature of capitalist society is the particular "work ethic" or "spirit of capitalism," as he refers to it, that

See also: Émile Durkheim 34–37 ■ Zygmunt Bauman 136–43 ■ Jeffrey Alexander 204–09 ■ Colin Campbell 234–35 ■ Karl Marx 254–59 ■ Bryan Wilson 278–79

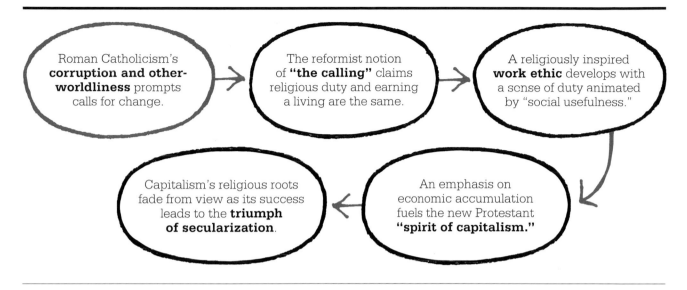

Roman Catholicism's **corruption and other-worldliness** prompts calls for change.

The reformist notion of **"the calling"** claims religious duty and earning a living are the same.

A religiously inspired **work ethic** develops with a sense of duty animated by "social usefulness."

An emphasis on economic accumulation fuels the new Protestant **"spirit of capitalism."**

Capitalism's religious roots fade from view as its success leads to the **triumph of secularization**.

drives modern economies and the pursuit of wealth and profit. He claims that this "work ethic" is founded on the values of rationality, calculability, individual self-regulation, and gain.

The pursuit of profit

Weber's focus on the part played by cultural factors was partly intended to counter Marx's view that the rise of capitalism was a natural and inevitable process. Weber rejected the notion that human history is driven by underlying, inexorable "laws" that determine the path society will take.

The buying and selling of goods and services for more than they are worth is, Weber says, not unique to capitalism. Throughout history people have always traded with one another with a view to accruing profit. What is historically unique

to capitalism, he argues, is that the pursuit of profit becomes an end in itself. A modern-day example is the transnational banking group HSBC, which made a pre-tax profit of US $22.6 billion in 2013. If this profit was distributed among all of the firm's employees they could stop working and still live materially comfortable lives. Instead, firms such as HSBC use the profit they make to reinvest in the corporation, improve its efficiency, and pursue further profit.

Where, wondered Weber, did this ideal—the unrelenting pursuit of profit, or wealth for wealth's sake—that animates the "work ethic" at the heart of capitalism, actually come from?

Weber believed that to answer this question, we must look not to changes in social solidarity or technology but to one of the oldest features of all human societies—religion. He looks back in time to religious developments that were taking place in 16th-century »

The vast profits of the US retail giant Walmart should, staff says, be redirected into paying better wages. The corporation came under scrutiny in 2014 as a low-paying employer.

Europe, when Protestantism emerged as a reaction to the perceived corruption and failings of the Roman Catholic Church. Nascent Protestantism offered a very different vision of the relations between God and his subjects and the ethics overseeing them.

The Protestant "calling"

Weber identified in particular the importance of "the calling" to the new Protestant system of ethics, by which was meant the position that God has called people to occupy in this world. Whereas the Roman Catholic Church urged monastic retreat from the world of mundane affairs (such as daily life and work), Protestantism demanded that its followers fulfilled their worldly duties and responsibilities.

In drawing attention to this difference in religious ideals, Weber identified the German theologian Martin Luther (1483–1546) as the man whose thinking was essential to the development of Protestant theology. Luther was the first person to suggest that fulfilling the duties of secular life also demonstrated reverence to God. He claimed that at the heart of the concept of "the calling" is the belief that earning a living and religious duty are one and the same thing.

Luther's ideas were taken up within two decades and developed in important ways by arguably the most influential of all the reformers, John Calvin (1509–1564). However, contained within the otherwise coherent ethical system Calvin formulated was a significant inconsistency or contradiction: if God is all-seeing and all-knowing, then our destiny as individuals is predetermined because God made the world and everyone in it.

Calvin's notion is referred to as the concept of the "elect." Because God already knows how we are fated to live our lives, he also knows whose souls he has elected to save and whose souls will be damned. The problem for Protestants, however, is that there is no way of knowing in advance the category—the saved or the damned—to which they belong. According to Weber, this unknown gave rise to "salvation anxiety" and led to psychological terror among the followers of Protestantism. To resolve their unease, Protestants convinced themselves and one

Calvinist church aesthetics stress simplicity: Protestantism focused on austerity and thrift in contrast to the grandeur and ostentation that was often associated with Catholicism.

another that there were certain distinct signs that revealed who was predestined to be saved.

Social usefulness

Protestants felt that the most obvious way in which they could tell whether or not they were saved was by succeeding in the world, especially in economic affairs. Essential to this outcome was, they believed, a specific work ethic—historically novel and uniquely Protestant—that emphasized the absolute need for austerity, self-monitoring, and self-control in the conduct of economic affairs. Weber referred to this as the "spirit of capitalism."

A further aspect of this spirit was the drive toward increasing rationalization, control, and calculability within the sphere of economic action. To prosper economically is to demonstrate to one's self and others adherence to the notion of "the calling": the more

Modernity and the Holocaust

For Weber, the spread of the values of calculability, rationality, and self-restraint that defined the Protestant work ethic were also central to the development of modernity.

German-Polish sociologist Zygmunt Bauman argues that the value-basis of that ethic also explains how the Nazi Holocaust was able to occur. Instead of the traditional view of the Holocaust as the triumph of irrationality and a regression to primitive, pre-modern ways of thinking and acting, Bauman sees it as a highly rationalized event. Not only did modernity's rationality make the Holocaust possible, it was a necessary condition for it because the extermination was run on bureaucratic, organized lines. Bauman argues that the high levels of rationality and self-discipline exhibited by the Holocaust's perpetrators are inextricably bound up with the religious culture and values that were found throughout Protestant Europe.

hard-working, austere, and self-controlled individuals are in their actions, the greater will be the economic rewards they reap; and the more wealth they accumulate, the more this is understood as proof of their religious purity and the promise of salvation.

The inverse of the Protestant ethic is to shy away from work—to commit the sins of idleness and indolence and to fail to prosper financially.

Secularization

With the steady decline of formal religion (secularization) from the Industrial Revolution onward, the Protestant ethic that underpins the "spirit of capitalism" has been eroded. When Weber claims that early Protestants "wanted to work in a calling" but that today "we are forced to," he is suggesting that although the values of hard work, self-control, and self-discipline upon which capitalism is founded have remained and are valued socially, their religious roots have disappeared from view.

In identifying the strong affinity between the work ethic contained within Reformation Protestantism—particularly the teachings of John Calvin—and the spirit of capitalism, Weber draws attention to a great historical irony. The Protestant Reformation was intended to salvage the message of God from the corrupting influences of the Roman Catholic Church. Nearly 500 years later, formal religion has gone into significant decline. What began as an attempt to salvage the Word has given rise to a work ethic that has been essential to the proliferation of capitalism. And as capitalism has developed, the power of formal religion to influence our actions has greatly diminished.

More than 100 years after its original publication in German, Weber's theory of the Protestant ethic remains hotly debated among contemporary sociologists and historians. The Italian sociologist Luciano Pellicani, for example, has argued that the spirit of capitalism arose much earlier than Weber suggests and that it was already present in medieval society.

In Weber's defense, English historian Guy Oakes points to the fact that medieval capitalism was fueled by greed rather than by the sober, mundane sense of duty promoted by Calvinism. However, the fact that industrial capitalism first took hold in the Protestant countries of Europe, such as the Netherlands, Britain, and Germany, confirms the link that Weber made between Protestantism and the enterprising impulse that was necessary for the development of capitalism. And

Fulfillment of worldly duties is... the only way to live acceptably to God.
Max Weber

in *The Romantic Ethic and the Spirit of Modern Consumerism* (1987), Colin Campbell uses Weber's theory to account for the rise of consumer culture in Europe and the US. This extension of Weber's ideas confirms that his religion-inspired account of the rise of capitalism continues to exert a powerful influence over sociological thought. ∎

The Protestant world view was shaped by the concept that worldly duties show reverence to God and promote his glory. Material success is interpreted as God's approval—a reward for effort, thrift, sobriety, and other "correct" ways of living.

TECHNOLOGY, LIKE ART, IS A SOARING EXERCISE OF THE HUMAN IMAGINATION
DANIEL BELL (1919–2011)

IN CONTEXT

FOCUS
Post-industrialism

KEY DATES
1850s–80s Karl Marx argues that the social power of the bourgeoisie, or capitalist class, derives from ownership of industrial machines.

1904–05 Max Weber's *The Protestant Ethic and the Spirit of Capitalism* points to the increasingly rational nature of modern culture.

1970s Leading US sociologist Talcott Parsons defends the values and advancement of modern industrial society.

1970–72 Daniel Bell forecasts the rise of the Internet and the importance of home computers.

From the 1990s The concept of post-industrialism informs the theories of globalization experts Ulrich Beck and Manuel Castells.

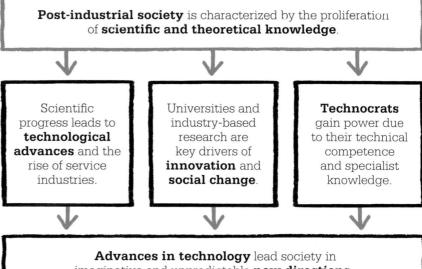

Post-industrial society is characterized by the proliferation of **scientific and theoretical knowledge**.

Scientific progress leads to **technological advances** and the rise of service industries.

Universities and industry-based research are key drivers of **innovation** and **social change**.

Technocrats gain power due to their technical competence and specialist knowledge.

Advances in technology lead society in imaginative and unpredictable **new directions**.

During the 1960s and 1970s profound changes swept through the economic basis of society in Western Europe and the US. In his influential work *The Coming of Post-Industrial Society* (1973), political journalist and sociologist Daniel Bell developed the concept of "post-industrialism" to refer to these changes. Having lived in New York and Chicago, Bell had first-hand experience of the rapid and extensive urban development that was taking place.

Bell agrees with Karl Marx that the bourgeoisie, or capitalist class, was the most powerful social group in industrial society because they owned the means of production—the factories and machines that produced the goods consumed by the wider population. In Bell's post-industrial society,

See also: Karl Marx 28–31 ▪ Manuel Castells 152–55 ▪ Ulrich Beck 156–61 ▪ Max Weber 220–223

however, the most valuable social "resource" is scientific and theoretical knowledge, and those who control it hold the power.

He also claims that social change occurs at an unprecedented pace as scientific progress and developments in technology interpenetrate and propel human societies into the future. The post-industrial era is therefore, he says, a period in the history of society in which advances in science and technology are as unpredictable and boundless as the human imagination.

Post-industrial society

According to Bell, post-industrial society differs from industrial society in three interrelated ways: first, the production of consumer goods is surpassed by the growth and progress of "theoretical" knowledge; second, developments in science and technology become increasingly intertwined as universities and industry-led

Modern cities are no longer dominated by the factories essential to manufacturing. In the post-industrial world of service industries, futuristic architecture has space to thrive.

initiatives form ever-tighter and interpenetrating relations; and finally, the number of unskilled and semiskilled workers declines as the majority of the population work in, and draw upon, the expanding service industries. Bell refers to service industries as those spheres of human activity that are devoted to managing and guiding the application of information and knowledge.

Another key aspect of post-industrial society, according to Bell, is the rise in power of "technocrats," or people who exercise authority through their technical knowledge and ability to solve problems logically. The social power of technocrats is determined by their skill in forecasting and guiding new scientific ideas.

Bell believes that technology encourages imagination and experimentation—in so doing, it opens up new ways of thinking about the world. He points to the fact that the Greek word *techne* means "art." For him, art and technology should not be seen as separate realms: technology, he says, is "a form of art that bridges culture and social structure, and in the process reshapes both." ▪

Daniel Bell

The influential social thinker, writer, and sociologist Daniel Bell was born in Manhattan, New York City in 1919. His parents were Jewish immigrants from Eastern Europe. His father died when Bell was just a few months old; his family's name was changed from Bolotsky to Bell when he was a teenager.

In 1938 Bell received a BSc from City College of New York. He worked as a political journalist for more than 20 years. As managing editor of *The New Leader* magazine and editor of *Fortune*, he wrote widely on social issues. In 1959, in recognition of his contribution to political journalism, he was appointed professor of sociology at Columbia University; he was later awarded a PhD from the same university, even though he did not submit a doctoral thesis. He was a professor of sociology at Harvard University from 1969 to 1990.

Key works

1969 *The End of Ideology*
1973 *The Coming of Post-Industrial Society*
1976 *The Cultural Contradictions of Capitalism*

THE MORE SOPHISTICATED MACHINES BECOME THE LESS SKILL THE WORKER HAS

HARRY BRAVERMAN (1920–1976)

IN CONTEXT

FOCUS
De-skilling

KEY DATES
1911 US mechanical engineer Frederick Winslow Taylor publishes *The Scientific Principles of Management*.

1950s The translation into English of Karl Marx's writing on alienation brings his work back into vogue in Anglophone sociology.

1958 US thinker James R. Bright publishes *Automation and Management*, which warns of links between automation and de-skilling.

1960s Mechanization causes widespread alienation among unskilled and semiskilled workers in the US.

1970s A US governmental report entitled *Work in America* concludes that significant numbers of workers are dissatisfied with their jobs.

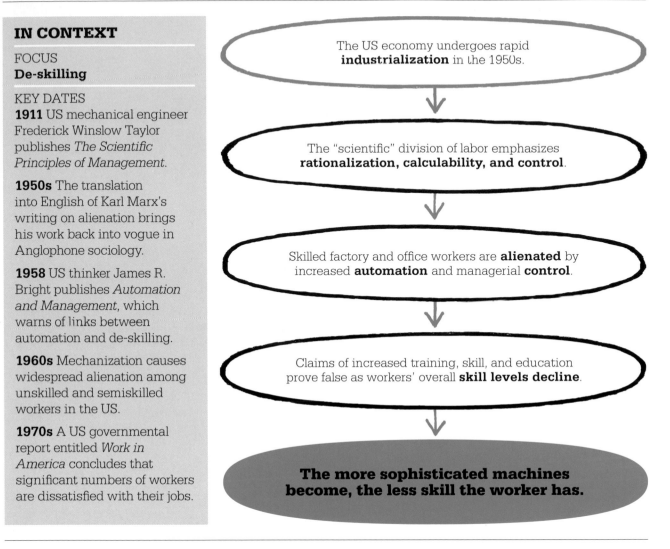

The US economy undergoes rapid **industrialization** in the 1950s.

The "scientific" division of labor emphasizes **rationalization, calculability, and control**.

Skilled factory and office workers are **alienated** by increased **automation** and managerial **control**.

Claims of increased training, skill, and education prove false as workers' overall **skill levels decline**.

The more sophisticated machines become, the less skill the worker has.

Since the 1950s, Karl Marx's concept of alienation has been the leading analytical lens through which sociologists from North America and Europe have sought to understand the modernization of employment and its effects on the workforce.

Both Marx and Max Weber had predicted that the rise of industrial technology would be accompanied by a drive toward ever-greater levels of efficiency, and the rationalization of the workforce into increasingly differentiated and specialized parts. Explicitly acknowledging that he is following in this intellectual tradition, Harry Braverman's classic 1974 study, *Labor and Monopoly Capital: The Degradation of Work in the Twentieth Century*, is a systematic inquiry into the nature of industrial work and the changing composition of the working class under the conditions of monopoly capitalism.

Braverman's analysis pivots on the notion of "de-skilling": that advances in industrial technology and machine production have led to the alienation and "deconstruction" of skilled members of the industrial working class and craftsmen. He believed that the de-skilling of work and the degradation of industrial workers was a process that had been gathering momentum since World War II. Although his focus was on factory workers, he also dealt with, albeit in less detail, office and clerical workers.

Myths of skilled labor
The idea that the industrialization of factory work is empowering for workers is tackled head on by Braverman and found seriously wanting. Drawing on his own

See also: Karl Marx 28–31 ▪ Max Weber 38–45 ▪ George Ritzer 120–23 ▪ Manuel Castells 152–55 ▪ Erich Fromm 188 ▪ Daniel Bell 224–25 ▪ Robert Blauner 232–33

> Industrial processes and... organization have robbed the worker of his craft and its heritage.
> **Harry Braverman**

experience of such factory work, Braverman challenges official statistics and governmental classifications of workers to demonstrate the progressive and ongoing "de-skilling" of the US working class.

So, for example, the notion that increasing technology in the workplace calls forth a more technically proficient and educationally qualified workforce is, he argues, simply not true. Terms like "training," "skill," and "learning" are vague and open to interpretation, and the amount of training required to operate factory and office machinery often takes only a matter of minutes or, at most, a few weeks. Merely pointing to the fact that workers can operate machinery does not necessarily mean their skill levels have increased significantly. Tending to machinery and knowing how to operate it—a good example is learning how to use a photocopier—does not mean that a worker should be reclassified as "skilled."

Moreover, Braverman found that while general levels of educational achievement have increased among the workforce, typically this has a negative and unintended consequence for the individual entering paid employment.

In the course of surveys and interviews undertaken by Braverman, it was often found that the attainment of educational qualifications made the experience of factory and office work even more frustrating, or lacking in fulfillment, because opportunities for individuals to utilize and apply the knowledge obtained from their schooling simply did not exist. Greater educational achievement can lead to a far more acutely perceived sense of alienation.

Progressive skills erosion

Before the Industrial Revolution, notes Braverman, material goods were made by skilled and semiskilled craftsmen and artisans. Advances in technology had enabled the scale of industrial production to reach unprecedented levels. The capacity for machines to perform so many of the tasks hitherto performed manually by skilled workers meant certain skills and technical knowledge were no longer required, while the need for new competencies and expertise grew in their place.

Understood in this way, argues Braverman, automation removes the need for some skills while creating a need for different, new skills in their place. Technological progress alone does not necessarily lead to a decline in workers' skill levels. Neither does alienation follow as a direct result.

Braverman was not arguing nostalgically for a return to the pre-industrial model of the craft worker; on the contrary, he acknowledges that automation can be a positive development. The effects become wholly negative, he claims, when automation of the workplace is coupled with radical changes to the social relations of production: the way in which the total labor process is organized, managed, and manipulated. He emphasizes the distinction between advances in science and technology and how those are implemented in the workplace on the one hand, and changes to the social relations of production— the drive for ever-more efficient ways to organize and divide up the labor force—on the other.

Just as machines are built to do jobs in the most efficient way, the workforce is structured to increase productivity and profit. Braverman's aim is to show that the embodied knowledge and technical competencies of skilled workers have been eroded and forgotten. »

The production line at Opel in 1950s' West Germany. Subdivision of labor improved efficiency but, claimed Braverman, such processes de-skilled and degraded the worker.

What Braverman means by the degradation of work is the decline in the number of jobs that require a worker to conceptualize and execute a task. He argues the workforce has been reorganized into a mass of workers, whose jobs require little conceptualization, and a smaller number of managers.

The rise of management

Influenced by the work of US engineer and industrialist Frederick Taylor, who had developed a theory of scientific management and workflows, Braverman argues that three novel and significant developments have accelerated and accentuated the de-skilling of the labor force.

First, knowledge and information of the entire labor process is known only to, and closely controlled by, management and not the workers. Second, and as a direct result of the first development, the worker performs his set task in the total division of labor on a "need-to-know" basis. Workers are kept completely in the dark about the impact of the tasks they perform and about the role these tasks play in the

> **"**
> The alienation of the worker presents itself to management as [a] problem in costs and controls.
> **Harry Braverman**
> **"**

overall labor process. Third, empowered by knowledge of the total labor process, management is able to control in highly exacting ways what it is that each individual worker does. Careful monitoring and regulation of productivity levels means that management is able to intervene whenever productivity is perceived to be dipping, or whenever a worker can be shown to be underperforming.

Braverman argues that the ultimate negative consequence of organizing work in a manner that above all else emphasizes efficiency, calculability, and

productivity is the separating out of what Braverman refers to as "conception" from "execution." Invoking a biological metaphor, Braverman states that the workers are like a hand, whose every move is controlled, supervised, and corrected by the distant brain of management.

The cold logic of capitalism

As the total range of skills possessed by workers diminishes over time, so in turn their value decreases. Workers can be paid less because the tasks they perform are increasingly menial and unskilled. Robbed of their expertise, they are more dispensable and, crucially, interchangeable. For Braverman, the cruel and unforgiving logic of the capitalist system inextricably ties his analysis to the concept of social class. The deconstruction of craftsmanship among the labor force works to ensure that entire sections of the population are prevented from climbing the social hierarchy.

Braverman's study focuses primarily on industrial factory work but his attention also turns to the de-skilling of office workers.

In Braverman's metaphor, managers are the brain and workers the hand of all-seeing management in the workplace. When labor is organized to maximize efficiency, productivity, and profit, there is a negative outcome for the workers. Braverman attributed this to the rise of management, which now observed, monitored, controlled, and regulated every action of the workforce. The effects of technology were first felt in factories; today, even retail outlets are supervised by distant, centralized head offices.

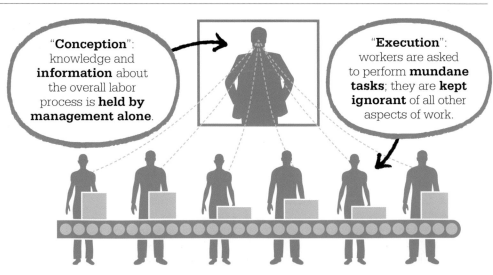

"**Conception**": knowledge and **information** about the overall labor process is **held by management alone**.

"**Execution**": workers are asked to perform **mundane tasks**; they are **kept ignorant** of all other aspects of work.

Female typists at a mail-order firm in 1912. By the early 20th century the profession of clerk had given way to large-scale, efficiently arranged, and scientifically managed offices.

He notes that control of the daily round of activities involved in clerical work—including bookkeeping, scheduling, and the responsibility that ensues from this—have been degraded to endless paper-chasing, photocopying, and other menial tasks. He also observes that because—at the time he was writing—office workers in Britain and the US were typically female, they could be paid less, which in turn reduces costs and maximizes profit.

Expertise diminished

Labor and Monopoly Capital is considered a classic contribution to the discipline of sociology, but it is the only academic book that Braverman ever wrote. The book's influence on the application of critical Marxist thinking to the empirical study of industrial work has been profound. Like Marx, Braverman never held a university post and it is perhaps for this very reason that he was able, without

fear of censorship, to write such a penetrating and biting critique of the injustices of industrial capitalism and their impact on the majority of the workforce. While Braverman was not the first or only thinker to identify and denounce the relationship between automation and de-skilling, his work was crucial for revitalizing the analysis of work across a broad range of disciplines, including history, economics, and political science. Since the publication of *Labor and Monopoly Capital*, Braverman's ideas have continued to generate debate among sociologists of work. Writing in 1979, US sociologist Michael Burawoy was strongly supportive of Braverman's work, as was US sociologist Michael Cooley in his study of computer-aided design.

While the conviction with which Braverman presented his arguments has led to criticism from some quarters (in the work of Robert Blauner, for example), his central ideas have survived and been carried forward in the work of Manuel Castells, the highly influential Spanish sociologist of globalization and the network society. ∎

Harry Braverman

Harry Braverman was born in 1920 in New York to Polish-Jewish émigré parents. He attended college for one year before leaving for financial reasons. He later worked as an apprentice coppersmith in Brooklyn, where he developed a powerful insight into the effects of science-based technology on the "de-skilling" of the working class.

Deeply affected by his experience, Braverman joined the Socialist Workers Party (SWP) and absorbed himself in the work of Marx and other socialist thinkers of the period. In 1953 he was expelled from the SWP, and went on to found the Socialist Union and to become editor of *The American Socialist*. In 1963 Braverman finally completed a BA from the New School of Social Research.

Key works

1974 *Labor and Monopoly Capital: The Degradation of Work in the Twentieth Century*

Marxism is not hostile to science and technology... but to how they are used as weapons of domination.
Harry Braverman

AUTOMATION INCREASES THE WORKER'S CONTROL OVER HIS WORK PROCESS
ROBERT BLAUNER (1929–)

IN CONTEXT

FOCUS
Alienation

KEY DATES
1844 Karl Marx introduces the concept of estrangement or alienation from the world in *Economic and Philosophic Manuscripts of 1844*.

1950–60 Increasing industrialization of the US economy leads to the significant occupational restructuring of society.

1960 The concept of alienation is imported into US sociology by theorists from the neo-Marxist "Frankfurt School."

1964 Robert Blauner's work redirects the focus of US, French, and British sociologists on alienation and automation.

2000–present Commercial organizations such as Apple and Microsoft seek to empower workers by using automated work processes.

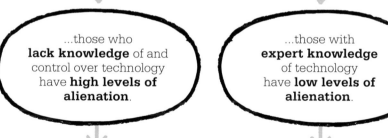

Workers in different industries experience **varying levels of alienation** in automated work processes...

...those who **lack knowledge** of and control over technology have **high levels of alienation**.

...those with **expert knowledge** of technology have **low levels of alienation**.

Knowledge of automation increases the worker's control over work processes and reduces alienation.

Alienation occurs when workers are disconnected from and lack control over their work, according to Karl Marx. In his influential book on industrial society, *Alienation and Freedom: The Factory Worker and His Industry* (1964), US sociologist Robert Blauner draws heavily on Marx's concept of alienation to examine the possibility that alienation in the workplace can be significantly reduced by the effective use of technology.

Blauner claims alienation is central to understanding the negative impact of automation on workers during and after the Industrial Revolution. His text critically assesses Marx's claim

See also: Karl Marx 28–31 ▪ Erich Fromm 188 ▪ Daniel Bell 224–25 ▪ Harry Braverman 226–31 ▪ Arlie Hochschild 236–43 ▪ Michael Burawoy 244–45

that all workers are necessarily alienated due to the increased automation of work. Blauner suggests, on the contrary, that automation can actually facilitate, empower, and liberate workers.

Using a wide range of data (including statistics, interviews with workers, and attitudinal surveys), Blauner examines four types of industry: craft printing, car assembly lines, textile machine-tending, and chemical-processing. Alienation levels are tested according to four criteria: job control, social isolation, sense of self-estrangement, and meaningfulness of work.

Technology and alienation

Blauner describes his results as conforming to an "inverted U curve." According to his study, alienation is typically very low among print workers. He suggests that the use of machinery is empowering for these employees because it provides them with greater control and autonomy. The same is true for workers in chemical-processing plants: again, these individuals are empowered,

Automated technology on car assembly lines should be organized and deployed in ways that enable the manufacturing workers to regain a sense of control over their environment.

> Alienation exists when workers are unable to control their immediate work processes.
> **Robert Blauner**

he proposes, because they possess expert knowledge of the relevant technology, which in turn is meaningful and fulfilling because it furnishes them with a significant degree of control over their work experience and environment.

By contrast, the automated technology used in car production and in textile factories leads to relatively high levels of alienation. These findings seem to contradict Blauner's claim that greater automation diminishes alienation. To explain this, however, he argues that it is not technology itself that alienates workers, but a lack of control over the way it is used, how work is organized, and the nature of the relationships between workers and management.

Blauner concludes that under the right organizational conditions, automation increases the worker's control over his work process and diminishes a sense of alienation in equal measure.

Blauner's study has greatly influenced the sociology of work, as testified by follow-up studies

Robert Blauner

Robert Blauner is an emeritus professor of sociology at the University of California, Berkeley. He was awarded his undergraduate degree from the University of Chicago in 1948.

Blauner was a staunch communist, and after graduating he worked in factories for five years, aiming to inspire a working-class revolution. Unsuccessful in those efforts, he completed his MA and PhD at Berkeley in 1962. His PhD thesis became the 1964 study that established his reputation. In addition to his contributions to the study of alienation and work, Blauner has made penetrating analyses of race relations in the US.

Key works

1964 *Alienation and Freedom: The Factory Worker and His Industry*
1972 *Radical Oppression in America*
1989 *Black Lives, White Lives: Three Decades of Race Relations in America*

conducted by sociologists in the US, as well as in Britain and France during the 1970s and 1980s. Furthermore, the "political" character of Blauner's work means studies of alienating work environments have fed into, and strongly influenced, commercial working directives and policies. The global technology firm Apple, for example, is renowned for investing heavily in training staff to use Apple technology to enhance their working experience as well as their own personal lives. ▪

THE ROMANTIC ETHIC PROMOTES THE SPIRIT OF CONSUMERISM
COLIN CAMPBELL (1940–)

IN CONTEXT

FOCUS
The Romantic ethic

KEY DATES
1780–1850 The Romantic movement in Europe reacts to the overly rationalistic, abstract ideals of the Age of Enlightenment.

1899 In *The Theory of the Leisure Class*, US social and economic thinker Thorstein Veblen suggests that consumption is driven by groups "emulating" one another to gain social status.

1904–05 Max Weber identifies a connection between the "Protestant work ethic" and the rise of capitalism.

Present Scholars such as US sociologist Daniel Bell and Italian sociologist Roberta Sassatelli draw heavily on Colin Campbell's ideas in their studies of consumption.

Why have Western Europe and the US developed consumer cultures? British sociologist Colin Campbell, emeritus professor at the University of York, discusses this question in his important study, *The Romantic Ethic and the Spirit of Modern Consumerism* (1987), intended as a sequel to Max Weber's similarly named and hugely influential *The Protestant Ethic and the Spirit of Capitalism* (1904–05).

Weber claims that the values of self-discipline and hard work, which lie at the heart of modern

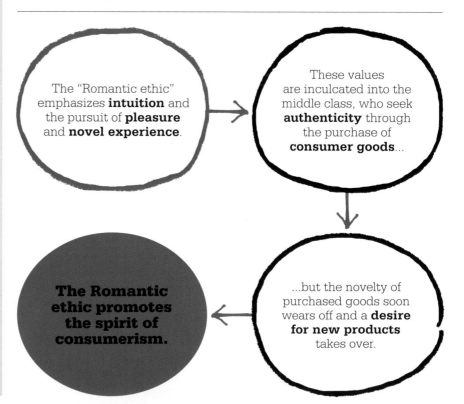

The "Romantic ethic" emphasizes **intuition** and the pursuit of **pleasure** and **novel experience**.

These values are inculcated into the middle class, who seek **authenticity** through the purchase of **consumer goods**...

...but the novelty of purchased goods soon wears off and a **desire for new products** takes over.

The Romantic ethic promotes the spirit of consumerism.

See also: Karl Marx 28–31 ▪ Max Weber 38–45 ▪ Herbert Marcuse 182–87 ▪ Jean Baudrillard 196–99 ▪ Thorstein Veblen 214–19 ▪ Daniel Bell 224–25

Designer goods stimulate the desire for purchase, possession, and for a lifestyle far removed from the mundane realities of existence. But desire, by its very nature, is insatiable.

capitalist societies, have their basis in the Protestant work ethic of the 16th and 17th centuries. Campbell, building on Weber's work, advances the theory that the emotions and hedonistic desires that drive consumer culture are firmly rooted in the ideals of 19th-century Romanticism, which followed on the heels of the Enlightenment and the Industrial Revolution.

Desire, illusion, and reality

The Enlightenment conceived of individuals as rational, hard-working, and self-disciplined. But the Romantics saw this as a denial of the very essence of humanity. They stressed intuition above reason, and believed that the individual should be free to pursue hedonistic pleasures and new and exciting feelings.

The Romantic ethic was inculcated into and carried forward by the burgeoning middle class, and by women in particular, Campbell argues. Within consumer culture this ethic is expressed as a self-perpetuating loop: individuals project their desire for pleasure and novelty onto consumer goods; they then purchase and make use of those goods; but the appeal of the product quickly diminishes as the novelty factor and initial excitement fade; the desire for excitement, fulfillment, and novelty is then projected onto, and restimulated by, new consumer items. And so the cycle of consumption, fleeting fulfillment, and ultimate disillusionment, repeats itself.

The engine of capitalism

The cycle described by Campbell is one of highs and lows for the consumer. Consumer desire is the very engine of capitalism because it drives individuals to search for that elusive yet satisfying experience amid the endless tide of new products. The consequences

of this process for economies based on consumption are vast because consumers are forever chasing the latest commodities.

Campbell's concept of the Romantic ethic has had immense influence on sociology and anthropology. His work not only dispels the overly simplistic view of humans as necessarily disposed to acquire things, but it also attempts to shed light on the more positive aspects of consumer society.

It is simply wrong, according to Campbell, to suggest that consumerism is an inherently bad thing. Instead, the pursuit and projection of our innermost desires onto consumer goods form a fundamental part of our own self-realization in the modern world.

Campbell's highly original and powerful correctives to more economically reductive and cynical accounts of consumerism have provided contemporary thinkers with fertile soil in which to develop more positive and historically informed appraisals of modern-day consumer society. ■

Consumerism as mass deception

The uniqueness of Campbell's focus on the Romantic ethic as the key to modern consumerism lies in its engagement with the impact of long-term historical processes. His ideas differ greatly from those of the highly influential French post-structuralist and postmodern thinkers such as Roland Barthes and Jean Baudrillard a decade or so earlier.

For them, unlike Campbell, the triumph of consumer culture is to be resisted at all costs.

They see the failed social and political revolutions of the late 1960s as signifying the "death of Marxism" and therefore also the triumph of capitalism. Barthes' work on semiotics identifies the advertising industry as playing a key role in blinding consumers to their true wants and desires, whereas for Baudrillard the media is responsible for overwhelming the consumer and concealing the vacuous nature of modern capitalist society.

IN PROCESSING PEOPLE THE PRODUCT IS A STATE OF MIND

ARLIE RUSSELL HOCHSCHILD (1940–)

IN CONTEXT

FOCUS
Emotional labor

KEY DATES
1867 Karl Marx completes the first volume of *Das Kapital*, which inspires Hochschild's concept of emotional labor.

1959 Canadian sociologist Erving Goffman publishes *The Presentation of Self in Everyday Life*.

1960s The burgeoning service industries of Europe and North America start to be heavily gendered toward women workers.

1970s Feminist thinkers begin to turn their attention to the negative consequences of capitalism for women.

2011 Sociologists Ann Brooks and Theresa Devasahayam publish *Gender, Emotions and Labour Markets*, which combines Hochschild's ideas with globalization theory.

When Karl Marx, in *Das Kapital*, expressed concern about mother-and-child factory workers and the "human cost" of labor, he said they had become an "instrument" of labor. This observation, and the environment of brutalizing physical work, led to his alienation concept, whereby lack of fulfillment and control leads workers to feel disconnected and estranged.

Alongside Marx's insights, two models of emotion emerged in the late 19th and early 20th century. The "organismic" model, built from the work of Charles Darwin, William James, and Sigmund Freud, identifies emotion as mainly a biological process: external stimuli trigger instinctual responses that people express in similar ways. From the 1920s, John Dewey, Hans Gerth, Charles Wright Mills, and Erving Goffman created an "interactional" model. They accepted emotion had a biological component, but they maintained that it is more interactive and differentiated by a range of social factors: culture is involved in the formulation of emotion and people manage feelings subjectively.

> 'Sincerity' is detrimental to one's job, until the rules of salesmanship and business become a 'genuine' aspect of oneself.
> **Charles Wright Mills**

Following the translation of Marx's work into English in the 1960s, alienation became a powerful analytical tool for sociologists trying to make sense of the changes then taking place to working conditions in North America and Western Europe.

A state of mind
Inspired by these various ideas, and drawing upon women thinkers such as Simone de Beauvoir, US feminist and sociologist Arlie Hochschild has made the analysis of the emotional dimensions of

New service industries require workers to possess **"emotional resources."**

Because women are stereotyped as more **emotional**, these industries are heavily **gendered toward a female workforce**.

Women workers are asked to act in ways that **create positive emotional states** to help ensure future custom.

Under capitalism, human emotions are commodified: in processing people, the product is a state of mind.

See also: Karl Marx 28–31 ▪ G.H. Mead 176–77 ▪ Erving Goffman 190–95 ▪ Harry Braverman 226–31 ▪ Christine Delphy 312–17 ▪ Ann Oakley 318–19

Children are exposed to "childhood training of the heart," says Hochschild. Whereas girls learn to be caring and to master aggression and anger, boys mask fear and vulnerability.

human interaction her life's work. More specifically, she concentrates on the ways in which social and cultural factors condition the experience and display of emotions in capitalist society.

Her work charts the rise of the service industries in North America from the 1960s onward, and the emergence of forms of employment in which the emotions of workers have become marketable commodities sold for a wage: "emotional labor," as she calls it.

Hochschild says that her interest in how people manage emotions probably began when she was growing up in a household where her diplomat parents acted as hosts to foreign embassy staff. Where, she wondered, did the person end and the act begin? Later, as a graduate, she was inspired by the chapter "The Great Salesroom" in Wright Mills' *White Collar*, in which he argued that we sell our personality when selling goods and services.

Hochschild felt that this had the ring of truth, but that it missed the sense of the active emotional labor involved in the selling. Unlike 19th-century factory work, where output could be quantified and it mattered little whether you loved or hated what you made, employment in a service industry is qualitatively different. It means that "the emotional style of offering the service is part of the service itself," which makes it necessary for the worker to sustain a certain outward appearance in order to produce a proper state of mind in others. Whereas for Marx the individual in the factory becomes alienated from the products they create, Hochschild argued that in the service-based economy "the product is a state of mind."

In Hochschild's view, the increasing use of emotionally based rather than manually based labor has a greater impact on women than men, because women are conditioned since childhood to supply feelings. But she believes that this can come at a cost to the individual, who may become estranged from their own emotions, which feel like they belong to their work rather than to them.

Managing interaction

One of the major influences on Hochschild is symbolic interactionist Erving Goffman. The idea underpinning his work is that selfhood is created during social interaction. Only by interacting with others—and managing the way we present ourselves—are individuals able to obtain a personal sense of identity. In essence, our innermost sense of selfhood is inextricably bound up with the social contexts in which we are implicated.

Hochschild extends this idea in a critical way by arguing that emotions, as well as being something external—residing in interactions between individuals and groups—are subject to self-management too. Emotions and feelings are also tied directly to behavior and are experienced by individuals as they prepare to act and interact with others.

In a similar way to the sensory faculty of hearing, "emotion communicates information," as Hochschild puts it. She likens emotion to what Freud referred **»** to as a "signal function," whereby messages such as fear or anxiety are relayed to the brain, indicating the presence of danger, and so on. Hochschild says that: "From feeling we discover our own viewpoint on the world." Emotions engender a mental component that reconciles past events with actual situations in which we put or find ourselves.

In addition to putting these emotional dimensions at the heart of social interaction, Hochschild stresses the myriad ways in which emotions are mediated and shaped by wider processes. Society and culture intervene in the emotional economy of the individual through socialization. For example, through primary socialization people learn to make sense of their emotions and, with varying degrees of success, manipulate and manage them. Hochschild is saying that emotions are not simply things that happen to passive human actors. Rather, individuals are actively involved in producing and creating their feelings and emotions.

Emotional work and rules

As individuals, claims Hochschild, we "do" emotions. Feeling emotional and acting in emotional

> ...the action is in the body language, the put-on sneer, the posed shrug, the controlled sigh. This is surface acting.
> **Arlie Russell Hochschild**

ways is purposively enacted. She calls this process "emotional work," and uses it to describe how people alter and intensify particular feelings, while simultaneously trying to suppress unpleasant emotions. She identifies three main ways that people work to produce emotion: cognitive emotional work, bodily emotional work, and expressive emotional work.

In cognitive emotional work, individuals use images, ideas, and thoughts in order to call forth, or stifle, the various emotions associated with those ideas. Bodily emotional work refers to any attempt to control the physical reaction accompanying a particular emotional state, such as sweating when anxious, or shaking when angry. Expressive emotional work involves attempting to manage the public display of particular emotions with a view to realizing a specific feeling, or set of feelings.

The purpose of Hochschild's typology of emotions is to highlight the extent to which individuals are actively involved in shaping and managing their inner emotional states in order to call forth certain feelings. Earlier work in this area focused on outward appearances: the physical behavior and verbal cues we use to communicate emotions; what Hochschild refers to as "surface acting." She extends her analysis to focus on "deep acting," referring to "method acting" when trying to explain it: "Here, display is a natural result of working on feeling; the actor does not try to *seem* happy or sad but rather expresses spontaneously, as the Russian theater director Constantin Stanislavski urged, a real feeling that has been self-induced."

It is not Hochschild's intention to suggest that people consciously manipulate or deceive one another,

Many women work in service-industry jobs, where employers ask them to exude real emotion to satisfy customers. All in the line of, as Hochschild puts it, "being nice."

although this is always possible. She is attempting to demonstrate the ways and extent to which people interact and work together to define a particular social situation and how, in turn, this feeds back into, and intimately shapes, their emotional states.

Hochschild maintains that rationalization and the marginalization of the more emotional aspects of human behavior have meant that the often tacit rules that underpin interpersonal conduct have begun to develop in new directions. To explain this, she introduces the notion of "feeling rules." These are socially learned and culturally specific norms that individuals draw upon in order to negotiate and guide the display and experience of emotions and feelings. In modern capitalist societies, there are two types: display rules and emotional rules. Display rules are, like "surface acting," the outward verbal and nonverbal cues people communicate to one another. Emotional rules refer to the level of people's emotions, the directions they take, and how long they endure. For example, if a loved one dies, there is a strong social expectation that the grieving process will take time to run its course. In essence, emotional rules exist that influence what constitutes an appropriate response to death, how powerful the response should be, and the length of time it should last.

Delta Airlines

The interconnected notions of emotional labor and emotional work were explored by Hochschild in her most celebrated book, *The Managed Heart: Commercialization of Human Feeling* (1983). The study focuses primarily on Delta Airlines. She demonstrates that the airline consistently hired people who it perceived could be controlled physically—in terms of their personal appearance—and emotionally. Keen to increase passenger numbers, Delta focused on employing young, attractive, single women, although a small number of men were employed too. The appeal of the women was that they were perceived to embody, in the most literal ways, the very specific ideals and image the corporation wanted to project to customers. Especially important was that flight attendants did not use surface acting when displaying emotion. In order to ensure passengers felt the emotional experience they were receiving was authentic, flight attendants were taught to practice "deep acting" by producing within themselves emotional displays that were sincere and genuine. Delta Airlines recognized that authentic displays of emotion and emotional performances are far easier to perform and sustain "when the

> In the case of the flight attendant, the emotional style... is... the service.
> **Arlie Russell Hochschild**

feelings are actually present." Training manuals and guidelines were issued so that flight attendants could perform emotional labor and produce authentic performances. The manuals taught an array of sophisticated strategies with which to produce corporately calculated emotional states and feeling repertoires. If these were genuine, passengers would feel »

Surface acting

Deep acting

I'm tired, fed up, and I want to go home.

You're my guest and I'm happy to help you in any way I can.

Champagne, sir?

Emotional labor is, according to Hochschild, the "commercialization of human feeling." Delta Airlines, she says, trained recruits so that they could transcend "surface acting," whereby postures or expressions are deceits and feel faked. The company urged trainees to imagine the cabin as their home, into which they welcomed customers as "personal guests." Once staff had mastered the art of "deep acting," feigning sincerity became unnecessary as real feelings were self-induced.

reassured, happy, and at ease. By evoking in passengers positive emotional states and feelings of comfort and safety, Delta believed it could secure the loyalty and future custom of passengers.

Ingenious and innovative as the corporate philosophy might at first seem, Hochschild argues that the deep acting and emotional labor demanded of flight attendants was ultimately damaging to their psychological well-being. Constantly having to control, manage, and subvert their own feelings, while simultaneously working to produce and display a range of positively authentic emotions, proved harmful.

She identified two particularly negative consequences arising from long-term emotional labor. First, the fusing together of the flight attendants' private sense of selfhood with their public self—the roles they played as attendants—was liable to lead to emotional and psychological burnout. Second, a sense of self-estrangement often

occurred: trying to manage the very real disparity between their personal feelings and the emotional states they strived to evoke in passengers, typically led to one of two outcomes among them—either they began to resent themselves emotionally or they developed resentment for the job.

Hochschild claims that even if individuals actively engage in strategies aimed at self-preservation, resenting the work as opposed to themselves, the net result is the same. The emotional and psychological well-being of the individual is harmed, with the result they feel increasingly alienated from their innermost self and their emotions too.

Gender inequality

As a feminist sociologist, Hochschild's study of Delta also provides a window onto the ways in which wider gender inequalities are sustained and reproduced within US society. Since the 1960s, increasing numbers of women have

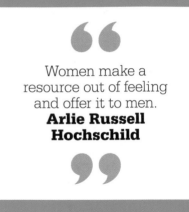

> Women make a resource out of feeling and offer it to men.
> **Arlie Russell Hochschild**

entered into the workforce, with many joining the burgeoning service industries. For Hochschild, this is not necessarily a positive development, because it serves to push the highly uneven division of emotional-labor characteristics of modern capitalist society further in the direction of women. In making this argument, Hochschild claims that women are more inclined to make a resource out of feeling, which they in turn sell back to men. Although the increasing numbers of working women seem to testify to a shift in the occupational status of women in modern society, a closer examination of the statistics shows that women are far more likely than men to work in the service industries—most retail associates, call-center operators, and hotel and bar staff are women.

Within modern capitalist society, it falls to women to undertake the vast majority of the total emotional labor. In the long term, this is a negative and

Many nurses claim their emotional labor is invisible to some colleagues. They give loving, daily care to patients, often in an attempt to compensate for the insensitivity of more senior staff.

unintended consequence of capitalism because it makes women more emotionally prone to burnout, and psychologically and socially susceptible to feelings of self-estrangement and alienation.

Insatiable capitalism

Hochschild's notion of emotional work and her analysis of the emotional labor performed by airline flight attendants marks a key moment in the history of sociological thinking. For Marx, capitalism leads to physical and mental degradation for the worker as the nature of work becomes increasingly repetitive, menial, and specialized. Social thinker Harry Braverman argued that automation of the workplace leads to the steady deconstruction of a once highly skilled workforce. Remaining with the Marxist tradition, Hochschild demonstrates that even the most personal aspects of individual selfhood—our emotions, feelings, and affective life—are turned into commodities and exploited by the capitalist market in order to make profit. Her ideas have been developed by many other scholars involved with the sociology of work and emotions, and applied to a

> ❝
> ...when a worker abandons her work smile, what kind of tie remains between her smile and her self?
> **Arlie Russell Hochschild**
> ❞

Call-center operators experience high levels of emotional burnout and distress, induced by their emotional labor, according to research by Dutch sociologist Danielle van Jaarsveld.

number of occupations, ranging from nurses and caregivers to waitresses, telemarketers, and call-center operators.

Hochschild gives particular credit to a cross-cultural study of emotion management, between Japan and the US, by Aviad Raz in his 2002 book *Emotions at Work*. She relates his story about "smile training" in which the Japanese managers at Tokyo Dome Corporation were not happy with the weak, "spiritless, externally-imposed smiles" that they thought managers in the US were prepared to settle for. Instead, the Japanese felt it necessary to appeal to the underlying *chi* ("spirit") of the workers. This they enticed from their employees through the culturally powerful force of shame. Cameras were placed at the cash registers of unfriendly sales clerks, whose videotaped behavior was shown later to their fellow workers.

The smile may now be a global fad but Raz confirms Hochschild's insight that capitalism exploits emotional aspects of culture. ■

Arlie Russell Hochschild

Arlie Russell Hochschild was born in 1940 and is a US feminist and sociologist of work and emotion. Her parents were both US diplomats. Hochschild claims that growing up in a social milieu defined by the need for people to control and manage their emotions in very subtle and convincing ways instilled within her a fascination with the emotional dimensions of modern social life.

Hochschild obtained her MA and PhD at the University of California, Berkeley. During this time she became a feminist and developed an ongoing interest in the dual roles women play as workers and primary caregivers in capitalist society.

The overtly political pitch of Hochschild's work has strongly influenced feminist thinking in the US and Western Europe. It has also led to an ongoing dialogue with captains of industry and high-level politicians.

Hochschild's work has informed social policy at a number of levels, including the US state of California's Child Development Policy Board as well as former US vice president Al Gore's working families' policy directives.

Key works

1983 *The Managed Heart: Commercialization of Human Feeling*
2003 *The Commercialization of Intimate Life: Notes from Home and Work*
2012 *The Outsourced Self: Intimate Life in Market Times*

SPONTANEOUS CONSENT COMBINES WITH COERCION
MICHAEL BURAWOY (1947–)

IN CONTEXT

FOCUS
Manufacturing consent

KEY DATES
1979 The effects of the global oil recession impact on US manufacturing industries, causing tension between workers and management.

1981 British sociologist Anthony Giddens refers to Michael Burawoy's book, *Manufacturing Consent: Changes in the Labor Process Under Monopoly Capitalism*, as "one of the most significant contributions to industrial sociology."

1998 In "Manufacturing Dissent? Burawoy in a Franco-Japanese Workshop," French sociologist Jean-Pierre Durand and British sociologist Paul Stewart apply Burawoy's concept of manufacturing consent to a Nissan automobile plant.

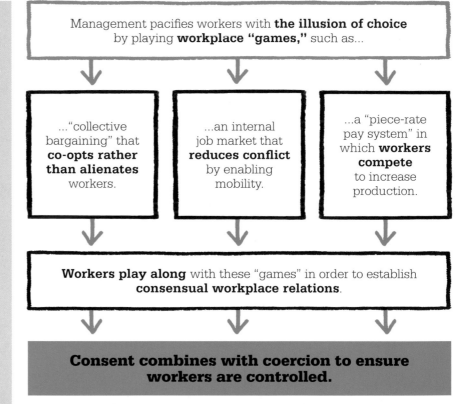

Management pacifies workers with **the illusion of choice** by playing **workplace "games,"** such as...

..."collective bargaining" that **co-opts rather than alienates** workers.

...an internal job market that **reduces conflict** by enabling mobility.

...a "piece-rate pay system" in which **workers compete** to increase production.

Workers play along with these "games" in order to establish **consensual workplace relations**.

Consent combines with coercion to ensure workers are controlled.

hy workers in the capitalist system work as hard as they do and how the interests of workers and management are negotiated are issues that Anglo-American sociologist Michael Burawoy analyses from within a Marxist theoretical framework. From this perspective, the interests of labor and capital are seen as being in fundamental opposition; Burawoy

See also: Karl Marx 28–31 ▪ Michel Foucault 52–55 ▪ Pierre Bourdieu 76–79 ▪ Anthony Giddens 148–49 ▪ Harry Braverman 226–31 ▪ Robert Blauner 232–33

contends that modern management now manufactures and channels workers' consent to work harder.

He rejects Marx's explanation that workers are simply exploited and coerced into working as hard as they do. The rise in the power of labor unions and workers' collectives has done a lot to curb the use of power by managers, which was once exerted through the bullying of workers. Burawoy acknowledges that within any organization there is always coercion and consent but their relative proportions and mode of expression have changed.

Management, he claims, now seeks to control workers by creating restrictive social relations and organizational structures that give them the "illusion of choice," but that ultimately serve to mask and maintain unequal power relations.

Workplace "games"

Burawoy worked in a factory called Allied Corporation, where he researched his ideas about the "games" played within the workplace, such as collective bargaining (negotiation of wages and conditions of work), ensuring internal job mobility for workers, and the piece-rate pay system, in which workers are paid more if they produce above quota. This system, he says, gives the illusion that work is a game; the workers are the players and compete with one another to "make out"—surpass their expected production quotas. Job satisfaction is achieved by mastering the intricate and often devious and informal strategies workers use to "make out" under various production conditions. Burawoy claims that the games

workers play are not attempts to reduce job discontent or oppose management, because often lower-level management participates in the games and the enforcement of their rules. Playing the game creates consent among workers about the rules upon which workplace games are based—and, crucially, the arrangement of social relations (owners–managers–workers) that define the rules.

Moreover, because managers and workers are both involved in playing games, the numerous opposing interests that define the social relations between the two are obscured, ensuring that manager–worker conflict is kept to a minimum. Burawoy claims such methods of manufacturing and eliciting cooperation and consent are more effective than the coercive measures of early capitalism.

Burawoy's work is a seminal contribution to the sociology of industrial relations and has inspired follow-up studies, including those by British social thinkers Paul Blyton and Stephen Ackroyd, focusing on workplace resistance and coercion. ∎

> ❝
> Conflict and consent are not primordial conditions but products of the organization of work.
> **Michael Burawoy**
> ❞

Michael Burawoy

Michael Burawoy is an Anglo-American Marxist sociologist at the University of California, Berkeley. He obtained his first degree in 1968 in mathematics from the University of Cambridge, England, before going on to complete his doctorate in sociology at the University of Chicago in 1976.

Burawoy's academic career has changed direction and focus over time. His early work involved a number of ethnographic studies of industrial workplaces in the US as well as in Hungary and post-Soviet Russia. In the latter part of his career he turned away from the factory floor to focus on raising the public profile of sociology by using sociological theories to address prominent social issues.

In 2010, in recognition of his considerable contribution to the discipline, and in particular to promoting sociology more widely to the general public, Burawoy was elected President of the International Sociological Association (ISA) at the XVII ISA World Congress of Sociology. He is editor of *Global Dialogue,* the magazine of the International Sociological Association.

Key works

1979 *Manufacturing Consent: Changes in the Labor Process Under Monopoly Capitalism*
1985 *The Politics of Production: Factory Regimes Under Capitalism and Socialism*
2010 *Marxism Meets Bourdieu*

THINGS MAKE US JUST AS MUCH AS WE MAKE THINGS
DANIEL MILLER (1954–)

IN CONTEXT

FOCUS
Material culture

KEY DATES
1807 In *Phenomenology of Spirit,* German philosopher Georg Hegel outlines his theory of "objectification," which describes how people transform their labor into material objects (a house, for example, is the result of considerable collective labor).

1867 Karl Marx introduces his ideas about the fetishization of commodities in *Das Kapital.*

1972 French sociologist Pierre Bourdieu publishes *Outline of A Theory of Practice,* which examines the life and material culture of the Kabyle Berber people in Algeria.

2004 Finnish sociologist Kaj Ilmonen examines how people externalize a part of themselves in the material objects they own.

Modern societies are **materialistic and consumerist**.

Consumerism is often perceived negatively—as a signifier of **wastefulness** and **superficiality**, for example.

But **material objects** and possessions can help **shape and strengthen** people's **self-identity** and their interactions and **relationships with others**.

Things make us just as much as we make things.

Sociologists, drawing on the pioneering work of Thorstein Veblen in the late 19th century, have traditionally conceived of consumer goods symbolically, as objects people acquire to communicate specific meanings to one another—for example, the type of lifestyle they lead and the amount of social status they possess.

However, British sociologist Daniel Miller in his book *Stuff,* published in 2010, points out that the myriad ways in which consumer goods inform personal identity, selfhood, and interactions with others have been understood primarily in negative terms. Consumerism is, he says, considered by the majority of commentators to be wasteful and bad; desiring consumer goods is thought to be superficial and morally reprehensible; and consumerism is alienating and socially divisive—it separates the "haves" from the "have-nots" and can lead to serious social problems, including theft.

Miller puts a very different slant on things by emphasizing the various positive ways in which material artifacts contribute to

See also: Karl Marx 28–31 ▪ Pierre Bourdieu 76–79 ▪ Herbert Marcuse 182–87 ▪ Thorstein Veblen 214–19 ▪ Colin Campbell 234–35 ▪ Theodor W. Adorno 335

making us who we are and how they mediate in our relationships and interactions with others.

Rethinking the house

Miller gives the example of his own family home. The architectural style and physical design, he says, feed into and shape his identity in relation to the property, but they also affect the interactions with and between family members.

His property retains "many of the original features," including an oak staircase, fireplaces, and window surrounds. These physical and aesthetic features frame his experience of and relationship to the house, he says. For example, his predilection for furniture and design by the popular Swedish furnishing store IKEA creates a tension within him: he feels that his taste for the modern, clinical, and clean lines that are characteristic of this brand means that he has "demeaned" and betrayed the house, that it deserves someone with "better taste." To resolve this tension, he describes

how ongoing discussions with family members enable him to find a compromise with regard to furnishing and decoration.

Miller claims that he and his family imagine and relate to the house as though it were a family member, with a unique identity and its own needs. His argument here is that the materiality of the house is not necessarily oppressive, alienating, or divisive; on the contrary, it not only positively shapes the relationships of the family to it, but also facilitates interaction and increasing solidarity between family members.

A counterbalance

Miller's work is designed to provide an alternative to the accounts of consumerism given by Frankfurt School thinkers such as Herbert Marcuse and Theodor W. Adorno, who read mass consumer culture as "symptomatic of a loss of depth in the world." At a time when the global economic and environmental crises have cast serious doubt over the

> Stuff... achieves its mastery of us precisely because we constantly fail to notice what it does.
> **Daniel Miller**

sustainability of a materialistic, consumer culture, Miller's work is thought by many, including sociologists Fernando Dominguez Rubio and Elizabeth B. Silva, to provide a provocative riposte to views that denigrate material culture in society. Miller's ideas are permeating sociological analysis and inform part of the increasing interest in the examination of material objects (the "materiality of cultural forms"), spearheaded by French sociologist Bruno Latour. ▪

Tight blue jeans are popular in Brazil because they are thought to enhance the natural curvature of a woman's buttocks.

The denim phenomenon

Since 2007, British sociologist Sophie Woodward, in collaboration with Miller and other sociologists, has been interested in blue denim as a phenomenon of consumerism. She suggests that despite being available everywhere, denim garments are often revered as highly personal items, with which their owners have an intimate relationship—a favorite denim jacket or pair of jeans, for example.

Drawing on ethnographic studies of denim jeans as fashion items throughout the world, Woodward has found that the appeal of denim is inextricably bound up with the cultural mores and frames of meaning specific to particular locales. In London, England, for example, blue jeans are often used by many different types of people to resolve anxieties about what to wear—their anonymity and ubiquity protect the wearer from negative judgement. In Brazil, however, jeans are often worn by women to emphasize their sensuality.

FEMINIZATION HAS HAD ONLY A MODEST IMPACT ON REDUCING GENDER INEQUALITIES

TERI LYNN CARAWAY

IN CONTEXT

FOCUS
The feminization of work

KEY DATES
From the 1960s The rise of globalization and industrialization in the developing world attracts the attention of feminist scholars of work.

1976 Michel Foucault's *The History of Sexuality, Volume I: An Introduction* claims that gender roles and relations are socially constructed discourses.

1986 Sylvia Walby publishes *Patriarchy at Work: Patriarchal and Capitalist Relations in Employment.*

1995 R.W. Connell's fluid conception of gender categories as things that are flexible and open to change is articulated in *Masculinities.*

More women are entering—and **feminizing**—the workforce.

↓

Although globalization has helped to erode **men's domination of the economy**, the **unequal gender division of labor** persists.

↓

Significant feminization of the industrialized economy can occur only if...

↓

...**labor demand** outstrips the capacity of the male workforce available.

...women are more available for work due to better **access to higher education and childcare**.

...the trade unions either support the access of women or are **unable to exclude them** from "male" occupations.

See also: Karl Marx 28–31 ▪ Michel Foucault 52–55 ▪ R.W. Connell 88–89 ▪ Roland Robertson 146–49 ▪ Robert Blauner 232–33 ▪ Jeffrey Weeks 324–25

In recent decades, despite a big growth in the participation of women in the workforce in Southeast Asia, the gender division of labor has been redrawn rather than eliminated. US feminist and sociologist Teri Lynn Caraway studied industries in Indonesia in her book *Assembling Women: The Feminization of Global Manufacturing*. Building upon the work of Michel Foucault, she says that gender in the workplace is fluid and constantly renegotiated, and it is even influenced by the ideas of femininity and masculinity held by factory managers, who may determine machine operations that suit male or female workers.

Caraway rejects mainstream economic theory because it views individuals as rational and genderless, reflecting the male, middle-class characteristics of those who developed it. She also dismisses Marxist analyses because they prioritize social class over gender. Whereas the conventional wisdom is that employers pay women lower wages, which has led to more women entering the global workforce, Caraway claims that this underestimates the power of gender in labor markets. Instead, ideas and practices about men and women providing distinct forms of labor—what she terms "gendered discourses"—play a key role in the feminization process.

Conditions for feminization

Caraway says three conditions are necessary for the feminization of industrial labor to occur. First, when demand for labor exceeds supply (for example, when there are insufficient male workers), industry turns to women. Second, only when family planning and mass education are available can women enter the workforce. And third, work for women becomes possible when barriers such as trade unions—which protect male-dominated workplaces from being undermined by cheap female labor—are no longer effective. In Indonesia, this happened when the state weakened Islamist organizations and trade unions, both of which are potential opponents of female labor.

Caraway notes the general assumption that some employers pay more to men because they perceive their work to be superior, while others consider women to be unreliable in the long-term (due to motherhood or marriage). In fact, Caraway argues, both are examples of complex "gendered cost benefit analysis"; how female workers are perceived and treated, and therefore why women are seen as better for certain types of labor, can be explained by wider cultural ideals, values, and beliefs about gender roles within a society. ■

Female factory workers in Indonesia, like these garment workers in Sukoharjo, receive equal wages with men. According to Caraway's research, this is not the case in East Asia.

Globalization and gender well-being

The economic changes created by globalization and the new, flexible requirements of labor markets are thought to benefit women. Although feminization "opens the door of job opportunity to women," as Teri Lynn Caraway puts it, the outcome is mixed. Caraway, Sylvia Walby, and Valentine Moghadam have all shown that female workers are far more likely to suffer ill health. Moreover, women's disproportionate burden of domestic work means that employment outside the home places greater strain on them.

German sociologist Christa Wichterich argues, in *The Globalized Woman* (2007), that rather than liberating women into the workplace, globalization has bred a new underclass. She shows how, from Phnom Penh to New York, women's lives have been devastated by having to respond to the demands of transnational corporations, surviving in low-paid employment, and coping with the erosion of public services.

> ❝ Employers feminize their workforces only if they imagine women are more productive than men.
> **Teri Lynn Caraway** ❞

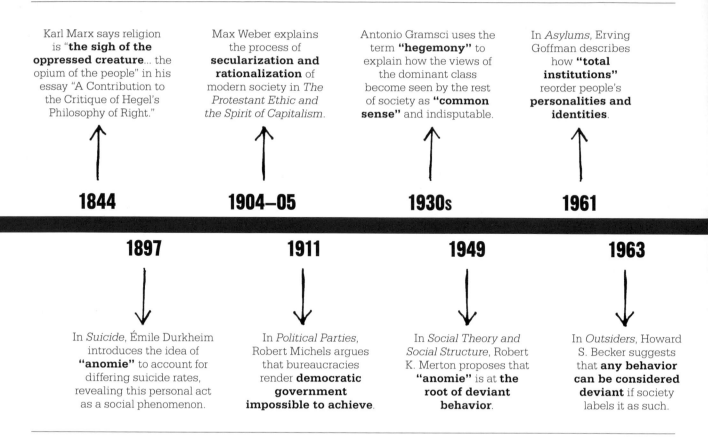

Karl Marx says religion is "**the sigh of the oppressed creature**... the opium of the people" in his essay "A Contribution to the Critique of Hegel's Philosophy of Right."

Max Weber explains the process of **secularization and rationalization** of modern society in *The Protestant Ethic and the Spirit of Capitalism*.

Antonio Gramsci uses the term **"hegemony"** to explain how the views of the dominant class become seen by the rest of society as **"common sense"** and indisputable.

In *Asylums*, Erving Goffman describes how **"total institutions"** reorder people's **personalities and identities**.

1844

1904–05

1930s

1961

1897

1911

1949

1963

In *Suicide*, Émile Durkheim introduces the idea of **"anomie"** to account for differing suicide rates, revealing this personal act as a social phenomenon.

In *Political Parties*, Robert Michels argues that bureaucracies render **democratic government impossible to achieve**.

In *Social Theory and Social Structure*, Robert K. Merton proposes that **"anomie"** is at **the root of deviant behavior**.

In *Outsiders*, Howard S. Becker suggests that **any behavior can be considered deviant** if society labels it as such.

For centuries, the dominant institutions in Europe were the Church and the ruling class of monarchs and aristocrats. It was not until the Renaissance that the authority of the Church was challenged by humanist ideas and scientific discovery, and republican democracy began to threaten claims of a God-given, inherited right to rule. The age of Enlightenment thought further weakened these institutions, and in the 18th century the old order was overturned with political revolutions in the US and France, and an Industrial Revolution spreading from Britain.

Secularism and rationalism
A recognizably modern society rapidly emerged, which was shaped by the rational ideas of the Enlightenment and the economic demands of industry. The social cohesion based on community values and shared beliefs gave way to new secular institutions, and government of society was transferred to representatives of the people. Together with this secularization came a rationalization suited to the increasingly material nature of modern society. Industrialization, and the capitalism that grew from it, required a much greater degree of administration, and the idea of bureaucracy spread from the sphere of commerce to government too.

The institutions of modern society evolved from these bureaucracies: financial and business institutions, government departments, hospitals, education, the media, the police, armed forces, and so on. The new institutions formed a prominent part of the social structure of modern society, and sociologists have sought to identify the roles they play in creating and maintaining social order.

Bureaucracies, however, are organized for efficiency and consequently tend to follow a hierarchical structure. As Robert Michels pointed out, this leads to their being ruled by a small elite, an oligarchy, which, far from helping to promote democratic government, actively prevents it. As a result, people feel as much under the control of the new institutions as they did under religious and monarchical rule. Michel Foucault later examined the nature of the (often unnoticed) power of institutions to shape society and

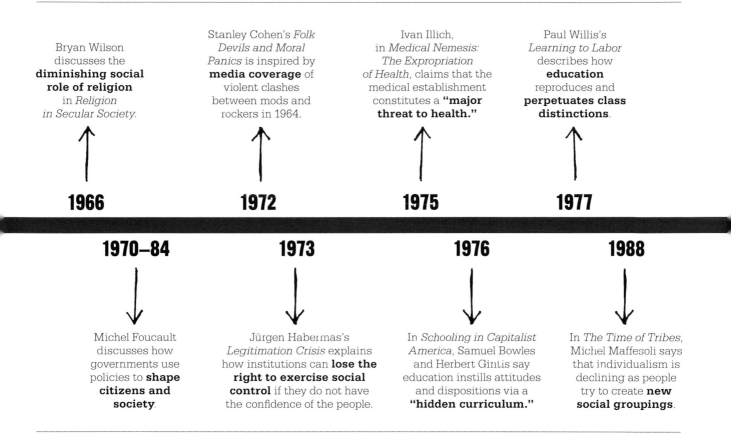

Bryan Wilson discusses the **diminishing social role of religion** in *Religion in Secular Society*.

Stanley Cohen's *Folk Devils and Moral Panics* is inspired by **media coverage** of violent clashes between mods and rockers in 1964.

Ivan Illich, in *Medical Nemesis: The Expropriation of Health*, claims that the medical establishment constitutes a **"major threat to health."**

Paul Willis's *Learning to Labor* describes how **education** reproduces and **perpetuates class distinctions**.

1966   **1972**   **1975**   **1977**

1970–84   **1973**   **1976**   **1988**

Michel Foucault discusses how governments use policies to **shape citizens and society**.

Jürgen Habermas's *Legitimation Crisis* explains how institutions can **lose the right to exercise social control** if they do not have the confidence of the people.

In *Schooling in Capitalist America*, Samuel Bowles and Herbert Gintis say education instills attitudes and dispositions via a **"hidden curriculum."**

In *The Time of Tribes*, Michel Maffesoli says that individualism is declining as people try to create **new social groupings**.

the behavior of its individual citizens—imposing social norms, and stifling individuality. Jürgen Habermas was similarly critical of institutional power, but argued that this can only be wielded so long as the institutions are trusted by the people. More recently (and controversially), Michel Maffesoli has suggested that as people become disillusioned with institutions, they form new social groupings along tribal lines, with corresponding new institutions.

The social influence of religious institutions, described famously by Karl Marx as "the opium of the people," declined with the growth of bureaucracies, and during the 20th century most states had (at least nominally) a form of secular government. Nevertheless, today some 75 percent of the world's population still identify themselves as belonging to a recognized faith community, and in many places religion is increasingly becoming a social force.

Individualism and society

As well as studying the nature and scope of institutions in society, sociologists in the latter part of the 20th century have taken a more interpretive approach, examining the effects of these institutions on the individual members of society. Max Weber had warned of the stultifying effects of bureaucracy, trapping people in the "iron cage" of rationalization, and later Erving Goffman described the effects of institutionalization, when individuals have become so used to living with an institution they can no longer do without it. A particular example of this is our increasing reliance on medicine as a means of curing all ills, as described by Ivan Illich. Education, too, came under scrutiny as an institutional means of fostering social attitudes and maintaining a desired social order.

But it was Émile Durkheim who recognized the conflict between individualism and institutional expectations of conformity. His concept of "anomie," a mismatch between an individual's beliefs and desires and those of society, was taken up by Robert K. Merton in his explanation of what was considered deviant behavior. Howard S. Becker developed this further, suggesting that any behavior could be considered deviant if an institution labels it as such, and, according to Stanley Cohen, the modern media demonizes things in just this way. ∎

RELIGION
IS THE SIGH OF THE
OPPRESSED
CREATURE
KARL MARX (1818–1883)

IN CONTEXT

FOCUS
Religion

KEY DATES
1807 German philosopher Georg Hegel's work *The Phenomenology of Spirit* introduces the concept of alienation.

1841 *The Essence of Christianity* by German philosopher Ludwig Feuerbach draws on Hegel's idea of alienation and applies it critically to Christianity.

1966 Religion has lost its authority, according to British sociologist Bryan Wilson in *Religion in Secular Society*.

2010 German sociologist Jürgen Habermas, in *An Awareness of What is Missing: Faith and Reason in a Post-Secular Age*, muses on why religion has failed to disappear.

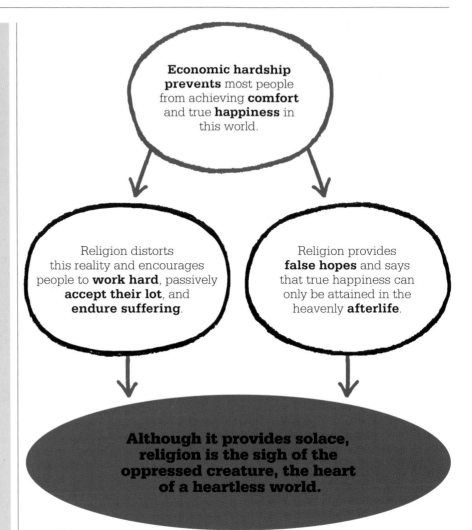

Economic hardship **prevents** most people from achieving **comfort** and true **happiness** in this world.

Religion distorts this reality and encourages people to **work hard**, passively **accept their lot**, and **endure suffering**.

Religion provides **false hopes** and says that true happiness can only be attained in the heavenly **afterlife**.

Although it provides solace, religion is the sigh of the oppressed creature, the heart of a heartless world.

According to the German philosopher Georg Hegel, liberty in a full sense consists of participation in certain ethical institutions. More infamously, he also said that only in the state "does man have rational existence." He believed that Christianity was the perfect ("consummate") religion for the emerging age of modernity because it reflected its spirit or *geist*—faith in reason and truth. However, because of the process of contradiction known as "dialectic" (in which, by its own nature, something can contain its

opposite), the social structures and institutions that people create to serve them can instead come to control and even enslave them. The process of rational self-discovery can lead to "alienation"— a concept of estrangement that went on to have a profound influence on the social sciences.

Ludwig Feuerbach, a German philosopher and former student of Hegel's, used the concept of alienation to criticize religion. Feuerbach argues that people endow God with human qualities and then worship him for those

qualities, so they unconsciously worship themselves. This prevents them from fully realizing their own potential; the divine is no more than a projection of alienated human consciousness. Karl Marx's collaborator, Friedrich Engels, acknowledged that Feuerbach's *The Essence of Christianity* had a profoundly liberating effect on them both in the 1840s.

Man makes religion
Karl Marx's father had converted from Judaism to Christianity merely to ensure his job security,

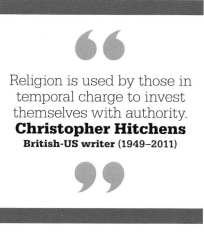

> Religion is used by those in temporal charge to invest themselves with authority.
> **Christopher Hitchens**
> **British-US writer (1949–2011)**

and yet he instilled in his son a belief that religion is necessary for morality. However, from a relatively young age, Karl Marx criticized the idea that a spiritual realm was needed to maintain social order. He later became convinced that secularization (decline in the social significance of religion) will liberate people from mystical forms of social oppression. He outlined many of his ideas about religion in "A Contribution to the Critique of Hegel's Philosophy of Right" (1844).

Expanding upon the idea of alienation, Marx argues that "man makes religion, religion does not make man." People, he says, have forgotten that they invented God, who has come to have a life of his own and now controls the people. What people have created, they can destroy. The revolutionary working class, he believes, will realize that the ideologies and institutions of capitalist society, which enslave

The wealth of the Catholic Church has been criticized by many. For Marx, religion serves capitalist interests and is a tool used by wealthy elites to control and oppress the working class.

them, are not natural or inevitable but can be overthrown. Until then, religion will remain as a symptom of the disease caused by material deprivation and human alienation, which creates such pain for its sufferers that they need the solace provided by religion.

Like the French philosopher Auguste Comte, for whom religious belief is an infantile state of reason, Marx believes in society progressing scientifically toward secularism. However, Marx is more critical of religion as a reflection of society, rather than as a set of beliefs. His goal is to liberate the working class from the oppression of capitalism, and he argues that the ideas of the ruling class are those dominating society—and one of the apparatuses transmitting those ideas is the Church.

The Church and the state

In 18th-century England, an unknown wit described the Church of England as a political party "at prayer." For Marx, any institution

that serves capitalist interests, including religion, has to be contested, and ultimately done away with. The replacement will be a humanist society based on socialism and communism.

According to Marx, religion is "consolation and justification" for the existing state and society. Churches proclaim that the authority of the ruling class is ordained by supernatural authority, thus the lowly position of the workers is inevitable and just. When a society is riven by inequality, injustice is perpetuated rather than eased. Marx declared: "The struggle against religion is, therefore, indirectly the struggle against that world whose spiritual aroma is religion." This sentiment was echoed in the 1960s by British sociologist Bryan Wilson, who claims that the role of the Church is to socialize each new generation into accepting their lot.

Marx aims to expose the illusory nature of religion and reveal it as an ideological tool of the »

Marx argues that religion is a belief system that enables the ruling class to maintain power in the present by promising the working class that things will be better in the hereafter. The poor find solace in moral teachings because, ultimately, they will reap a reward for their suffering; social change is averted because religion stabilizes society and upholds the status quo.

The hereafter

The here and now

ruling class. Because a belief in the hereafter serves as a comfort to the poor and the oppressed, Marx described religion as "the opium of the people." Russian revolutionary Vladimir Ilyich Lenin said it is "spiritual gin": religion deadens the harsh realities of working-class life, and through it people are drugged into accepting their lowly positions in return for a better afterlife. In effect, religion can be understood as a potent form of social control that keeps the poor in their place and obstructs social change.

Religion and radicalism

Marx does not overlook the fact that Christianity is a religion that grew out of oppression, and that it has sustained and comforted those who are miserable and without hope. Religious suffering is both an "expression of real suffering and a protest against real suffering"— it is the "sigh" of oppressed people,

which suggests that religion has a radical or potentially revolutionary aspect. In 17th-century England, for example, Puritanism led to the execution of a king and the establishment of a republic. However, Marx says that religion is the "*illusory* happiness of

the people" when the situation demands their *real* happiness: "To call on them to give up their illusions about their condition is to call on them to give up a condition that requires illusions." The task of history and philosophy, he declares, is "to unmask self-estrangement in its unholy forms once the holy form of human self-estrangement has been unmasked."

Marx agreed with German sociologist Max Weber's premise that Protestantism had played a big role in establishing capitalism because it better satisfied the commercial needs of 16th-century merchants and later industrialists. Hard work accompanied by reward was at the heart of Protestant philosophy, and Calvinists in particular looked upon material success as a sign of God's favor.

Marx describes the Reformation as Germany's revolutionary past— a revolution that began in the brain of a monk, as he puts it. Luther, he says, "overcame bondage out of *devotion* by replacing it with bondage out of *conviction*"; Luther turned priests into laymen because he turned laymen into priests. In Marx's view, Protestantism did

---

Feminism and religion

Elizabeth Cady Stanton, 19th-century US author of *The Woman's Bible*, said the Word of God was actually that of a man and was used to subjugate women. Feminist theories of religion since then have generally echoed this theme of sexism and gender inequality.

Women tend to participate more than men in religious observation, but they are usually marginalized and discriminated against, with fewer rights and heavier punishments. Egyptian

writer Nawal El Saadawi says religion may be used to oppress women, but the cause is patriarchal forms of society, which has reshaped religion. Many Muslim women use their religion and dress to symbolize their liberation, notes British sociologist Linda Woodhead.

Within some religions, the position of women is changing significantly; since the Church of England permitted female ordination in 1992, women now make up one in five of the clergy.

not offer the true solution to the problem, but it did provide a "true setting" whereby a man's struggle was now no longer against the clergy outside but the "priestly nature" inside himself.

Meanwhile, the social status quo presented a further obstacle to real human emancipation. Whereas the landowners and capitalists became richer in this world, the reward for the working class for toiling long hours for little pay was a place in heaven; suffering is made into a virtue. Marx is concerned by the role of the Church as a landowner and employer in the 19th century and sees this as further evidence that religion is once more ideological tool used by the ruling classes to control the workers.

An irreligious workforce

In Britain, the establishment feared that working people were losing touch with organized religion and turning instead to other Christian religious groups or working-class political movements, such as Chartism. For this reason, a Census of Religious Worship was carried out in 1851. This revealed working-class apathy as well as a divide in society between the conservative, established Church of England and the meeting houses and chapels where followers of newer, popular religions, such as Quakerism and Unitarianism, gathered.

Methodism—a Protestant denomination focused on helping the poor—was extremely popular in many working-class areas in the manufacturing centers of Britain.

Christian groups like the Quakers were perceived as a threat to the religious-political status quo. Opposed to war and slavery, and refusing to swear oaths to others, they rejected the idea of hierarchies in the Church.

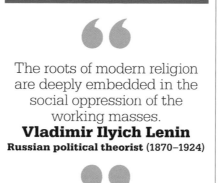

> The roots of modern religion are deeply embedded in the social oppression of the working masses.
> **Vladimir Ilyich Lenin**
> **Russian political theorist (1870–1924)**

It also attracted the new factory owners, who were both perturbed by the apparently irreligious nature of their workers and shocked by their vices, such as drunkenness. Offering Marxists further evidence of religion being used as an ideological tool by the ruling classes, some owners coerced workers into attending services, Bible study classes, educational talks, and hobbies in an attempt to "educate" them into a "decent," sober, existence—one that would enable them to work more efficiently. Divesting them of energy

in this way also thwarted their revolutionary potential and ensured they became the compliant workhorses of industry.

Western intellectuals such as A.C. Grayling, the late Christopher Hitchens, and Richard Dawkins, sometimes branded the "New Atheists," share many of Marx's sentiments about religion. Namely that, as arguably the first attempt at philosophy, religion is interesting but is a form of alienation, both emotional and intellectual, and a poor substitute for social justice and happiness. However, Marx himself—in his observations about the Reformation—acknowledged religion's potential for radical thought and social action. The part that Nonconformist religions played in Britain during more than a century of progressive social reform later demonstrated this. In seeking an answer as to why religion has not faded away by the 21st century, Jürgen Habermas acknowledges the important public role played by religious communities in many parts of the world. Today, in spite of widespread secularization, no one speaks of the extinction of religions or the religious. ∎

THE IRON LAW OF OLIGARCHY
ROBERT MICHELS (1876–1936)

IN CONTEXT

FOCUS
Oligarchy

KEY DATES
1904–05 Max Weber's
*The Protestant Ethic and the
Spirit of Capitalism* sees the
rationalization that results
from bureaucracy as an
inevitable feature of modernity.

1911 In *Political Parties*,
German social and political
theorist Robert Michels
contends that organizational
democracy is an impossibility.

1916 Italian sociologist
Vilfredo Pareto argues that
democracy is an illusion; the
elite will always serve itself.

2009 The launch of the Chilcot
Inquiry in the UK into the 2003
invasion of Iraq shows the
extent to which officials, such
as ex-Prime Minister Tony
Blair, are protected from being
publicly accountable for their
actions. Many argue that Blair
should be tried for war crimes.

Bureaucracy is an enemy of
individual liberty, according
to Robert Michels. In the
early 20th century, he pointed
out the link between bureaucracy
and political oligarchy (the rule
of the many by the few). In his
observations of political parties
and unions, he saw that the size
and complexity of democracies
require hierarchy. A leadership,
with a clear chain of command,
and separate from the masses, is
needed—resulting in a pyramid-
like structure that places a few
leaders in charge of vast and
powerful organizations.

Michels applies Max
Weber's idea that a hierarchy of
responsibility increases efficiency,
but argues that this concentrates
power and endangers democracy.
The interests of the elites of
organizations, rather than the
needs of the people, become
the key focus, despite professed
democratic ideals. Michels stresses
that the self-interest of those at
the top of organizations always
comes to the fore.

Keeping their positions of power
becomes an important role of
bureaucracies such as political
parties; and maintaining an air
of mystery and superiority through
complex voting systems, use
of arcane language, and sub-
committees helps to ensure this.
Officials tend to be well-insulated
from the consequences of their
decisions—bureaucracy protects
them against public accountability.
Oligarchy thrives in the hierarchical
structure of bureaucracy and
frequently undermines people's
control over their elected leaders. ∎

> Who says organization,
> says oligarchy.
> **Robert Michels**

See also: Karl Marx 28–31 ▪ Max Weber 38–45 ▪ Friedrich Engels 66–67 ▪
Michel Foucault 270–77 ▪ Jürgen Habermas 286–87

HEALTHY PEOPLE NEED NO BUREAUCRACY TO MATE, GIVE BIRTH, AND DIE
IVAN ILLICH (1926–2002)

IN CONTEXT

FOCUS
Iatrogenesis

KEY DATES
c.460–370 BCE Hippocrates, a physician in ancient Greece, believes medics should not cause harm to their patients; iatrogenesis becomes a punishable offence.

1847 Hungarian physician Ignaz Semmelweis recommends surgeons wash their hands to reduce infection-related deaths.

1975 Ivan Illich, in *Medical Nemesis*, claims that the medical establishment constitutes a major threat to human health.

2002 David Clark, professor of medical sociology, argues that terminal cancer patients are given ravaging chemotherapy treatments as a result of human-centered treatment that offers false hope.

S ociety has become acutely aware of the dangers posed by medicine. Over-use of diagnostic x-rays in pregnancy, which can lead to childhood cancers, and harmful prescription-drug interactions are examples. The Greek word "iatrogenesis"— "brought forth by a healer"—is used to describe such problems. Radical Austrian thinker Ivan Illich argues that the medical establishment has become a serious threat to human life because, in conjunction with capitalism, it is an institution that serves itself and makes more people sick than it heals.

Illich suggests there are three main types of iatrogenesis. Clinical iatrogenesis is when a harm arises that would not have occured without medical intervention; less resistance to bacteria from the over-prescription of antibiotics, for example. Social iaotragenesis is the medicalization of life: more and more problems are seen as amenable to medical intervention, with expensive treatments being developed for non-diseases. Minor

Hospital births, uncommon before the 20th century, are cited by some as an example of social iatrogenesis— the increasing, and unncecessary, medicalization of life.

depression is, for example, often treated with habit-forming drugs. The agencies involved, such as drug companies, have a vested interest in treating people this way.

Even worse, for Illich, is cultural iatrogenesis—the destruction of traditional ways of coping with illness, pain, and death. The over-medicalization of our lives means that we have become increasingly unwilling to face the realities of death and disease: doctors have assumed the role of priests. ∎

See also: George Ritzer 120–23 ▪ Robert Putnam 124–25 ▪ Ulrich Beck 156–61 ▪ Erving Goffman 264–69 ▪ Michel Foucault 270–77; 302–03

SOME COMMIT CRIMES BECAUSE THEY ARE RESPONDING TO A SOCIAL SITUATION
ROBERT K. MERTON (1910–2003)

IN CONTEXT

FOCUS
Anomie or strain theory

KEY DATES
1897 In *Suicide*, Émile Durkheim uses the concept of anomie to account for differing suicide rates among Protestants and Catholics.

1955 US criminologist Albert Cohen, a former student of Talcott Parsons, says the disadvantages faced by lower-class men cause status frustration, or strain, leading to delinquency, which is seen as a way to command respect.

1983 British criminologist Steven Box says some accounts of delinquency, such as those of Albert Cohen, fail to explain the crimes of the powerful in society.

1992 US sociologist Robert Agnew insists that anomie, or strain theory, can be used to explain crime and deviancy but should not be tied to class.

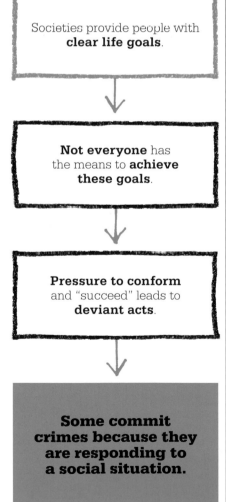

Societies provide people with **clear life goals**.

Not everyone has the means to **achieve these goals**.

Pressure to conform and "succeed" leads to **deviant acts**.

Some commit crimes because they are responding to a social situation.

Deviance is universal, normal, and functional, according to French theorist Émile Durkheim. He argues that when people no longer feel integrated into society and are unsure of its norms and rules—for example, during times of rapid social change—they are more likely to turn to deviant acts or suicide. This condition is known as *anomie*, a Greek word meaning "without law." In his article "Social Structure and Anomie," published in 1938, US sociologist Robert K. Merton adapts Durkheim's analysis of deviance, applying it to contemporary US society and arguing that such behavior occurs as a direct result of strain.

The American Dream

Merton suggests that the ideals and aspirations connected with individual "success" in the US—the "American Dream" of, for example, material prosperity, and home and car ownership—are socially produced. Not everyone can achieve these goals through legitimate means because certain constraints, such as social class, act as barriers to achieving them. According to Merton, deviance

See also: Richard Sennett 84–87 ▪ Robert D. Putnam 124–25 ▪ Max Weber 220–23 ▪ Howard S. Becker 280–85 ▪ Talcott Parsons 300–01

The American Dream of leading a charmed life, owning a home and a car, and accumulating wealth is a fantasy for many, especially those caught in the clutches of poverty and unemployment.

(which is also socially constructed) is likely to occur when there is an obvious tension or discrepancy between social expectations and the ability or desire to attain them. This "strain theory," for Merton, explains the direct correlation between unemployment and crime: for example, a lack of money means that the legal routes to buying a car, a house, or other items are not accessible, but the pressure to conform to what is expected can lead people to theft.

Rebel or conformist?

Merton extends his theory by dividing people into five categories according to their relationship to culturally accepted goals and the means of achieving them. "Conformists," he suggests, have invested in the American Dream and, through the accepted routes of education and gainful employment, are able to attain it. "Ritualists" do not aspire to society's cultural goals, but nevertheless respect the recognized means of achieving them. They may, for example, go to work every day and perform their duties conscientiously, but they do not attempt to climb the corporate ladder to "success."

"Innovators" (often seen as criminals) are those who believe in the goals of society but choose less legitimate and traditional means to achieve them. "Retreatists" are society's dropouts—they reject not only conventional goals but also the traditional means of attaining them. Finally, "Rebels" are similar to Retreatists, but they create alternative goals and means of achieving them and seek to advance a counterculture. It is this group (which often includes terrorists and revolutionaries) that, according to Merton, can effect social change.

Merton's strain theory has been criticized for focusing on individual deviancy at the expense of group or gang behavior. It is also argued that the theory relies too heavily on official crime statistics, which often obscure middle-class crime. ▪

Robert K. Merton

Robert K. Merton was born as Meyer R. Schkolnick in 1910 in Philadelphia. His parents were working-class Russian-Jewish immigrants; the first few years of his life were spent living above their dairy shop (which later burned down). He adopted the stage name Robert Merlin at the age of 14 as part of his magician act, but changed it to Robert K. Merton when he won a scholarship to Temple University.

Merton is credited with coining the phrases "self-fulfilling prophecy" and "role models," and is said to have pioneered the focus-group research method. He was elected president of the American Sociological Association in 1957.

Key works

1938 "Social Structure and Anomie"
1949 *Social Theory and Social Structure*
1985 *On the Shoulder of Giants: A Shandean Postscript*

> Antisocial behavior is... 'called forth' by... differential access to the approved opportunities for legitimate... pursuit of... cultural goals.
> **Robert K. Merton**

TOTAL INSTITUTIONS STRIP PEOPLE OF THEIR SUPPORT SYSTEMS AND THEIR SENSE OF SELF

ERVING GOFFMAN (1922–1982)

IN CONTEXT

FOCUS
Institutionalization

KEY DATES
1871 Henry Maudsley, a British psychiatrist, argues that asylums adversely affect individuals' sense of self.

1972 *Psychological Survival*, Stanley Cohen and Laurie Taylor's study of a men's prison in Durham, UK, reveals that inmates adapt behavior and identity in order to survive.

1975 French thinker Michel Foucault's *Discipline and Punish: The Birth of the Prison* considers the ways in which prisons and asylums maintain social order and conformity.

1977 In *Decarceration,* US sociologist Andrew T. Scull contends that the trend to reduce the number of institutions for the mentally ill and prisoners leads to a greater lack of care.

When dealing with the bureaucratic procedures that typify the modern world—and the frustrations they engender—most of us can escape into our private lives to maintain a sense of balance. However, there are people for whom this is not an option because they spend all their time in structured institutions, such as prisons or asylums.

US sociologist Erving Goffman was interested in how people deal with things when they cannot escape everyday rules and regulations. For his seminal study *Asylums*, published in 1961, he investigated how the "self" adjusts to living in permanent and omnipresent bureaucracy. He contended that the most important factor for a patient in a mental hospital was not the illness but the institution—and that the reactions and adjustments the affected person makes are found in inmates of other types of institution too.

Total institutions

Institutions that are closed off from the outside world—often physically by walls, fences, and locked doors—are what Goffman

> These establishments are the forcing houses for changing persons in our society. Each is a natural experiment, typically harsh, on what can be done to the self.
> **Erving Goffman**

calls "total institutions." Asylums, prisons and concentration camps, and even boarding schools and monasteries, are examples of this extreme form of organization.

In "total institutions," not only are the inmates physically separated from the outside world, they are frequently isolated for extended periods of time, sometimes involuntarily. Due to these peculiar circumstances, such organizations develop particular ways of going about

The goal of "total institutions" is **to influence the lives of individuals** comprehensively.

A person's former identity and **sense of self is broken down**...

...and they are **forced to adapt and become adjusted** to the goals of the institution.

"Total institutions" strip people of their support systems and their sense of self.

See also: Émile Durkheim 34–37 ▪ Michel Foucault 52–55; 270–77 ▪ G.H. Mead 176–77 ▪ Ivan Illich 261 ▪ Howard S. Becker 280–85

their business. Within such places, says Goffman, a relatively small number of staff supervise a much larger group of inmates. They do so using surveillance techniques to achieve compliance—an observation made by Michel Foucault in his 1975 study, which depicted prisons as all-seeing, all-powerful machines. Goffman's additional insight was that inmates responded to "total institutions" by fashioning a new mode of life.

Functionalist theory holds that society is glued together by social consensus—an agreed sense of purpose. A "total institution" works because it has goals, and everything within it is targeted on those goals. Goffman, who worked in a US asylum between 1955 and 1956, argues that alongside the official aims of the organization, there exist other, invisible goals and practices that constitute a crucial part of its functioning. He calls this the "underlife of public institutions" and he concentrates on the world of the asylum patients to understand this "underlife."

Bethlem Royal Hospital, London's notoriously chaotic asylum, from which the word "Bedlam" is derived, was founded in 1247. It is now a modern psychiatric facility.

Alcatraz prison, US, is a powerful symbol of institutional dominance. Foucault saw prison as omnipotent, but Goffman argues inmates of institutions try to fashion life to meet their needs.

Using his own observations and drawing upon a range of published material, such as autobiographies and novels about similar institutions, Goffman concludes that identity is shaped, and adjusted, through interaction with others. He states that if the organization's key goals are to be met, it is sometimes necessary to sideline official practices and ideals while giving the impression they are being upheld.

Goffman maintains that the social relationships and identities that patients possessed before they entered a mental institution give way to wholly new identities that are built around the ways in which they adapt to life in their new institutional home.

Breaking down the self

The process begins with the breaking down of the old self. The patients are sometimes either forcibly committed or tricked by family members and health professionals into entering an institution, and discover that these same people are stripping them of their rights. In this way, they lose their autonomy and experience humiliation and a challenge to their identity, perhaps by having their actions or their sanity questioned.

The admission to the hospital continues this breaking-down process: being photographed, having personal possessions confiscated, fingerprints taken, and undressing—all these procedures chip away at the "old self." Goffman argues that our sense of self is partly invested in our appearance, the things we own, and the clothes we wear; if these are changed or taken away, people are given a message that they are no longer the person they were. Once admitted, this feeling is continually »

"Mortification of the self"

is Goffman's term for an institutional process whereby an individual is stripped of a sense of self. A personal identity is transformed into an organizational identity—as "patient" or "inmate." At the outset, the "old self" is partly defined by trappings, such as possessions and clothes. Within the institutional maze, by becoming a number, getting a haircut or a uniform, having freedom curtailed through physical restraints, and one's behavior modified by rules, or perhaps through medication, a compliant "new self" is forged.

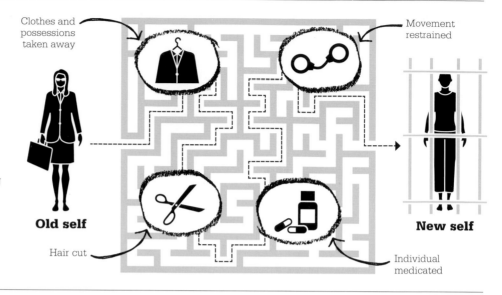

Clothes and possessions taken away

Movement restrained

Old self

Hair cut

Individual medicated

New self

---

emphasized; for example, by having to ask permission to go to the toilet. This adds to what Goffman calls a "mortification of the self," which is brought about by the humiliations and degradations of such a life.

Usual face-saving ways of coping with these situations, such as sarcasm or profanity, are not possible in "total institutions" because punishment will ensue. Inmates have to make a primary adjustment to this organizational demand, and often end up in a placid state where they can be easily controlled, enabling the institution to function effectively. The system of privileges and reward used by the institution, in return for work in the kitchen or elsewhere, can help to focus an inmate's energy and attention, and give a new sense of purpose and meaning, while keeping them compliant.

In some cases, the institution can overwhelm the inmate, resulting in either "conversion" or "colonization." In an asylum, conversion is when a patient accepts a hospital's definition of them—for example, as being emotionally disturbed—and then

tries to conform to what is expected of the ideal patient. Colonization, according to Goffman, is when the institution's regime engulfs the inmate, so that the world "inside" seems preferable to that outside and the inmate would be unable to function in the world outside the institution.

Salvaging identity

The second stage of a mental patient's progress is the salvaging of some sense of individuality.

> Many total institutions… seem to function merely as storage dumps for inmates, but… usually present themselves to the public as rational organizations.
> **Erving Goffman**

Although "total institutions" are focused on producing standardized behavior, many inmates find ways to adjust. Goffman suggests that humans can develop complex responses to the types of demands on the self required by such organizations. He maintains that a process of secondary adjustment enables individuals to create a new self, centered on the organization, which inhabits the spaces not taken by the rules and regulations.

These secondary adjustments comprise the "underlife" of the institution and are a means for the inmates to get by on a day-to-day basis, produce a degree of autonomy, and retain some personality. The most popular way this is done, according to Goffman, is by "playing it cool"; generally getting along with staff while carving out an identity and "working" the system without overtly clashing with the rules. Inmates can find and use what he refers to as "damp corners" in the organization—spaces such as kitchens, workshops, or the sick bay—that provide an opportunity to exert control over self and situation. In such places, the inmates can create new currencies—for example, bargaining with tobacco or sweets—or develop particular ways of communicating through a creative use of language. Some may try to maintain a defiant feeling of independence by discreetly urinating on a radiator, which will evaporate any signs of misbehavior, rather than ask for permission to go to the toilet. Institutions will often turn a blind eye to such relatively minor indiscretions in the knowledge that these keep the inmate tractable for the most part.

Not everyone is successfully socialized into the norms of "total institutions." Although Goffman does not focus in detail on this, some inmates may retain a spirit of resistance and rebel by sabotaging the plumbing, organizing mass refusal of particular foods, riots, or even arranging for a member of staff to have "an accident."

Self-serving institutions

Despite writing in a cool, detached tone, Goffman has been accused by some of over-identifying with the patients he observed. Others, such as the US sociologist and criminologist John Irwin, have suggested Goffman's study was a little narrow in its focus and was limited by only observing inmates while in the institution.

Nevertheless, in seeing "total institutions" as places that, rather than operating in the best interest of inmates, effectively dehumanize them, Goffman's work has been cited as precipitating changes in the treatment of mental health patients. He lays bare the ways in which "total institutions" are self-legitimatizing organizations—through defining their goals they legitimate their activity, which in turn legitimates the measures they take to meet those goals.

His work is also important for the sociology of identity because of his claims that names, possessions, and clothes are symbols imbued with meaning and importance for identity formation. He highlights the clear gap between officially imposed definitions of the self and the self that the individual seeks to present.

Goffman's studies remain of social relevance. Despite the fact that, in Britain, many mental health

One Flew Over the Cuckoo's Nest, a novel by Ken Kesey, is set in an asylum. It deals with patients adopting coping strategies, and how institutions crush challenges to their authority.

facilities have been closed from the 1960s onward as part of a process of deinstitutionalization in favor of domiciled ("in the community") care, a significant proportion of people will still end their days in an institution. An aging population means that many citizens may be unable to live independent lives and therefore have to spend time in nursing or care homes, which can exhibit some of the negative hallmarks of "total institutions." ∎

US city jails confine those arrested but not yet charged or convicted. It is argued such institutions expose normal citizens to inmate culture.

A crisis of incarceration

John Keith Irwin had a different kind of first-hand experience of a "total institution" than Goffman: in 1952, he served five years in prison for robbery. He used that time to study and later gained a PhD in sociology, becoming an expert in the US prison system and the forms of social control demanded by society.

Based on his own insight and interviews with prisoners, Irwin wrote *The Jail: Managing the Underclass in American Society* (1985), which he dedicated to Erving Goffman. He argued that city jails, which confine those arrested but not yet charged or convicted, degrade and dehumanize people. Rather than controlling the disreputable, they indoctrinate inmates into particular ways of behaving.

He claims that these jails are designed to manage the "underclass," or "rabble," who are seen as threatening middle-class values. The jails are perceived to be holding-tanks for petty thieves, addicts, and sexual nonconformists, which confirms their outsider status.

GOVERNMENT IS THE RIGHT DISPOSITION OF THINGS

MICHEL FOUCAULT (1926–1984)

IN CONTEXT

FOCUS
Governmentality

KEY DATES
1513 In *The Prince*, Florentine political theorist Niccolò Machiavelli offers advice on how to maintain power.

1567 French writer Guillaume de la Perrière argues in *Le Miroir Politique* that the word "governor" can apply to a broad array of people and groups.

1979 Michel Foucault publishes an article entitled "On Governmentality."

1996 British sociologist Nikolas Rose examines how institutions such as prisons and schools shape the behavior of citizens.

2002 German sociologist Thomas Lemke applies Foucault's concept of governmentality to modern day neo-liberal societies.

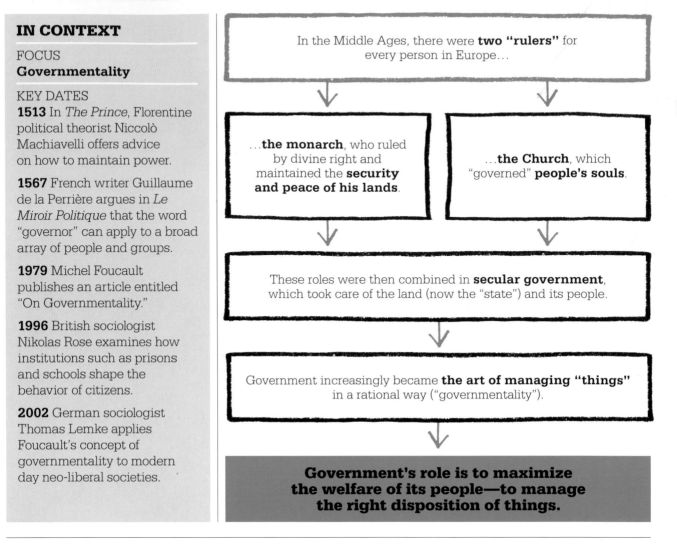

In the Middle Ages, there were **two "rulers"** for every person in Europe…

…**the monarch**, who ruled by divine right and maintained the **security and peace of his lands**.

…**the Church**, which "governed" **people's souls**.

These roles were then combined in **secular government**, which took care of the land (now the "state") and its people.

Government increasingly became **the art of managing "things"** in a rational way ("governmentality").

Government's role is to maximize the welfare of its people—to manage the right disposition of things.

Throughout history, people have been concerned with the nature of government, where and how it is needed, and the question of who has the right to govern other people. French philosopher Michel Foucault focused his study on the workings of power, and became particularly interested in the processes and legitimacy of government in Western Europe from the 16th to 20th centuries.

As a professor at the prestigious Collège de France in Paris between 1970 and 1975, Foucault delivered a series of lectures that became a prominent feature of intellectual life in the city. One of these lectures was later published in the influential journal *Ideology and Consciousness* in 1979, under the title "On Governmentality." In this work, Foucault argues that it is impossible to study the formation of power without also looking at the practices—the techniques and rationality—through which people are governed. This rationality is not an absolute that can be reached by pure reason, as most philosophers have suggested, but a changing thing that depends on both time and place. What is "rational" in one space and time may be thought irrational in others. To summarize this concept, Foucault joined the French words *governeur* (governor) and *mentalité* (mentality) to create a new term—governmentality—to describe the way that a government thinks about itself and its role (its "rationality").

Foucault's approach to philosophical analysis focuses on the "genealogy of the subject." So rather than relying on the

See also: Michel Foucault 52–55; 302–03 ▪ David McCrone 163 ▪ Norbert Elias 180–81 ▪ Max Weber 220–23 ▪ Robert Michels 260

traditional approach to inquiry, where philosophers look for the universal and invariant foundations of knowledge, Foucault looks at how a subject is constituted across history, and how this leads to its modern appearance.

Foucault's series of lectures on governmentality examined the ways in which the modern idea of an autonomous, individual self developed in concert with the idea of the nation-state. He was particularly interested in seeing how these two concepts co-determined each other's existence, and changed with the political rationality of the time.

Medieval governance

Foucault's investigations trace the shifts in ways of governing that have taken place in different eras and places. Looking back to Europe in the Middle Ages (c.500–1500), he says that the modern nation-state as we know it did not exist; nor did governmentality. People lived in a "state of justice" that imposed blunt laws and customs, such as putting

> " I wanted to study the art of governing, that is to say, the reasoned way of governing best and, at the same time, reflection on the best possible way of governing.
> **Michel Foucault**

offenders in the stocks, in order to integrate people into their community. This was the age of feudalism, when monarchs, who were seen as God's divine representatives on Earth, relied on various lords to keep the local people under control. The network of lords with allegiance to a king offered a way of maintaining order across large areas of land.

The lords earned their titles, castles, and land rights by providing military service and support to the monarch. Eventually these privileges became hereditary. Peasant farmers, or serfs, were obliged to work the land, making large profits for their rulers. Such a system, in which there was a very clear and obvious exercise of power by individuals, meant that there was little sense of coherent governance: the various nobles often ruled in very different ways. Conflict and internal warfare were also common. Monarchs' subjects did not think of themselves as bound to a national identity but instead were tied to their locality and aligned to their feudal lord.

Peasant farmers worked on the land during the Middle Ages making vast profits for their lords. Feudal systems imposed control on people, rather than coherent government.

A new way to govern

According to Foucault, the question of governing became a far greater problem in the 16th century when medieval feudalism fell into decline. As the ideas of empire and territorial expansion began to take hold, the question of how to govern the individual, the family, and the state became a central issue. Governmentality was born.

The break with the feudal system also led to a rise in conflict between states. As a result, it became increasingly important that a state knew both its own capacity and strength and the strength of its rivals. Foucault claims this is why the phenomenon of the "police" emerged in the 16th century. These forces not only provided the government with security but were also able to measure and assess the strength of the state. The police enabled the easy governance of »

German priest Martin Luther led the Protestant Reformation, which challenged the power of the Catholic Church and, argues Foucault, marked the beginning of a shift in governance.

citizens, ensuring that individuals under surveillance remain productive and compliant.

The 16th century also saw a significant shift in religious practice in Europe. The Protestant Reformation, which began in 1517, was a major challenge to the Catholic Church and its power. According to Foucault, the conflict that took place between the Protestant and Catholic Churches, together with the rise of territorial states, led early modern theorists of government to combine two very differing ways of thinking. Theologians had always approached governance from a spiritual perspective: the pastoral leader's ultimate duty was to save souls by watching over his "flock" as a shepherd would guard his sheep. Secular statesmen had approached the art of government in much more worldly terms— seeing their role as managing conflict, protecting the territory, and securing peace. These two ways of thinking, Foucault argues, came together to form a new hybrid art of governance in the late 16th and 17th centuries.

Death of the prince

For the first time, it seemed possible that the citizens and their rulers could be brought together in a system that was mutually beneficial. The personal interest of the rulers was no longer the sole guiding principle for ruling; with this shift, the idea of "ruling" was transformed into "governing." Foucault traces the shift from a sovereign notion of power to

government as an efficient mode of operation through an examination of the political treatise *The Prince* (1513), by Florentine diplomat Niccolò Machiavelli. In this short work, the prince is seen as being fundamentally concerned with maintaining and expanding his territories; his subjects living on those lands are of little interest or consequence, as long as they are behaving themselves. The prince remains morally detached from his territory—he owes no one any obligation or debt. This is the way of thinking that came to an end as monarchs lost their sovereign rights, the Churches lost power, and new technologies (such as the printing press) allowed for the spread of revolutionary ideas.

From the late Middle Ages to the 17th century, the Renaissance ushered in a return to classical ideas of freedom and democracy, followed by more revolutionary thinking that threatened the physical safety of monarchs as well as their right to rule. In England, for

example, King Charles I's belief that he had a divine right to rule brought him into armed conflict with parliamentary forces in the English Civil War. Charles was tried, convicted of high treason, and executed in 1649.

Benevolent government?

Foucault highlights French Renaissance writer Guillaume de la Perriere's 1567 definition of government, which was significant because of its lack of reference to "territory." Instead, government was described here as the correct disposition of things, organized to lead to a convenient end. Under an ideology of benevolence, the responsibilities of governments were expanded to include the welfare of their citizens, although in reality, this form of governance was really concerned with managing people's lives—and the material products of their efforts—in order to maximize the nation's strength. Ensuring the growth of wealth was seen as crucial in governing, but it was also important to have a healthy populace that would multiply if the government wanted to secure long-term prosperity and productivity. Foucault says that from this point onward, "men and things" (the relation people have to wealth, the environment, famine, fertility, the climate, and so on), rather than territories, needed to be administered in an efficient way. Governance was now an "art."

Citizen or subject?

Foucault contends that early liberal ideas of civil society, as espoused by John Locke and Adam Ferguson in the 18th century, made a social government possible. The liberal art of government has as its organizational principle "the rationale of least government"; in other words, it advocates less state intervention and an increased focus on the role of the population. At this time the concept of a "population" and its centrality to the success of the state became paramount, and led to the idea of "an individual member of the population" as a living, working, and social being. The new idea of an autonomous individual was to lead to many new political questions, including the rights and responsibilities of the individual and the state. In what ways can an individual be free, if he or she is governed by the state? The link between the "autonomous" individual's self-control and political control became an important issue, as did the possibility of domination and economic exploitation.

In examining this period, Foucault revisited his work on "passive bodies." In *Discipline and Punish*, he had traced how the body was seen as a target (to be used and improved) by those in power during the 17th and 18th centuries. He also examined how techniques of surveillance drawn from monasteries and the army were used to control people's bodies and produce passive subjects who were incapable of revolt.

In this earlier work, Foucault maintained that discipline creates docility, but when focusing on governmentality, he began to think this placed too much emphasis on domination and was too simplistic an argument. Individuals, he now said, have more opportunities to modify and construct themselves than he had thought previously.

> Let us not... ask... why certain people want to dominate... Let us ask, instead, how things work at the level of... processes, which subject our bodies, govern our gestures, dictate our behaviors.
> **Michel Foucault**

Governmentality refers to the ways in which societies are decentered and citizens play an active role in their own self-governance; it is the relationship between public power and private freedom that is central.

The art of government

Foucault claims that govermentality is important because it provides a link between what he calls the "technologies of the self" (the creation of the individual subject) and the "technologies of »

Dieters regulate and discipline themselves according to mass standards and cultural requirements rather than through individual choice.

Governing the body

Weight-loss organizations, such as Weight Watchers and Jenny Craig, illustrate Foucault's notion of governance of the self that sits in line with "normal" ideas of the time. While these organizations develop a person's sense of self and worth, they also envelop them in a web of power that ultimately benefits huge corporations.

Many feminists, such as US writer Kim Chernin, have argued that the quest for the perfect body through dieting places women within a "tyranny of slenderness."

Slimming companies and diets constitute disciplinary practices that promise an "improved self," but they also subject women to patriarchal (male-dominated) ideas about what a woman "should" look like and how she should behave. This necessity to conform to current standards of "normal" transforms dieting from an eating behavior into a moral imperative. US feminists Sandra Bartky and Susan Bordo argue that this is indicative of the ways in which women become, simultaneously, both subjects and subjected.

> If one wants to analyze the genealogy of the subject in Western civilization, he has to take into account not only techniques of domination but also techniques of the self.
> **Michel Foucault**

domination" (the formation of the state). This is because, according to Foucault, "government" does not have a purely political meaning. From the 18th century until relatively recently, government was a broad concept that embraced guidance for the family, household management, and guidance for the soul, as well as more conventional politics. Foucault describes this all-embracing form of government as "the conduct of conduct." In the modern world, governing is more than simple top-down power relationships, Foucault says; it rests on a multi-layered web. Where once governing rested on violence—or the threat of violence—this is now just one element of control. Other systems that hold sway in current forms of governing are coercive strategies, and those that structure and shape the possible forms of action citizens may take. Governing by fear and violence is much less effective than employing more subtle forms of control, such as defining limited choices or using disciplinary institutions like schools to guide the behavior of individuals. In this way, self-control becomes linked to political rule and economic exploitation. What appears to be individual choice just "happens to be" also to the benefit of the state. In this way, Foucault suggests that the modern nation-state and the modern autonomous individual rely on one another for their existence.

Governmentality in action

Foucault's view of governmentality as the effort to shape and guide choices and lifestyles of groups and individuals has been further developed by many contemporary scholars. For example, US anthropologist Matthew Kohrman

> The dream or nightmare of a society programmed… by the "cold monster" of the state is profoundly limiting as a way of rendering intelligible the way we are governed.
> **Nikolas Rose**
> British sociologist (1947–)

considered governmentality in relation to cigarette smoking among Chinese physicians. His 2008 paper "Smoking Among Doctors: Governmentality, Embodiment, and the Diversion of Blame in Contemporary China" looks at the ways smoking among health professionals was suggested to be the cause of high smoking rates among the public. Public health campaigns targeted these doctors, blaming them for tobacco-related diseases in China and calling on them to govern their own bodies and stop smoking.

The individual and the state

The individual became recognized as important in politics, Foucault claims, when the ideas of the divine right of kings and the infallibility of the Catholic Church were challenged. The task for any government then became how to find a way to conspicuously act for the people, while nevertheless continuing to build its own strength.

Domination by the monarchy and the Church (c.6th–16th centuries).

The rise of the individual (late 16th–17th century).

Citizens participate in their own governance (from the 18th century).

Foucault's vision of the modern nation-state as a governmentalized whole is not without its critics. He has, for instance, been charged with being vague and inconsistent in his definition of governmentality. Philosopher Derek Kerr has argued that Foucault's definition "beheads social subjectivity," by seeming to do away with free, subjective choice. Canadian sociologists Danica Dupont and Frank Pearce accuse Foucault of taking a rather simplistic and idealistic reading of Western political history, seeing it as "the growth of a plant from a seed," which overcomes obstacles to realize its true potential (as though this were always implicit, in some way).

Neo-liberalism

Nevertheless, Foucault's idea of governmentality remains a powerful conceptual tool with which to unpick and critique neo-liberalism. This is the post-war, post-welfare politics and economics of the late 20th century, whereby the state, in many respects, rolled back its responsibilities to its citizens. In his lectures, Foucault discussed neo-liberalism in three post-war states: West Germany, France, and the US. This form of governance has been described as the triumph of capitalism over the state, or as "anti-humanism," owing to its emphasis on the individual and the destruction of community bonds. In neo-liberal thinking, the worker is viewed as a self-owned enterprise and is required to be competitive.

Neo-liberalism relies on the notion of responsible, rational individuals who are capable of taking responsibility for themselves, their lives, and their environment, particularly through "normalizing technologies"—the

agreed-upon goals and procedures of a society that are so "obvious" that they are seen as "normal." In the 21st century these include behaviors such as recycling, losing weight, being involved in Neighborhood Watch schemes, or quitting smoking.

Foucault claims that the ways we think and talk about health, work, family and so on, encourage us to behave in particular ways. People govern themselves and others according to what they believe to be true. For instance, many societies view monogamous, heterosexual marriage as the "correct" environment for bringing up children, and this "truth" is

Barack Obama's 2008 US presidency campaign had supporters chanting "Yes We Can!," implying government by the people. The tactic echoes Foucault's concept of self-government.

established in many ways, from cultural artifacts to government discourse on family values. Political policies may also be used to put weight behind particular ideas, such as the family, through incentives such as tax breaks.

British academic Nikolas Rose, drawing on Foucault's key ideas, has written persuasively on the "death of the social" and the ways in which the individual in the neo-liberal state has to govern his or her access to state services with little or no help. It is through perspectives such as this, Foucault says, that we can see the ways in which power is repressive, even while it appears to be acting in the interests of the individual. Foucault argues that political control—the art of governance—is most effective when it presents everything it offers as an act of free choice. Modern neo-liberalist governments have found perhaps the most dangerous way to govern—by giving the impression that they are not governing at all. ∎

> 66
> Foucault's work permanently changes one's understanding of how people are governed in modern society.
> **Brent Pickett**
> **US political scientist**
> 99

RELIGION HAS LOST ITS PLAUSIBILITY AND SOCIAL SIGNIFICANCE
BRYAN WILSON (1926–2004)

IN CONTEXT

FOCUS
Secularization

KEY DATES
1904–05 Max Weber claims there is a strong relationship between rationalization and secularization.

1966 Austrian-American sociologists Peter Berger and Thomas Luckmann suggest that the loss of religion's authoritative voice has led to a legitimation crisis.

1978 British sociologist David Martin argues that the alleged decline of religion cannot be measured in statistical terms.

1985 US sociologists Rodney Stark and William Bainbridge claim that religion is here to stay because people need the solace of the supernatural.

1992 Traditional religions have had to adapt and become less "religious" in order to survive, according to British sociologist Steve Bruce.

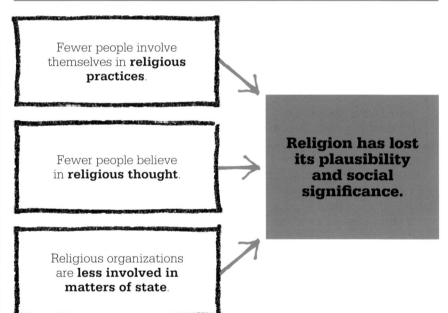

Fewer people involve themselves in **religious practices**.

Fewer people believe in **religious thought**.

Religious organizations are **less involved in matters of state**.

Religion has lost its plausibility and social significance.

Towns and cities across Britain contain churches and chapels that have been converted into pubs, showrooms, and apartments. British sociologist Bryan Wilson, writing between the 1960s and early 1990s, argues that a process of secularization is taking place. By this he means that the importance of the supernatural and the sacred is declining; religion, he suggests, has less influence on social life, institutions, and the individual. Using statistical data on various aspects of religious life, he notes that, according to polls, fewer children are being baptized in the Church of England, fewer people take part in the Easter communion, and more people say that they do not believe in God.

Wilson cites modernity—industrialization, the development of the state, and the advances in

See also: Auguste Comte 22–25 ▪ Karl Marx 28–31; 254–59 ▪ Émile Durkheim 34–37 ▪ Max Weber 38–45; 220–23 ▪ Jürgen Habermas 286–87 ▪ Michel Maffesoli 291 ▪ Michel Foucault 302–03

science and technology that come with it—as contributing to this decline in the importance of religious thought in society.

Initially, he suggests, religion was not defeated outright in the modern world, but had to compete with other claims to truth. But eventually science became too formidable an adversary. There has been a consequent disengagement of state and church into separate domains, in contrast to their closeness in the Middle Ages. And the role of religion in schools is negligible, as it is in the workplace, where the principles of organization have little room for religious myths.

God is dead?

Wilson, like Karl Marx, believes that world religions such as Christianity and Judaism play a role in maintaining the status quo by socializing new generations into accepting social divisions. But with modernity, religion has lost its authority to instruct people in what to believe and how to behave. He states that churches are aware of

their marginalized position and have to adapt to changing moral values. As old orders crumble, people seek new assurances.

Social fragmentation has brought with it cultural pluralism: alternative beliefs compete for popularity, and religions have become more private. In this sense, for Wilson, secularization is linked to a decline in community. Rather than being indicative of the longevity of religion, he sees new religious movements (NRMs), such as Scientology, as "anti-cultural": they symbolize a destructuring of society and do not contribute to the maintenance of social order and control. They are unable to channel their religious expression into a form that might have significant repercussions in modern society.

Many key thinkers of the 19th century, such as Marx, Durkheim, and Comte, believed that religion would lose its significance with the advent of industrialization. But in recent years, despite having several supporters, including British sociologist Steve Bruce, the

The Unification Church is one of several new religious movements that, according to Wilson, point to fragmentation and secularization in the modern world.

idea of secularization has received stark criticism. British journalist Michael Prowse, for example, says the idea is out of date and that there is evidence for the continuing vitality of religion. The popularity of church-going in the US and the growth of non-Christian religions in Britain, particularly Islam, certainly endorse this view. ▪

[The] content of the message that the churches seek to promote, and the attitudes and values that it tries to encourage, no longer inform much of our national life.
Bryan Wilson

Bryan Wilson

Bryan Ronald Wilson was born in Leeds, England, in 1926. He was awarded his PhD from the London School of Economics and went on to become a lecturer at the University of Leeds, where he taught for seven years. He then moved to the University of Oxford, and remained there for 30 years, until his retirement in 1993. Wilson was president of the International Society for the Sociology of Religion from 1971 to 1975. Although an agnostic, he had a lifelong interest in new religious movements and sects, and was a staunch advocate of freedom of religious thought. In addition to his fascination with religion, he wrote extensively on youth culture and education. Wilson suffered from Parkinson's disease for several years. He died in 2004, aged 78.

Key works

1966 *Religion in Secular Society*
1973 *Magic and the Millennium*
1990 *The Social Dimensions of Sectarianism*

OUR IDENTITY AND BEHAVIOR ARE DETERMINED BY HOW WE ARE DESCRIBED AND CLASSIFIED

HOWARD S. BECKER (1928–)

IN CONTEXT

FOCUS
Labeling theory

KEY DATES
1938 Austrian-US historian Frank Tannenbaum argues that criminal behavior is the result of conflict between one group and the community at large.

1951 *Social Pathology*, by US sociologist Edwin Lemert, introduces the idea of primary and secondary deviancy.

1969 Authorities create deviant identities, says US sociologist David Matza in *Becoming Deviant*.

1976 US sociologist Aaron Cicourel suggests that the police operate with a stereotype of the deviant as a young, working-class male; these youths are therefore far more likely to be sentenced than middle-class youths who commit crimes.

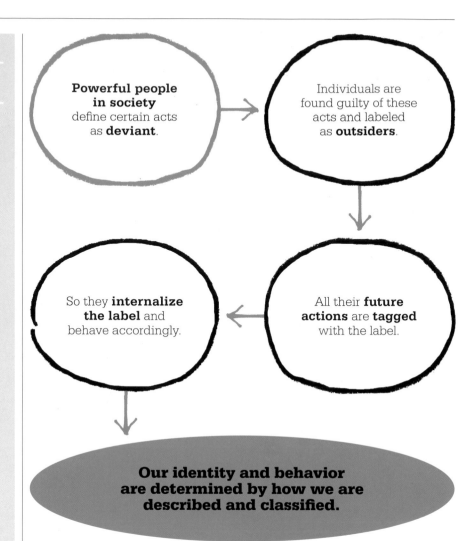

Powerful people **in society** define certain acts as **deviant**.

Individuals are found guilty of these acts and labeled as **outsiders**.

So they **internalize the label** and behave accordingly.

All their **future actions** are **tagged** with the label.

Our identity and behavior are determined by how we are described and classified.

A lthough many people in society break the law—for example, by exceeding the speed limit or stealing stationery from work— only some are regarded as real criminals. Labeling theory, which emerged from a mistrust of government powers in post-war Britain and the US in the 1960s and 70s, considers why this is so.

Proponents of labeling theory argue that criminologists once tended to conceptualize criminals as types of people, asking why particular individuals, or groups of people, committed crime. In contrast, labeling theory questions why some acts are thought to be deviant and who has the power to label some people's behavior as deviant; it then examines the impact of such labeling on society and the individual.

Consider this example: If a group of young, middle-class men on a stag night are drunk and disorderly in a town center, the authorities are likely to attribute their behavior to youthful exuberance. But if a similar disturbance is caused by young, working-class men, they are far more likely to be labeled as hooligans or criminals.

According to labeling theorists, this is because rule-makers, such as judges and politicians, tend to be middle or upper class and treat the infractions of their own kind more leniently than the deviance of working-class people. Our concept of deviance comes, the theorists argue, not so much from what people do, as how others respond to it—labeling is a political act. This school of thought—which has connections with the work of Émile

See also: Émile Durkheim 34–37 ▪ Ferdinand Tönnies 32–33 ▪ Edward Said 80–8 ▪ Elijah Anderson 82–83 ▪ G.H. Mead 176–77 ▪ Erving Goffman 190–95 ▪ Samuel Bowles and Herbert Gintis 288–89 ▪ Stanley Cohen 290

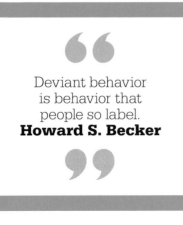

> Deviant behavior is behavior that people so label.
> **Howard S. Becker**

Durkheim, G.H. Mead, and the Chicago School in the US—is particularly associated with the work of US sociologists Howard S. Becker and Edwin Lemert.

Types of deviancy

Lemert distinguished between the ideas of "primary" and "secondary" deviancy. According to him, primary deviance is when a crime or other act is committed, but is not officially labeled as deviant, either because it went unnoticed or because the perpetrator was considered to be acting out of character. Either way, it does not attach a label of "deviant" to the individual. Secondary deviance is the effect that society's reaction has on an individual. If someone commits a crime, and is caught and labeled as criminal or deviant, they may change their behavior in the future to live up to that label.

In *Outsiders* (1963), Becker developed a number of Lemert's ideas and laid the foundations for what became known as labeling theory. He argued that there is no such thing as a deviant act: how we respond to an act depends on whether a particular form of

behavior has become sanctioned within a given society. For example, "terrorists" are accused of murder, but the army may legally kill terrorists. And among Western nations, as recently as the 1990s, a husband forcing intercourse on his wife was not guilty of rape, according to the law. Becker claims that it is not the act itself that is deviant; the response of society defines it as such and, crucially, the responses of the powerful determine how society is expected

to view such behaviors. Only those who have power can make a label stick; institutions such as the criminal justice system can ensure that a deviant label will follow an individual. Rather than being universal, deviance is relative— it depends on who commits it and how it is responded to.

Moral entrepreneurs

Coining a label that has proved extremely useful in the social sciences, Becker identifies »

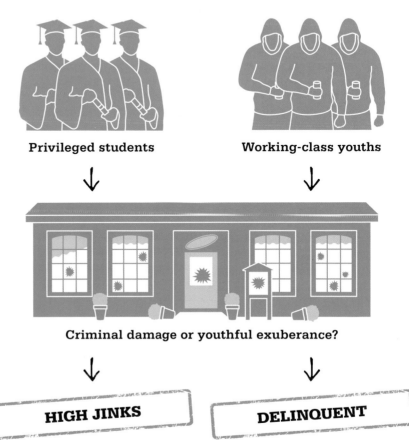

A group of privileged undergraduates who smash up a restaurant when fueled by alcohol may be accused of student high jinks, while a group of working-class boys displaying identical behavior may be labeled as delinquents.

Privileged students   **Working-class youths**

Criminal damage or youthful exuberance?

HIGH JINKS   **DELINQUENT**

The film *Reefer Madness* (1936) was a thinly disguised piece of propaganda that charts the downfall of a respectable high-school couple who are corrupted by marijuana use.

"moral entrepreneurs" as the people in society who have the power to label others. They task themselves with the role of persuading others to see the world in a way that suits their own moral beliefs. They fall into two types: rule creators and rule enforcers. The position and identity of moral entrepreneurs varies between societies, but they are always people in positions of relative power, who use that power to get their own way by either imposing their will on others, or by negotiating with them.

Becker illustrated the actions of moral entrepreneurs through the case study of a publicity campaign that was run by the Federal Bureau of Investigation (FBI) in the US in 1937. The goal was to ban the recreational use of marijuana. The moral entrepreneurs' distaste for public displays of enjoyment or ecstasy, coupled with a Protestant concern for respectability and self-control, led to the push for legal change. The FBI, according to Becker, used various means to achieve their goals; these included propaganda such as the film *Reefer Madness*, as well as public debate and political lobbying.

Deviant "careers"

Becker was particularly interested in individuals who internalized the label of deviancy, making it their defining characteristic, and went on to adopt lifestyles with deviancy as a central feature. He studied marijuana users to investigate how they progressed through the various stages of a deviant "career" and noted that first-time marijuana smokers had to learn how to perceive and subsequently enjoy the effects of the drug. Without this learning process, he said, taking the drug could be unpleasant or apparently have no effect whatsoever. Learning was central to the meaning of the deviant act— people only willingly learned what was meaningful to them—and individuals became fully fledged "dope smokers" only when they learned how to hide the habit from the "straight" or "square" world. If the smoker was caught and charged or arrested, their deviant status was likely to be confirmed. Becker reasoned that following a deviant career has its rewards, though they do not come from wider society; instead, they come from feeling a sense of belonging to a group that is united by its opposition to the world at large.

Labeling critics

Despite its influence and continued popularity, a number of criticisms can be leveled at labeling theory. The British sociologist Jock Young, for example, points to the fact that much labeling theory focuses

> The process of making a criminal... is a process of tagging, defining, identifying, segregating.
> **Frank Tannenbaum**
> Austrian-US historian (1893–1969)

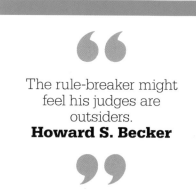

> The rule-breaker might feel his judges are outsiders.
> **Howard S. Becker**

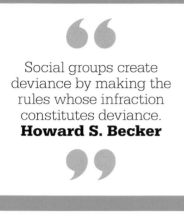

> Social groups create deviance by making the rules whose infraction constitutes deviance.
> **Howard S. Becker**

on marginal deviancy rather than more "serious" crimes, and therefore ignores the fact that some crimes, such as murder, are almost universally condemned, and are not subject to alternative perceptions of deviancy. Alvin Gouldner, a US sociologist, has

In a study of jazz musicians, Becker proposed that their "deviant" lifestyle set them apart from society, which caused them to develop values that reinforced their deviancy.

complained that Becker's deviants passively accept the labels forced upon them, rather than fighting back. Gouldner challenges Becker's theory by saying people frequently fight back in their own defense: free will is far stronger than Becker's work implies.

Academics such as Becker have also been accused of romanticizing the underdog; in response, Becker has stated that "unconventional sentimentality… is the lesser evil." But Becker's work forces us to ask important questions about power relationships and justice in society and has been significant for a number of theorists who focus on deviancy. US sociologist David Matza, for instance, develops many of Becker's ideas by arguing that what becomes a crime is the outcome of decisions and actions taken by governments and agents of the state. According to this process, both the criminal and their act are seen as abnormal and yet from the perspective of the deviant, the deviancy is entirely normal behavior. ■

Howard S. Becker

Born in Chicago, US, in 1928, sociologist Howard Saul Becker became involved in the world of music from an early age. By the age of 15 he was working as a semi-professional pianist in bars and clubs and was regularly exposed to the drug culture that he later made the subject of his studies. After studying sociology at the University of Chicago, most of his academic career was spent at Northwestern University. Becker has received many awards during his academic career, including the Award for a Career of Distinguished Scholarship from the American Sociological Association in 1998. Becker is known for his academic generosity—although mainly retired, he continues to help doctoral students with their work and offers advice on how to publish their theses. Music—jazz in particular—remains a subject of personal and research interest for him.

Key works

1963 *Outsiders: Studies in the Sociology of Deviance*
1982 *Art Worlds*
1998 *Tricks of the Trade*

ECONOMIC CRISIS IS IMMEDIATELY TRANSFORMED INTO SOCIAL CRISIS
JÜRGEN HABERMAS (1929–)

IN CONTEXT

FOCUS
Legitimation crisis

KEY DATES
1867 In *Das Kapital*, Karl Marx suggests that capitalism is prone to economic crises.

1929 The stock exchange crash on Wall Street, New York, leads to a ten-year economic depression that affects all Western economies.

1950–60s Talcott Parsons discusses legitimation and soical order, claiming that through socialization people acquire values that lead them to conform to social norms.

2007 Global economic recession results in a swing across Europe to parties of the political right.

2009 Chilean sociologist Rodrigo Cordero Vega argues, contrary to Habermas, that Marx remains relevant to contemporary society.

Late-capitalist societies experience periodic **economic downturns**.

↓

Policies to cope with this may seem **unfair** to the majority of voters.

↓

When this happens, citizens **question the authority** of government.

↓

Demonstrations and protests threaten the legitimacy of the state.

↓

Economic crisis is immediately transformed into social crisis.

Karl Marx argued that capitalist societies are prone to economic crises and that these will worsen over time, culminating in a workers' revolution. But why is it that when a society has such a crisis, a somewhat different change in the political climate often follows?

This was the question posed by the German sociologist Jürgen Habermas in the early 1970s. He was intrigued by the relationship between capitalism and crises, having seen the system survive a series of extraordinary events such as the Wall Street Crash of 1929 in the US, the subsequent Great Depression, the rise and fall of fascist movements in Europe, World War II, and the Cold War.

Habermas suggests that traditional Marxist theories of crisis tendencies are not applicable to some Western late-capitalist societies. This is because these societies have become more democratic and have changed significantly thanks to welfare-state policies, such as free healthcare provision, that aim to make up for economic inequalities. In addition, he says, collective identities have fragmented

See also: Adam Ferguson 21 ▪ Karl Marx 28–31 ▪ Herbert Marcuse 182–87 ▪
Daniel Bell 224–25 ▪ Michel Foucault 270–77 ▪ Stanley Cohen 290

and there is evidence of increased individualization and fewer class-based conflicts.

Crisis of legitimacy

Although the economic cycles of prosperity and recession continue, policy measures by nation-states have enabled them to avert major crises. Unlike earlier capitalist societies, under state-regulated late-capitalism, the primary site of crisis and conflict has shifted to the cultural and political spheres.

The crisis of modern Western society is, according to Habermas, one of legitimation. Legitimacy has become the focal concern because the state, as manager of the "free market" economy, has simultaneously to solve economic problems, ensure democracy, and please the voters. If the public feels government policies are unfair, it withdraws its support for the government. The state therefore

has the difficult task of balancing the pursuit for capital with maintaining mass support. In other words, state policies must favor business and property owners while appearing to represent the interests of all. This means the conditions exist for government institutions to suffer a large-scale loss of legitimacy.

If citizens sense that the government is just and benevolent, then they will show support. If, however, they feel that policies are not in their interests, people will respond with political apathy or even large-scale discontent and protests. Given a threat to the status quo, a government may try to appease its citizens with short-lived social welfare measures.

Habermas says democratic capitalism is an "unfinished project," implying the social system can be further improved. Western governments' actions since the global financial crisis began in 2007 have exposed many social tensions between narrow capital interests, the public interest, mass democracy, and the need to secure institutional legitimacy. ∎

Riot police in Athens, Greece, in 2011 confront demonstrators claiming that government austerity measures to deal with sovereign debt favor the few at the expense of the many.

Jürgen Habermas

Born in Düsseldorf, Germany, in 1929, Jürgen Habermas's political awakening came when, as a teenager in the Hitler Youth, he witnessed the aftermath of World War II and the Holocaust—events that inform much of his work.

Habermas is one of the world's foremost contemporary social thinkers. Many of his writings are concerned with knowledge communication and the changing nature of the public and private spheres. He was born with a cleft palate, which affected his speech and, at times, left him socially isolated in his youth. The experience influenced his work on communication.

He studied sociology and philosophy in Frankfurt at the Institute for Social Research, under Max Horkheimer and Theodor Adorno, who both helped originate critical theory, and in the late 1960s he became director of the Institute for Social Research.

Key works

1968 *Knowledge and Human Interests*
1973 *Legitimation Crisis*
1981 *The Theory of Communicative Action*

SCHOOLING HAS BEEN AT ONCE SOMETHING DONE TO THE POOR AND FOR THE POOR

SAMUEL BOWLES (1939–) AND HERBERT GINTIS (1940–)

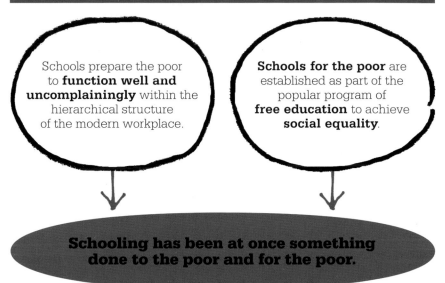

Schools prepare the poor to **function well and uncomplainingly** within the hierarchical structure of the modern workplace.

Schools for the poor are established as part of the popular program of **free education** to achieve **social equality**.

Schooling has been at once something done to the poor and for the poor.

IN CONTEXT

FOCUS
The hidden curriculum

KEY DATES
1968 In *Life in Classrooms,* US sociologist Philip W. Jackson claims that children are socialized in the classroom via a "hidden curriculum."

1973 According to Pierre Bourdieu, the reproduction of "cultural capital" (the ability to recognize cultural references, to know how to act appropriately in different social situations, and so on) explains middle-class success.

1978 Kathleen Clarricoates' British study indicates that gender inequity, to the detriment of girls, forms part of the implicit curriculum.

1983 Henry Giroux, US cultural critic, suggests that hidden curriculums are plural, operating along lines of gender and ethnicity as well as social class.

Schools exist to prepare children for adulthood and society, but in the 1960s the benign consensus about this fact of modern life began to fragment. At the end of that decade the term "hidden curriculum" was coined by Philip W. Jackson, who claimed that elements of socialization take place in school that are not part of the formal educational curriculum. Although Émile Durkheim had observed this imparting of values decades earlier, it was now given a less favorable interpretation and since then several sociological approaches have developed.

The most radical perspective comes from US economists Samuel Bowles and Herbert Gintis, who argue in *Schooling in Capitalist America* (1976) that education is not a neutral sphere but one where the needs of capitalism are reproduced by implicitly creating attitudes among young people that prepare them for work that alienates them in their future lives.

See also: Émile Durkheim 34–37 ▪ Pierre Bourdieu 76–79 ▪
Erving Goffman 264–69 ▪ Paul Willis 292–93 ▪ Talcott Parsons 300–01

According to Bowles and Gintis, schools exist to reproduce social inequalities. Therefore, the best predictor for a child's future is the economic status of parents, rather than academic achievement or intelligence. Although the explicit curriculum is about equality of opportunity, education's prime role is not to teach the skills needed in the world of work, but to instill into children the "hidden curriculum."

Working-class children are taught their place in society and learn that qualities such as working hard, deference, punctuality, and following orders are prized. These traits are rewarded, while creativity and independent thought are not valued. This maintains the economic status quo, which needs industrious, uncritical employees.

Bowles and Gintis claim that early 19th-century schools in the US were set up to assimilate immigrants into the "American" work ethic. Crucially, there is a "correspondence" between the hierarchical social relations within the school system and those found in the economic system. The nature of work also has similarities: pupils have little control over what they study and neither do they study for the inherent value of knowledge; like workers, they are "alienated." Schools teach children that social inequalities are just and inevitable, and therefore education can be seen as a form of social control.

Class matters

In France, Pierre Bourdieu took a different view and suggested that the hidden curriculum is achieved through the cultural reproduction of knowledge. The dominant class is able to define its culture and values

> The structure of social relations in education… inures the student to the discipline of the workplace.
> **Samuel Bowles & Herbert Gintis**

as superior and this shapes what is taught, thus people learn to respect things perceived as upper class and deride those considered working class. For example, working-class children might be taught that classical music is superior to popular music, and that it is too difficult for them to understand, whereas middle-class children are taught how to appreciate it. In a similar way, middle-class children are taught the qualities that will enable them to become leaders. So, lower-class children face systematic bias against them in the system.

Many sociologists, such as British academic Diane Reay, contend that schools have not become vehicles for economic opportunity. The work of Bowles and Gintis still has much resonance because there has been little progress for the working classes over the last century. The poor are simply better educated than in the past. Throughout Western society, "real" incomes for the poorest have been falling, inequality has been increasing, and it is common to find graduates in low-paid work. ■

Samuel Bowles and Herbert Gintis

Both Samuel Bowles, born in New Haven, Connecticut, and Herbert Gintis, born in Philadelphia, Pennsylvania, received doctoral degrees from Harvard University and they have since worked extensively with one another. They were invited by the US civil rights leader Martin Luther King Jr. to write educational background papers for the Poor People's March of 1968. Much of their work, which has been described as Marxist, argues that many social institutions, such as schools, are characterized by the disciplinary exercise of power.

They were both hired in 1973 to join the economics department at the University of Massachusetts. Gintis still works there, but Bowles left in 2001 to join the Santa Fe Institute as research professor and director of behavioral sciences, and he is also a professor of economics at the University of Siena. Recent collaborations have focused on cultural and genetic evolution, asking why large groups of unrelated individuals gather together cooperatively.

Key works

1976 *Schooling in Capitalist America: Educational Reform and the Contradictions of Economic Life*
1986 *Democracy and Capitalism: Property, Community, and the Contradictions of Modern Social Thought*
2005 *Unequal Chances: Family Background and Economic Success* (eds.)

SOCIETIES ARE SUBJECT, EVERY NOW AND THEN, TO PERIODS OF MORAL PANIC
STANLEY COHEN (1942–2013)

IN CONTEXT

FOCUS
Moral panics

KEY DATES
1963 *Outsiders: Studies in the Sociology of Deviance*, Howard Becker's study of labeling, lays the foundations for moral panic theory by discussing how people's behavior can clash with societal norms.

1964 Media exaggeration of clashes between "mods" and "rockers" youth subcultures in the UK sparks a moral panic.

1971 In *The Drug Takers: The Social Meaning of Drug Use*, Scottish academic Jock Young, a friend of Stanley Cohen, discusses the idea of moral panic in relation to the social meaning of drug-taking.

1994 US sociologist Erich Goode and Israeli academic Nachman Ben-Yehuda develop Cohen's ideas in their book *Moral Panics: The Social Construction of Deviance*.

So important is the sociological concept of "moral panics" that the term is now widely used by journalists and politicians. The idea emerged in the 1970s, partly from South African-born sociologist Stanley Cohen's *Folk Devils and Moral Panics* (1972), which was inspired by media-aggravated conflicts in 1964 in the UK between youth groups known as mods and rockers.

Cohen examines how groups and individuals are identified as a threat to dominant social values, and how the media plays a key role in amplifying this, presenting them in negative or stereotyped ways, thus creating a national panic. The media is an influential institution that often reflects the values of the powerful and represents issues so that the public are enticed to agree with "experts" (politicians and the police, for example) on how best to deal with the problem.

Those seen as blameworthy become scapegoats, or what Cohen terms "folk devils," for problems that often lie with the state; moral panics reflect deep-seated anxieties. Media attention may create a "self-fulfilling prophecy" by encouraging the behaviors it reports. Moral panics can be short-lived and die down when they are seen to be dealt with, or they may form part of a larger, ongoing panic.

The concept of moral panics continues to be used by academics, such as British sociologist Angela McRobbie, to describe the role the media plays in creating deviant acts and justifying increased social control of marginalized groups. ∎

The 9/11 attacks in New York, sparked moral panics about "terrorism," leading to widespread Islamophobia—prejudice against Muslims or those perceived as Muslims.

See also: Harold Garfinkel 50–51 ▪ Edward Said 80–81 ▪ Herbert Marcuse 182–87 ▪ Stuart Hall 200–01 ▪ Howard S. Becker 280–85

THE TIME OF THE TRIBES
MICHEL MAFFESOLI (1944–)

IN CONTEXT

FOCUS
Neo-tribalism

KEY DATES
1887 Ferdinand Tönnies identifies an important shift in social ties from *Gemeinschaft* (community) to *Gesellschaft* (society).

1970s and 1980s Building on the work of US sociologist Robert Merton, subcultural theorists argue that youths form ties based on class and gender.

1988 French sociologist Michel Maffesoli's *The Time of Tribes: The Decline of Individualism in Mass Society* is published.

1998 British sociologist Kevin Hetherington expands Maffesoli's concept and argues that neo-tribes, a reaction to the fragmentation of postmodern society, are communities of feeling.

We live in "the time of the tribes," according to French sociologist Michel Maffesoli. In a world of rapid change, characterized by risk and unpredictability, individuals need new ways to find meaning in their lives. New collectives, or tribes, have emerged, says Maffesoli: they are dynamic, fleeting, and "Dionysiac" (after the Greek god Dionysus: sensual, spontaneous). A shared social experience, or collective aesthetic sensibility, is far more important to the tribes than individuality, and the repetition of shared rituals is a way of forging strong group solidarity.

The rave movement of the 1980s and early 1990s, featuring "raves" (parties with rhythmic music and a specific dance style), was characterized less by a common identity than a shared consciousness (love of rave music and dance). Not as fixed as class-based subcultures such as punk, the movement exemplifies the tribal forms of solidarity described by Maffesoli. Unlike traditional

> The metaphor of the tribe... allows us to account for... the *role*... each person... is called upon to play within the tribe.
> **Michel Maffesoli**

institutions and ties, those new forms of belonging and community are actively achieved, rather than being something one is born into.

Maffesoli sees the modern-day tribes as short-lived, flexible, and fluid rather than fixed, so a person can move between different groupings in everyday life and achieve a fulfilling plural existence. Tribal membership, says Maffesoli, must be worked at and requires a shared belief or consciousness to maintain coherence. ■

See also: Ferdinand Tönnies 32–33 ▪ Pierre Bourdieu 76–79 ▪ Zygmunt Bauman 136–43 ▪ Benedict Anderson 202–03

HOW WORKING-CLASS KIDS GET WORKING-CLASS JOBS

PAUL WILLIS (1950–)

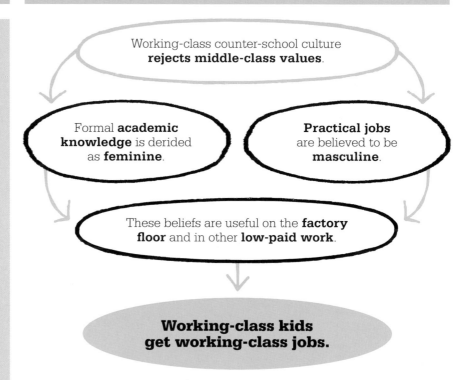

Working-class counter-school culture **rejects middle-class values**.

Formal **academic knowledge** is derided as **feminine**.

Practical jobs are believed to be **masculine**.

These beliefs are useful on the **factory floor** and in other **low-paid work**.

Working-class kids get working-class jobs.

IN CONTEXT

FOCUS
Cultural reproduction and education

KEY DATES
1971 Influential research by British sociologist Basil Bernstein suggests that working-class children are disadvantaged in the education system.

1976 US academics Samuel Bowles and Herbert Gintis suggest that schools are institutions that teach people their place in society.

1979 British journalist Paul Corrigan's *Schooling the Smash Street Kids* argues that working-class boys reject middle-class understandings of success through hard work.

1994 A study by British sociologist Máirtín Mac an Ghaill, *The Making of Men*, reflects some of Paul Willis's findings, showing how "macho lads" react against school.

A repeated claim is that society is meritocratic: people can achieve to the level of their ability. But Paul Willis, in his study of working-class youths in an industrial town in England in the 1970s, asks why it is, then, that working-class boys end up in working-class jobs.

Following 12 boys, or "lads" as he refers to them, in their final two years of school and first year of employment, Willis claims it is the culture and values surrounding these young men that inform their life choices. They develop a counterculture that resists the philosophy of school, namely that

See also: Michel Foucault 52–55 ▪ Friedrich Engels 66–67 ▪ Pierre Bourdieu 76–79 ▪ R.W. Connell 88–89 ▪ Stuart Hall 200–01 ▪ Samuel Bowles and Herbert Gintis 288–89

academic hard work will lead to progress. Through language, dress, and practices such as smoking and drinking, they make clear their rejection of middle-class ideals, and instead emphasize their belief in practical skills and life experience, developing what Willis sees as a chauvinistic or patriarchal attitude.

School's out

The boys see academic knowledge as "feminine," and pupils who aspire to achieve—the "ear'oles" (conformists)—as "sissies" and inferior. Factory work and similar employment is viewed, says Willis, as suitably masculine. Many of the boys work part-time, for example as shelf-stackers or key-cutters, and learn the value of and culture connected to such work.

Their attitudes to girls are exploitative and hypocritical ("sexy" girls are desired but also become figures of contempt), and are based, Willis claims, on a belief in the gendered division of labor. Another challenging aspect of their culture is racism, which serves to distinguish their white, working-class group identity. The factory or shop floor culture mirrors the boys' experiences in school—with a stress in both places on having a laugh and resisting too much work.

Factory fodder?

Willis argues that, in effect, the boys' "performance" of working-class masculinity supports both patriarchy and—crucially, from a Marxist perspective—capitalism by providing the low-paid (male) workforce. The lads, however, experience their employment as a matter of their own free choice rather than as exploitation.

Willis says that this is not simply an example of Friedrich Engels' "false consciousness," whereby the dominant ideology is imposed from above. Instead, ideas about class, gender, and ethnicity also emerge from within their culture; they are very aware that they would have to sacrifice their class identity to move up the social ladder. Their teachers often have low expectations of the boys, leading them to gradually give up on the idea of teaching them. Schools thus play a crucial role in reproducing cultural values, economic divisions, and working-class trajectories.

New questions

Willis's work has been criticized, for example, by British sociologists David Blackledge and Barry Hunt, for being based on insufficient sampling. But in the 1990s British sociologist Inge Bates reframed Willis's question to ask why working-class girls end up with working-class and gender-stereotyped jobs. One of her studies showed that girls who wanted to

The fierce opposition to school exhibited by working-class boys in the UK is evident, according to Willis, in their "struggle to win symbolic and physical space from its rules."

work in childcare ended up in training programs for care of the elderly. Another study focused on girls who wanted to enter the gender-stereotyped world of fashion. These aspirations confirm, says Bates, that working-class girls have limited horizons. Overall, Bates suggests that a constrained labor market, few qualifications, and socialization into "choosing" gendered jobs means there is little evidence of social mobility. ▪

Paul Willis

A cultural theorist, sociologist, and ethnographer, Paul Willis was born in Wolverhampton, UK. After graduating from the University of Cambridge with a degree in literary criticism, he studied for his PhD at the Centre for Contemporary Cultural Studies at the University of Birmingham.

From 1989 to 1990, Willis was a member of the Youth Policy Working Group for the Labour Party. Much of his recent work has focused on ethnographical studies of culture; in 2000 he cofounded the journal *Ethnography*. Having been a professor of social and cultural ethnography at Keele University, he is now a professor in the sociology department of Princeton University.

Key works

1977 *Learning to Labour: How Working Class Kids Get Working Class Jobs*
1978 *Profane Culture*
2000 *The Ethnographic Imagination*

FAMILIES
INTIMACI

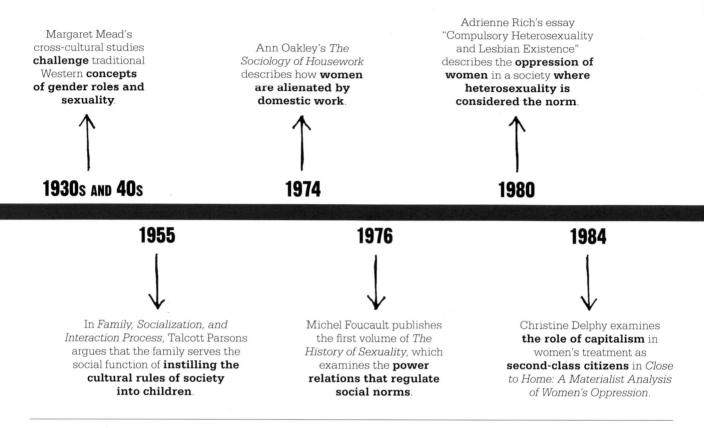

Margaret Mead's cross-cultural studies **challenge** traditional Western **concepts of gender roles and sexuality**.

Ann Oakley's *The Sociology of Housework* describes how **women are alienated by domestic work**.

Adrienne Rich's essay "Compulsory Heterosexuality and Lesbian Existence" describes the **oppression of women** in a society **where heterosexuality is considered the norm**.

1930s and 40s

1974

1980

1955

1976

1984

In *Family, Socialization, and Interaction Process*, Talcott Parsons argues that the family serves the social function of **instilling the cultural rules of society into children**.

Michel Foucault publishes the first volume of *The History of Sexuality*, which examines the **power relations that regulate social norms**.

Christine Delphy examines **the role of capitalism** in women's treatment as **second-class citizens** in *Close to Home: A Materialist Analysis of Women's Oppression*.

For many years, sociologists had used scientific methods to study institutions and the structure of society as a whole. However, the middle of the 20th century saw a shift in emphasis toward understanding the social actions of individuals—a study of reasons and meanings rather than quantities and correlations. This came to be known to sociologists as the interpretative approach.

From the 1950s, the scope of this interpretive method widened slightly to include the study of families, which could perhaps be seen as a social unit somewhere between the individual and institutions. As such, it was possible to identify not only the relationships between individuals and their families, but also the connections between families and wider society. This area of study progressed to examine interpersonal relationships and how they are shaped by society.

Family roles

Among the first sociologists to examine the family in this way was US scholar Talcott Parsons, who combined the interpretive approach of German social theorist Max Weber with the concept of functionalism. For Parsons, the family is one of the "building blocks" of society, and has a specific function in the working of society as a whole. Its primary function, he argued, was to provide an environment in which children can be prepared for roles they will later play in society, by instilling in them its rules and social norms. Adults too benefit from another function of the family unit—to offer a framework in which they can develop stable relationships.

Others were more critical of the conventional notions of family. Traditionally, families reflected the norms of wider society—patriarchal in their structure, with a male breadwinner and a female child-carer and houseworker. But attitudes changed rapidly after World War II. The idea of the stay-at-home mother was increasingly regarded as a form of oppression, and feminist sociologists such as Ann Oakley and Christine Delphy described the alienation that these women experienced.

Gender roles within the family and, by extension, within society as a whole, began to be challenged, as did the idea that there is such a thing as a "typical" or "normal"

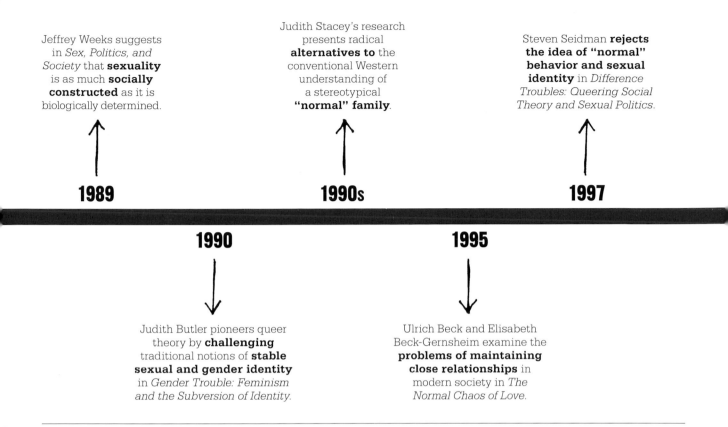

Jeffrey Weeks suggests in *Sex, Politics, and Society* that **sexuality is as much socially constructed** as it is biologically determined.

Judith Stacey's research presents radical **alternatives to** the conventional Western understanding of a stereotypical **"normal" family**.

Steven Seidman **rejects the idea of "normal" behavior and sexual identity** in *Difference Troubles: Queering Social Theory and Sexual Politics*.

1989

1990s

1997

1990

1995

Judith Butler pioneers queer theory by **challenging** traditional notions of **stable sexual and gender identity** in *Gender Trouble: Feminism and the Subversion of Identity*.

Ulrich Beck and Elisabeth Beck-Gernsheim examine the **problems of maintaining close relationships** in modern society in *The Normal Chaos of Love*.

family. As a result of the decline of the traditional patriarchal family model, the conflicting pressures of home and work now affect both partners in many couples, putting a strain on their relationship. The nature of families, according to Judith Stacey, is continually changing to meet the demands of the modern world and also responding to and shaping social norms, so that, for example, single-parent families and same-sex couples are no longer considered unusual in Western societies.

Interpersonal relationships

The more liberal attitude toward sexual relationships and sexuality in the West was, however, slow in coming. In the 1930s and 1940s, the anthropologist Margaret Mead helped to pave the way with her study of gender roles and sexuality in various cultures around the world, showing that ideas of sexual behavior are more a social construction than a biological fact. In the West, despite increasing secularization, religious morality continued to influence the social norms of heterosexual relationships within marriage.

Attitudes toward relationships changed greatly during the 1960s. An anti-establishment youth culture helped break taboos surrounding sex, advocating hedonistic free love and a relaxed view of homosexuality. This change in culture was echoed by the academic work of French scholar Michel Foucault and others.

Foucault believed that the new openness toward intimate relationships of all kinds was a way of challenging the sexual norms imposed by society, and his ideas paved the way for the sociological study of sexuality itself.

In the 1980s, Jeffrey Weeks applied the idea of sexual norms as a social construct to his study of sexuality, and specifically homosexuality, while Christine Delphy described the experiences of lesbians in a predominantly heterosexual society. Perhaps the most influential sociologist in this field of study, however, is Judith Butler, who advocated challenging not only notions of sexuality, but the entire concept of gender and gender identity too, opening up a new, and radical, field of study now known as queer theory, which calls into question conventional ideas of what constitutes normal sexual behavior. ∎

DIFFERENCES BETWEEN THE SEXES ARE CULTURAL CREATIONS
MARGARET MEAD (1901–1978)

IN CONTEXT

FOCUS
Variation in gender roles across different cultures

KEY DATES
1920 Women in the US are given the right to vote.

1939–45 Women in the UK and subsequently in the US prove themselves capable of doing "men's work" during World War II; factory worker Rosie the Riveter becomes a US icon of female capability and economic potential.

1972 British sociologist Ann Oakley argues in *Sex, Gender, and Society* that gender is a matter of culture.

1975 In her article "The Traffic in Women: Notes on the 'Political Economy' of Sex," US cultural anthropologist Gayle Rubin argues that heterosexual family arrangements give men power and oppress women.

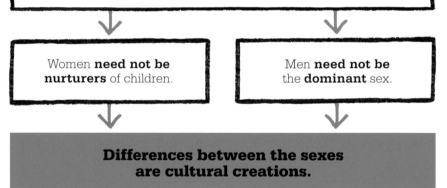

Men and women **learn their gender roles** through systems of reward and punishment...

↓

...but definitions of **"natural" tendencies** of men and women **vary from culture to culture**.

↓ ↓

Women **need not be nurturers** of children.

Men **need not be** the **dominant** sex.

↓ ↓

Differences between the sexes are cultural creations.

I n early 20th-century US society, a man's role was to provide for his family, while women were relegated to the private sphere and considered responsible for childcare and housework because they were thought to be naturally more inclined to such roles. Margaret Mead, however, believed that

gender is not based on biological differences between the sexes, but rather reflects the cultural conditioning of different societies.

Mead's investigations of the intimate lives of non-Western peoples in the 1930s and 1940s crystallized her criticisms of her own society: she claimed that the ways in which US society

See also: Judith Butler 56–61 ▪ R.W. Connell 88–89 ▪ Talcott Parsons 300–01 ▪ Ann Oakley 318–19 ▪ Jeffrey Weeks 324–25

expressed gender and sexuality restricted possibilities for both men and women. Mead claims that men and women are punished and rewarded to encourage gender conformity, and what is viewed as masculine is also seen as superior.

Comparing cultures

Mead takes a comparative approach to gender in her studies of three tribes in New Guinea. Her findings challenge conventional Western ideas about how human behavior is determined. Arapesh men and women were "gentle, responsive, and cooperative" and both undertook childcare—traits the West would see as "feminine."

Similarly, it was the norm for Mundugumor women to behave in a "masculine" way by being as violent and aggressive as the men. And in a further reversal of traditional Western roles, women in Tchambuli society were dominant, while men were seen as dependent.

The fact that behaviors coded as masculine in one society may be regarded as feminine in another, leads Mead to argue that temperamental attitudes can no longer be regarded as sex-linked.

Her theory that gender roles are not natural but are created by society established gender as a critical concept; it allows us to see the historical and cross-cultural ways in which masculinity, femininity, and sexuality are ideologically constructed.

Change can happen

Mead's work laid the foundations for the women's liberation movement and informed the so-called "sexual revolution" of the 1960s onward. Her ideas posed a fundamental challenge to society's rigid understandings of gender roles and sexuality.

Following on from Mead, feminists such as US cultural anthropologist Gayle Rubin argued that if gender, unlike sex, is a social construction, there is no reason why women should continue to be treated unequally. Viewing gender as culturally determined allows us to see, and

Gender roles are cultural creations, according to Mead. There is no evidence that women are naturally better than men at doing the housework or caring for children.

therefore challenge, the ways in which social structures such as the law, marriage, and the media encourage stereotyped ways of conducting our intimate lives.

In comparison to the early 20th century, gender roles for both men and women in the 21st century have become far less restrictive, with women participating more in the public sphere. ▪

Margaret Mead

Margaret Mead was born in Philadelphia in 1901. Her father was a professor of finance; her mother was a sociologist; she herself became curator emeritus of the American Museum of Natural History, New York.

Mead received her PhD from Columbia University in 1929, and went on to become a leading cultural anthropologist, best known for her studies of the people of Oceania. Her early work on gender and sexuality was labeled as scandalous and she was denounced as a "dirty old woman." She nevertheless

became a popular figure, lecturing widely on key social issues such as women's rights, sexual behavior, and the family. Mead was the author of more than 20 books, many of which were part of her mission to make anthropology more accessible to the public. She died in New York in 1978.

Key works

1928 *Coming of Age in Samoa*
1935 *Sex and Temperament in Three Primitive Societies*
1949 *Male and Female*

FAMILIES ARE FACTORIES THAT PRODUCE HUMAN PERSONALITIES
TALCOTT PARSONS (1902–1979)

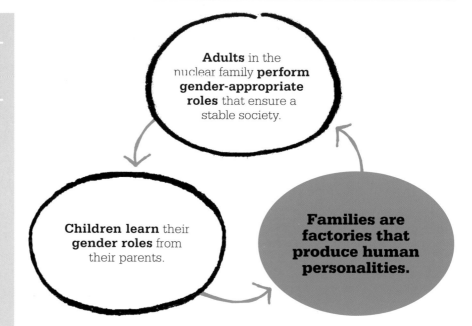

Adults in the nuclear family **perform gender-appropriate roles** that ensure a stable society.

Children learn their **gender roles** from their parents.

Families are factories that produce human personalities.

Many of the writings of the sociologist Talcott Parsons focused on American society in the 1940s and 1950s. Parsons (influenced by the work of Émile Durkheim and Max Weber) claimed that the US economic order required a smaller family unit. The family, Parsons believed, is one of several institutions, such as the education system and the law, that have roles that support one another and enable the stable functioning of society as a whole.

From Parsons' perspective, the modern nuclear family—in which a husband, wife, and their children live relatively isolated from their extended family and community—is the prime agent of socialization. People derive status and roles from their various positions in the family. Although during World War II

See also: Émile Durkheim 34–37 ▪ Max Weber 38–45 ▪ Margaret Mead 298–99 ▪ Judith Stacey 310–11 ▪ Ulrich Beck and Elisabeth Beck-Gernsheim 320–23

women showed that they were perfectly able to do work previously considered "men's work," many non-feminist authors typically assume a natural division of labor between men and women, and Parsons is no exception.

Happy families

The separation of home life and paid employment, with women remaining at home, is logical, according to Parsons, because women are natural carers. Men are then able to take the lead in the role of breadwinning. This division is considered efficient because there is less competition for the family wage. Staying out of paid employment allows women to focus on their caring role: child-rearing and the stabilization of adult personalities.

In addition to cooking and cleaning, this role demands psychological management to ensure a happy household. Parsons is of the opinion that personality is not born but made, and the family is the first place this happens.

He argues that women are able to use their emotional bond with children to steer them into becoming socialized human beings. For example, children learn their sex roles by identification with their same-sex parent. These roles are internalized so that girls become "feminine" women and boys become appropriately "masculine" men, ready to take their place in heterosexual family life. So, in much the same way as a factory produces goods, each stable family unit produces grounded individuals who are groomed to contribute positively to society.

Nuclear power

For Parsons, this neat division avoids tainting the household with the rational, competitive outside world, although the father can provide the link between the outside world and the home when the child is ready. The nuclear family, from a Parsonian perspective, can be seen as the lynchpin of civilization and crucial for the moral health of society.

The nuclear family was once considered the traditional family unit. But the existence of diverse family types is now acknowledged, including same-sex and single-parent families.

This way of understanding families remained dominant in the social sciences until the 1970s and 1980s, when feminists, among others, began to question it. The nuclear family, it is argued, only pertained to privileged white, middle-class Western families and ignored the differing realities of many other groups in society. It also served to justify and perpetuate inequality between the genders. ▪

The importance of the family and its function for society constitutes the primary reason why there is... differentiation of sex roles.
Talcott Parsons

Talcott Parsons

Talcott Parsons was born in Colarado in 1920 and belonged to one of the oldest families in US history. His father was a liberal academic and a congregational minister.

Parsons graduated from Amherst College with a degree in philosophy and biology and thereafter studied at the London School of Economics and at the University of Heidelberg, Germany. He was a fierce critic of both fascism and communism, and a staunch advocate of US

society. For most of his academic career, he was based at Harvard University until he retired in 1973, after which he continued to develop theories and give lectures. Parsons died of a stroke in 1979 in Munich, Germany, where he had been lecturing.

Key works

1937 *The Structure of Social Action*
1951 *The Social System*
1955 *Family, Socialization, and Interaction Process*

WESTERN MAN HAS BECOME A CONFESSING ANIMAL
MICHEL FOUCAULT (1926–1984)

IN CONTEXT

FOCUS
The will to truth

KEY DATES
1782 Jean-Jacques Rousseau, Swiss political philosopher, publishes *Confessions*, one of the first autobiographies to focus on worldly life, rather than religious experiences and inner feelings.

1896 Austrian neurologist Sigmund Freud introduces the term "psychoanalysis."

1992 Sociologist Anthony Giddens suggests in *The Transformation of Intimacy* that men are reluctant to disclose feelings publicly and rely on women to do the emotional work in relationships.

2003 Frank Furedi's *Therapy Culture: Cultivating Vulnerability in an Uncertain Age* sees the will to talk and reveal as potentially damaging.

Why do people talk so much about sex these days? This is one of the key questions posed by the influential French philosopher Michel Foucault in *The History of Sexuality: Volume I* (1976). Foucault claims there is an important relationship between confession, truth, and sex. He suggests that to understand sexuality in the West, we must consider how knowledge operates and how particular forms of knowledge, such as the science of sexuality (*scientia sexualis*) and

The Christian Church requires confession to **absolve "sins of the flesh."**

Psychiatry and psychology require confession of **sexual desires** and obsessions **to reveal who we really are**.

We are told that telling all **to unveil the "truth"** will cure us.

Western man has become a confessing animal.

See also: Michel Foucault 52–55; 270–77 ▪ Norbert Elias 180–81 ▪ Arlie Hochschild 236–43 ▪ Karl Marx 254–59 ▪ Jeffrey Weeks 324–25

In confessing, we give power to "experts" (priests, therapists, doctors) to judge, punish, and correct us. The confessor suffers an endless cycle of shame, guilt, and more confession.

psychology, have increasingly dominated our ways of thinking about gender and sexuality.

These knowledges are a form of "discourse"—ways of constructing knowledge of the world that create their own "truths." Incitement to discourse, says Foucault, began in the West four centuries ago. The Christian Church's emphasis on "sins of the flesh" in the 17th century led to a greater awareness of sexuality, and to the rise in the 18th century of "scandal" books—fictional accounts of illicit sexual behavior. The discourse culminated in the 19th-century science of sex that created modern sexuality—from being an act, it was transformed into an identity.

The confession

With the advent of psychiatry and psychology at the end of the 19th century, the Christian ritual of confession—admitting to sins and seeking penance from a priest in order to regain the grace of God— became reconstructed in scientific form. Revealing sexual habits and desires was seen as a way to unearth the "authentic" self.

According to Foucault, the confession has become one of the most valued ways to uncover "truth" in our society. From being a ritual, it has become widespread and is now part of family life, relationships, work, medicine, and policing. As Hungarian sociologist Frank Furedi posits, confession now dominates personal, social, and cultural life, as evident in reality TV shows and in social media platforms such as Facebook and Twitter.

Healthy relationships, we are continually assured, require truth-telling. Thereafter, an "expert" (a therapist or doctor, for example) is required to reveal our "authentic" self. The compelling promise of the confession is that the more detailed it is, the more we will learn about ourselves, and the more we will be liberated. A person who has experienced trauma is often told that retelling the experience will have a curative effect. But this "will to truth" is a tactic of power, says Foucault, that can become a form of surveillance and regulation. Confession, he claims, does not reveal the truth, it produces it.

Foucault's work has had an immense impact on feminism and studies of sexuality since the 1980s. In particular, his ideas have influenced British sociologist Jeffrey Weeks, who uses Foucault to unearth the ways in which legislation has served to regulate gender and sexuality in society. ▪

Therapy culture

The Hungarian sociologist Frank Furedi, emeritus professor of sociology at the University of Kent, UK, argues that we are obsessed with emotion in the modern age. Experiences and emotions that were once thought normal, such as depression and boredom, are now believed to require treatment and medical intervention.

We read constantly about sports stars' addictions and celebrities' sex lives. And in order to heal, the emotionally injured are encouraged to share their pain with others, to ignore the boundaries separating public and private. To seek help publicly—through a revealing autobiography, for example— is seen as a virtue in a therapeutic culture. Emotions have come to be seen as defining features of identity and we are encouraged to understand them as being indicators of illness. This phenomenon, Furedi argues, is intensely disabling. Ironically, the supposedly "therapeutic" culture leaves society feeling vulnerable.

> " Everything had to be told... sex was taken charge of, tracked down.
> **Michel Foucault** "

HETEROSEXUALITY MUST BE RECOGNIZED AND STUDIED AS AN INSTITUTION

ADRIENNE RICH (1929–2012)

IN CONTEXT

FOCUS
**Compulsory
heterosexuality**

KEY DATES
1864 The Contagious
Diseases Act in Britain
punishes prostitutes who
are infected by their clients.

1979 *Sexual Harassment of
Working Women*, by US lawyer
Catherine A. MacKinnon,
argues that women occupy
markedly inferior positions
in the workplace and are
sexualized as part of their job.

1993 Marital rape is finally
recognized as a crime by
every state in the US.

1996 In *Theorizing
Heterosexuality: Telling it
Straight*, British sociologist
Diane Richardson introduces
a series of key essays that
critique the institution of
heterosexuality.

What if heterosexuality
is not innate or the only
"normal" sexuality?
Heterosexuality is often seen as
a "natural" foundation for society,
but Adrienne Rich challenges
this idea in her important essay
"Compulsory Heterosexuality and
Lesbian Existence" (1980). Rich
was influenced by the French
intellectual Simone de Beauvoir,
who argues that women have been
urged to accept the roles placed
upon them in a society that views
women as inferior.

Rich suggests that, far from
being natural, heterosexuality is
imposed on women and must be
seen as a system of power that
encourages false binary thinking—
heterosexual/homosexual, man/
woman—in which "heterosexual"
and "man" is privileged over
"homosexual" and "woman."
Compulsory heterosexuality, she
says, presents "scripts" to us that
are templates for how we conduct
relationships and "perform" our
gender. We are, for example,
encouraged to think of men as
being sexually active and women
as sexually passive, even though
there are no studies to prove this.

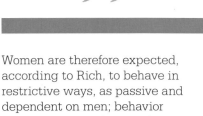

The most pernicious message
relayed by pornography is
that women are natural sexual
prey to men and love it;
that sexuality and violence
are congruent.
Adrienne Rich

Women are therefore expected,
according to Rich, to behave in
restrictive ways, as passive and
dependent on men; behavior
that does not conform to these
expectations is considered deviant
and dangerous. Sexually active
women, for instance, are labeled
as abnormal or called promiscuous.
Patriarchy (a power system that
assumes male superiority) is a
useful conceptual tool for Rich in
explaining women's oppression
over time; she suggests that it is
necessary to think about male

Heterosexuality
is constructed
as **normal**; men are
seen as active and
women as passive.

Heterosexuality
is **promoted** and
maintained by
ideology and **force**;
lesbianism is
denied and **denigrated**.

**Heterosexuality
must be recognized
as an institution and
a system of power
that benefits men
and subjugates
women.**

See also: Karl Marx 28–31 ▪ Judith Butler 56–61 ▪ R.W. Connell 88–89 ▪ bell hooks 90–95 ▪ Sylvia Walby 96–99 ▪ Steven Seidman 326–31

power over women as the key to understanding women's subordinate position.

The power of ideology

Rich discusses many of the ways in which the ideology of compulsory heterosexuality "forces" women into sexual relationships with men. The unequal positions of men and women in the labor market, for instance, can result in women being financially dependent on men. And the pervasive myth that women are at risk of male violence in public spaces, and should restrict their movements and seek male protection, is another example of how women are coerced into heterosexual relationships. Women are encouraged to view themselves as sexual prey, and men as "natural" sexual predators (reinforced by beliefs such as stranger danger), so entering into heterosexual relationships offers women a (false) sense of security.

Despite increasing numbers of people opting to delay marriage, many young women still perceive it as a normal and inevitable part of their lives: this expectation is an important aspect of Rich's argument about the compulsory nature of heterosexuality. Once again, ideology helps shore up heterosexuality through the promotion of romantic narratives in films such as *Titanic* and fairy tales like *Cinderella*.

So prevalent is the idea of heterosexuality in society that people are assumed to be heterosexual unless they declare otherwise. The irony then is that when lesbians or gay men "come out" they are viewed as being more sexual than those who do not have to. Heterosexuality therefore carries with it an insidious assurance of normality.

Oppressive tactics

Karl Marx argued that capitalism is, in part, maintained through violent actions such as conquest and enslavement. Heterosexuality, Rich contends, can be viewed in a similar way. Under conditions of compulsory heterosexuality, men and women no more choose to be heterosexual or homosexual than a worker chooses wage labor.

Alongside the symbolic violence of ideology, physical violence is often used to control the behaviors of women. Acts such as female genital mutilation and punishment for female adultery or lesbianism »

Hollywood films such as *Basic Instinct* that depict lesbians as killers provide an ideological endorsement of lesbianism as threatening and deviant and heterosexuality as normal.

Modes of dress that restrict women's movements are designed, Rich argues, to inhibit women's freedom and prevent them from moving outside and participating in the public sphere, independent of men: they can then, she says, be kept under control by men within compulsory heterosexuality.

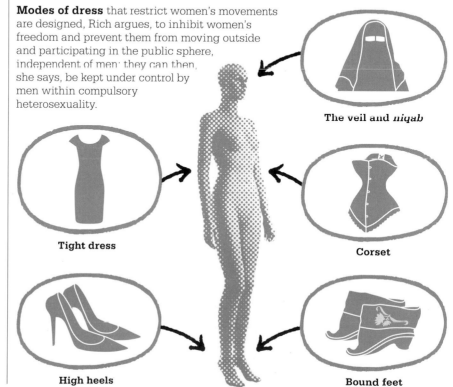

The veil and *niqab*

Tight dress

Corset

High heels

Bound feet

deny women sexuality. Child and arranged marriage, pornographic images that depict women enjoying sexual violence and humiliation, child sexual abuse, and incest—all force male sexuality on women. Rape is another violent tactic; marital rape was not recognized in many Western nations until the 1990s—a reflection of the belief that a woman must be sexually submissive to her husband. And Rich says that "using women as objects in male transactions" is another oppressive tactic of compulsory heterosexuality—as revealed, for instance, in the trafficking of women for sexual exploitation and the use of prostitutes for sexual pleasure.

The view, persistent in some cultures, that it is preferable to send the son to school because sons will stay in the family, whereas girls leave to join the husband's family after marriage, means that across the globe only 30 percent of girls get a secondary-school education. A poor education will inevitably mean poor employment prospects.

Another method whereby male power is maintained is through the barring of women from exclusive

[Heterosexuality] has had to be imposed, managed, organized, propagandized, and maintained by force.
Adrienne Rich

clubs, and from leisure pursuits such as golf where important business deals might be made.

It is in these many different ways that heterosexuality can be understood as an institution that operates through rigid social constructions of gender and sexuality. Considerable social control, including violence, is used to enforce these ideas of gender. The effect is to keep women inside heterosexuality and to ensure that they remain subordinate within it. A direct consequence of heterosexuality, for Rich, is the oppression of women.

Erasure and denial of lesbianism in history and culture is one of the ways in which heterosexuality is maintained. Rich contends that society is male-identified, meaning it is a place where men and their needs are placed above women's needs. Women feel the need to look beautiful for men, and place more value on romantic relationships with men than on their friendships with women. Rich calls upon women to try and reshape their lives around other women—in other words, to be woman-identified. This does not mean that she urges all women to give up men and sleep with women but, rather, she wants all women to experience that which has arguably only been available to lesbian communities—namely, to love other women.

The lesbian continuum
Rich challenges preconceptions about what a lesbian is—it is not someone who hates men or sleeps with women, but simply a woman who loves women. This idea is known as "political lesbianism": Rich and others saw it as a form of resistance to patriarchy rather than simply a sexual preference.

Adrienne Rich

Feminist, poet, and essayist Adrienne Rich was born in 1929 in Maryland. Her home life was tense, due to religious and cultural divisions between her parents.

Despite later identifying as a lesbian, Rich married, in part to disconnect from her family. During this time she took a teaching post at Columbia University. Her experiences as a mother and a wife impeded her intellectual potential and radicalized her politics. She was committed to anti-war protests, and was also actively engaged in feminist politics and the civil

rights movement. In 1997, in protest against the inequalities in the US, she refused the National Medal of Arts from President Bill Clinton.

Key works

1976 *Of Woman Born: Motherhood as Experience and Institution*
1979 *On Lies, Secrets, and Silence: Selected Prose, 1966–1978*
1980 "Compulsory Heterosexuality and Lesbian Existence"

Lesbianism can, then, be placed on a continuum, which includes those who are sexually attracted to women and those who may be heterosexual but are politically connected to other women. This does not mean there are degrees of lesbian experience, with those who are "less" lesbian being more socially acceptable. Instead, Rich is suggesting that there have always been women who have resisted the compulsory way of life and existed in and out of the continuum for hundreds of years—from the many women in Europe, in the 16th and 17th centuries in particular, who were hanged or burned as witches, often for living outside of patriarchy, to the late 19th-century "Wigan Pit Brow Lasses," colliery workers who caused scandal in Britain by insisting on wearing trousers.

Rich's idea of a lesbian continuum has caused considerable debate, partly because it can be seen as desexualizing lesbianism and allows feminists to claim to be part of the continuum without examining their heterosexuality.

Sheila Jeffreys, a British radical feminist, argued that it allowed heterosexual women to continue their relationships with men while feeling politically validated. But the strength of Rich's work is that rather than critiquing heterosexual women, it critiques heterosexuality as an institution.

Rich's ideas also challenge the hetero/homo binary and thus anticipate queer theorists such as US scholar Eve Kosofsky Sedgwick, who argues that sexual identity is a construct of Western culture. Sedgwick also opposes the assumption that these constructions of sexuality are only an issue for "minority" groups such as lesbians and gay men.

A conceptual shift

The ideas put forward in Rich's 1980 essay have arguably provided the most important conceptual shift in studies of sexuality by inviting an examination of heterosexuality as an institution. This had never been done before because, as British sociologist

Carol Smart suggests, heterosexual identity, like white colonial identity, has maintained an effortless superiority and an ability to remain invisible because it has constructed itself as the norm. Heterosexual feminists such as British sociologist Stevi Jackson have gone on to unpick heterosexuality as a direct result of Rich's work. French feminist Monique Wittig argued in 1992 that heterosexuality is a political regime that relies on the subordination and appropriation of women.

The recent revelation in the UK of the sexual abuse of girls by celebrities and the abduction of more than 200 schoolgirls in Nigeria, Africa, by the militant Islamist group Boko Haram, are glaring examples of how heterosexuality is still forced on women and girls. The arguments put forward by Rich thus continue to inform important explorations of heterosexuality as a social and political structure. ∎

> ❝
> The patriarchal institution of motherhood is not the "human condition" any more than rape, prostitution, and slavery are.
> **Adrienne Rich**
> ❞

WESTERN FAMILY ARRANGEMENTS ARE DIVERSE, FLUID, AND UNRESOLVED
JUDITH STACEY

IN CONTEXT

FOCUS
The postmodern family

KEY DATES
1970 US radical feminist Kate Millet argues that the nuclear family is a site of subordination for women.

1977 In *Haven in a Heartless World: The Family Besieged*, US social critic Christopher Lasch gives an anti-feminist account of how traditional family values are eroded in the modern world.

1997 In *Lesbian Lifestyles: Women's Work and the Politics of Sexuality*, British academic Gillian Dunne argues that lesbian relationships are more egalitarian than heterosexual partnerships.

2001 In *Same Sex Intimacies: Families of Choice and Other Life Experiments*, Jeffrey Weeks and others state that families are increasingly becoming a matter of choice.

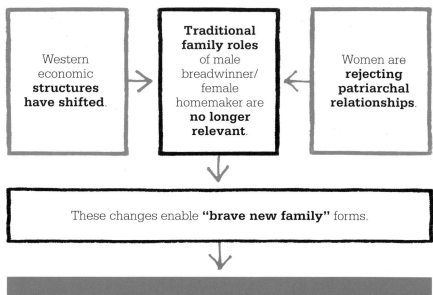

Western economic **structures have shifted**.

Traditional family roles of male breadwinner/female homemaker are **no longer relevant**.

Women are **rejecting patriarchal relationships**.

These changes enable **"brave new family"** forms.

Western family arrangements are diverse, fluid, and unresolved.

The "modern" US family unit, praised by the likes of Talcott Parsons, is a dated and potentially oppressive institution. This is the view of Judith Stacey, professor emerita of social and cultural analysis at New York University, whose work has focused on the family, queer theory, sexuality, and gender. Based on her detailed research into families in Silicon Valley, California, Stacey suggests that, in line with demands from a changing economic structure resulting in poverty and unemployment, the family has undergone a radical shift. Marriage is also weaker because women are rejecting patriarchal relationships. Instead,

See also: Sylvia Walby 96–99 ▪ Talcott Parsons 300–01 ▪ Adrienne Rich 304–09 ▪ Ulrich Beck and Elisabeth Beck-Gernsheim 320–23 ▪ Jeffrey Weeks 324–25

there is a move toward blended families, lesbian and gay families, cohabitating couples, and single parents—all of which are part of what she calls the "postmodern" family (although many have argued that these forms have always existed and that Parson's nuclear family was only relevant for a few privileged middle-class families). To reflect this new reality, Stacey insists that the work structure needs to ensure equal pay for men and women, and universal health and child care should be provided.

A pioneering spirit

The economic role of the family has declined, Stacey argues, and as a result, intimacy and love have become more important. Despite the decline of marriage, Stacey does not believe that individuals no longer form meaningful social ties, but rather that complex ties continue to be formed as a result of divorce and remarriage.

Because traditional roles and legal- and blood-ties within the family are less relevant today than they were in the past, family members now have greater choice and are therefore creating more experimental intimacies. She suggests that the heterosexual/homosexual binary is becoming less stable and is being replaced by a "queering" of family relations. These "brave new families" are endeavoring to fully embrace change and diversity and forge more unconventional and egalitarian relationships.

Stacey is in line with other key thinkers, such as Jeffrey Weeks and British sociologist Gillian Dunne, in suggesting that lesbian and gay families are at the forefront of

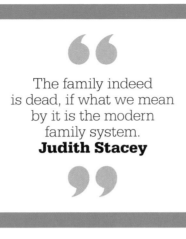

> The family indeed is dead, if what we mean by it is the modern family system.
> **Judith Stacey**

creating more democratic and equal relationships. For her, these relationships represent an ideal of postmodern kinship for which traditional roles are less applicable.

Equal love?

The British sociologist Anthony Giddens is in agreement with Stacey when he suggests that contemporary family forms bring greater equality to relationships and undermine stereotypes and traditional gender roles. In contrast, recent studies in Britain have revealed that in heterosexual couples, women are still largely responsible for housework.

Some have questioned the extent to which same-sex relationships are more equal. Canadian researcher Janice Ristock, for example, has pointed to the prevalence of domestic abuse among same-sex couples. Others, such as sociologists Beck and Beck-Gernsheim, have emphasized the many difficulties associated with living a detraditionalized life. Nevertheless, Stacey contends that social experiments in ties of love are ongoing. ▪

Gay parenthood

Stacey notes that US pressure groups are claiming that the country is facing a crisis due to fatherlessness: heterosexual men are abandoning pregnant partners or opting not to have children at all. New technologies and the availability of contraceptives have separated sex from procreation. And having a child no longer guarantees a future income for parents. Thus Stacey argues that parenting is now more about emotion than finances.

Yet increasing numbers of gay men are opting for parenthood, even though they face many more challenges than lesbian and heterosexual couples, including access to the means of reproduction (eggs and a womb). When straight couples adopt, they are often given healthy babies. Gay men tend to be offered older children or those who are unwell or thought of as "difficult" in some way. Thus it is gay men, says Stacey, who are giving homes to some of society's most needy children.

Gay men who choose to become fathers challenge many of society's stereotypes about masculinity, fatherhood, and gay promiscuity.

THE MARRIAGE CONTRACT IS A WORK CONTRACT

CHRISTINE DELPHY (1941–)

Within a patriarchal system, **heterosexuality** is a **socially constructed** institution that **encourages marriage**.

Marriage enables the husband, as head of the household, to **exploit his wife**, by benefitting from her **unpaid labor**…

…**around the home**.

…**in support of his job**.

…**in producing and looking after children** (his legitimate heirs).

The marriage contract is a work contract.

For hundreds of years in many societies, marriage has been the destiny and often the dream of every young girl. Numerous cultural artefacts—from fairy tales to novels and films—have reinforced this view. However, in the 1980s, feminists such as Ann Oakley and Christine Delphy argued that, in reality, marriage is a highly abusive institution that is fundamental in aiding men's continuing oppression of women.

Christine Delphy is a Marxist theorist, who claims that the only way to investigate oppression of any sort is through a Marxist-style analysis that looks at the material benefits accruing to any party. But where Marx investigated oppression through examining class structure, Delphy investigates women's oppression through the power structure of patriarchy (the power and authority held by men). She says that within a patriarchal system, heterosexuality (and the resulting male–female couple) is not an individual sexual preference but a socially constructed institution, which acts to maintain male domination. This is demonstrated,

she argues, in the way that women are channeled into marriage and motherhood, so that their labor can be exploited by men.

Domestic production
Delphy argues that Marx's concepts can be applied to the home environment, which she sees as a site of the patriarchal mode of production. Within this workplace, men systematically take advantage of, and benefit from, women's labor. Under these conditions, women labor for the male head of the household, carrying out

The narrative of films such as *Pride and Prejudice,* adapted from the novel by Jane Austen, reinforce the idea that what every woman wants is to find the "perfect" man and marry him.

potentially limitless work. This role, she says, has no job description, no agreed wage, and no limit in terms of the hours. In any other working position, such conditions would be viewed as exploitative. And in marriages where a woman is engaged in paid employment outside the home, she is also in most cases—expected to be responsible for household and childcare duties. According to Delphy, when the domestic situation is viewed in these materialist terms, it becomes obvious that married women are working for nothing.

Delphy points out that for Marxists, classes only exist in relation to one another: there can be no bourgeoisie (owners of the means of production) without the proletariat (the workers). Friedrich Engels wrote extensively on how

the development of a class society is the basis for women's oppression. He said that with the rise in private property during the 19th century, there was a corresponding rise in inequality because men increasingly controlled the public sphere of production, and so became increasingly wealthy and powerful. In addition, men wanted to ensure that their property would be inherited by their legitimate male heirs, and the most effective way of doing this was through the institution of the monogamous patriarchal family. In this way, marriage became a relationship of property.

Unpaid assistants

Demand for labor increased during and following the Industrial Revolution. Women were required to produce more children to supply that demand. But the more children a woman had, the more tightly she was tied to the household and unable to work elsewhere. Delphy also suggests that unmarried women become "wives" too, in

the sense that their labor was often appropriated by brothers, fathers, or employers. This view was partly influenced by the book *Married to the Job*, by British sociologist Janet Finch. This work documents how women are co-opted by employers into a male relative's job, but without pay. This might be through indirect help, such as entertaining (for businessmen or politicians); direct involvement, such as acting as an assistant (for tradesmen or academics); or providing welfare, for example cooking and cleaning (for members of the clergy).

Materialist feminism

Delphy sees capitalism and patriarchy as two distinct social systems, both of which share the appropriation of labor, and which influence and shape each other. Her materialist feminist approach to the family marks a departure from earlier forms of feminist analysis, which did not consider the role of capitalism. Delphy pointed out, however, that a »

Women's exploitation in the home is, says Delphy, a consequence of the combined effects of patriarchy and capitalism, both of which function to perpetuate male dominion and control.

Surveys conducted among OECD countries (Organisation for Economic Co-operation and Development) between 2009 and 2011 have shown a hugely unequal division of labor in the home, with women spending far more time than men caring for family members (preparing food, for example) and doing domestic chores.

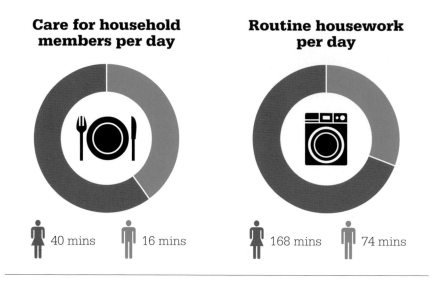

Care for household members per day

40 mins   16 mins

Routine housework per day

168 mins   74 mins

wife's obligation to perform domestic duties is institutionalized on entering marriage, making marriage a labor contract.

This idea has proven to be controversial, but has received support from other academics including the British political theorist Carole Pateman. Drawing on the ideas of British philosopher John Locke, who envisaged a social contract whereby individuals act as good citizens and in return receive protection from the state, Pateman saw heterosexual relations in terms of a sexual contract. Women might be seen to receive protection from men by being married, but husbands had acquired a right to their wives' work and their bodies ("rape in marriage" was not yet a criminal offense in England when Pateman wrote her book *The Sexual Contract* in 1988).

Delphy claims that it is not simply a case of women's work being devalued, as some feminists have argued. The problem will not go away by paying women more. This is because—as Marxist class analysis has shown—the system only works if there is a group that can be exploited. If there is no exploited group, there is no profit. The creation of an exploitable group in turn depends on the existence of a dominant ideology that runs throughout a society, continually positioning a group of people in a certain way. In a capitalist, patriarchal society, this ideology is sexism (prejudice against women because of their sex).

One critique raised against Delphy's ideas is that they do not take account of the fact that some women benefit from marriage, financially and/or sexually. Delphy does not deny this; she claims, however, that there is an unequal exchange. Wives may enjoy some of the tasks they complete for their own sake and because they love their husbands, but this does not mask the fact that they are expected to do large amounts of unpaid work. Writing with Diana Leonard, Delphy notes that married men and women may love each other—but "loving women does not prevent men from exploiting them."

A woman is made, not born

Delphy argues that a person's sex is far from self-evident: maleness is not determined solely by the presence of a penis or chest hair, for example, nor is femaleness a function of being able to bear children. Sex is emphasized in society because we live in a world where the simple binary division by gender gives men priority over women, and values heterosexuality over homosexuality. In this way, gender dictates, or "precedes," sex, and the classification of people by sex maintains hierarchies and power structures.

Delphy argues that using sex as a system to classify people is misguided and leads to serious errors in thinking. Why should a person's sex be more prominent than other physical traits that are equally distinguishable? Why is biological sex the only physical trait that splits the world's

> "The fact that domestic work is unpaid is not inherent to the particular type of work done, since when the same tasks are done outside the family they are paid for.
> **Christine Delphy & Diana Leonard**
> British sociologist (1941–2010)

Signing a marriage contract means entering a legal partnership. This has different implications in different countries, but Delphy suggests it always benefits the man.

population into two groups, which are then loaded with apparently "natural" traits and roles? This idea of sex as a wholly false classification is a crucial concept within Delphy's radical appraisal of patriarchy because it undermines the notion of sex being used to differentiate between those who will dominate (financially, socially, and sexually) and those who will be dominated.

In developing her theories, Delphy was greatly influenced by the writings of the French feminist Simone de Beauvoir, who argued that men had made women "other" in order to support an unequal patriarchal system. By challenging the categories of "men" and "women" as meaningful, Delphy's ideas can be seen as a precursor to queer theory, which questions previously accepted ideas of sex, sexuality, and gender, and their role in establishing identity.

Feminism and Marxism
Delphy's ideas created a furor in feminism when they were first published. This was at a time when feminists were interested in domestic labor and how to understand it, but there was considerable disagreement about the relationship between feminism and Marxism. Some Marxist feminists, such as British scholars Michele Barrett and Mary McIntosh, were extremely hostile to the accusation that men benefit from their wives' labor and therefore directly exploit them. Others argued that it is impossible for two modes of exploitation (patriarchy and capitalism) to exist at the same time in a given society.

Continuing inequality
Delphy and many other feminists since the 1980s have taken on board these criticisms and worked them through in detail, making Delphy's work a continuing influence on feminists around the world. US philosopher Judith Butler, for instance, has used many of Delphy's concepts in her work, in particular her questioning of the sex/gender distinction. In developing Delphy's ideas, French feminist Monique Wittig has argued that the division of society into two sexes is the product, not the cause, of inequality. In *The End of Equality* (2014), journalist and campaigner Beatrix Campbell charted the ways in which women continue to be exploited in their intimate relationships; for instance, there are few societies in the world where men equally share the work of childcare with women. For Campbell, contemporary global capitalism has served to strengthen and further men's domination over women.

Material oppressions in forms other than economic exploitation, such as the ongoing debate about abortion in some countries, also benefit from Delphy's analysis. If child-bearing and -rearing are understood as labor extorted from women, as Delphy suggests, men may fear that women will escape this form of exploitation by limiting births. In this way the withdrawal of the right to abortion in places such as Northern Ireland, and the fierce debates about abortion in the US, can be seen as a form of male control over women's choice, keeping them as an exploited class so as to sustain both capitalism and patriarchy. ∎

Christine Delphy

Christine Delphy was born in France in 1941 and educated at the universities of Paris, France, and California, Berkeley. Inspired by the political protests in Paris in 1968, she became an active member of the French women's liberation movement. In 1977 she cofounded the journal *New Feminist Issues* with French philosopher Simone de Beauvoir.

Delphy was a member of Gouines Rouge (Red Dykes), a group that attempted to reclaim the insulting term "dykes" used for lesbians by referring to it as a revolutionary position. More recently, she voted against the law that banned Muslim girls from wearing the *hijab* (veil) in French schools, calling the act a piece of racist legislation.

Key works

1984 *Close to Home: A Materialist Analysis of Women's Oppression*
1992 *Familiar Exploitation* (with Diana Leonard)
1993 *Rethinking Sex and Gender*

HOUSEWORK IS DIRECTLY OPPOSED TO SELF-ACTUALIZATION
ANN OAKLEY (1944–)

IN CONTEXT

FOCUS
Housework as alienation

KEY DATES
1844 Karl Marx introduces his theory of the workers' alienation from their work.

1955 Sociologist Talcott Parsons sees housework as an integral part of the female role.

1985 In *Contemporary Housework and the Houseworker Role*, British sociologist Mary Maynard reveals that working women do far more housework than their working husbands.

1986 British sociologists Linda McKee and Colin Bell claim that when men are unemployed, they do less housework: their masculine identity is seen as threatened and wives are unwilling to weaken it still further by asking them to accept greater domestic responsibility.

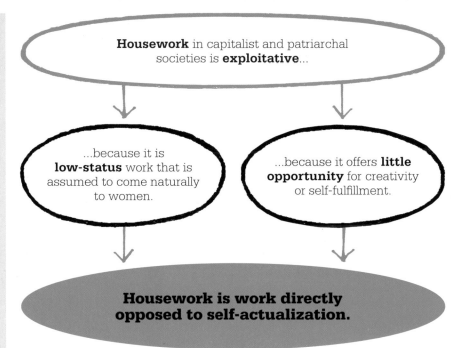

Housework in capitalist and patriarchal societies is **exploitative**...

...because it is **low-status** work that is assumed to come naturally to women.

...because it offers **little opportunity** for creativity or self-fulfillment.

Housework is work directly opposed to self-actualization.

The majority of women's work is still domestic labor that takes place in the home. More than a generation ago, in 1974, sociologist Ann Oakley undertook one of the first feminist sociological studies of domestic labor when she interviewed 40 London housewives between the ages of 20 and 30, all of whom had at least one child under five. The pioneering study looks at housework from the perspective of these women.

Oakley argues that housework should be understood as a job in its own right and not a natural extension of a woman's role as a wife or mother. This was a controversial standpoint at a time

See also: Sylvia Walby 96–99 ▪ Harry Braverman 226–31 ▪ Robert Blauner 232–33 ▪ Arlie Hochschild 236–43 ▪ Talcott Parsons 300–01 ▪ Christine Delphy 312–17

when housework was not seen as "real work." Women are compelled to engage in domestic duties for no wages—an essential form of exploitation that enables capitalism to function and succeed: by providing the needs of the male worker, housewives ensure male workers are able to provide the needs of the economy.

A woman's role?

Domestic duties have often been regarded as natural for women, due to their ability to give birth; although why that capacity means a woman is better able to iron out creases in clothes is unclear. Arguably, it does not occur to most women to demand wages for the work they give "for free."

Karl Marx's argument that male workers are exploited in paid employment is applicable to women's exploitation in the home. Ideology serves to disguise this fact by presenting housework as "natural" for women and also not worthy of a wage. Oakley contends, however, that gender, and gender

roles, should be seen as reflecting cultural and historical processes, rather than as being tied to biology.

Alienation

Marx claims that workers, in a system of private ownership, experience alienation or estrangement from their work because they do not own the fruits of their labor. Similarly, Oakley insists, the majority of housewives are dissatisfied with their lot, finding nothing inherently satisfying about their work, which is lonely, monotonous, and boring. They resent the low status that is associated with being a housewife. Like factory workers, they find their jobs repetitive, fragmented, and time-pressured.

Oakley's studies reveal that women report feelings of alienation from their work more frequently than factory workers. This is due in part to their sense of social isolation as housewives—many of them had careers before marriage, which they subsequently gave up. These women, Oakley says,

> Women's domesticity is a circle of learned deprivation and induced subjugation.
> **Ann Oakley**

have no autonomy or control; responsibility for the work is theirs alone and if it is not done they risk an angry husband or sick children.

Viewed in this way, housework prevents women from reaching their full potential. Oakley's findings remain significant today: recent research by, among others, British sociologist Caroline Gatrell shows that 40 years later women are still doing most of the housework, despite engaging more in paid employment. ▪

Ads for household products from the 1950s stereotype women as happy housewives who have an emotional attachment to the cleaning agents that form such a key part of their lives.

Ann Oakley

The sociologist and feminist Ann Oakley was born in the UK in 1944. She is professor of sociology and social policy at the University of London. After completing a degree at Oxford, where she was one of the first students to take a sociology option, she wrote two novels but was unable to find a publisher for them. She then enrolled for a PhD and her first academic book, *Sex, Gender, and Society*, introduced the term "gender" into everyday use.

Oakley's first novel, *The Men's Room*, was published in 1988 and in 1991 it became a popular BBC series starring Bill Nighy. Oakley remains committed to feminism, and much of her work addresses gender issues. She also has an interest in developing environmentally friendly cleaning products.

Key works

1972 *Sex, Gender, and Society*
1974 *The Sociology of Housework*
1974 *Housewife*

WHEN LOVE FINALLY WINS IT HAS TO FACE ALL KINDS OF DEFEAT

ULRICH BECK (1944–2015) AND ELISABETH BECK-GERNSHEIM (1946–)

IN CONTEXT

FOCUS
The chaos of love

KEY DATES
1992 Anthony Giddens' *The Transformation of Intimacy* presents an optimistic view of egalitarian relationships in a reflexive (self-aware) society.

1994 US right-wing thinker Charles Murray asserts that traditional family values need to be emphasized to halt a breakdown in society.

1998 British sociologist Lynn Jamieson suggests that "intimacies" is the most useful term for describing the organization of our personal relationships.

1999 British academics Carol Smart and Bren Neale suggest parental relationships with children are far more enduring than fragile intimate partnerships.

S ustaining a happy, intimate relationship can be a difficult and tiring business, yet at the same time a compelling one. In *The Normal Chaos of Love* (1995), German husband-and-wife team Ulrich Beck and Elisabeth Beck-Gernsheim try to explain why this is so. They trace the development of a new social order that has transformed the ways in which we conduct our personal lives, arguing that one of the main features of this new order is "a collision of interests between love, family, and personal freedom." The traditional nuclear family—"built around gender status"—is disintegrating "on the issues

See also: Ulrich Beck 156–61 ■ David Held 170–71 ■ Colin Campbell 234–35 ■ Talcott Parsons 300–01 ■ Adrienne Rich 304–09 ■ Judith Stacey 310–11

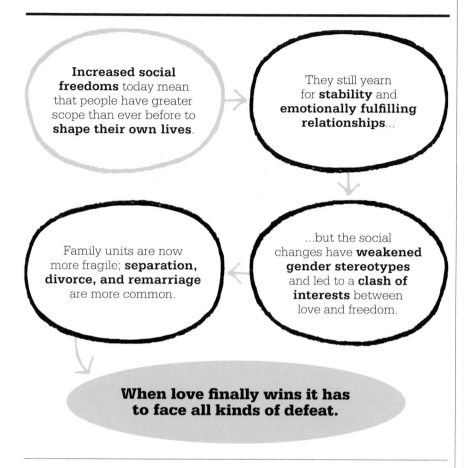

Increased social freedoms today mean that people have greater scope than ever before to **shape their own lives**.

They still yearn for **stability** and **emotionally fulfilling relationships**...

...but the social changes have **weakened gender stereotypes** and led to a **clash of interests** between love and freedom.

Family units are now more fragile; **separation, divorce, and remarriage** are more common.

When love finally wins it has to face all kinds of defeat.

Elisabeth Beck-Gernsheim

Born in Freiburg, Germany, in 1946, Elisabeth Beck-Gernsheim is a sociologist, philosopher, and psychologist. Her partly Jewish heritage meant that many of her family members fled Nazi Germany in the 1930s, with some of her uncles moving to London.

She has produced several key works in collaboration with her husband, Ulrich Beck (who had his own links to London through the LSE), but has also written extensively on issues from social change to biotechnologies. More recently, she has developed an interest in transnational marriage, migration, and ethnic identities. She is currently a senior research fellow at the Institute for Cosmopolitan Studies, University of Munich. (See pp.156–61 for Ulrich Beck.)

Key works

1995 *The Normal Chaos of Love* (with Ulrich Beck)
2002 *Individualization* (with Ulrich Beck)
2002 *Reinventing the Family*

of emancipation and equal rights." The fading away of traditional social identities means that the antagonisms between men and women over gender roles emerge "in the very heart of the private sphere," with the result that more couples are divorcing or separating, and different family forms are taking shape. All this is part of "the quite normal chaos called love."

Individualized living

Following on from Beck's earlier *Risk Society* (1986), which suggests that women are torn between "liberation" and the continuance of traditional gender roles, the couple makes the case that a new age of "reflexive modernity" has produced new risks and opportunities. The particular social and economic conditions of global capitalism have led to a greater sense of individual identity; life is less predictable and personal narratives have more of a sense of "do-it-yourself."

The couple explains that "individualization" is the opposite principle to that used in Germany's Code of Civil Law in the late 19th-century, which established that "marriage is to be viewed [as] a moral and legal order independent of the will of the spouse." Individualization has facilitated new forms of personal and social experimentation. »

"

People marry for... love and get divorced for... love.
Ulrich Beck & Elisabeth Beck-Gernsheim

"

The pursuit of love and marriage remains a feature of modern society, despite the fact that the pressures on our lives mean that marriages are more likely to end in divorce than in the past.

The couple's views echo those of Anthony Giddens who, in *The Transformation of Intimacy* (1992), argues that in contemporary society we make our identity rather than inherit it. Such a change has, he says, altered how we experience the family and sexuality.

According to Giddens, in the past, when marriages were economic partnerships rather than love matches, expectations were lower and disappointments fewer. Now that men and women are increasingly compelled to reflexively create their identity through day-to-day decisions, Giddens argues that they are able to choose partnerships on a basis of mutual understanding, leading to what he describes as "pure relationships"—entered for their own sake and only continuing while both parties are happy. Such partnerships, he says, bring greater equality between individuals and challenge traditional gender roles.

Intimate but unequal

Although Beck and Beck-Gernsheim agree with Giddens that there is far more scope in the modern world for men and women to shape their own lives and thus weaken gender stereotypes, they are not wholly optimistic.

Individuals are subject to forces beyond their control; life may be do-it-yourself but it is not do-as-you-like. Women and men, say the couple, are "compulsively on the search for the right way to live"—trying to find a model of the family that will offer a "refuge in... our affluent, impersonal society."

Individualization may have released people from the gender roles prescribed by industrial society, but the material needs of modern life are such that they are forced to build up a life of their own that is adapted to the requirements of the labor market. The family model, Beck and Beck-Gernsheim say, can mesh "one labor market biography with a lifelong housework biography, but not two labor market biographies," because their inner logic demands that "both partners have to put themselves first." Inequality will persist until men become more accepting of women's participation in the workplace and until men engage in more domestic labor.

Fragile yet resilient

Beck and Beck-Gernsheim contend that, for the most part, intimate relationships cannot be egalitarian; if equality is what is required, then relationships must be abandoned: "Love has become inhospitable."

Men and women face choices and constraints that differ significantly from those faced by their counterparts in previous eras because of the contradiction between the demands of relationships of any kind (family, marriage, motherhood, fatherhood) and the demands of the workplace for mobile, flexible employees. These choices and constraints are responsible for pulling families apart. Rather than being shaped by the rules, traditions, and rituals of previous eras, Beck and Beck-Gernsheim argue that contemporary family units are experiencing a shift from a "community of need," where ties and obligations bound us in our intimate lives, to "elective affinities" that are based on

> 66
> For individuals who... invent... their own social setting, love becomes the... pivot giving meaning to their lives.
> **Ulrich Beck & Elisabeth Beck-Gernsheim**
> 99

choice and personal inclination. In spite of these difficult changes, the lure of the romantic narrative remains strong. In an uncertain society, "stripped of its traditions and scarred by all kinds of risk," as Beck and Beck-Gernsheim put it, love "will become more important than ever and equally impossible."

Individuals now have a greater desire for emotionally fulfilling relationships, which has fueled industries such as couples' therapy and self-help publishing. But the ties that bind are fragile and people tend to move on if perfection is not achieved. As the couple say, even when individuals do fall in love ("when love finally wins"), there are often more battles ahead—division, resentment, and divorce, for example.

Beck and Beck-Gernsheim suggest that nurturing personal relationships and attending to the demands of a rapidly changing economic world require a delicate balancing act; as a consequence, there is a rise in divorce. Yet so strong is the hope of happiness that many divorcees marry again.

The importance of children
While Beck and Beck-Gernsheim argue that we have come too far to return to old ways, and neither men nor women would wish to, the pressures of an individualized life mean that it can be tinged with nostalgia and a longing for certainties that perhaps never existed—those "family values" that governments often hark back to. The more fragile our relationships are, the more we hanker after love.

One way in which this yearning for the past exerts itself is through the increased significance placed upon children in contemporary society. While love between adults might be viewed as temporary and vulnerable, love for children becomes more important, with both parents investing emotionally in their children, who are seen as providing unconditional love.

In this respect, Beck and Beck-Gernsheim suggest that men may be challenging women for the role of emotional caretakers in the family. This can be seen in the increased numbers of fathers who seek custody of their children post-divorce and the rise of groups advocating equal parenting rights for fathers, such as Fathers4Justice.

The feminist academic Diana Leonard supports this view, saying that parents are "spoiling" their children with gifts to keep them close to them. Connection with

The child... promises a tie... more... profound and durable than any other in... society.
Ulrich Beck & Elisabeth Beck-Gernsheim

the child in this context becomes ego-driven and intense, providing a feeling of permanence not found in the chaos of adult relationships.

Inevitably, criticisms have been leveled at Beck and Beck-Gernsheim's arguments. Several theorists, including Swedish scholars Diana Mulinari and Kerstin Sandell, have objected to the implication that women are responsible for the increased divorce rates. Nevertheless, *The Normal Chaos of Love* transformed academic work on the family—from being seen as an institution that responds to social change, it was acknowledged as one that actually contributes to change. ∎

Marriage and divorce rates in the Western world during the past 50 years have altered significantly. Changes in the law and society have seen marriage decline and divorce increase. Although the pattern seems to have stabilized, the family unit is now more fragile.

1960:
  Marriage
  Divorce

2012:
  Marriage
  Divorce

* Divorce not permitted in Spain until 1981. Earliest data is from 1990.

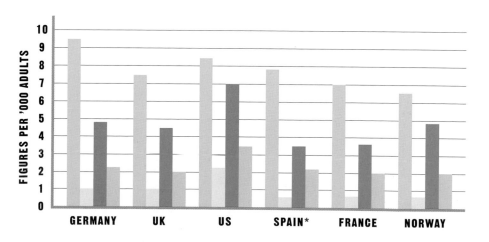

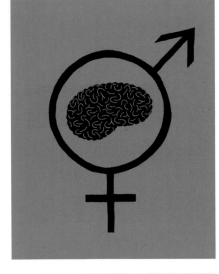

SEXUALITY IS AS MUCH ABOUT BELIEFS AND IDEOLOGIES AS ABOUT THE PHYSICAL BODY
JEFFREY WEEKS (1945–)

IN CONTEXT

FOCUS
The social construction of sexuality

KEY DATES
1885 The Criminal Law Amendment Act is passed in the UK, recriminalizing male homosexuality and strengthening the laws against prostitution.

1968 An essay by British sociologist Mary McIntosh, "The Homosexual Role," helps promote the view that sexuality is socially not biologically determined.

1976 *The History of Sexuality: Volume I*, by French philosopher Michel Foucault, examines the role of "experts" in the classification of sexuality.

2002 Same-sex couples are legally entitled to adopt in the UK.

2014 Same-sex marriage is legalized in the UK.

Jeffrey Weeks, arguably the most influential British writer on sexuality, offers a detailed historical account of how sexuality has been shaped and regulated by society. He sees sexuality not so much as rooted in the body, but as a social construct that is ideologically determined.

Inspired by the work of British sociologist Mary McIntosh, he argues that industrialization and urbanization consolidated gender divisions and increased the stigma of male same-sex relations.

Weeks examines how Victorian society used the new "sciences" of psychology and sexology (the study

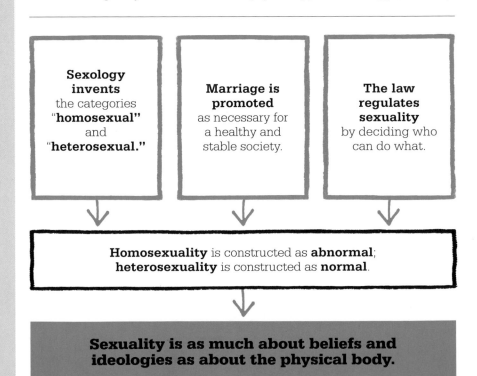

Sexology invents the categories **"homosexual"** and **"heterosexual."**

Marriage is promoted as necessary for a healthy and stable society.

The law regulates sexuality by deciding who can do what.

Homosexuality is constructed as **abnormal**; **heterosexuality** is constructed as **normal**.

Sexuality is as much about beliefs and ideologies as about the physical body.

See also: Sylvia Walby 96–99 ▪ Margaret Mead 298–99 ▪
Michel Foucault 302–03 ▪ Adrienne Rich 304–09 ▪ Steven Seidman 326–31

Oscar Wilde was tried and convicted in the late 19th century of "gross indecency" with other men. The trials of the Irish writer helped construct homosexuality as a social problem.

of sexuality that claimed to be a science but was often undertaken by wealthy amateurs) to pass sentence on homosexuals.

The growing interest in classifying sexuality assumed that women were naturally sexually passive and men were naturally active, without having any evidence for such assumptions. Anything contrary to these "essentialist" views (that sexuality reflects biology) was often considered abnormal. The new sciences thus firmly upheld existing patriarchal ideas.

Weeks observes that there was an increasing tendency to view the institution of marriage as essential to the maintenance of a stable, "healthy" society. There was also, therefore, a concern to regulate men's "natural" lustfulness by steering them toward marriage. At the same time marriage was

heralded as the norm and essential for society, "homosexuality," Weeks says, was invented. Acts that might be homosexual had been criminalized previously, but for the first time in history, sexologists identified a new type of people: "homosexuals" (the category "heterosexuality" was invented soon after). Many of the studies on sexuality were influenced by the teachings of the Christian Church.

Sexuality as social control

Male homosexuality was viewed as a perversion and, increasingly, as a social problem, leading to tighter legal and social control. The 1885 Criminal Law Amendment Act, for example, broadened and redefined the legal definition of homosexual acts. This construction of homosexuality as abnormal, along with essentialist ideas of femininity and masculinity, served to support the belief that heterosexuality was normal and the only legitimate form of sexual behavior.

It is possible, Weeks suggests, to see this defining of sexuality as both a social construction and a form of social control. The law can decide who is allowed to marry, adopt children, have sex, and at what age. Religion can instruct society that any sex that does not lead to procreation is sinful.

But cultural ideals about who should have sex, and who should not, can have a significant negative impact. There has, for example, been a notable rise in sexually transmitted diseases among the over-50s in the UK and the US because ideas that sex between older people is, among other things, distasteful, has led to fewer older people seeking medical care. ∎

Jeffrey Weeks

The social historian Jeffrey Weeks was born in Rhondda, Wales, UK, in 1945. His work has been influenced by his early participation as a gay rights' activist in the Gay Liberation Front (GLF).

Weeks was a founding member and editor of the journal *Gay Left*, and his work continues to be informed by ideas from lesbian and gay politics, socialism, and feminism. He has published over 20 books and numerous articles on sexuality and intimate life, and is currently a research professor at the eponymous Weeks Centre for Social and Policy Research at South Bank University in London, England. In 2012, he was awarded an OBE for his services to social science.

Key texts

1977 *Coming Out: Homosexual Politics in Britain*
1989 *Sex, Politics, and Society*
2001 *Same Sex Intimacies: Families of Choice and Other Life Experiments*

> Social processes construct subjectivities not just as categories but at the level of individual desires.
> **Jeffrey Weeks**

QUEER THEORY QUESTIONS THE VERY GROUNDS OF IDENTITY

STEVEN SEIDMAN (1950–)

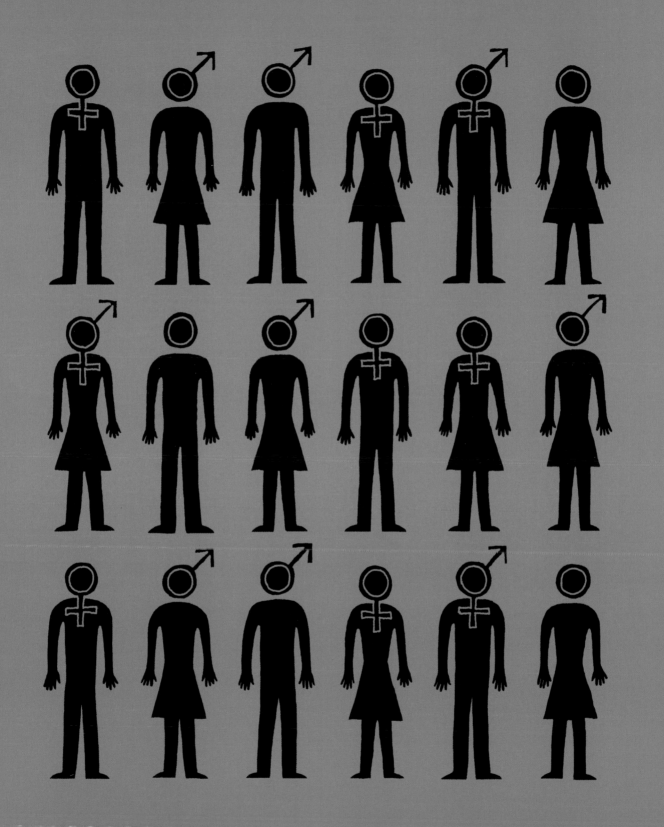

IN CONTEXT

FOCUS
Queer theory

KEY DATES
1976 Michel Foucault's work
*The History of Sexuality.
Volume I: An Introduction*
traces the social construction
of sexuality; he sees sexual
identities emerging through
history and produced by
power, and thus not based
on nature or biology.

1987 ACT UP (AIDS Coalition
to Unleash Power) forms in
New York as a response to
homophobic AIDS campaigns.

1990 In *Gender Trouble*,
Judith Butler argues that
gender is socially constructed
and produced from actions
and behaviors that are
constantly repeated.

1998 US academic Judith
("Jack") Halberstam examines
masculinity without men in
Female Masculinity.

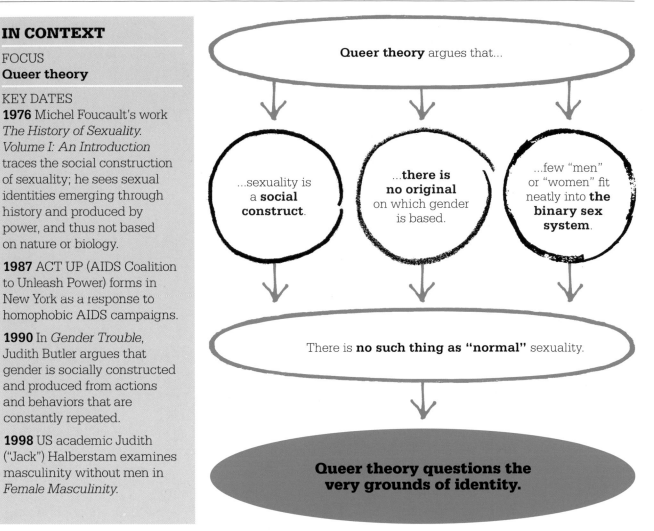

In the early 1980s, the AIDS crisis was wrongly identified in the public mind as an epidemic that mainly affected gay men. The resultant health panic and growth of homophobia made the lesbian and gay community feel isolated and marginalized.

Politically activist gay men and lesbians responded by originating "queer" politics and theory, trying to deprive the term "queer" of its derogatory power. As a reverse affirmation of a pejorative word, "queer" is still a contentious term for some. In its widest sense it includes any category that debunks the heterosexual male–female "natural" model—not just gays and lesbians, but transgendered people, cross-dressers, and others, including heterosexuals who reject the "norm."

Queer theory and its political approach has grown out of feminist and lesbian and gay theory. Influenced by Michel Foucault and Judith Butler, the key queer theorists, such as Eve Kosofsky Sedgwick, Gayle Rubin, and Steven Seidman, have disrupted traditional unitary identity—or social—categories, believing that the differences within categories such as "woman" or "gay" undermine their usefulness. Queer theory, like some feminist theory, was also initially critical of the lesbian and gay communities, which were seen as assimilationist—seeking to enter the mainstream by campaigning for things such as marriage rights.

Constructed sexuality

Steven Seidman is an important figure in the history of queer thinking due to his interpretation

See also: Judith Butler 56–61 ▪ R.W. Connell 88–89 ▪ Michel Foucault 302–03 ▪ Adrienne Rich 304–09 ▪ Christine Delphy 312–17 ▪ Jeffrey Weeks 324–25

and critique of other queer theorists. Seidman argues, like Foucault and British sociologist Jeffrey Weeks, that sexuality is "constructed." Industrialization and urbanization, which gendered social space by creating the public male world of work and the private female world of the home, produced significant changes in how we understand masculinity and femininity, and the regulation of sexuality. Many of the qualities of gender and sexuality that we now see as natural ("heteronormative" means heterosexuality deemed to be the normal sexual orientation) were established at this time, such as women being seen as nurturing and caring, men being regarded as sexually active, and homosexuality being viewed as a perversion.

Seidman suggests that up until the late 20th century, the study of sexuality can be seen as a history of homosexuality. To the sciences of the 19th century, as well as to sexology and Freudian psychology, heterosexuality was normal and not in need of examination. In effect, this moment in history established

In India, the Supreme Court in 2014 upheld the right of transgender individuals, an ancient group called *hijra*, to self-identify their sex, thereby creating a third gender status in law.

many of the social inequalities that persist, such as the divisions between men and women.

Questions of identity

Because queer theorists such as Seidman regard identity as socially constructed, it is considered unstable and lacking coherence; even something seemingly as stable as biological sex is questioned. Few individuals fit neatly into the categories "man" or "woman"—when tested on chromosomes, hormones, genes, or anatomy most will fit somewhere on a continuum. Some men may look very masculine but have high levels of "female" hormones, or a micropenis, while some women may be very tall or hairy, which are qualities we are encouraged to view as masculine.

When babies are born with ambiguous sex, surgeons have often intervened, removing a boy's small penis and suggesting that he be brought up a girl: a paradoxical response that is at one and the same time essentialist, by assuming that a characteristic of "real" men is that they have large penises, and social constructionist, by implying that identity is really a matter of social conditioning. By challenging the idea of unitary identity, such as straight, and rejecting binary ways of thinking, such as man/woman, Seidman is fundamentally critiquing identity-based theory and politics.

Feminism and the lesbian and gay movements emerged as forms of identity politics to challenge patriarchal and heteronormative society. However, critics argued that these movements were promptly dominated by the white

Let's declare war against the center, against all centers, all authorities in the name of difference.
Steven Seidman

middle class (and men, in the case of lesbian and gay politics). At times, such groups also took essentialist approaches to identity, meaning that they saw identities as rooted in biology and therefore natural or normal. As Butler argues, in this context the marginalized identities themselves, by producing fixed meanings, become complicit in reaffirming the binary regimes. Seidman argues that queer theory provides a necessary challenge to the normative gay and lesbian politics because these sexual identities reproduce the processes of power they seek to challenge.

Challenging the norm

In his influential text *The Trouble with Normal: Sex, Politics, and the Ethics of Queer Life* (1999), Michael Warner argues that the concept of "queer" is not just about resisting the norm but challenging the very idea of normal behavior. Because "queer" is about attitude rather than identity, anyone who challenges the norm or the expected can be "queer"—for instance, couples who decide not to have children. »

Seidman, in *Difference Troubles: Queering Social Theory and Sexual Politics* (1997), while acknowledging the important contribution that queer theory has made to modern politics and culture, explores the difficulties that can arise for those who champion the politics of difference. How do social thinkers conceptualize differences, such as sexuality or race, without falling into the trap of reducing them to inferior status?

His pragmatic response is to argue for what he calls a "less repressive view of difference"—a social postmodernism in which "queer" is a verb, describing actions, and no longer a noun.

His aim is to challenge all norms by recognizing difference and having "an affirmative politics of difference" rather than an "illiberal kind of identity politics," such that "difference and democracy might coexist." Seidman insists that queer theorists must, just as other social thinkers do, take into account other forms of social theory and continue to critique key social institutions and examine how people live their lives.

There are many criticisms of the "queer" concept and its theoretical approach. Although it argues against the concept of identity, it has nevertheless become an umbrella term that particularly

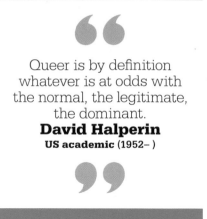

> Queer is by definition whatever is at odds with the normal, the legitimate, the dominant.
> **David Halperin**
> US academic (1952–)

refers to gay men, lesbians, bisexuals, and transgender people. In essence, "queer" can be seen as a new label for an old concept. In this way it has been used to unify many diverse categories of people and has been accused of ignoring important differences and inequalities.

A flawed approach?
Because queer theorists such as the American David Halperin have understood "queer" as a position that can be taken by anyone who feels they have been marginalized due to their sexual preferences, Australian academic Elizabeth Grosz warns that it could be used to validate ethically questionable practices, such as those by "sadists, pederasts... pimps."

Queer theory has been accused of focusing on sexuality to the exclusion of other categories: when Warner argues that pornography is "queer" because—as a result of its uninhibited enactments of sexual fantasies—it is the opposite of "normal," he ignores the ways in which the use of women in much pornography relies on assumptions of "normal" masculinity. In *Queer Race*, South African academic Ian

Groups asserting self-identification sexuality have in recent years challenged the assumption that male–female heterosexuality is the normal sexual orientation. The symbols below are just a few of the many now used to declare to the mainstream that different sexual identities exist.

Self-identification symbols

Symbol	Orientation	Inspiration
⚢	Female couple	Paired mirror of Venus astrological and alchemical signs, traditionally used to denote an organism of female gender.
⚣	Male couple	Paired shield and spear of Mars astrological and alchemical signs, traditionally used to denote an organism of male gender.
◯	An intersex or genderless person	The circle element of the Venus and Mars signs, without the gender-defining additions.
⚧	A transgender person	A combination of the male and female gender signs.
☽☾	A bisexual person	The double-moon symbol is widely used in northern Europe, in preference to a "reclaimed" Nazi-era pink triangle used in some countries.

Barnard contends that queer theory has created a whitewashed, Western version of "queer" that ignores race. British historian Jeffrey Weeks has accused it of ignoring the material constraints, such as a lack of money, that mean the decision to be transgressive is not available to all. It could, then, be argued that queer theory has become a white, middle-class, gay male position.

Queer theory also claimed to be the first social theory to challenge the sex/gender distinction. But as British sociologist Diane Richardson points out, this claim is exaggerated: radical feminists such as Christine Delphy, author of *The Main Enemy* (1970), had begun this task as early as the 1970s.

Despite such criticisms, queer theory has influenced a range of academic areas, particularly in studies of masculinity. For example, the work of US academic Judith Halberstam has been lent a "queer" bent by arguing that if we want to understand masculinity it is important to consider marginalized or subordinate forms such as female masculinity. Seidman contends that a queer theory

approach also yields a great deal when applied to novels and films. He argues that the goal of contemporary literary criticism has been to deconstruct the binaries present in much literature—and "queer" makes this possible.

For those whose sexualities are marginalized and who often find that their representations are limited, a "queer" reading that reinterprets the narrative opens up possibilities that the author or creator may not have foreseen—for example: Conan Doyle's *Sherlock Holmes* novels can suggest a

"Queer" interpretations have now been given to many films. In *Alien Resurrection*, Ellen Ripley—part human, part alien—has a potentially erotic liaison with a female android.

romantic friendship between Holmes and Watson; the cross-dressing in Shakespeare's plays can also be given a "queer" interpretation; and films in the *Alien* series are open to a new twist on the "predatory female" trope. "Queer" has also filtered into TV shows such as the US reality series *Queer Eye for the Straight Guy.* ∎

US drag king Murray Hill (shown here) is described by Halberstam as "transforming masculinity and exposing its theatricality."

Female masculinity

Judith ("Jack") Halberstam argues that masculinity can exist without men, and challenges the ways in which "masculine" females, such as tomboys, are denigrated. Femaleness does not necessarily produce femininity; maleness does not always lead to masculinity.

This idea poses a fundamental challenge to the gender/sex distinction whereby socially constructed gender (masculinity) is perceived as the natural expression of biological sex (man). Halberstam, whose work is

understood as "queer," argues that there has been a tendency to lump all gender-"queer" women under the umbrella term lesbian; but words like "lesbian" and "gay" are not sufficient to explain the broad array of erotic activity that is not conventionally heterosexual. Female maleness becomes a gender rather than an imitation.

"Drag kings" (women who dress as men) highlight the ways in which male masculinity is not based on an authentic essence but is produced through repeated everyday actions.